God's Little Things

365 Inspirational Devotionals

Val D. Harvey

CrossBooks™
1663 Liberty Drive
Bloomington, IN 47403
www.crossbooks.com
Phone: 1-866-879-0502

©2009 Val D. Harvey. All rights reserved.

No part of this book may be reproduced, stored in a retrieval system, or transmitted by any means without the written permission of the author.

First published by CrossBooks 11/16/2009

ISBN: 978-1-6150-7005-3 (sc)

Library of Congress Control Number: 2009937791

Printed in the United States of America
Bloomington, Indiana

This book is printed on acid-free paper.

To my family

Jim, my husband, who encouraged me to be all God created me to be;
Mark and Judy Harvey, who serve the Lord in Singapore as
International Mission Board missionaries;
Martha, who continually blesses my life with her thoughtfulness and love,
and my grandchildren,
James Philip and his wife Jen, who serve as local missionaries to ethnic groups,
and sweet Jordan, who is just beginning her journey through life.

Introduction

The truth expressed by the songwriter, "Little is Much When God is in It," has always challenged my thinking. Bible study confirms this truth with many examples of how God accomplished His purposes with small or sometimes overlooked people or objects. An invitation is extended to you for a one-year discovery of some of God's **little** things.

The outline for each day is as simple as letters in the alphabet. The purpose and presentation for the daily study is designed for:

- **A**—Advice from the Bible. A key verse is selected for the focal study.
- **B**—Biblical Example. A brief summary of the total scripture passage is presented.
- **C**—Contemporary Application. The question, "How does this study relate to me today?" is answered.
- **D**—Directed Prayer. A focused prayer thought is suggested

Significant calendar events are presented and various theme devotionals are used such as: the Fruit of the Spirit; Seven Churches of the Revelation; and the devotionals for December are in chronological order (when possible).

Little is significant when God is involved. From remnants to Gideon's little army, the Bible reveals interesting happenings and miracles explained only by God's awesome power.

Enjoy this year of a daily quiet time with a big God who is interested in **Little** things.

Val D. Harvey

January 1

Nehemiah's Little Building Project
Getting the job done.
(Nehemiah 1—2)

A—Advice from the Bible

Come, let us rebuild the wall of Jerusalem.
(Neh. 2:17, NIV)

B—Biblical Example

The Book of Nehemiah begins in Babylon. Years of exile had forced God's people to leave their homeland of Israel and be subjected to an environment of non-Hebrew control. Nehemiah had become a participant in the court of King Artaxerxes. However, this high place of honor did not relieve this layman of his love and concern for his homeland, especially Jerusalem. Bad news filtered back to the exiles concerning the conditions of the Holy City and Nehemiah experienced a great shock at the reports. Prayer to the *Lord God of heaven* was his first reaction. Being a man of courage, he boldly sought permission to return to Jerusalem to get the job done. The project included enlisting people to help rebuild the walls of the city. Needs were assessed and plans were made to accomplish the task. Good news: the wall was rebuilt in 52 days!

C—Contemporary Application

Happy New Year! Today begins another year of your life. Perhaps last year wasn't all that great and so you have resolved to start over and do better. Some people make New Year's resolutions, but find that keeping those goals lasts about a month. One problem a person faces with high ideals is that some times what they want to accomplish is too much for them to achieve. I have some good news for you. Include God in your plan-making. Seek His desires for your life through daily Bible study and prayer. In addition to your time alone with God, read a book on organizational skills or suggestions for better health. A friend of mine refers to this type of progress as "Eating an Elephant"—one bite at a time. Eventually the project gets smaller and smaller and you have succeeded. Consider having a plan for accomplishing your personal goals or dreams. And like Nehemiah, the plan must be worked. At this point, preparation is a priority. The exiled Hebrew knew what had to be done for his people and for God, so the great task became a challenge to him and the Jews who remained in Israel.

Here are some how-to-suggestions:
- Commit this new year to God.
- Make a list of some needed endeavors or changes.
- Think in terms of days or weeks when setting goals.
- Each month check your "list" to see if you are getting the job done.

D—Directed Prayer

Lord, help me as I begin a new year rebuilding areas of my life.

January 2

A Little Mustard Seed

The smallest quantity of faith enables a person to do incredible feats!
Luke 17:5-6

A—Advice from the Bible

"If you have faith the size of a mustard seed" . . .
(Luke 17:6, HCSB)

B—Biblical Example

Luke 17 contains a collection of four of Jesus' sayings. None of the teachings seem to be related, but are addressed to His disciples. The situation concerning today's verses occurred when a man brought his demon-possessed son to Jesus for healing. At this time, helping the physically impaired was a major part of Jesus ministry. Demon possession was experienced in many of the towns and cities. The disciples had tried to exorcise the demon at an earlier time, but were unsuccessful. Their inability to heal presented a request by the disciples for more faith. Jesus told the apostles that if they exercised what faith they already had, amazing results would follow. The issue was about genuine faith versus doubt. Jesus used the illustration of a small mustard seed to make His point. This tiny seed, that you can barely see, seemed insignificant. However, Jesus emphasized that the problem was not quantity of faith, but quality of faith. Just a little true faith, like a mustard seed, could do mighty things.

C—Contemporary Application

The local church needed to relocate. Lack of parking spaces and rooms for educational purposes were needed. The structure needed major remodeling. This historical downtown church had provided worship and education for several generations of families. Weddings and funerals of loved ones somehow made the building seem special to the survivors. Opposition to the "moving" idea was expected. However, the person I thought would be most vocal against the relocation, became the advocate. His faith was expressed in believing that God would bless the church and help reach more lost people at the new site. He was totally committed the proposal to putting the church somewhere else. He tirelessly worked on encouraging the "resisters" to see the need for reaching more people for Christ. His faith inspired other members of lesser faith. He watched the final relocation from heaven.

How can a Christian better understand the meaning of faith?

- A Christian does not need more faith.
- A Christian needs to use the faith already possessed.
- A Christian's unused faith is not faith at all.
- A Christian's **little** faith, if utilized, is enough.

D—Directed Prayer

Lord, help me as I begin a new year to use the faith I already have to do mighty things for You.

January 3

A Little Woman Judge

God has leadership roles for women.
Judges 4:4-24

A—Advice from the Bible

Deborah, a prophetess . . . was leading Israel at that time.
(Judges 4:4, NIV)

B—Biblical Example

The Book of Judges is a continuation of The Book of Joshua and is often called the "Dark Ages" of the Israelites. Joshua had no successor when he died. Each tribe decided to act independently. A pattern of behavior soon developed. The people would forsake God and God would forsake His people. One phrase best summarizes this book: *Everyone did as he saw fit* (17:6).

The book reads like a script for a play. The characters include villains and heroes. Deborah appears in Act 4. She is identified as a prophetess and married to Lapidoth. Her authority as a judge allowed for the summoning of Barak, a potential commander for Israel's army. A battle was necessary to free her people from Jabin and the Canaanite oppression. The site for the war would be Mount Tabor. Then an unbelievable thing happened, Barak refused to go to battle without Deborah. Assurance was needed or maybe his lack of faith was the problem. A great storm came and confused the enemy. The situation ended in victory. God and the people worked together to bring about peace from persecution.

C—Contemporary Application

The headlines read, "Slavery is a major issue and must be abolished." These words were printed in the Commonwealth paper of Boston. Julia Ward Howe and her husband promoted antislavery messages. This courageous, career woman was later described as an abolitionist, social activist, and poet. A visit in 1861 to a Union army camp during the Civil War awakened within her the need to do something to stop the fighting. Returning home, Julia could not sleep. The lines of a poem began to form in her head. She wrote down these words, "Mine eyes have seen the glory of the coming of the Lord." This great song, *The Battle Hymn of the Republic* was published in 1862. She received $5 for her efforts.

God still calls individuals to fight the battles of injustice. Consider these truths:
- God provides the needed strength as we struggle with feelings of inadequacy.
- God calls us to overcome obstacles of fear and pride and depend only on Him.
- God brings victory through His people as they depend on Him.
- God calls men and women to accomplish His will.

D—Directed Prayer

When the battles of life come, I must remember to depend on You for the victories.

January 4

Nicodemus' Little Secret

Can there ever be a secret disciple?
John 3:1-8

A—Advice from the Bible

This man came to Jesus at night . . .
(John 3:2, HCSB)

B—Biblical Example

A very religious man named Nicodemus came to Jesus at night. He wanted to learn from Him. He discovered that worshiping and living for God involved more than practicing laws. He was not only one of the Pharisees, a very religious branch of the Jews in Jerusalem, he also was one of their leaders, a member of the Sanhedrin, and a teacher of the Scriptures. The Pharisees believed that the way to please God was to keep all of His laws in every detail. They rejected people who did not follow this practice. Sometimes they appeared to make the law more important than people. The Pharisees felt that the people closest to God were those who had descended from Abraham. When Nicodemus encountered Jesus and the subject of religion or rebirth came up, this seeker was confused. He realized that spiritual rebirth or being born again was an even greater miracle than being physically born. Jesus continued to lead Nicodemus to understand His teachings by using a Scripture from the Old Testament. Remember the serpent on a pole? Apparently, this secret disciple did not reveal his identity as a follower of Jesus until John 7:50-53.

C—Contemporary Application

Nicky, a young teen, went to his first summer Christian youth camp with a school friend. He didn't have a clue about what the week would involve. He discovered that everything was so different from the religion of his East Asian parents. He listened and compared the teachings with his home religion. During a time of commitment, Nicky felt an unfamiliar stirring in his heart. Yes, he did believe Jesus was the Savior. But he kept this discovery private. Ten years later, Nick still thought about that summer experience and felt sure of his belief in the Savior, but he kept this discovery a secret. Ten more years passed and Nick continued to be a secret disciple. One day at his office, a fellow attorney invited Nick to worship at his church. The time had come to let people know about his decision to follow Jesus twenty years earlier. No more secrets!

Consider the answers to these questions:
- How would you define the word *secret*?
- What is a disciple?
- How then would you describe a secret disciple?
- How would you determine a way to take a public stand for Christ?

D—Directed Prayer

Lord, help me share my testimony about You in a public setting.

January 5

Hannah's Little Baby

The importance of making vows to God
1 Samuel 1:1-20

A—Advice from the Bible

Hannah conceived and gave birth to a son.
(1 Sam. 1:20, NIV)

B—Biblical Example

Hannah's husband, Elkanah, had two wives which was a common practice in his day. The second wife, Peninnah, had several children and constantly ridiculed Hannah because she had none. Every year the family traveled to Shiloh to worship the Lord. The ceremony included the offering of an animal sacrifice and a festival of celebration. This joyous occasion was to establish good relations between God and His worshipers. Peninnah increased her torment of Hannah. This problem caused much grief and Hannah dreaded the annual trip to Shiloh. Elkanah's second wife received special recognition because of her children and makes fun of Hannah. In desperation, this barren woman prayed to God. She reminded Him that she had been his faithful servant. She pleaded with God for a son and made a solemn vow that if He would answer her prayer she would give him to the LORD all the days of his life. After bringing her needs to God, Hannah felt release from her frustrations. As she prepared for motherhood, she knew that eventually her son would be released to serve the Lord. In time, Hannah became pregnant and delivered her first son, naming him Samuel. Later, God gave her more children.

C—Contemporary Application

The snow began falling in the night and by morning southwestern Oklahoma looked like a winter wonderland. This beautiful setting was both good news and bad news for me. The good news was that today I would give birth to our second child. The bad news was our hospital was in another town and snow packed roads separated us. The journey to the hospital began and we finally arrived in time for Martha's birth. I made two vows to God that day. Before the birth, I prayed for her physical needs, a strong body and sound mind. The second vow was made following her birth. I promised God that I would model for her how to love the Lord and serve Him. This beautiful princess has been such a blessing to me all these years. God heard and answered my prayer.

You, too, can find help from the Lord during your time of need. Express your opinion to the following questions.

- How should a person approach God when faced with a serious need?
- When God does not respond immediately to your request, how should you react?
- How do you feel about making a bargain with God to get what you want?
- Why do you think God expects you to keep your promises to Him?

D—Directed Prayer

Thank You, Lord, that You hear and answer the prayers of faithful servants.

January 6

God's Little Environmental Policy

Christians should be concerned about our earth.
Genesis 1:26-31

A—Advice from the Bible

Then God said . . . rule over all the earth.
(Gen. 1:26, NIV)

B—Biblical Example

Nothing happened by chance when the world began. God's plans for earth were brought into being at His command. A scientific explanation isn't necessary. The *who* and *why* of creation is, however, emphasized. Following the creation of plant and animal life, God created man in His own image. The concept for humankind included males and females. The assignment to be trustees over the earth was issued. The project as announced by the Creator was to develop and produce good things. The result of the finished creation brought pleasure to God. He proclaimed that His work was "good" six times and then added the word "very good" for the seventh time. Man with his intelligence was to control the created order of earth. He gave names to all nature and the animals. The environment at this time was peaceful and beautiful. Later, David expressed his appreciation to God by writing, "You made him ruler over the works of your hands; you put everything under his feet" (Ps. 8:6). From generation to generation, humankind has been subduing and controlling the world of nature. No one can predict what will happen in the future, but the environment does depend on thoughtful care in order to survive.

C—Contemporary Application

The sight is difficult to describe. Standing on the rim of the Grand Canyon National Park and viewing the great chasm always prompts me to worship the God who created such a wonder. One of the men responsible for protecting this beautiful place was President Theodore Roosevelt who died on January 6, 1919. He loved the land west of the Mississippi and ultimately sought ways to protect this environment. This controversial national leader established the United States Forest Service and in 1906 designated 18 areas as national monuments. No persons or organization could use this land for personal interests—the citizens were the benefactors. Roosevelt is remembered for his environmental contributions such as 150 national forests, 51 wildlife refuges, and many other natural places of beauty.

How can I participate in protecting the environment?
- Replace vegetation, such as trees.
- Recycle appropriately.
- Purchase biodegradable products.
- Conserve energy

D—Directed Prayer

I thank You, Lord, for Your greatness and goodness in creating our world.

January 7

The Lame Beggar's Little Miracle

Unexpected opportunities to share our faith happen in simple everyday living.
Acts 3:1-16

A—Advice from the Bible

A man who was lame from his mother's womb . . .
(Acts 3:2, HCSB)

B—Biblical Example

The apostles performed many miracles, but only Luke recorded this one initiated by Peter and John. The purpose of the miracle was to show the power of the Holy Spirit operating in the first-century church. The Jewish pattern of worship, three times a day, was still followed by the apostles. However, this ritual became an opportunity for fellowship and spiritual strength for the believers in Christ. The hopelessness of a man's condition would serve as a miracle-moment for the early church. Obviously the man had never walked. People carried him wherever he went. Peter and John saw this lame beggar as they approached the Temple. Compassion filled their hearts when they observed his physical condition. Peter went into action by insisting the beggar look at him instead of crying for alms. The beggar expected money from these interested men, but God had another plan in mind. The man's crippled feet and ankles became strong instantly. Physical healing had occurred. The apostles clearly stated that the healing power was not theirs, but from God. This miracle became a ready-made opportunity for Peter to preach the gospel.

C—Contemporary Application

Ana is an eight-year-old girl from Guatemala. A missionary team from our church had gone to help build a church and school building in Guatemala City. The crew heard about a little girl who had been randomly shot and was not expected to survive. The bullet was lodged somewhere in her abdomen. The local physician made an effort to locate the projectile, and in the process a problem developed from surgery. When the mission team met Ana, she was beginning to stoop over, because of the scar tissue. If medical help did not intervene soon, she would never stand straight again. God had a plan and He used these willing people as tools in the miracle. Ana was brought to the United States. A famous surgeon in Nashville agreed to repair the damage to her little body. Other doctors became involved in the process of making Ana whole again. This beautiful miracle would not have happened without Christian people seeking an opportunity to serve God.

How can this beggar's miracle help me grow in Christ?
- My thoughts and actions are valuable to the Kingdom work.
- My spiritual life can continue to develop as I study God's Word.
- My concern for all types of people is important.
- My faith in Christ needs to be demonstrated daily.

D—Directed Prayer

Lord, help me to take advantage of every impromptu happening to share the gospel.

January 8

Little Unbelief Delays

People have to reach out in the midst of danger.
Numbers 13:30—14:10

A—Advice from the Bible

But the men said . . . "we can't."
(Num. 13:31, NIV)

B—Biblical Example

Almost a year passed before Israel began the march from Sinai to Canaan. During that time God instructed them in His laws and gave them plans for the construction of the tabernacle. Early in the journey some problems surfaced. Continuous complaining became the norm. This attitude provoked Moses and displeased God. The time came to send out a spying party into Canaan to explore the conditions of the land and the strength of the people. After a six weeks absence, the twelve scouts returned with ripe fruit and one positive report. Caleb brought a call for action. He and Joshua advocated immediate possession of the land of Canaan. However, the other 10 spies said Israel was too weak to capture the land. In this situation in Israel's life, obeying God would have resulted in moving into the Promised Land immediately, instead 40 years of wandering in the wilderness was the sentence. Caleb and Joshua said, "We are well able . . ," but the other men said, "We are not . . . ."

C—Contemporary Application

Many separate battles were fought in the early years of establishing the United States. One name that stands out during these difficult times is General Andrew Jackson. One major triumph occurred when he defeated the Creek Indians, who were allies of the British. The result of that victory earned Jackson the name, "Old Hickory." Another call to arms was issued in the War of 1812 against New Orleans. The British army, comprised of veteran soldiers, was in command of this important southern city. The battle plans were made by General Jackson and his irregular army of Kentucky riflemen. The outlook was similar to that of the negative spies in the wilderness who refused to conquer the Promised Land. However, on January 8, 1815, this unlikely army won an amazing one-sided victory over the British. This battle was a major success for the United States. One man felt that his men could overcome any obstacle as they advanced into the city. Caleb would have liked this challenge!

Think about your journey in life today:
- How are you rebelling against God?
- What causes you to be afraid to take risks?
- How can you lose sight of God's plans and goals for your life?
- What are some "giants" that come between you and God?

D—Directed Prayer

Lord, help me to remember that sometimes the minority is right.

January 9

The Blind Man's Little Pool

You can be faithful in sharing Jesus even when others reject what you say.
John 9:1-35

A—Advice from the Bible

Go wash in the pool of Siloam
(John 9:7, HCSB)

B—Biblical Example

Jesus and His disciples were in Jerusalem to celebrate the Feast of Tabernacles. This miracle of healing probably occurred during that time. The experience is unique in the Gospels because it is the only instance in which the sufferer was supposedly born with his affliction. The disciples wondered if perhaps the man had sinned thus causing his blindness. Jesus shattered the old, traditional beliefs when He stated that neither the blind man nor his parents were responsible for the handicap. The Lord took advantage of this incident to impress upon His followers the urgency of performing their ministry at the moment of opportunity. The mission of Jesus and the works that He did were both commissioned and empowered by God. The method Jesus used to heal was unusual. The use of spit for various reasons was common in ancient times. A command was given to go wash in a pool. The beggar had to exercise a measure of faith to go to the pool. He obeyed and washed off the clay. Some people believed the man could see, others decided he was just a person who looked like the blind man. Then the Pharisees became involved and as usual controversy followed. Their final action was to cast the healed man away from their presence.

C—Contemporary Application

A group of senior adults was driving to Tuscumbia, Alabama, to attend the performance of *The Miracle Worker*. This outdoor play is presented at the home of Helen Keller. The story of her remarkable life unfolds on the stage. At age 19 months, Helen, for some cause, became deaf and blind. The entrance of Anne Sullivan into Helen's life caused a modern day miracle. First, Helen learned to read Braille. As a result of this achievement, her world of darkness and silence began to improve. Ten years later, the still deaf and blind girl was able to attend Radcliffe College. The rest of her amazing life is recorded in history. Her lectures and travels around the world encouraged other handicapped people to seek a better life. Her shared experiences brought hope to caregivers and parents of disabled children everywhere.

Lesson learned from this beggar's miracle and Helen's experience:

- Illnesses are not always the result of personal sin.
- Be ready to minister when opportunities come.
- Provide an undeniable testimony before people who know you.
- Share your faith even when others reject what you are saying.

D—Directed Prayer

Lord, I promise to continue to be Your witness in any situation.

January 10

Naomi's Little Grandson

God can bring a great blessing out of tragedy.
John 9:1-35

A—Advice from the Bible

Then Naomi took the child . . . and cared for him.
(Ruth 4:16, NIV)

B—Biblical Example

Naomi is a case study in hardship. During a time of famine in Israel, her family became refugees in a foreign land called Moab. This relocation brought added sorrow to this Jewish mother. She became a widow and her two sons died. The future seemed to offer nothing but old age and loneliness. Despite Naomi's trials, one ray of hope surfaced when she decided to return to her homeland. Ruth, a daughter-in-law, chose to return with Naomi. The rest of the book reveals God at work in a family and Naomi's changing attitude from bitterness to joy. The reason for this change in her life was a grandson named Obed. She had faced many personal challenges, but now the marriage of Ruth and Boaz provided a way for the family lineage to be extended. When Obed was born, Naomi loved her grandson and cared for his needs. She was secure and confident again. In the past God had cared for her needs by enabling her to endure times of material and family loss. Now God had blessed this woman by providing security and fullness of life. She once again rejoiced in God's goodness.

C—Contemporary Application

I have decided that first-time grandparents are really odd. Speaking from experience, the day our grandson James was born brought a special kind of joy to my life. A smile came on my face that January 10 afternoon that stayed in place for a week. Eighteen months later, James went with his parents to the mission field of Hong Kong. I thought my heart would break the day we said goodbye. However, God's plan was much more important to His kingdom work than my feelings. The years passed and James became a teenager. Wonderful electronic mail provided daily contact with our faraway family. Time for college approached and God blessed us in another special way. James wanted to live with us as he attended a local college. What joy these last two years have been for me! Caring for my grandson, watching him grow in Christ, and now seeing him prepare for mission work in the future brings fullness to my life. I have learned the value of letting God's plans for my family take priority over my uncertainties.

Lessons learned from a grandmother's experience:
- Maintain an ongoing trust in God.
- Offer your grandchildren to God for His service.
- Times of family loneliness will come, but God's grace is sufficient for the time..
- Believe that God will provide for now and eternity.

D—Directed Prayer

Father, thank You for creating grandchildren for us to love.

January 11

A Little Hospitality

Provide for those who are involved in vocational Christian service.
3 John 1-14

A—Advice from the Bible

> *You are showing your faith by whatever you do for the brothers and . . . strangers.*
> (3 John 5, HCSB)

B—Biblical Example

Third John is addressed to an individual Christian name Gaius. He probably occupied an influential role in the local church and the Christian community highly respected this man. John loved this Christian brother with the genuine kind of love shown by God. Despite the letter's highly personal nature, John also expressed thoughts he wanted Gaius to share with other Christian acquaintances. The *elder* (John) had confidence in Gaius's spiritual progress because he had heard about his testimony from the brothers. One factor in this man's character was his hospitality to other believers. He lived a balanced Christian life, adhering to both truth and love. Christians rejoice when they learn that believers remain faithful to Christ and to His people. John pointed to one particular aspect of how Gaius was living in the truth. He commended Gaius for his hospitality to visiting Christians even though they were strangers. The early church depended on the evangelistic and teaching ministries of traveling missionaries. These workers, in turn, relied on the hospitality and gifts of church members. The hospitality of John's friend sprang from genuine love and so John urged him to continue demonstrating kindness to these Christian workers.

C—Contemporary Application

The Christian message was spread rapidly along the Atlantic Coast in the 1700's. One person credited with much success was Jonathan Edwards (1703—1758). This man began as a preacher in his grandfather's Northhampton Church, Massachusetts Bay Colony. His life took a different direction after meeting George Whitefield, an evangelist. Together they started a great revival movement. Traveling on horseback and staying in homes of Christians, they covered the area with the gospel message. Later, Edwards became a missionary to the Housatonic River people. The hospitality provided by believers, such as Gaius in the Scripture for today, made sharing the message of salvation possible for traveling missionaries and strangers who were welcome in Christian homes.

Truths from these passages:

- We should rejoice when other believers are faithful to Christ and His people.
- We should pray and give financial support to vocation workers.
- We should follow the example of godly believers.
- We should welcome friends and strangers into our home.

D—Directed Prayer

Father, help me support Your workers through encouragement, prayer, hospitality, and financial gifts.

January 12

Gideon's Little Scare

In times of trouble, you can seek God's assurance.
Judges 6:1-24

A—Advice from the Bible

"But Lord . . . how can I save Israel?"
(Judges 6:15, NIV)

B—Biblical Example

Gideon was an unlikely Old Testament hero. He lived at a time when the well-being of his nation was constantly threatened by the powerful Midianites. Judges 6 begins by describing a bleak situation. The Israelites had stopped obeying God's law and now were suffering the consequences. This young Israelite was a farm boy from an undistinguished family. He was busy at work when a messenger of God appeared to him with an announcement that he had been chosen to become a military leader. Gideon was skeptical. He was concerned that the Lord had abandoned His people. The conversation revealed that this farmer lacked faith in himself and God. The Lord then revealed a specific assignment and Gideon responded with objections. God asked him to trust His judgment and to depend on Him. Gideon's pleas of inadequacy were rejected by the Lord. The determining factor for his success was the presence of the Lord. Gideon's excitement was growing. Hope was mounting in him. The scare Gideon felt was soon replaced when God declared that he would not die, but would live to lead God's forces against the Midianites.

C—Contemporary Application

Brigadier General Chuck Yeager is an American hero. This United States Air Force volunteer was an ace fighter pilot in World War II, a famous post-war test pilot, and a pioneer in the space program. He is perhaps best known as the first pilot to fly an airplane faster than the speed of sound. Many scares occurred during his years of service, but he continued to achieve the tasks set before him. Yeager came from humble beginnings in rural West Virginia. He never attended college. According to his autobiography published in 1985, his natural mechanical abilities were developed while watching and helping his father work on gas drilling equipment. His story typifies the American dream that through hard work a talented person can overcome times of trouble and achieve his goals. The fact that Yeager was from a small town and possessed no college degree did not prevent him from successfully serving his nation.

Lessons we can learn from Gideon's encounter with God:

- God was not angry about Gideon's doubts.
- God saw potential leadership in this young man.
- God promised to be with Gideon.
- God gave Gideon a task and then promised to help him accomplish the challenge.

D—Directed Prayer

Thank You, Lord, that Your assurances come through Your Word.

January 13

A Little Light and Darkness

Seek to live in daily fellowship with God.
1 John 1:5-11

A—Advice from the Bible

The darkness has blinded his eyes.
(1 John 1:11, HCSB)

B—Biblical Example

Every form of life has enemies. The enemy of the Christian is sin. With this fact established, the Apostle John makes an important announcement—*God is Light*! This good news emphasized the majesty, splendor, and glory of God. Light erases all kinds of darkness. God has no connection with anything evil. Notice that three statements for Christian living begin with the phrase "If we claim." Rather than attacking the false teachers, John instructed his own people on doing right. Walking in the light means living a sincere, open, and honest life. A believer will not consciously tolerate sin. In the area of personal conduct, "light" means personal purity; "darkness" means personal evil. John boldly states that if you claim to have a close personal relationship with God and don't follow His instructions, you are a liar! Two blessings come from this lifestyle. First, Christians experience fellowship with each other. The second blessing comes from God, as He forgives and cleanses from sin. The writer concluded that true light removes darkness.

C—Contemporary Application

His was a routine admission to busy Belleview Hospital, New York City, a charity case, one of many every night. Just a bum from the Bowery with a slashed throat. He lived in the darkness of filth, loneliness, cheap liquor, drugs, and disease. He accidentally fell and cut himself on the sink. The night was January 13, 1864 and the victim was Stephen Collins Foster. A friend seeking him was directed to the local morgue. The bum was finally identified. Once upon a time he had written the beautiful songs that made the whole world sing. And now at age 37, he was silenced. Remember these favorites? "Camptown Races"; "Oh! Susanna!"; "Beautiful Dreamer"; "My Old Kentucky Home." His lyrics became deeply rooted in our rich American heritage. So, what happened to this forgotten man? He chose darkness rather than light. All his worldly possessions were 38 cents in his pocket and a penciled scrap of paper with a line for a new song.

Evaluate the quality (good, bad, nothing) of your relationship with God and with others. Complete the following sentences:

- The quality of my relationship with God is_____.
- The quality of my relationship with Christian friends is _____.
- The quality of my relationships with non-Christians is _____.
- My goal for living in the light this week is _____.

D—Directed Prayer

Father, help me to know more than just the facts about You.

January 14

Elijah's Little Pity-Party

God provides ways for healing when you experience depression.
1 Kings 19:1-18

A—Advice from the Bible

"I have had enough, LORD."
(1 Kings 19:4, NIV)

B—Biblical Example

The prophet Elijah was literally on top of the world! He had successfully faced 450 prophets of Baal on Mount Carmel. The contest of the century followed. The Baal prophets ranted, chanted, prayed, and self-mutilated in an emotional frenzy, but their gods did nothing. Elijah prayed boldly before the people and with much dignity. God then sent fire to consume the sacrifice. The prophets of Baal were slain and the worship of the one true God was restored in Israel. God also sent rain to break the drought that had caused a famine throughout the land. Elijah was so exited about the previous events that he ran the 17 miles from Mount Carmel to the capital Jezreel. He was feeling good, but then something happened. Jezebel, the queen, sent a threatening message to Elijah, saying she would get even for his actions. The prophet became very depressed and plunged into total despair. Everything in his life looked hopeless. The long journey into depression began with fear. However, his journey ended when Elijah calmed down enough to hear the quiet voice of God. The Lord always stands ready to help.

C—Contemporary Application

My parents were married during the worldwide economic slump that began in 1929. Wall Street crashed and eventually most banks closed. The farmers in Southwest Oklahoma seemed to suffer the most. Drought and dust storms hit the Midwest and especially the southwest. This crisis was called "The Great Depression." My family began to make daily sacrifices in order to have food and jobs. Times of personal hopelessness were felt by most people, yet many did not run away from this problem. Years later, after the nation recovered under the leadership of President Franklin D. Roosevelt, the subject of this great depression would eventually be included in conversations. The lesson I learned from their example was that most people did not give up. Most people experience low times. However, some depressing moments are more severe than others. Elijah's mood swing was caused by a threat. He finally called out to God for help and God provided the resources to alleviate depression

Discover answers to the following questions:

- Why do I sometimes feel so bad about things?
- What is depression, and how can I deal with this problem?
- How can God help me overcome my mood swings?
- How can I help a depressed friend?

D—Directed Prayer

Lord, I am so grateful that when I listen, I can find You in the quietness.

January 15

Paul's Little Road Trip

You are accountable for sharing your testimony.
(Acts 26:12-23)

A—Advice from the Bible

I appoint you as a servant and a witness of things you have seen.
(Acts 26:16)

B—Biblical Example

The Apostle Paul shared his testimony many times about meeting Christ on the Damascus road. However, the experience in today's passage was probably the most dramatic. His enemies had accused him of being a revolutionary and with bringing a Gentile into the sacred part of the Jewish temple. An arrest was certain. The Roman soldiers took him from Jerusalem to Caesarea, a Roman city far away from the Jewish leaders. After several encounters with Governor Festus, Paul asked to be sent to Rome rather than return to Jerusalem. The desire to share his testimony was one of the reasons for this decision. King Agrippa II requested an audience with the apostle. This opportunity to talk about Jesus was just what the missionary desired. The reasons for Paul's imprisonment were explained to this Jewish ruler. Then the prisoner was allowed to speak. He recounted the experience on the road to Damascus and how because of Christ and this life-changing event, Paul was never the same again. He had to be a witness!

C—Contemporary Application

John Warr, an 18th century apprentice shoemaker, was determined to be a faithful witness for Christ. He did not realize at the time how difficult this commitment would be. Another young apprentice was hired who didn't want to be bothered with spiritual things. One day this unbeliever was caught taking a shilling that did not belong to him. The young man's guilt led to great humiliation and so he asked John Warr for help and prayer. Time passed and finally the man put his faith in Christ and became a committed disciple. What difference did the witness of John Warr make? That fellow apprentice was William Cary, who later became a remarkable missionary to India. The impact of one witness brought glory to God and untold blessing to multitudes of people around the world.

Practice writing your personal testimony by using the following outline:

- How I lived before I accepted Christ: _____
- How I accepted Christ as my Savior _____
- How my life has changed since I accepted Christ _____
- The name a person I may witness to today is_____

D—Directed Prayer

Father, lead me to witness with my life, not just my words.

January 16

Zechariah's Little Pep Talk

You can have hope for the future.
(Zechariah 14:1-9)

A—Advice from the Bible

A day of the Lord is coming.
(Zech. 14:1)

B—Biblical Example

The Book of Zechariah presents hope for God's people and introduces the minor prophet who would be God's spokesperson. The setting was during the time the Jews returned from Babylonian captivity to rebuild the Temple in Jerusalem. The local people living in and around Jerusalem strongly opposed the work and presence of these returnees. However, God spoke through His prophet and promised that He would reestablish the Jews in their homeland, away from enemy rulers. He would make them victorious over their enemies. Even beyond the days of the prophet, God promised to send His Messiah to bring eternal peace to His people and His world. Chapter 14 presents God saving Jerusalem, His people. A defeated Jerusalem had been robbed and humiliated. God's comforting words assured total victory over all the nations opposed to God. On "that day," the Lord would dramatically change all of His creation. Waters would flow in all directions and the seasons will be altered. The climax of "the day of the Lord" is that all people will recognize God as the one and only God.

C—Contemporary Application

History books remind us that evil rulers have always been present in the world. People have been abused in horrific ways. The first Persian Gulf War began on January 16, 1991, and ended six weeks later when the allied military coalition drove Iraq's armies out of Kuwait. That media presentation was my first introduction to the evil man named. Saddam Hussein, president of Iraq (1979-2003). This man's brutal rule was marked by costly and unsuccessful wars against neighboring countries. Saddam launched an invasion of Iran's oil fields in September 1980. He caused thousands to flee to refugee camps along the country's northern border. Untold thousands more were murdered, many simply disappearing into the regime's prisons. Saddam was finally captured by U.S. soldiers without firing a shot. Victory over the enemy had come.

A letter from God might begin and end with: Dear people—Forever yours, God:

- I have always loved you.
- I have always offered hope for you.
- You can be secure in My love.
- You can experience My blessings forever.

D—Directed Prayer

- Begin today thanking God for your spiritual hope-chest.

January 17

Little Army of Locust

God uses individuals to give His warnings.
(Joel 1:1-12)

A—Advice from the Bible

The destroying locust has eaten everything.
(Joel 1:4)

B—Biblical Example

Joel was a prophet to Judah and may have lived in Jerusalem. The immediate occasion for Joel's prophecy was a plague of locust which had devastated the entire country. The severity of the destruction of these insects is indescribable. Joel saw in this tragedy a warning of the coming day of the Lord and he called his countrymen to repentance. The prophet desired to get the attention of all the people. Four groups of people were challenged to recall things from their past that had been painful. Old men, drunkards, worshipers, and vinedressers were addressed. Without a change in Judah's actions, they could not expect God's protection, restoration, and blessing. What the people were about to experience would be worse than anything in their past. Swarm after swarm of locust would continue to devour everything in their path. Now that Joel had the attention of the people, he began his lament, his announcement of the day of the Lord, and His call to repentance. Verse 7 contains a vivid description of what would remain after the invasion.

C—Contemporary Application

The cotton crops were the best the farmers had seen in years. A prediction of a good harvest was what these men needed. The Oklahoma fields were beautiful with their green leaves and flowering boles. However, the past hail storms could not be blamed for what happened in a few hours. I watched as a dark cloud seemed to be moving across the countryside. My small town became disturbed about the potential unknown danger. The enemy was a swarm of locust coming from nowhere. These destructive insects attacked the cotton fields and stripped away all the green leaves and finished by chewing the stems to the ground. Tears flowed from the eyes of these land owners. All hope of a harvest was gone. More bank loans would be required for survival until the next planting season. However, an interesting fact occurred about this plague. The farmer with the most land was named Joel!

Christian disobedience can result in locust-like problems:
- Disobedience means something or someone is more important than God.
- Continued disobedience can destroy the joy and happiness of a life.
- Ongoing disobedience brings separation from God and His Word.
- Complete disobedience devastates a family and a church.

D—Directed Prayer

Thank You, God, for Your invitation to repent.

January 18

A Little Report from Timothy

Christians experience joy when they share the gospel.
(1 Thessalonians 3:6-13)

A—Advice from the Bible

We were encouraged about you through your faith.
(3:7)

B—Biblical Example

The Apostle Paul had feared that the Thessalonians might not withstand persecution and remain faithful. He had sent Timothy to visit the church to help them and then return to him with a report. Timothy met Paul at Corinth and gave him the glad news that things were going well at Thessalonica. Paul was extremely happy about Timothy's information. Two items about the account were especially important to him. The first was that the people were standing fast in faith and in love. His joy caused him to turn to God with a prayer of thanksgiving for the Thessalonian Christians and their steadfastness in the faith. Paul also wanted to know how these believers felt about him. He knew enemies were present in the fellowship and they did not want to see him again. Verses 11-13 are a prayer containing a request that Paul be able to serve them by helping them grow spiritually. Some time passed before the prayer was answered. (Read Acts 20:1-3.) Timothy's news gave him new strength for his ministry.

C—Contemporary Application

Our son is a missionary in the Philippians. Many Bible study groups were formed during Mark's first term in Manila. These students lived in a place called "the squatter's area." These people are the poorest of the poor, yet, they long to know about Jesus. When the time came for Mark and Judy to return for a year's stateside assignment, concern became the issue for these new Christians. Who would check on these people? What if they ceased to meet because no one showed an interest in them? Mark prepared them for his absence as best he could and then prayed for their continued spiritual growth. One day about six months into the absence, an email arrived telling Mark that each house-group was continuing to study and grow. This report brought a sigh of thanksgiving and a joyous celebration of this good news. Many missionaries have to leave behind the work they have established. Some of their disciples fail to follow; others serve the Lord.

What is God teaching me from this Scripture passage today?

- Express thanksgiving for those who have inspired you to be more faithful.
- Be a blessing to others by praying <u>for</u> them.
- Be a blessing to others by praying <u>with</u> them.
- Express your love for others in the Lord.

D—Directed Prayer

Father, thank You for all the people whom You have sent to bless my life.

January 19

Mephibosheth's Little Limp

God enables you to care for others.
(2 Samuel 9:1-9)

A—Advice from the Bible

"Is there anyone still left whom I can show kindness?"
(2 Sam. 9:1)

B—Biblical Example

King David's loyalty and personal affection for Jonathan caused him to seek out his remaining son. Who was Mephibosheth? His father Jonathan was David's special friend, and his grandfather was Saul, king of Israel. The young man was lame in both feet (4:4) as a result of fleeing with his nurse during political violence. His father was killed when Mephilosheth was four-years-old. For years he hid, afraid of being killed by the king who replaced his grandfather. Without David's personal commitment made years earlier, Mephibosheth, who by now had his own son, would have perished. This example of the kindness of one person for another is demonstrated by a king who actively sought ways to be gracious to other people. The former royal received many benefits from his new benefactor. The land of his grandfather was restored and his status in the kingdom was recognized. He and his family were invited to eat at the royal table as a frequent guest. David demonstrated his faith in God and also found a way to decrease Mephibosheth's potential threat to his throne.

C—Contemporary Application

Plans were being made for the summer vacation from school. However, this summer would be different. An outbreak of polio had occurred in our county. Four people had developed this disease; one of my friends died. The fear of this crippling disease was relieved when Dr. Jonas Edward Salk (1914-1995), American doctor and epidemiologist, developed the first vaccine against poliomyelitis. Salk's work in the 1940s on an antiinfluenza vaccine led him and his colleagues to develop a vaccine against polio in 1952. After successful wide-scale testing in 1954, the vaccine was distributed nationally and greatly reduced the disease. The following summer, most of the fears had been replaced with thankfulness for the medicine needed to eradicate this disease. This man's concern for others made a difference in the lives of many children.

Specific reason why you need to care for people who are potential enemies:

- They are no longer a threat to you.
- They are easier to get to know.
- They make you feel more at ease.
- They have a lifestyle you will try to understand.

D—Directed Prayer

Father, what would it cost me to be kind to someone this week?

January 20

A Little Discipleship

True discipleship involves sacrificial devotion to Jesus.
(Mark 8:34-38)

A—Advice from the Bible

He must deny himself and take up his cross and follow me.
(Mark 8:34)

B—Biblical Example

The disciples of Jesus had just heard some distressing news from the Lord. He began to speak to them about His coming death. These men had no idea about the method of His passing. Jesus continued by discussing the price all His followers must pay to follow Him. Two things are commanded in verse 34: denial of self and cross-bearing. The word "cross-bearing" was new to the listeners. Of course, they understood crucifixion. The Roman's preferred this method of execution and chose public areas for humiliation of the victim. Another command is given to "follow me." Our self-denial is to be like Jesus' denial of Himself. This makes us more understanding of His life and His message to us. Jesus then offers more advice by stating that the road to true discipleship is by the pathway of human rejection. He knew that some would-be disciples might become timid in the presence of those who would be hostile to the gospel. They could be ashamed of Jesus and His words. A true disciple of Jesus will never be embarrassed in the presence of non-Christian friends.

C—Contemporary Application

The remarkable life of a true disciple is Susannah Annesley Wesley. She was born in London, England on January 20, 1669. She married Samuel Wesley and bore him 19 children. The last two are familiar to Christians. John and Charles Wesley were the founders of Methodism and Charles wrote the lyrics to some of my favorite hymns such as "O for a Thousand Tongues to Sing." Susannah was a devoted preacher's daughter and gave her allegiance to the Church of England. She was a successful preacher's wife. She was an unusual mother. Stories of her life tell how each child had a special audience every week with their mother. In the privacy of her sitting room, she instructed each child in the way of the Lord. She taught them to understand the Bible and to accept a sacrificial life of true discipleship to Jesus Christ.

Discipleship is a process by which we become more like Jesus.

- It involves discomfort, pain, fear, and failure.
- It involves growing stronger and more effective.
- It involves ministering to broken families.
- It involves faithfulness to your church.

D—Directed Prayer

Father, thank You, for allowing me to take up my cross and follow You.

January 21

Bezalel's Little Skills

Giving to the Lord includes giving your abilities.
(Exodus 35:30-35)

A—Advice from the Bible

The LORD has chosen Bezalel.
(Ex. 35:30)

B—Biblical Example

After Moses told the people of Israel about the tabernacle, they brought their possessions to be used in building and furnishing this place to worship God. The Lord called Bezalel by name to head up the building of the tabernacle. He came from the tribe of Judah, one of the largest tribes in the Israelite community. His job description was the chief engineer, the architect, and the job contractor for the project. His name means "in the shadow of God," indicating that he lived under God's protection. As a divine choice, the Spirit of God empowered him. In addition to spiritual knowledge and understanding often provided by the Holy Spirit, intellectual aid, artistic guidance, and technical skills also were bestowed. This leader not only designed the tabernacle, but he taught others how to build the facility. Just imagine working with metallurgists, stonecutters, woodcarvers, engravers, designers, embroiders, and weavers! Bezalel was now ready to do God's task.

C—Contemporary Application

Two people come to mind when I think about using personal abilities to serve the Lord. Brother Dave was a member of our first pastorate after seminary graduation. He and his wife were a quiet couple, who lived in a small house, and lived frugally. Many times, when my husband was at his study in the church basement, he would hear footsteps upstairs. Checking out who might be in the building, he would find Brother Dave with a little can of oil fixing the windows so they would open, or using his screwdriver to tighten anything that was loose. Nothing was ever said by him, he just did his job.

The other person is a woman named Sandy. She is a gourmet cook and caters many fancy celebrations. However, she loves to use her abilities in our church kitchen. Our meals are served with style and delicious taste. Recently she volunteered to cook the meals for our Room at the Inn ministry to homeless men. Both people find great joy in servicing the Lord.

Which of the abilities do you feel describe you?

- Leading others to serve the Lord.
- Caring for others who are in need.
- Being a generous steward of all God has provided for you.
- Working with the details involved in a project or ministry.

D—Directed Prayer

Lord, I want to put my abilities into action for You.

January 22

Little Miracles

You must believe to belong.
(John 10:24-38)

A—Advice from the Bible

The miracles I do in My Father's name speak for me.
(John 10:25)

B—Biblical Example

Chapter 10 focuses on the Lord's confrontation with Jewish leaders. The passage begins with a familiar story of shepherd and sheep. Jesus then makes the fourth great I AM statement in John's Gospel, when He declares that He is the good Shepherd. About two and a half months later, John records an encounter Jesus had with the same Jews. The Feast of Dedication (Hanukkah) was taking place and these men were celebrating the rededication of the temple by Judas Maccabeaus in 164 B.C. The words of Jesus in verse 38 proclaim that He had been set apart by the Father and sent into the world. These leaders decided the time had come for a "showdown," and they did not want Him to evade the issue of whether He was the Messiah or not. When the Lord said that He was one with the Father, the Jews shouted "blasphemy." The miracles that had occurred should have convinced these enemies that He was God. However, the simple matter of examining the evidence still was rejected. They were unwilling to accept the truth. The session ended with an attempt to arrest Jesus, but He left the area completely and did not return until Palm Sunday, when He presented Himself as Israel's King.

C—Contemporary Application

Harry Houdini was an American magician, who fooled people with his magic. Some press releases referred to him as the greatest performer of "miracles" in the world. His career began in 1882 as a trapeze performer. Subsequently, he became famous for his performances of feats of magic. He showed astounding ability in extricating himself from handcuffs, ropes, locked trunks, and bonds of any sort. Houdini attributed all his feats of magic to natural, physical effects and explained how many of his tricks were performed. He exposed the tricks of fraudulent spiritualistic mediums, often producing "spiritualistic" phenomena himself. Fake miracles fool the people; true miracles are rejected by many people.

Jesus was the true miracle worker:
- He used them to heal people.
- He used them to prove His divine identity.
- He used them to offer salvation.
- He used them to explain that He was the Good Shepherd.

D—Directed Prayer

Thank You, that You offer the miracle of salvation to all people.

January 23

Joshua's Little Military Expedition

A Christian can be courageous because God is with you.
(Joshua 1:1-11)

A—Advice from the Bible

You will lead these people to inherit the land.
(Josh. 1:6)

B—Biblical Example

When Joshua accepted God's role of leadership, he became an important part of Israel's history. He was introduced early in the account of Israel's journey from slavery in Egypt to freedom in Canaan (Ex. 17:8-16). Before Moses died, God directed him to commission Joshua as his successor. The Lord spoke directly to His chosen leader and gave the next step in Israel's journey. The crossing of the Jordan River was the most dramatic event for Israel since the crossing of the Red Sea. God, then, gave the new guide a vision of the land that they would conquer. His enemies would be enemies of God. Strength and courage were essentials for the task ahead. The *law* was probably parts of the Book of Deuteronomy. Joshua was to practice and proclaim the *law*. Practicing God's law would result in prosperity and success. Discouragement was to have no part in this journey. The nomadic Israelites were now ready to be a nation. God had been preparing the people and Joshua had the wisdom to delegate responsibility to them. The provisions were gathered and the military expedition was ready. Possess the land!

C—Contemporary Application

Dwight David Eisenhower (1890-1969) was one of my favorite American military leaders. I remember seeing pictures of the war at the movies (our only source of information at that time). His great popularity as Allied supreme commander during World War II led to his appointment as supreme commander of the Allied Expeditionary Force for the invasion of France. In the months leading up to the invasion on June 6, 1944, he supervised the preparation of air, sea, and land forces and all other strategic planning. In the autumn of 1945, Eisenhower became army chief of staff. During his tenure in that office, he had the dual role of demobilizing the wartime army while maintaining a suitable defense force. He returned to Europe as supreme commander for the North Atlantic Treaty Organization.

A leader is one who:

- Knows the way.
- Goes the way.
- Shows the way.
- Lives the Way.

D—Directed Prayer

Father, Your courage and strength are so special to me.

January 24

A Little Fight against False Teachers

God is not looking for volunteers.
(Jude 17-23)

A—Advice from the Bible

Snatch others from the fire and save them.
(Jude 23)

B—Biblical Example

Jude is the brother of James and the half-brother of Jesus and his epistle is written in military fashion. The writer seems to be sounding the trumpet, calling the faithful to war. The captain of the army is Jesus, who has carefully watched and guarded His followers. The purpose for writing the letter is to make Christians aware that salvation involves more than a personal, private experience. We are to identify, label, and avoid false doctrines. The enemies of the believers mocked the Christian faith as a whole; therefore, defending the faith was necessary. Remember that we are not fighting personal enemies, but the enemies of God. Four instructions are given to prepare for the spiritual fight:
1. Remember God's Word by memorizing Scripture.
2. Remember the inspired writers of the Word and how they remained firm in the faith.
3. Remember select passages of Scripture to use in standing firm in the faith.
4. Remember why many writers of the Bible wrote about the spiritual warfare.

C—Contemporary Application

I am a fan of professional football. Each winter I look forward to the Super Bowl, played about this time of the year. This annual championship game of the National Football League (NFL) is the only major professional American football league in the United States. All spring and summer the men prepare for this encounter. In fact, the sport is one of the most popular American events. It is played between the champions of the American Football Conference (AFC) and the National Football Conference (NFC). The teams know their "enemy." Drills have been created to defeat the other team. Equipment is the best possible for defending the players. The similarities between spiritual battles and the sports battle are interesting. Each team knows the rules and wants to be the victor. The Christian receives affirmation from God; the winning football player receives a ring.

What can we do about false teachers?
- Know the Word of God.
- Have the courage to defend the Truth.
- Watch and pray.
- Be careful where you send your money.

D—Directed Prayer

Father, lead me to stand firm against Your enemies.

January 25

Abram's Little Exodus

Christians need to respond to the promises of God.
Genesis 12:1-9

A—Advice from the Bible

So Abram left as God told him.
(Gen. 12:4)

B—Biblical Example

A pioneer's necessary character traits of courage, perseverance, boldness, and innovation were evident in this Old Testament patriarch. Abraham was the original pioneer. God presented this man with a challenge and a vision of a new land. However, Abraham had to take the risk and claim the promise. He gave up a secure present for the promise of a great future. The details of how God spoke to Abraham are not available, but the fact remains that this believer understood the message. Being obedient to God's call affected many people at that time, especially their family. What if something terrible happened to Abraham? Sarah would be without any support in a strange land. Nevertheless, this family chose to follow God's directive. With no guarantee other than the promise of God, he set out on what would prove to be a perilous journey. His example of faith was measured by his obedience. The whole plan of God was not revealed to Abraham all at once, but step-by-step. God clarified the course and issued new instructions. Abram followed.

C—Contemporary Application

Peter Marshall (1902-1949) was a well-known Presbyterian pastor and Chaplain of the U.S. Senate (1947-49). He was recognized for his powerful prayers for our nation and his kindness to all people. One of his sermons was titled, "Under Sealed Orders." The topic was selected from Abraham's experience and the principle involved is that faith in God is ongoing. Government leaders must make nation-changing decisions without a written plan of how the project will be completed. He died at an early age on January 25, 1949, but his name became famous through the publication of his biography, *A Man Called Peter,* written by his widow, Catherine Marshall. Abraham and Marshall's faith and obedience marked them as spiritual pioneers of all who believe that their greatest joy comes by responding to the promises of God.

Faith is best expressed as:

- Expecting God to keep His promises.
- Looking beyond the known into the unknown.
- Accepting risks.
- Knowing none of the answers.

D—Directed Prayer

Lord, help me to share with others what faith in God means to me.

January 26

A Little Encouragement and Hope

A Christian leader can be the source of great encouragement to fellow believers.
2 Thessalonians 2:13-17

A—Advice from the Bible

God gave us eternal encouragement and hope.
(2 Thess. 2:16)

B—Biblical Example

Paul based his thanksgiving for the Thessalonians on the fact that they were brothers and they were beloved of the Lord. This firm foundation in the Lord was the reason for the apostle encouraging the church to "stand firm" and continue doing what they had been taught. Apparently his first letter to the church had been misunderstood and now disturbing news came back to Paul in Corinth that the church had severe problems. The confusion seemed to center around the second coming of Christ and their false interpretation of this doctrine. The Christians seemed to have forgotten that their salvation and sanctification was a call to share in the glory which was Christ's. These believers were contending with many problems. Major troubles were disrupting the fellowship of the church. Persecution from outside forces was a constant threat. A solution was offered by Paul that emphasized they hold fast to the truths taught to them by Paul, Silvanus, and Timothy. The gospel, the good news of salvation in Jesus Christ, was the basic content of the traditions they were urged to maintain. A beautiful benediction is pronounced in verse 16. An everlasting confidence and assurance was expressed that nothing would keep them from ultimately being with Christ.

C—Contemporary Application

The apostle Paul enjoyed what God had called him to do and wanted the Thessalonians to share in his joy. The story is told about Thomas Edison, who worked hard and long in his laboratory with no time off. His wife was concerned that he might ruin his health. She therefore urged him to take a vacation and get away from his lab for awhile. He asked his wife were he should go on a vacation and she answered "Go and do the thing you want to do more than anything else in the world." The next morning, Thomas Edison rose early and went directly to the lab and began work. He found encouragement and hope in his life-purpose.

God has always provided leadership for His people, who:
- Faithfully preach His Word.
- Faithfully teach His Word.
- Faithfully follow His commands.
- Faithfully witness to "the utter most parts of the earth."

D—Directed Prayer

Father, allow me the opportunity to encourage someone this week.

January 27

Abraham's Little Test

Faith is the ability to see God in the dark.
Genesis 22:1-14

A—Advice from the Bible

God tested Abraham.
(Gen. 22:1)

B—Biblical Example

Abraham and Sarah were real people who lived in a real world. God promised great blessings: descendants, a land, and hope. During the years of moving around, the Lord promised a son to Abraham. If Isaac's birth was the joyful high point in Abraham's life, God's call for Abraham to sacrifice his son was one of the lowest points. After all Abraham's successes and failures, after all he had learned about God—then came the test and it came from God. The main question in this encounter with Abraham and God is, "Did Abraham love God even more than his only son?" The story of this test was to focus on Abraham's obedience and faith. This father and son went out into the wilderness to the foot of the mountain called Moriah. And he intended to do what God had asked—offer his son as a sacrifice. However, God did provide an animal for the sacrifice. God had seen Abraham's faithfulness and Abraham had seen God's. "The Lord will provide" did not want Abraham to offer Isaac. Rather, he wanted this patriarch's faith to be so great that he was willing to do what was commanded. The test was complete. God began the test; He directed the test, and heaven graded Abraham on the spot. He passed!

C—Contemporary Application

A noted English preacher, William Sangster, tells an experience when visiting a young girl in the hospital. The doctors were working in vain to keep a serious disease from causing blindness. With sadness the girl said to her pastor, "God is going to take away my sight." Reverend Sangster waited a few minutes, then answered, "Don't let Him, Suzie. Give your eyes to Him." The young girl didn't understand what he meant. The preacher explained, "Pray this prayer: 'Father, if I must lose my sight, help me to give them to You.'" Abraham surrendered Isaac as a love-offering and God honored his actions. An old hymn has these lines: *Some through the water; some through the flood, Some through the fire . . . but God gives a song.*

God designs what we go through; we decide how we got through the situation:

- Sometimes we become angry with God.
- Sometimes we threaten to leave His church.
- Sometimes we lose the joy of our salvation.
- Sometimes we walk through the valley with God.

D—Directed Prayer

Lord, help me to remain ready to obey when Your testing comes into my life.

January 28

Making a Little Difference

What we do will last longer than what we say.
Titus 2:11-15

A—Advice from the Bible

Say "No" to ungodliness and worldly passions.
(Titus 2:12)

B—Biblical Example

Titus was one of Paul's most reliable helpers and missionary companions. At the time Paul wrote the letter to Titus, he was a young teacher and preacher on the island of Crete. Some of the believers were surrounded by false teachers and pagan lifestyles. Living for Jesus was difficult. These pagan actions concerned the apostle, so he sent his advice to Titus in the form of an epistle. Paul taught that sound doctrine leads to a lifestyle that makes a difference. Obviously, belief in Jesus Christ must show itself in everyday living. Without Titus 2:11-15, all of the chapter would seem like a list of legalistic rules. However, beginning in verse 11, Paul identified the foundation for all Christian behavior and attitudes. From God's grace comes the spiritual power to live God's way. The apostle both challenged and affirmed Titus. This young adult could have felt inadequate because of his youthfulness. Yet, the missionary had confidence in Titus' ability to teach, encourage, and correct people of all ages. Based on sound doctrine and a consistent lifestyle, Titus could exercise all authority. This chosen way of living would make a major difference in the people of Crete.

C—Contemporary Application

Thomas Obadiah Chisholm was born in Franklin, Kentucky, in 1866. A limited education kept him as a teacher in a one-room school house he had attended as a child. By age 27, he was working on a newspaper when he became a believer in Christ. The revival he attended changed his life and he soon became an ordained Methodist preacher. He pastored a church for one year, when poor health prevented him from continuing in the ministry. He returned home, sold some insurance, and began to write music as personal therapy. A friend asked Thomas to compose some words for a new song he had written. "Living for Jesus" was born and published in 1917. Other familiar songs of Mr. Chisholm are: "Great Is Thy Faithfulness" and "O to Be Like Thee."

Test your effectiveness for Christ by placing a checkmark by a recent action:
- Used Scripture to help a friend.
- Showed kindness to someone.
- Worked to reconcile a broken relationship.
- Spent time praising God for His grace and salvation.

D—Directed Prayer

Father, I want to live a life that is true and meaningful.

January 29

Daniel's Little Confession

How blessed are Christians who stand on the victory side of the cross!
Daniel 9:1-12

A—Advice from the Bible

I prayed to the LORD my God and confessed.
(Dan. 9:4)

B—Biblical Example

Faithful Jews never ceased to believe that they were people of destiny. Their prophets kept alive the messianic hope, and this sustained the people when they were discouraged. Their concept of the Messiah often was more national than spiritual. Although Daniel probably never met Jeremiah, he apparently had been a student of prophecy, particularly the prophecies that related to the fate of his people. Perhaps he was referring to Jeremiah 25:1-14. As he read that the captivity was to be 70 years, Daniel realized that the time was almost complete and felt the need to pray for himself and his people. In verses 3-12, the nation's sins were confessed. He recited the history of his people's rebellion. Then he prayed an agonizing prayer for the sinful Israelites to be forgiven and restored to God. This captive Hebrew knew that repentance and forgiveness must happen if the children of Israel were ever to return to their homeland. His prayer is one of the greatest examples of intercession in the Bible.

C—Contemporary Application

Old Brother Russell was the eldest member of his small local church. Many changes had occurred during the last seventy years. Some good things had happened; some unpleasant events had almost destroyed the fellowship. Things were happening at this time that caused this faithful Christian to grieve. The present leadership was leading the congregation away from the values and principles of God's Word. Brother Russell tried to talk with the deacons about his concerns, but they refused to listen to this faithful follower of God. Finally, he decided to intercede for his church. Prayer was real to him and many times God had heard and answered his requests. He started praying for the return of worship that honored God; for a time of renewal and repentance; for change in the direction the church was going; and for the church to be in the world, but not let the world in the church. His prayer journal was read at his memorial service.

Daniel knew how to pray and believed that God:

- Knew about the suffering and desolation of His children.
- Answered the prayers of His people when they were faced with suffering.
- Would give victory to those who trusted in Him.
- Might not bestow His answers immediately.

D—Directed Prayer

Lord, lead me to be faithful in intercessory prayer.

January 30

Little Careless Words

Believers reveal their true character by their conversation at unguarded moments.
Matthew 12:33-37

A—Advice from the Bible

Men will have to give account for every careless word they have spoken.
(Matt. 12:36)

B—Biblical Example

Chapter 12 is concerned with the response of a group known as the scribes and the Pharisees. This religious body was bitter and vindictive against anyone who reacted to their established beliefs. Jesus was a real threat to them by His freedom and spiritual power. Of course, these enemies were not able to control the Savior, nor could they make Him fit into their system. His main accusation against them was blasphemy. Jesus said that blasphemy against the Holy Spirit would never be forgiven, in this world or the coming one. They could not even thank God for the miraculous healing of the man on the Sabbath. Dozens of signs and miracles had been done in their presence, but these men rejected the work of the Holy Spirit. The real tragedy of this experience is that the Pharisees knew that God was working in Jesus. The Holy Spirit had convicted them of this truth. However, by their words, the work of the Holy Spirit was called the work of the devil. To reject the Spirit means that the door of communication is closed to forgiveness and salvation.

C—Contemporary Application

My first encounter with a computer was very frightening. I marveled at the use and management of words and soon appreciated the ability to delete certain things I had written, but the words that come from our lips often cannot be removed. Bess had a reputation for hurting people by the use of words. She formed opinions of visitors to her church and soon spread gossip about who these people were. How sad that this middle-age woman was a believer in Jesus and yet, blasphemed her fellow Christians! One day, a friend challenged Bess about her unkind words. The pastor's sermon urged the believers to use words to encourage other worshipers. That afternoon, Bess called several members and spoke against some of the individuals the pastor had mentioned. This friend encouraged her to seek forgiveness and take responsibility for the result of bad words.

People respond to God in different ways and with different words:
- Some react to the gospel with true responsibility.
- Some remain faithful to the gospel, no matter what happens.
- Some choose selected passages of Scripture and ignore the rest of the Bible.
- Some completely reject the message and the Messenger.

D—Directed Prayer

Father, help me to say nothing today that needs deleting.

January 31

Little Worthless Idols

We will be disappointed if we trust in something other than God.
Jeremiah 2:5-13

A—Advice from the Bible

They follow worthless idols.
(Jer. 2:5)

B—Biblical Example

The prophets of the Old Testament explained God's judgment as coming to people who reject God, His words, and His ways. Chapter 2 is a powerful sermon dealing with the sin of idolatry. Jeremiah fervently pleaded with the people to turn from idolatry and return to the Lord. His appeal begins with three questions found in verses 5-8. A connection between the past generations and the present revealed that idolatry was present when Israel first settled the land of Canaan. God wanted to know what was lacking in His relationship with His children that had caused them to turn to another. The people had turned from the life-giving power of God to that which was worthless. Israel had produced nonexistent gods and gained nothing. They had gone after worthlessness and had become worthless. People could not mix their faith in the Lord God with the worship of idols. Israel had forgotten their great deliverance from Egypt, so God summarized their salvation history for them. Pagan worship of idols had polluted the natural beauty of the land. The leaders were held responsible for the idolatry. The priests had become indifferent and irresponsible. Israel had exchanged God for non-gods and suffered a great loss.

C—Contemporary Application

Most third-world countries have idols. These images are placed in prominent locations in yards or in a house. I recall walking down a street in Hong Kong and shopping in the various stalls where local merchants displayed their wares. Each place had an idol. Candles and incense were the most frequent objects around the false gods. These idols could be purchased for a small amount of change. As I stood looking at these worthless images, my thoughts focused on the one true God. How I longed for these people to know Him and His superiority to anything they made or worshiped! Our missionary son was there to help declare the good news about a worthy God.

Old Testament people named their gods. What do some people call their gods today?

-
-

D—Directed Prayer

God, lead me to have a positive influence on the spiritual condition of my friends.

February 1

The Hostess of Shunem's Little Baby

Caring for others brings personal blessings from God.
2 Kings 4:8-37

A—Advice from the Bible

"You have gone to all this trouble for us. Now what can be done for you?"
(2 Kings 4:13, NIV)

B—Biblical Example

Elijah, the aggressive prophet of Israel, had trained Elisha, the pastor-prophet, to become his successor. This new spokesperson for God was sensitive to the needs of hurting people. Most of his miracles involved deeds of kindness and mercy.

The experience in this passage resulted from Elisha following a familiar path for traveling. Along the way, a Shunammite couple became his friends. Their hospitality included adding an extra room on their house as a resting place for the prophet. He desired to show his appreciation for their thoughtfulness. The question, "What can I do for you?" was answered by meeting her need for a baby. A son was born, but a heatstroke took his young life. The miracle that followed was preceded with prayer, *Elisha . . . prayed to the LORD* (v. 33). The woman's generosity brought two personal blessings: a miraculous conception and the miracle of resurrection from death.

C—Contemporary Application

Every day people are encountered who need our attention. Personal needs and activities often prevent us from seeing hurting people. This Bible couple saw an opportunity to help ease the lifestyle of God's prophet by providing a permanent place to lodge during his travel from town to town. Janet and George are my Christian friends. This couple has a great love for people from Guatemala. The caring began on a mission trip to that country. After meeting the people and helping build the Shalom Baptist Church, an love-interest developed that now extends for many years. People from that country have been house guests many times. A Mexican child, who needed specialized surgery was housed in their home. God seems to give willing people a heart for less fortunate individuals. Sometimes these people are from a different country or background. My friends have a suite for their Mexican friends and provide for all their needs.

The following statements suggest a personal response you might make when an opportunity surfaces for ministry. Which attitude best describes your behavior?

- You hesitate helping people you don't know.
- You are always ready to make a new friend.
- You wonder what the person will want from you in return for kindness.
- You see this experience as a way to help a person in need.

D—Directed Prayer

Lord, how can I show a caring spirit to other people?

February 2

Capernaum's Little Emergency

Following Jesus provides opportunities to minister to all kinds of people.
Luke 7:1-10

A—Advice from the Bible

A Centurion's slave . . . was sick and about to die.
(Luke 7:2, HCSB)

B—Biblical Example

Capernaum was located on the northwestern shore of the Sea of Galilee. This important city had a synagogue where Jesus often taught. Nearby Nazareth was Jesus' hometown and the place of rejection for His work. Sometimes hometowns don't recognize the importance of their sons and daughters. Jesus and His disciples relocated to this Roman controlled city and established their Galilean headquarters. Simon Peter was a local boy from Capernaum.

An emergency had surfaced in the home of a centurion. This man commanded 100 infantrymen and was part of a Roman legion. He also must have been very compassionate toward the slaves who served in his household. One slave in particular was special to this military man. Apparently the centurion had become impressed by the religion of the Jews. A delegation of Jewish elders wanted to help this generous man, so they came to Jesus with a request. The Lord did not hesitate to interrupt what He was doing and go to the Roman soldier's house.

The faith of this slave owner presents a powerful lesson to all who follow Jesus. He believed in Jesus and His power to heal. Verse 10 presents the rest of the story.

C—Contemporary Application

Sally's mother returned from the medical clinic with bad news. A terrible disease had invaded her body and immediate treatment was necessary. More bad news! This single mom has five children. Sixteen-year-old Sally is the oldest and provides financial support through a food service job. The husband and father abandoned the family years earlier. The church has never been part of this family lifestyle. However, recently a student Bible study group invited Sally to meet with them. The recent bad news has caused Sally to tell the group about her mother and the problems the family faces. Where can she go for help? Her simple faith in her new Christian friends has been expressed. How would you go about helping Sally find assistance and also leading her to accept Christ as her Savior?

- Simple faith can be expressed by a person of no spiritual heritage or background in the Scriptures.
- Simple faith can be expressed by a person who hears the good news about Jesus and believes in His power.
- Simple faith can be expressed by believers who see the needs of hurting people.
- Simple faith can be expressed in deeds of kindness and ministry.

D—Directed Prayer

Only believe, only believe, all things are possible, only believe.

February 3

Lot's Little Land Deal

Family conflicts can be resolved when you put others before yourself.
Genesis 13:1-18

A—Advice from the Bible

So Lot chose for himself the whole plain of Jordan.
(Gen. 13:11, NIV)

B—Biblical Example

Abram and his nephew, Lot, had been dwelling together for some time. Lot's father had died and Uncle Abram and Grandfather Terah raised him. Lot became a successful businessman. Both family members were rich in livestock. The increase of animals was making pasture land insufficient. The herdsmen began to argue over the rights to certain grazing areas. Abram realized that some action was needed to prevent further conflicts. He took the initiative in resolving the problem. Normally, rank and power rated first choice in dividing the property. However, Abram allowed Lot the first option. Negative character traits were soon revealed in his nephew. He was greedy and self-centered, choosing the well-watered plains of Jordan for his herds. The green fertile region would provide Lot with more wealth and possibly greater influence with the people in Sodom.
Abram basically got the left-overs. The land of Canaan had hills and rocks.

C—Contemporary Application

A young farmer settled on a small farm in western Oklahoma. Hard work and sacrifices soon produced money to buy more land. Early in 1900, this land-lover owned many sections of land in Washita County. He was respected in the agriculture community. Two sons were born and farming also was their choice vocation. The father realized that division of his wealth might cause family problems, so in his will specific farms were designated for each son. Death came to the patriarch and each son received his inheritance. The younger man seemed to have gained the best land, with water and good soil. The older son received the farms that prospered the least. Farming was difficult because of bad soil and no irrigation possibilities. The younger man prospered, was recognized in the community, built a great house in town, and seemed to have everything going for him. One day an oil company was leasing land in the area. The farm of choice belonged to the older son. Oil wells were soon pumping day and night. The father had known that oil existed on the poor land and gave the best to his hard working son.

Godly ways to respond to family conflicts:
- Be first to resolve the problems.
- Be willing to get less than you desire from the situation.
- Be willing to put family peace before personal desires.
- Be sincere about seeking God's will in the family conflict.

D—Directed Prayer
- Dear Lord, help me to know how to settle family problems when they surface.

February 4

The Wild Man's Little Cave

God wants you to share the gospel with others.
Mark 5:1-20

A—Advice from the Bible

He lived in the tombs . . .
(Mark 5:3, HCSB)

B—Biblical Example

Jesus and His disciples sailed across the Sea of Galilee toward the eastern shore. No doubt the disciples were still wondering about Jesus' controlling the recent storm. The boat landed in the region of the Gadarenes, a territory largely inhabited by Gentiles. A demon-possessed man met the boat. The pathetic condition of the demoniac moved Jesus to compassion. This outcast was alienated from his people because he was so violent and unmanageable. Trying to restrain him proved impossible. His mental condition caused a display of self-destructive actions. However, Jesus loved him and commanded the demons to leave. The Lord's purpose in casting out the unclean spirits was to show that the Son of God had power over all destructive forces. The exorcised demons then entered a nearby herd of swine. The healed man was fully clothed and in full possession of his senses. The townspeople reacted by begging Jesus to leave their area. The former demented man begged to go with Jesus and join the band of disciples but Jesus had a far different and more difficult task in mind for Him. He told him to "go back home and tell what has happened to you." The Gadarene obeyed and witnessed to his circle of friends and throughout all Decapolis, a region of ten cities.

C—Contemporary Application

A baby girl was born in 1888 who would grow-up and impact China with the gospel message. Her name was Bertha Smith. This faithful missionary arrived in China and became aware of a deep need for Christian revival. A movement among the Chinese for a deeper understanding of God became her passion. The Shantung Revival was God's answer to her prayer. Not only did the revival change many Chinese, but Miss Bertha's life as well. She later recorded in her book, *Go Home and Tell,* how her life and love for God became more real year-by-year. The book is a spiritual journey through decades of telling others the good news about Jesus Christ. A friend said of Miss Bertha at her burial, "She was an inspiration to everyone during her 100 years of life."

What will I go home and tell about?

- My life before I became a Christian.
- How I realized I needed Christ.
- How I became a Christian.
- What being a Christian means to me.

D—Directed Prayer

Lord, help me keep my personal testimony up-to-date.

February 5

Solomon's Little Benediction

Worship is more than a service in a church building.
1 Kings 8:22-24,56-61

A—Advice from the Bible

May the LORD our God be with us as He was with our fathers.
(1 Kings 8:57, NIV)

B—Biblical Example

God's great promises to Abraham concerning his descendants and land were fulfilled. King David now ruled and asked God to allow him to build God a suitable dwelling place in Jerusalem. God declined his offer, but promised the king that his son, Solomon would succeed him and build the Temple. No expense was spared in materials or decorations. Seven years later the Temple was completed. King Solomon called for a national assembly to dedicate the new place of worship. The first event was to transfer the ark from the tent of meeting to a permanent dwelling place. The second event was Solomon's public benediction, a spoken blessing. The king offered a beautiful prayer by praising God for being faithful to David. The conclusion of the prayer was a benediction in which he issued a call both to God and to His people to remember and keep their covenant. God's abiding presence was desired for the people. Peace had finally come. Solomon realized that the blessings he experienced and those of his nation were gifts of God's grace and presence. He also blessed God for His goodness and His fulfilled promises. The king desired that the Temple be a place where people could meet with God.

C—Contemporary Application

Sunrise was on the horizon one Arizona morning. A congregation of believers gathered on a vacant lot for one purpose—to worship and honor God. The land had been recently purchased to relocate the downtown church. Space was needed for educational expansion and parking. This gathering was the first of several to follow before the building was completed. The worship service began with Scripture and music. The ending of this special celebration was a benediction sung by the worshipers.

Peter Christian Lutkin (1858—1931), Dean of Music at Northwestern University, Evanston, Illinois, wrote a benediction for his church choir that is familiar to most Christians today. The words call for God's blessing on His people. Remember the words?

The Lord bless you and keep you, The Lord lift His countenance upon you; and give you peace, and give you peace . . . .

The truths from Solomon's benediction still apply to our generation.

- God wants everything we do and say to show our loyalty to Him.
- God wants everyone to know that He is the one and only God.
- God will stand with His people.
- God will be with each generation as He was with previous generations.

D—Directed Prayer

Lord, teach me to make every worship service meaningful to You.

February 6

John's Little Children

Keep obeying God's commands.
1 John 2:1-11

A—Advice from the Bible

My little children . . .
(1 John 2:1, HCSB)

B—Biblical Example

John was Jesus' most intimate earthly friend. He observed first hand the Savior's love for people. The apostle was in his advanced years when this letter was written. First John was sent to the churches around Ephesus. These Christians needed assurance in their faith. "My little children" expressed John's affection for these believers. His purpose for writing was clear: he did not want them to sin at any time. A warning was issued to any one who claimed to know the Lord, yet continued to disobey His commands. The strong word "liar" was used to describe this behavior. However, the good news is that some of these Christians were obeying God's commands. They were sincere seekers of God's will. This group of followers pleased the aging writer. John made his message clear by stating that God expects His earthly children to follow the path of His Son.

C—Contemporary Application

John and Mary Fawcett were faced with an opportunity to leave their poor peasant parishioners and move to a more affluent pastorate. The bond of love with these people in Wainsgate, England for seven years was precious to this family. Pastor John decided to write a poem about the value of Christian fellowship before their departure. At the close of his sermon, he read the words from this poem titled, "Brotherly Love." The wagons were loaded and the tearful congregation met for a final farewell. Mary said, "We can't leave these people." The order was given to unload their possessions. For the next 54 years this couple remained obedient to God in their little village. John's successes in evangelism, preaching, scholarship, and writing became well known in England. Prosperous offers were made through the years yet, this couple remained with their little flock. His poem became a favorite hymn called "Blest Be The Tie That Binds." Remember these words, "Blest be the tie that binds our hearts in Christian love; the fellowship of kindred minds; is like to that above?" Pastor Faucett died in 1817 after a remarkable life of obedience to Christ.

The Apostle John suggested some ways to keep away from sin:
- Avoid selfish attitudes and negative thinking.
- Avoid secret sins.
- Avoid hatred.
- Avoid becoming a stumbling block.

D—Directed Prayer

Lord, awaken me to the fact that I do not have to sin.

February 7

Daniel's Little Circus

God will provide the strength you need in difficult times.
Daniel 6:1-23

A—Advice from the Bible

They brought Daniel and threw him into the lions' den.
(Dan. 6:16, NIV)

B—Biblical Example

When King Nebuchandnezzar conquered Judah, he took a number of choice young men to Babylon for training in the Babylonian culture and language. He planned to use them later in his service. Daniel and his three friends were clearly superior to all the other young men who went through the king's training program. This Hebrew became an important member of the king's court. Political jealousy caused his enemies to seek ways to discredit him with the king, because Daniel was a man of another race and religious creed that was exalted above them! A royal Persian law was issued by the king to treat him like a god for one month. Daniel, however, refused to give up his devotional life with God. Once Daniel made his decision to be faithful to God, he never wavered. As a result, the king was tricked into sending Daniel to the lion's den as punishment for his disobedience. God miraculously delivered Daniel by shutting the lions' mouths and soothing their savage nature. Daniel calmly greeted the king like nothing had happened.

C—Contemporary Application

A big event in my grade school was the annual visit of Ringling Brothers Circus to a nearby town. A school bus provided transportation for us to attend the matinee. We became excited days before the field trip. Our favorite attractions were the clowns and the lions. The clowns made us laugh; the lions scared us. I remember the first time I ever heard the great king of the beasts roar. I put my hands on my ears! For some reason, the bus-talk on the way home ended up with the story of Daniel in the lions' den. The conversation centered on how scared Daniel must have been and how did God stop such a big animal? All kinds of theories were suggested. One comforting result of this discussion was the fact that we knew the end of the story. Daniel was not eaten. God did something big! Every time I see a lion on television or in a zoo, the testimony of the Hebrew boy's faith always comes to mind. Daniel's faithfulness to his convictions and his heritage motivates me to evaluate my obedience to God's commands.

Lesson to be learned from this Old Testament story:
- Non-Christians may resent a lifestyle of high moral standards.
- Christians should determine their actions by what is right.
- God never deserts His own.
- Christians need to have a consistent pattern of prayer.

D—Directed Prayer

Lord, help me to be faithful to my commitment to You.

February 8

A Little Lower than the Angels

Our worth and dignity are God's gifts.
Psalm 8:1-9

A—Advice from the Bible

You made him a little lower than angels
(Ps. 8:5, NIV)

B—Biblical Example

The oldest hymnal in the world may be the collection of Psalms. The Israelites' songbook was used in regular occasions of worship and on festive occasions. Pilgrims probably sang these psalms as they traveled toward Jerusalem. The title of Psalm 8 identifies the writer as David. This king recognized two aspects of God's nature. First, he realized God's bigness as in His majesty and glory. Second, God's nearness means that humankind is cared for by the Father. God's great creative activity included putting the stars where they would be needed. A question is asked by David that perhaps we would like to ask God, "What is a human being?" The moon and the stars have been in place forever. The years of a person's life are short by comparison, therefore, what is our significance in contrast to the universe? Our worth and dignity are God's gifts. He made us, and He placed us in charge of everything on earth. People are the highest order of creation. As far as our earthy ministry is concerned, we are less than God and angels. We are less than God because He created us. We are less than angels because they dwell in God's heavenly presence and minister to us.

C—Contemporary Application

The first time I sang "This Is My Father's World," I was attending a youth camp. The tune seemed so gentle and the words so meaningful to my teenage heart. I later read the hymn story about a remarkable young student at Syracuse University named Maltbie Babcock. He could have been a success in any chosen profession, however, God called him to the ministry of preaching. Following his education, he served several very successful Presbyterian churches. One of his favorite things to do was to "go and see my Father's world." His church gave him a pilgrimage to the Holy Land. Maltbie departed by ship with great excitement. However enroute to Naples, Italy, he was seized with a fever and died on May 18, 1901. We are grateful to his wife for compiling his writings, including my favorite, "This Is My Father's World."

Reflect on how great God is and how good He is to you:
- Our smallness in comparison to the vast universe humbles us.
- Our superiority to the rest of creation gives us dignity.
- Our responsibility to manage His beautiful earth challenges us.
- Our awareness of how valuable we are to God provokes our praise to Him.

D—Directed Prayer

My God and Creator, I praise You as my Redeemer and Sustainer.

February 9

Little Actions of Love

You can demonstrate your love for others by your actions.
Luke 10:25-37

A—Advice from the Bible

. . . he had compassion . . . and took care of him.
(Luke 10:33, HCSB)

B—Biblical Example

Our Lord's parables provide us with a special look into the meaning of a "teachable moment." The Parable of the Good Samaritan is an example of this. Jesus often encouraged questions from His listeners. This "earthly story with a heavenly meaning" developed from a question by a scribe who was an expert in Jewish law. His major problem was defining the meaning of a neighbor. The scribe turned this question over to Jesus, who described what might have been an actual event. A man was traveling down the Jerusalem-to-Jericho road, known for many large rocks that could hide robbers. The traveler was wounded by an ambush. The story continues with a parade of people, who chose how to respond to this wounded man. The priests and Levites served in the Temple on a rotating system. They were now on their way home. A callous indifference is expressed by their behavior. They did stop and look at the man, but offered no assistance. Then a Samaritan came along and took time to help. No people were more unneighborly than Jews and Samaritans. Our Lord made the significant statement that when this Samaritan saw the wounded man, he had love for him. First aid was given and then the injured traveler was transported to the nearest inn. The example of a thorough commitment to another's physical welfare is presented. Love demands action.

C—Contemporary Application

Oscar and Suella recently retired from military service and moved to our town. The local church became the base for developing friendships. One Sunday the pastor asked them to bring a senior adult woman, so she could attend worship. The couple agreed to help with this ministry. Little did they realize that their obedience would make such a difference in the life of this lonely lady. Phone calls, shopping trips to the mall, and doctor's appointments soon became common experiences. The demonstration of their love for this needy individual was a blessing to our church. Mildred had been abandoned and grieved over the loss of family love. God sent her a new family and she knew she was loved.

Jesus' parable contained several messages:
- Love calls for response.
- Love is an action not just an emotion.
- Love seeks to meet the needs of all persons.
- Love needs to be expressed outside one's immediate family and friends.

D—Directed Prayer

Father, lead me to show Your kind of love to wounded people today.

February 10

The Children of Israel's Little Gifts

How can my giving help the work of God?
Exodus 35:4-29

A—Advice from the Bible

Everyone who is willing is to bring the Lord an offering.
(Ex. 35:5, NIV)

B—Biblical Example

The wandering Hebrews had been camped at Mount Sinai for about six months after leaving Egypt when God called Moses to come up on the mountain. After 40 days, Moses related to the people what God had instructed him to do with the Ten Commandments and plans for the tabernacle. God not only commanded the erection of the tabernacle as a place of worship, but He also gave instructions about the way this portable place of worship would be financed—the people would voluntarily provide the materials with offerings from their own possessions. Moses listed the specific needs for building the tabernacle. Having heard the challenge, the people went to their homes to gather the needed materials. Everyone contributed. The gifts were brought as a love offering to the Lord. The tabernacle was built and extra materials were available.

C—Contemporary Application

Church members have often been challenged to give love offerings for special occasions. At one of our early pastorates, extra money was needed to complete the educational building. An appeal was made on a Sunday morning to give generously for this need. Here are some ways the members responded to this challenge. Sister Ruth sold some of her antiques and gave the money generously and cheerfully. Brother John wasn't sure the building should cost so much. "The light fixtures are a little too fancy," he said. Plus he felt all the labor could have been done by the men. He also waited to see if the goal was reached and then he wouldn't need to give anything. The Parkers were selective about giving because they support the work of two missionaries and that expense took most of their extra money. They also help para-church groups with offerings. Some of these groups had proved unworthy of their giving, but nevertheless their television show made them look good. In spite of these problems, the church met the love offering challenge and exceeded the necessary amount for completing the facility.

Four kinds of givers are usually identified with a local church. Read the following list and determine which word best describes your giving attitude.

- A cheerful giver.
- A reluctant giver.
- A hesitant giver.
- A selective giver.

D—Directed Prayer

Lord, help me to enjoy giving to Your causes.

February 11

The Little Church at Ephesus

Christ expects all His people to maintain their love for Him.
Revelation 2:1-7

A—Advice from the Bible

You have abandoned the love you had at first.
(Rev. 2:4, HCSB)

B—Biblical Example

The focus of these devotionals for the next seven days will be the seven churches in the Book of Revelation. First century Ephesus was an important seaport of Asia Minor. The worship of the goddess Artemis attracted many people to the area. Jesus commended the life and conduct of the faithful church members in this wicked city. However, the Ephesian believers had one tragic flaw—they had lost a passionate love for Christ. They probably were doctrinally correct and busy in Christian activity, but lacking their initial purpose. Jesus issued a warning that contained three commands. The Ephesian Christians were to remember how they once loved Jesus. They were to repent of their coldness, and they were to do as they had done at first, that is, stand against false teachers and their sinful lifestyles. Each of the seven letters closes with the phrase, *Anyone who has an ear should listen to what the Spirit says to the churches.* The letter concludes with a promise to the overcomer. The victor is the person, who by faith, shares in Christ's victory in the Christian life for eternity.

C—Contemporary Application

Through the years numerous religious groups or sects have formed. Many denominations began as sects, then evolved into churches. Some of these small groups have ceased to exist because they did not maintain their love for Christ. For the next seven devotionals, seven of these little known groups will be presented. One common thread connects each sect—they lost their first love. For example, in 1881 Claas Epp, a leader of the Mennonite Brethren, pronounced that he was meeting Elijah in the skies and proceed with him to heaven. He proclaimed that Christ was to appear on March 8, 1889. Later Epp claimed to be a "son of Christ." His followers remained faithful until the fall of 1902 when they almost starved to death. The sect died out because the focus was removed from Christ to Claas Epp. Jesus calls all believers to affirm and to maintain their love for Him.

What actions can you plan that will ensure that you maintain your love for Christ?

- Continue to remember who Jesus is.
- Continue to maintain a close fellowship with Him through prayer and Bible study.
- Continue to stand against false teaching.
- Continue to correct sinful behavior.

D—Directed Prayer

Lord, I thank You that You will help my church remain focused on You.

February 12

The Little Church at Smyrna

To be a dedicated Christian will cost you something.
Revelation 2:8-11

A—Advice from the Bible

Don't be afraid of what you are about to suffer.
(Rev. 2:10, HCSB)

B—Biblical Example

Smyra (now Izmir, Turkey) was called the "Crown of Asia." Temples to Cybele, Apollo, Asclepios, and Aphrodite lined the streets. The heathen splendor that surrounded the Christians could have smothered the church out of existence, but the idol worshippers failed. Another factor working against the church was the great centers of Caesar worship. Emperor worship had become compulsory under Domition. Once a year a Roman citizen was required to burn a pinch of incense on the altar to the godhead of Caesar. This act was a test of a person's political loyalty. Everyone was to say, "Caesar is Lord." The Christians would not participate. Persecution came as a result of this choice. Caesar worship placed the church in great peril. Two words were used in the letter to describe what the Christian had to face—*tribulation* and *poverty*. Verse 11 contains the final promise to the person who would overcome. The individual who is faithful unto death dies to live again.

C—Contemporary Application

The Millerite Movement was started by a man named William Miller. He was a farmer of Low Hampton, New York, and an ardent student of the Bible, especially the "chronological portions." He became convinced that many events had been predicted to occur with a specific time and had always transpired according to chronology. Various passages in Daniel and the Revelation were his favorite scriptures. Miller began to lecture in 1821 to prove his theories. Crowds became interested and many converts were made among preachers and members of the various denominations. He reasoned that the Lord's return would come on October 22, 1844. His group, now called Adventists, gathered for the return, which did not happen. Most of the believers renounced their faith. Persecution soon followed for the remaining members who believed in the imminent second advent. The Seventh Day Adventists came from the work of William Miller.

When the pressure to conform in order to escape persecution comes, as in Smyrna, what can we do?

- Exercise our faith in God.
- Remain a person of honesty and integrity.
- Realize that more people suffer for the wrong than for the right.
- Maintain Christlike goodness even though opposition may be provoked.

D—Directed Prayer

Father, help me to endure any persecutions with grace and dignity.

February 13

The Little Church at Pergamum

Something is wrong when a Christian church compromises with the world.
Revelation 2:12-17

A—Advice from the Bible

"You have some there who hold to the teaching of Balaam."
(Rev. 2:14, HCSB)

B—Biblical Example

John commended the church at Pergamum for their faithfulness while enduring persecution, yet among the membership were people whose practices were extremely displeasing to God. Pergamum, like Smyrna, was a center of Caesar worship. Therefore, to be a Christian in that city was to enter a danger zone, or as John said, "where Satan dwells." The believer had to make a choice to be primarily loyal to Christ, and at the same time live under earthly authority. The temptation to compromise one's allegiance to Christ in favor of earthly powers and thus gain momentary relief from persecution became a reality. One martyr is mentioned by the name Antipas. He was a faithful witness for Christ. Despite their faithfulness, some church members were holding to the teaching of Balaam and were eating meat offered to idols and practicing sexual immorality. The message came to these people to repent. The letter ends with a promise of the "white stone" bearing an unknown name.

C—Contemporary Application

In the early American revival period, the doctrine of perfectionism began to run wild. Charles G. Finney was a supporter of that theory. Following his emotional conversion in 1818, he reportedly said, "So far as I could see, I was in a state in which I did not sin." His ministry as a holiness preacher was identified as hostile toward luxury, personal adornment, and other "worldly" practices. His followers became known as a Perfectionist sect. Some characteristics of their belief were the "second blessing"—an emotional experience that must follow conversion. The guidance of the Holy Spirit was sought in visions and gifts. They regarded themselves as the true church. Any modern scholarship was opposed by these fundamentalists. A number of dissatisfied members started their own groups such as the Methodist Episcopal Church and the Methodist Protestant Church. Some of the Perfectionist still exist today.

To avoid compromising with any teachings and actions that misrepresent Christ and lead others astray, a Christian must:
- Be alert to the pressure to conform to worldly practices over your better judgment.
- Be alert to issues that are not easily discernable.
- Be alert to being overly tolerant.
- Be alert to the distinction between false teaching and different interpretations.

D—Directed Prayer

Lord, lead me to identify the correct Christian response to compromise.

February 14

The Little Church at Thyatira

Refuse to be submissive toward evil.
Revelation 2:18-28

A—Advice from the Bible

But hold onto what you have until I come.
(Rev. 2:25, HCSB)

B—Biblical Example

Thyatira was a small, unimportant city and a center for trade. A cult of Caesar existed that called Caesar the son of God. The Christians claimed Jesus was the Son of God. Jesus saw everything going on in the church—both good and bad. Their works of love at the beginning were demonstrated in service to the needy. The Lord was pleased with what they *had* done. At the present time, however, He accused them of being too tolerant and permissive toward evil. A woman in the church was specifically leading others into evil. Her nickname was Jezebel. She claimed to be a prophetess, having the power and gifts of the Holy Spirit like the prophets of old. This fake leader enticed Christians to commit sexual sins. She used her powers to seduce and deceive the believers away from God. Jesus called on her to repent, but she persistently refused. He then described the "false doctrine" and explained the consequences of such a teaching. The faithful church was promised the "bright and morning star" by which to chart their course in life.

C—Contemporary Application

This part of the devotional continues to look at groups, cults, and sects that have evolved through the years as a result of some particular church leader. Many denominations began as sects, then evolved into churches. The people followed a certain leader, often without questioning the doctrine being taught. One sect was called the Latter Rain Movement. A revival, characterized by the baptism of the Holy Spirit, began in East Tennessee and North Carolina. Evidence of Spirit baptism was "speaking in other tongues as the Spirit gives utterance." A. J. Tomlinson, the founder and general overseer of the Church of God, took charge of the movement in 1906. Church members from various parts of the country visited these revival meetings. The group became known as the Outpouring of the Latter Rain. For the next 40 years, these churches functioned throughout the United States. Differences on points of doctrine finally divided the believers. Today about 60 congregations exist.

Our growth as disciples of Jesus Christ includes:

- Continuing to serve Him faithfully.
- Refusing to be permissive toward evil.
- Clinging to godly principles.
- Holding to biblical doctrines.

D—Directed Prayer

Lord, help me to continue to serve You faithfully.

February 15

The Little Church at Sardis

Our lifestyle must be consistent with the thinking of Jesus.
Revelation 3:1-6

A—Advice from the Bible

You have a reputation for being alive, but you are dead.
(Rev. 3:1)

B—Biblical Example

Sardis was located on a main road and was prosperous commercially. A thriving wool industry helped the economy. Yet, to Jesus, the city was dead. He looked at the heart of the church people and found that they were deceased. The Christians were meeting in a lively place, but it was a façade—they were fake. If they did not repent, Jesus warned that He would come to them in sudden and unexpected judgment. The Lord basically said, "Wake up!" This dead church in a dead city had a few people who remained faithful and consistent in their lives before the Lord. He made three promises to the disciples who would overcome. First, they could be clothed with holiness, purity, and righteousness if they would leave their former lifestyle. Second, their names would not be blotted out of the book of life. Third, He would intercede, speaking for them before the Father in heaven. Their part in this process was to show gratitude to Him by doing the kinds of works in their lives that were consistent with what He expected.

C—Contemporary Application

The Shaker doctrine was formulated by Ann Lee, a textile worker in Manchester, England. "Mother Ann," in 1758 converted to the "Shaking Quakers." After enduring persecution for noisy worship services, she had a series of revelations, after which she regarded herself as the second Incarnation of Christ. She developed an elaborate theology and established celibacy as the cardinal principle of the community. After Mother Ann's death (1784), the Shaker church came under the leadership of Elder Joseph Meacham. The first Shaker community, established at New Lebanon, New York, in 1787 spread through New England and westward into Kentucky, Ohio, and Indiana. By 1826, 18 Shaker villages had been set up in eight states. The Shaker movement reached its height during the 1840s, when about 6,000 members were enrolled in the church. By 1905 only a 1,000 members remained. Today one working Shaker village exists at Sabbath Day Lake, near New Gloucester, Maine. Fewer than 10 members serve in this dying church.

Consider this prescription for a dying church:
- Wake up.
- Get up.
- Stand up.
- Go to work doing what there is to do.

D—Directed Prayer

Father, lead me to witness with my life, not just my words.

February 16

The Little Church at Philadelphia

Relying on God's promises enables us to remain faithful.
Revelation 3:7-13

A—Advice from the Bible

You have kept my command to endure.
(Rev. 3:10)

B—Biblical Example

Philadelphia was located on a high plateau and produced wine along with leather and textile goods. The city is still prosperous with a population of around 15,000 people. According to this Scripture, three descriptions of the church at Philadelphia are identified. They were a missionary church, lovers of God's Word, and a humble, faithful church. For these reasons, no word of reproof was given. In fact, the Savior gave three wonderful and encouraging promises to these believers: (1) He would take care of their enemies; (2) He would keep them from tribulation; and (3) He would honor them. An interesting observation is that Jesus characterized Himself as the Messiah, the Savior God promised to the Jews. Based on what the Lord knew of the people, He made a promise that the door to His kingdom was open to these faithful followers. What an assurance that no human being can undo what God does for us when He saves us and gives us His kingdom! The church was commended for what they had done and needed to "keep on keeping on." This letter concludes with the church being given a new name. The name of Jesus the Savior and Lord was to be inscribed on them for eternity.

C—Contemporary Application

Little groups of devotees have continued to follow certain leaders. Most of these believers no longer are part of the original plan. For example, Reconstructionism was begun by the Jewish Reconstructionist Foundation in 1940. The key leader of this movement was Mordecai M. Kaplan. The goal was to examine Jewish life and follow six or more directives. The most familiar today was the establishment of a homeland for Jews and their culture in Palestine. The training in old Hebrew ritual was to be emphasized Kaplan was a coeditor of the *Reconstructionist Sabbath Prayer Book* (1945), in which, among other unorthodoxies, he denied the literal accuracy of the biblical text. As a result, the Union of Orthodox Rabbis of the United States and Canada declared his theories unacceptable. We may wonder what Jesus would have said to this organization?

Descriptions of the church at Philadelphia might cause us to identify with the message:

- Doors of opportunity are before us.
- Jesus opens the door.
- We must work.
- Jesus closes the door and we must wait.

D—Directed Prayer

Begin today thanking God for promising us His acceptance and security.

February 17

The Little Church at Laodicea

We can't help anyone if we are lukewarm.
Revelation 3:14-22

A—Advice from the Bible

So because you are lukewarm, I am going to vomit you out of My mouth.
(Rev. 3:16)

B—Biblical Example

The seventh church in the Book of Revelation that Jesus sent a message to was the church at Laodicea. This groups was the only one of the churches that received no approval from the Lord. They were a lukewarm, foolish, body of believers. The city was prosperous from farming, banking, and manufacturing and most of the citizens focused on this success. However, these same people did not get too excited about their relationship with Jesus or about their worship of Him. The church thought of itself as rich and wealthy; they needed nothing. But Jesus saw them as they were. Their indifference was not appealing to Christ. Yet He offered His invitation of love and fellowship to them. The people deceived themselves or were deceived by their riches into a false security. Jesus then told the people what he was going to do about their spiritual condition. He persistently pleaded with them to recognize their spiritual poverty. Verse 20 is the Lord's invitation to be right with Him and do the works that had been neglected.

C—Contemporary Application

The religious painting that has impressed me most is titled, "The Light of the World." This work of art was completed in 1854 by the artist Holman Hunt. Public opinion was at first hostile toward Hunt, but the picture of Christ knocking at the door of the human soul, brought him his first public success. The artist continued interpreting religious scenes until his vision failed and he could no longer see his canvas. The appeal of this work is for all Christians to renew their fellowship with Christ. He is seeking us. Mary Slade wrote the words to an old hymn based on this picture. Remember these words?

Who at my door is standing, Patiently drawing near, Entrance within demanding? Whose is the voice I hear? Sweetly the tones are falling; "Open the door for me! If thou wilt heed My calling, I will abide with thee." A warning is repeated again as in all seven churches, "He that hath an ear, let him hear."

In the Christian life there are three spiritual temperatures:
- A burning heart on fire for the God.
- A lukewarm heart
- A cold heart.
- Your heart.

D—Directed Prayer

Thank You, God, for Your invitation to repent.

February 18

A Righteous Little Job

A believer's righteousness can be tested for truth.
(Job 1:1-5)

A—Advice from the Bible

He was a man of perfect integrity.
(Job 1:1)

B—Biblical Example

The traditional Jewish mind of Job's day had a very simplistic solution. If one lived according to God's law, things would work out well and adversity would never come to him. If, on the other hand, a person violated the divine instructions from God, suffering would surely occur. The writer of the book suggested that Job's fear of God caused him to avoid wrongdoing. The patriarch's family is introduced first. He had seven sons and three daughters. Each of his sons owned a house. A big family signified God's blessings. "Happy is the man who has filled his quiver with them [children]" (Ps. 127:4-5). Job's business was evident by all his possessions. No wonder he was called "the greatest man among all the people of the East." Another look into Job's life suggests good family relationships. He cared enough to offer sacrifices for them just in case they had sinned. This patriarch was a very religious person, as well as a wealthy one. However, nothing in Job's conduct or character will explain why he had so much suffering.

C—Contemporary Application

Martin Luther was born on November 10, 1483. In 1501, at the age of 17, he enrolled at the University of Erfurt in Germany, intending to study law. In the summer of 1505, however, he entered the Augustinian monastery. This decision surprised his friends and appalled his father. In the monastery he observed the rules imposed on a novice but did not find the peace with God he had expected. Nevertheless, Luther made his profession as a monk in the autumn of 1506, and his superiors selected him for the priesthood. Ordained in 1507, he approached his first celebration of the mass with pure delight. During his study of the New Testament, he came to believe that Christians are saved, not through their own efforts, but by the gift of God's grace, which they accepted in faith. He was banned and excommunicated for these convictions. By 1537, Luther's health had begun to deteriorate. Old and sick, he went back home, and died on February 18, 1546.

Four characteristics describe Job. Do they describe you?

- He was sincere in his dealings with God.
- He was upright or honest with other people.
- He was a worshiper of God.
- He turned away from evil practices.

D—Directed Prayer

Father, help us to face suffering with courage and faith as Job did.

February 19

A Little Coping with Life

Many Christians are surprised by life's trials.
1 Peter 4:12-19

A—Advice from the Bible

Do not be surprised at the painful trial you are suffering.
(1 Pet. 4:12)

B—Biblical Example

This epistle was written to believers scattered throughout Asia Minor. Nero was the Roman Emperor at this time and he had just murdered his mother. In A.D. 64, he was accused of burning down Rome in order to have space to build a new palace. Of course, he blamed the Christians! These followers of Christ did not deserve to suffer for their faith. Remember that the world does not persecute "religious people," but it does persecute righteous people. Whatever glorifies God will anger the enemy and he will attack. The Gentile Christians were not experienced in suffering; the Jews had always faced abuse by other groups or nations. Peter summarized his letter by pointing out two things Christians should do: commit and continue. To *commit* means to deposit for safekeeping. The term is used in banking. The decision to deposit your life in God's bank means that you receive eternal dividends on your investment. Suffering for our faith is a matter of God's will. Therefore, we should *continue* to entrust our total being to God—body, soul, and spirit.

C—Contemporary Application

My friend passed this morning. She has suffered with cancer for several years. Sometimes the disease would go into remission, only to reoccur at a later time. Frances did not deserve to suffer this physical attack on her body. Let me tell you about some of her legacies.

- She was a gifted Bible teacher who focused mainly on single women.
- She was a woman of prayer and taught other women how to pray effectively.
- She was compassionate about hurting people and often visited in care centers.
- She used her spiritual gifts with the church family.
- She demonstrated faith and works.
- She was a faithful wife and loving mother to her family

Four guidelines in coping with undeserved suffering:

- Rejoice (vv. 13-14).
- Examine your life (vv. 15-16).
- Glorify God (vv.16-18).
- Commit yourself to God (v. 19).

D—Directed Prayer

Lord, help me not to complain about personal suffering.

February 20

A Little Wisdom

Wisdom is the principle thing.
Proverbs 4:1-9

A—Advice from the Bible

Get wisdom.
(Prov. 4:5)

B—Biblical Example

The Psalms are referred to as the Hebrew hymnbook; in Proverbs, a manual for daily righteousness is presented. In this passage, the writer appeals to his students to pay close attention to his teachings. The teacher traditionally would address his students as a father to his sons. The home was and would remain the most important setting for the education of children. Wisdom for living, like life itself, should start at home. These verses present the value of moral instruction from one generation to another. The writer declares that our great concern—the principle thing—should be to acquire wisdom and understanding. Such an attainment is within reach of every person. As James wrote, "If any of you lack wisdom, he should ask God, who gives generously to all without finding fault, and it shall be given him" (James 1:5).

C—Contemporary Application

The date was February 20, 1962. An astronaut named John Herschell Glenn, Jr. became one of the pioneers of space exploration, as the first American to orbit the Earth in space. He will forever be remembered for this distinctive achievement. No one else can share this unique honor. However, the greatest concern for John Glenn was not fame, but a safe launch and recovery of his *Friendship 7* spacecraft. The three-orbit flight covered approximately 81,000 miles in 4 hours, 55 minutes. As a pilot in the US Marine Corps, he flew 149 combat missions in World War II and the Korean War. As a test pilot, in 1957, he became the first person to make a non-stop supersonic transcontinental flight, from Los Angeles to New York. John Glenn had been instructed by teachers who were experienced in his field of study. From their instruction, wisdom became possible. His successful skills in the military continued to add to his ability to go into outer space. Today, he is retired, but was allowed one last trip in October 1998. He flew on a mission aboard the space shuttle Discovery.

The benefits of wisdom make life easier.

- The "things" of life begin to fall in place.
- Anxieties seem less important.
- Peace replaces fear and worry.
- God's will is easier to understand and apply.

D—Directed Prayer

Thank You, God, for placing wisdom within reach.

February 21

Three Little Words

Love is the supreme Christian quality.
1 Corinthians 13:13

A—Advice from the Bible

Now these three remain: faith, hope, and love. But the greatest of these is love.
(1 Cor. 13:13)

B—Biblical Example

Some of the Apostle Paul's greatest Scripture passages are set in the contexts of controversy. Chapter 12 was addressed to the church in Corinth, that was threatened with division over spiritual gifts. Chapter 14 begins with one particular gift, "speaking with tongues," that was a major cause of disruption in the church. He acknowledged the validity of spiritual gifts and the responsibility of Christians to exercise them. However, in between these two chapters, Paul wrote a beautiful prose/poem on Christian love in which he insisted the use of gifts be guided and motivated by love. The meaning of this love is found in the nature of God. The LORD Himself is love and this quality will last as long as He does, which is forever. Faith will remain because it is the heart of our relationship with God. Hope remains because it describes the result of our relationship with God. However, love will survive the things of this life and is greater even than faith and hope. The most important conclusion to draw from this chapter is the use of spiritual gifts. To use gifts without love is to misuse them.

C—Contemporary Application

Love is portrayed in the world today in many forms. One of the most frequently used during February is Cupid, whose name means "desire." In Roman mythology, he was the son of Venus, goddess of love. His father was Mercury. His counterpart in Greek mythology was Eros, god of love. This image is best known as the handsome young god who falls in love with the beautiful maiden Psyche. The story goes that this mischievous boy wounds both gods and humans with his arrows, thereby causing them to fall deeply in love. You have seen Cupid represented in art as a naked, winged infant, carrying a bow and a quiver of arrows. Jokes abound about Cupid's matchmaking, but this symbol of love is just that—"a symbol." A believer knows that God is love and this is the truth!

The meaning of Chapter 13:13:

- Love behaves in a distinctive way.
- Love will never come to an end.
- Love is an example of God's nature.
- Without love, life equals zero.

D—Directed Prayer

Father, help me to remember that faith is commitment, hope is assurance, and love is rooted in You.

February 22

A Little Burning Bush

God will help you deal with your problems.
Exodus 3:1-13

A—Advice from the Bible

"Why does the bush not burn up?"
(Ex. 3:3)

B—Biblical Example

The Book of Exodus begins with the children of Israel in Egypt experiencing ever-increasing persecution. They had been in bondage for 400 years. The identity of Moses was known. He was a Hebrew. So he attempted to take justice into his own hands by killing an Egyptian taskmaster. Now, we find him in the land of Midian as a fugitive. His new vocation was tending sheep for his father-in-law, Jethro. The day was like any other until the LORD appeared to him in a flame coming out of the midst of a burning bush. Moses moved closer to investigate the phenomenon. At this point, God called him by name. The LORD then told Moses that his new assignment would be to lead His people out of slavery. The Hebrew slaves had not been forgotten. God was moving to solve the cruel situation. At first, Moses must have been excited at God's announcement. The people were promised deliverance from bondage, but also God was providing for them a place of great potential. God was going to do something about the suffering of His people and His plan involved a human leader, Moses.

C—Contemporary Application

George Washington, (1732-1799), was born on February 22, 1732 in Westmoreland County, Virginia. He became the commander in chief of the Continental army during the American War of Independence, and later the first President of the United States. He symbolized qualities of discipline, duty, military skills, and persistence in adversity that displayed marks of mature political leadership. Washington's place in American history is a fascinating chapter in the intellectual life of the nation. He was God's leader at a critical time and was honest, hard working, and displayed true patriotism. The president long served as a symbol of American identity along with the flag, the Constitution, and the Fourth of July. Once again, a human leader was chosen to make a difference in the suffering of God's people.

God's plan often involves a human leader.

- Someone who is an effective spiritual leader.
- Someone who can handle responsibilities.
- Someone who is prepared.
- Someone who is willing to pay the price for training.

D—Directed Prayer

Father, You are the great I AM and our Leader.

February 23

A Little Persecution

Faithful service for Jesus Christ must continue.
Acts 5:33-42

A—Advice from the Bible

> *The Pharisee's wanted to put them to death.*
> (Acts 5:33)

B—Biblical Example

The church in Jerusalem faced several challenges during the early days of Christianity. The interaction between the apostles and the Sanhedrin, the highest Jewish court, focused on opposition and persecution. Remarkable examples of faithful service are included in Acts, Chapter 5. The apostles explained the reasons for their commitment to Jesus. They were witnesses because of what they had experienced with Him. The members of the Sanhedrin were so angered with the testimony of these followers of Christ that they wanted to put these men to death. A Pharisee named Gamaliel brought logic and calm to the chaotic murderous environment. He suggested a wait-and- see policy about this religious group. The other Jews decided to follow his advice. A flogging was administered to the innocent men and they were ordered not to preach or teach about Jesus. Rather than feeling humiliated, they felt honored to suffer for the name of Christ. Despite the severe persecutions, the apostles continued to witness for Christ every day.

C—Contemporary Application

The martyrdom of Polycarp, the bishop of Smyrna (today Izmar, Turkey), serves as one of the great examples of loyalty unto death. The crowds were involved in a festival day and were in a highly volatile state. The cry from the crowd went up to seize Polycarp, the Christian bishop, who probably knew the disciples of Jesus. Even the Jews joined in the mob-mentality. He confessed without hesitation that he was a Christian and was given a choice—worship Caesar or die! To that challenge, Polycarp gave his immortal answer, "Eighty and six years have I served Him, and he has done me no wrong. How can I blaspheme my King who saved me?" His burning at the stake occurred on a Sabbath day. As he died, the mob heard him praying. He was thanking God for the privilege of dying for Him. On the Christian calendar, February 23 is set aside as a feast day to remember this great Christian.

Christians can serve faithfully because:

- God gives opportunities for service.
- Service means doing what God wants.
- We can rejoice in the midst of suffering.
- We can face threats and still continue to serve Christ.

D—Directed Prayer

Father, help me to endure any persecution with grace and dignity.

February 24

The Exiles' Little Letter

God is with you and will help you during times of trouble.
(Jeremiah 29:1-11)

A—Advice from the Bible

This is the text of the letter that the prophet Jeremiah sent from Jerusalem.
(Jer. 29:1)

B—Biblical Example

The setting for this Scripture is both Babylon and the besieged city of Jerusalem. King Nebuchadnezzar of Babylon took the significant Jewish leaders into captivity. While in Babylon, the people suffered more than physical troubles. They also suffered spiritual troubles. Word returned to Jeremiah that the captives had refused to make the best out of living in this alien country, so he wrote a stern letter to encourage these Hebrews. First, he reminded the Jews why they were in captivity. Sinning against God was unacceptable. He urged the Jews in exile to settle down and make the best of the opportunities given them. They were free to have their own social, religious, and even political organizations. However, they were still prisoners of war. Jeremiah wrote advising them to treat their captors kindly. The people were warned not to listen to false prophets, but to trust only in God. A day would come when God would restore His people to their homeland. The words of the letter reassured the people that God still loved them very deeply. He also had plans for His people. God offered them a future and a hope.

C—Contemporary Application

One place I wanted to visit on our trip to Massachusetts was the city of Concord. A favorite writer of mine is Louisa May Alcott (1832-1888). Her books for children are characterized by their intimate depiction of family life and loyalties. Her father was an educator and philosopher. While touring her home, I discovered that she was tutored by the American writers Ralph Waldo Emerson and Henry David Thoreau. However, one point of interest to me was that while serving as a nurse during the American Civil War, Alcott wrote letters to her family. Many are on display today. The purpose in writing was to encourage her often poverty-stricken relatives to look for better days. She overcame their problems by writing and selling magazine articles for publication. Years after her death, a book was compiled of all her letters titled, *Hospital Sketches* (1863).

Words to help strengthen your faith:

- Troubles and difficulties are a part of everyone's life.
- God remains with His people in the midst of troubles.
- God expects His people to make the best out of troubled situations.
- God can be trusted to bring His people through their present troubles.

D—Directed Prayer

Lord, may personal troubles become opportunities to share and grow in our faith.

February 25

Little Times of Revenge

The weapon against revenge is kindness.
Romans 12:9-21

A—Advice from the Bible

Do not take revenge, but leave room for God's wrath.
(Rom. 12:19)

B—Biblical Example

Previous verses in this chapter have emphasized the conduct of an individual. The Apostle Paul now shifts to the conduct of an individual in the community where they live. The ruling theme is love, but Paul also went on to give constructive admonitions about the moral and spiritual life of a believer. He was realistic enough to recognize that some people in the world take advantage of other people. At times this treatment was severe enough for him to call it "persecution." When someone causes pleasant relationships to be broken, the response of a Christian should not be anger, but leave "the wrath to God." The world says, "Don't get mad, get even!" A Christian's love for all humans should keep him from getting even. Doing so would only make more discord and reconciliation more difficult. Love looks toward redemption, which is followed by peace. Paul wanted the Roman believers to let God deal with their enemies. He stated that Christian love leaves no place for a follower of Christ to indulge in retaliation. The final thoughts on the subject are that only God could appropriately exercise His wrath in vengeance.

C—Contemporary Application

Chechenya is a republic in southwestern Russia. When the breakup of the Soviet Union occurred in 1991, the Chechens declared themselves an independent republic on December 11, 1994. The world was horrified when Chechen rebels massacred hundreds of people held hostage in a school in Beslan, Russia. Many of the victims were children, including six belonging to two brothers, who were active in Christian ministry. One of the fathers responded in the way of the world; the other brother said, "Yes, we have an irreplaceable loss, but we cannot take revenge." He believed what the Lord said in Romans 12:19, "Vengeance is Mine, I will repay." Let go of bitterness and put any personal injustices into God's hands.

The reaction of a Christian to mistreatment by other people should be:
- Think well.
- Speak well.
- Praise well.
- Pray for those who mistreat you.

D—Directed Prayer

Father, You said, "Love your enemies . . . pray for those who persecute you," so I am.

February 26

Gideon's Little Attack

Look for new spiritual challenges.
Judges 7:2-21

A—Advice from the Bible

You will be encouraged to attack the camp.
(Judg. 7:11)

B—Biblical Example

Gideon was called by God to deliver His people after seven years of oppression under the Midianites. His experiences are recorded in three chapters of the Book of Judges. The invasion of this enemy army was an annual event. The Israelites cried to God for relief and He responded by preparing a simple man with all his weakness to obtain victory over the enemy. More than thirty thousand fighting men responded to Gideon's call for help. However, God had other plans in this circumstance. The volunteer army was to be reduced to 300! When the command was given to attack the Midianite camp, the Holy Spirit took the fearful leader and gave him unusual wisdom for the battle. An interesting observation is that this scared leader's first response before going to battle was to worship God. The Lord was faithful to the promise He made at the beginning of this calling when He said, "The Lord is with you." The weapons for the attack were trumpets, torches, and pitchers." Confusion in the camp caused the enemy army to panic and Gideon and his three hundred men were victorious.

C—Contemporary Application

Many efforts have been made, throughout history, by people who desire to see change in public life. Local citizens often "take on city government" and seek to better their living conditions. Sometimes an unassuming person will surface as a leader to combat the evils of the world. Lord Shaftsbury (1801-1885) of England had planned his career with the goal of becoming a Member of Parliament. However, the faces of the poor people on the streets of London began to haunt him. Instead of serving his government, he would give himself to helping the underprivileged. His attack on the social failures of his day inspired the passing of five basic laws that changed the lives of the women and children of England. In the case of Gideon, his weakness was used by God to win a battle for the Israelites. What spiritual challenge can you find in the little things of life?

Some things that make a believer win in the battle of life are:
- Obedience to God's commands.
- Trusting in God's wisdom.
- Faithfulness in daily Christian opportunities
- Encouragement found in reading the Word.

D—Directed Prayer

Father, help me to face my human limitations honestly.

February 27

Gracious Little Words

Some people still want Jesus to prove Himself by performing miracles.
Luke 4:17-24

A—Advice from the Bible

All were amazed at the gracious words that came from His lips.
(Luke 4:22)

B—Biblical Example

Jesus returned to Galilee and made a visit to Nazareth. The people who heard Him speak were impressed. However, some of the hometown citizens were puzzled. His background as a child and youth were known by most of the individuals. Questions were exchanged about this person being the son of Joseph. The Lord responded to their opinion of Him. He knew by their actions that they were not going to believe Him. Many miracles and healings had occurred in Capernaum. Now the time had come to do something great in Nazareth. Jesus commented on their unbelief in words that have become a familiar proverb to us, "No prophet is accepted in his own country." Some people have a tendency to discount that which is close and familiar. The reason may be that they want to feel superior to those they ordinarily associate with, or it may be that they cannot appreciate something they think they can explain in their own words. Unfortunately people today have some interest in Jesus or appreciation for Him, but not as Savior.

C—Contemporary Application

A first-time tourist to the Holy Land brings home many souvenirs. Olive wood carvings are favorite gifts, so I was surprised when one woman selected amulets for her family and friends back home. These bracelets are worn as a charm, and include New Testament Scripture. The ancient Egyptians wore amulets around their neck, with either an inscription or figures engraved on it. Some wearers believed it was a guard against sickness or witchcraft. The Egyptians wore amulets, sometimes in the form of necklaces. Among the Greeks, such a protective charm was called *phylaktçrion* and the Hebrew boxes contained passages of the Torah written on parchment, worn as a sacred reminder of God's Law. Today they contain words spoken by Jesus. Throughout the Middle East the practice of wearing amulets is almost universal. As for my friend, she wanted to share the gracious words of Jesus with other people.

Why do some people show an interest and appreciate Jesus, but not as Savior?

- They don't think they need saving.
- They would rather continue struggling with their problems.
- They witnessed an answer to prayer one time.
- The burden of their need isn't bad enough yet.

D—Directed Prayer

Lord, thank You for Your gracious words we read in the Bible.

February 28

The Little Mountain of the LORD

False authority must be condemned.
Micah 4:1-5

A—Advice from the Bible

Come, let us go up to the mountain of the LORD.
(Micah 4:2)

B—Biblical Example

The message of the Minor Prophet, Micah, focuses on the subject of authority. Dishonest princes, false prophets, and selfish priests in Israel and Judah had departed from the true standards of government. The only hope for God's people was in the coming of the Ruler to Israel. Rulers who judge for reward, priests who teach for hire and prophets who divine for money, are repulsive to God and will be judged by Him. Micah lived about 20 miles southwest of Jerusalem, near Gath. He predicted the ruin for all nations and leaders who were oppressive toward others. Throughout the book are prophecies about Jesus, the Messiah, who will gather the people into one nation. True faith in God generates kindness, compassion, justice, and humility. Chapter 4 introduces "the mountain of the LORD," which is Mount Zion. This period in time will introduce an era of peace and blessings. The world will never find true peace until all people have honored the King of kings and live under His control. This permanent message of Micah continues to warn generation after generation that the ultimate authority in all the affairs of men is God.

C—Contemporary Application

An English medical missionary was born Feb.28, 1865, in England. He found God's way for his life by being a tireless benefactor of the people of Labrador. While still a medical student at London University in 1887, Wilfred Grenfell was impressed by the sermons of the American evangelist Dwight L. Moody. During the next five years he served as surgeon on the first hospital ship dispatched to the North Sea fisheries. In 1892 he initiated missionary service to the fishermen of Labrador and soon became absorbed in improving the living conditions of the inhabitants of the Labrador coast. When Grenfell retired (1932), the following structures existed, 6 hospitals, 4 hospital ships, 7 nursing stations, 2 orphanages, 2 large schools, 14 industrial centres, and a cooperative lumber mill. He was knighted in 1927. Labrador became his mountain for the LORD

A good purpose for Bible study is to learn the ways of God:
- God will put an end to war.
- God will speak through His people about righteousness and justice.
- God will protect the oppressed and deceived.
- God will restore fellowship between man and God.

D—Directed Prayer

Thank You for helping me learn Your ways, O Lord.

February 29

A Thousand Little Years

God is not on our timetable.
2 Peter 3:8-14

A—Advice from the Bible

With the Lord a day is like a thousand years.
(2 Pet.3:8)

B—Biblical Example

Peter's second letter was written for believers living in the five provinces of Asia Minor: (Pontus, Galatia, Cappadocia, Asia, and Bithynia). The purpose of the letter was to strengthen the hope of believers. Peter, also, encouraged these people to make progress in their Christian life. Encouragement to live a godly life is found in all the things that God had provided. His promises gave motivation for growth. False teachers used the second coming of Christ to keep the learners away from the Truth. Some of the Christians could not understand why the second advent of the Lord was taking so long. The apostle explained that what appears to be a delay is really an expression of the mercy of God. On that day the world as we know it will cease to exist. Time will mean nothing to a believer. He admonished the faithful to face the future with positive hope as that day will usher in the new and eternal age.

C—Contemporary Application

Poor, Hugh! He only celebrates a birthday every four years. He refers to himself as "a leap-year baby." The time taken for the Earth to complete its orbit around the Sun is approximately 365.25 days. To account for the odd quarter day, an extra calendar day is added every four years. This addition was first begun in 46 BC, with the establishment of the Julian calendar. The following thoughts about time are interesting:
Father Time doesn't make round trips: We are but minutes—little things.
Each one furnished with 60 wings, with which we fly on our unseen track,
And not a minute ever comes back. We are but minutes; use us well,
For how we are used, we must one day tell.
Who uses minutes, has hours to use,
Who loses minutes; whole years must lose.
Make a special effort to celebrate with your leap-year friends.

God's promises strengthen our hope by:
- Encouraging us to fear not.
- Trusting in His Word.
- Providing spiritual gifts.
- Leading believers to obey God's timely opportunities.

D—Directed Prayer

Father, help me remain faithful to Your timetable.

March 1

Europe's First Little Convert

God may call you to help start a new church
Acts 16:9-15

A—Advice from the Bible

A woman named Lydia was listening.
(Acts 16:14, HCSB)

B—Biblical Example

Sometimes the word *Little* can be used in reference to importance. The second missionary experiences by the Apostle Paul and his companions were not going as planned. God had redirected the mission to a seemingly smaller task. The city of Philippi, a Roman colony, became the next destination for preaching the gospel. The missionary team entered the city and began looking for a synagogue, but the small number of Jewish residents did not have an established meeting place. Not a person to be discouraged, Paul located a prayer meeting already in progress on a riverbank, led by a group of women. The missionary and his team joined in this special time with the women. A worshiper of God, named Lydia, listened as the missionary gave faithful witness to the truth about the gospel. This prosperous career woman responded to the good news. The phrase, *the Lord opened her heart,* presents a fact for our remembrance—the Holy Spirit leads people to a faith in God. Our witness is the method He sometimes uses. The result of this riverside encounter was the beginning of a new church. One of Paul's favorite New Testament letters is Philippians. Read the epistle and discover how God continued to minister to the apostle through this congregation.

C—Contemporary Application

Beth loves her large city church. Her pastor has a love for missions and continues to lead the church in mission giving and going. An opportunity developed for starting a new church on the other side of the city. The pastor's appeal to the congregation was for some members to commit to a six-month, in-service ministry at the new location. Beth was gifted in working with single adults, but leaving the comfort of her present service was not something she would consider. However, she agreed to pray about the project. God has a way of speaking to a person's heart about His desires. Beth went, stayed a member, and experienced Christian growth.

Consider an answer to the following questions:

- Should a new church or Bible study group be started in your area?
- How could you participate in a mission Vacation Bible School this summer?
- How would you help a person respond to the gospel message?
- What would prevent you from taking a short-term international mission project?

D—Directed Prayer

Lord, help me to catch a vision of personal involvement in a mission opportunity.

March 2

Nehemiah's Little Water Gate

Special places of worship can bring spiritual renewal.
Nehemiah 8:1-18

A—Advice from the Bible

> . . . *all the people assembled as one man in the square before the Water Gate.*
> (Neh. 8:1, NIV)

B—Biblical Example

The walls around Jerusalem were completed. The focus was now on the people of the city and their dedication to God. The material building was over. The time had come to rebuild the people spiritually. A time for celebration was appropriate. Ezra the priest-scribe had returned to Jerusalem to help Nehemiah dedicate the new walls. A special request was made by the people. Ezra was asked to read from God's law. A hunger for better knowledge and understanding of the Word was desired. The people gathered at the Water Gate from early morning to midday, probably listening to the words from the Book of Deuteronomy. What an impressive scene that must have been! The people wept tears of regret for long ignoring the laws of Moses and the failure to obey these laws. Sometime during the reading, a time of remembrance occurred. The Feast of Booths (Tabernacles) was rediscovered (Lev. 23:40-43).

The people had two weeks to prepare for the celebration. The pattern found in Leviticus 23 was carefully followed. Great happiness swept through the crowds. God's Word was read for seven days and the people recalled God's provisions throughout their wilderness wanderings and in the harvest just gathered.

C—Contemporary Application

A special celebration, during my high school years, always brought me closer to God. Each spring in southwestern Oklahoma, an Easter pageant was held in the nearby mountains. People came from miles around to see actors portray the last week of Jesus' life. Special scenes were visible from different locations on the mountainside. The resurrection scene was presented as the sun came up on that hillside. My Sunday school class attended this season of remembrance for several years. The first year I wept when Jesus was beaten. One year, I wanted to defend the Lord during His trial. The next year, I rejoiced when He rose from the tomb. The memories of that event still linger in my mind.

The Bible produces the same results today as in Nehemiah's time.

Consider these truths:

- Reading God's Word can bring conviction for past sins.
- Understanding God's Word can bring great rejoicing.
- Obedience to God's commands leads to real contentment.
- Reading God's Word daily encourages continued spiritual renewal.

D—Directed Prayer

Express to the Lord your gratitude for His written Word and times of special renewal.

March 4

A Little Prayer for Missions

One way to participate in world missions.
2 Thessalonians 3:1-2

A—Advice from the Bible

Finally, pray for us, brothers . . .
(2 Thess. 3:1, HCSB)

B—Biblical Example

In Paul's day, Thessalonica was the capital city of Macedonia and a leading seaport. The apostle made his way to this area on his second missionary journey around A.D. 50 and many converts to the gospel were made during his visit. However, hostile Jews soon forced Paul to leave the city. He was greatly concerned about leaving these new believers. The church of the Thessalonians consisted primarily of converts from paganism. Paul needed to know about their spiritual condition, so Timothy brought good news that they were standing firm. Paul encouraged them in this letter to pray for Christian workers. The request was to "keep on making us the subject of your prayers." Paul needed deliverance from wicked and evil men. He did not want his preaching to be silenced. Paul and his companions wanted nothing to hinder them from telling the good news of salvation in Jesus Christ. The apostle believed that prayer could make a difference in protecting the gospel message.

C—Contemporary Application

The local church dedicated their memorial prayer room and began a sign-up for prayer around the clock. Members would select a one-hour time period to come to the prayer room and intercede for local, national, and international needs. Some people doubted that they could pray for one hour, however, their testimony after fulfilling their commitment was "that hour goes by so fast, I don't get through." The following suggestions will help you practice praying for an hour.
Twelve categories of prayer are listed. Pray five minutes for each request.
1. Praise the Lord (Heb. 13:15); 2. Pray the Word (Ps. 119:105); 3. Meditate on the Word (Joshua 1:8); 4. Confess your personal sins (1 John 1:9); 5. Intercede for others including missionaries (1 Sam. 12:23); 6. Be still and listen (Ps. 46:10); 7. Pray for teachers of the Word (Prov. 30:5); 8. Ask for your needs (James 4:2); 9. Pray for your church staff (1 Thess. 5:12); 10. Pray for your church (Eph. 5:25-27); 11. Pray for the world leaders (1 Tim 2:1-2); 12 Give thanks to God (Ps. 136:1-26).

What personal attitudes would improve your missionary praying?
- Be willing to learn how to pray for the missionaries.
- Be supportive during special weeks of prayer
- Be a participant when asked to pray at certain times of the day.
- Be sensitive to prayer needs around the world.

D—Directed Prayer

Lord, help to pray more effectively for missionaries by name.

March 5

Hezekiah's Little Throne

Worshiping the Lord includes helping other people.
2 Chronicles 29:1-3,20-26

A—Advice from the Bible

In the first month of the first year of his reign . . .
(2 Chron. 29:3, NIV)

B—Biblical Example

Hezekiah began his reign as the 13th king of Judah, the Southern Kingdom. His personal godliness led him to call his people back to the faith of their fathers. This reformer began his rule by reopening the doors of the house of God. King Ahaz, his father, had gathered all the furnishing from the temple and took them away. The late king nailed shut the door and set up altars at every street corner in Jerusalem. Hezekiah assumed the ruins from his father's reign and immediately instigated civil and religious reforms. Several strengths are characteristic of his personal life. He maintained a personal growing relationship with God. The result of this relationship is seen in restoring the Passover as a national holiday and promoting a revival in Judah. Another strength was his powerful prayer life and he honored the Lord by reading from His Word. The king had portions of Proverbs 25 copied by his men and read at each worship service. The result of this good king's life is summarized in 2 Kings 18:5,6: *Hezekiah trusted in the LORD, the God of Israel. There was no one like him among all the kings of Judah, either before him or after him. He held fast to the LORD and did not cease to follow him; he kept the commands the LORD had given Moses.* Hezekiah gave back to the people the privilege of worshiping the Lord.

C—Contemporary Application

Not many individuals have the honor of meeting a real king. My husband, Jim, had this privilege when he was invited to Uganda, Africa, to teach in a seminary. One day, a message was received from King Wilburforce inviting the missionaries to visit him. Jim and some companions went to the king's house. The presentation of the guests happened in the throne room, a very modest place. These honored guests soon discovered that their host was a Christian and wanted his people to know more about God. He understood the relationship between worshiping God and helping others. This ruler cared about his people and wanted them to be taught from the Bible. One of Jim's traveling companions was an agricultural specialist from Florida. The king wanted information on how to grow better crops and he welcomed Christians and wanted a better life for his people.

Giving and worship are still practiced through:

- Financial support.
- Attendance.
- Participation in worship.
- Sharing of talents.

D—Directed Prayer

Lord, help me to understand how giving and worship belong together.

March 6

Elijah's Little Bonfire

God's work may lead you into conflicts and confrontations.
1 Kings 18:36-46

A—Advice from the Bible

Then the fire of the LORD fell...
(1 Kings 18:38, NIV)

B—Biblical Example

One of the boldest, most colorful people in the Old Testament was Elijah. This prophet's model of courage is outstanding. Serving God led him into conflicts as he confronted a religion that was challenging God's people and their faith in Him. The Jews were about to betray Him by worshiping the Canaanite god of fertility called Baal. The ruling Hebrew monarch was King Ahab; the queen was the infamous Jezebel from Tyre. This political marriage brought impending disaster to God's children. Her zeal for idol worship had to be stopped. God used Elijah to accomplish this feat. God's prophet immediately began to prove the impotence of the Canaanite god. An unfolding drama in this passage of Scripture reveals how God would honor His servant's prayer. A showdown with the priests of Baal happened on Mount Carmel. The contest began with sacrificing a bull. Each side in the challenge was to call down fire from his god to consume the bull. You remember the rest of the story. Baal didn't; God did! Elijah's prayer was heard and answered. The earth was scorched and the water dried up. God had demonstrated His power and presence.

C—Contemporary Application

Sometimes my mind pictures places and events in exaggerated proportions. My husband and I were planning a trip to San Antonio, Texas. Our traveling habit was to read in advance about the site we would visit. The Alamo was on our list of tourist things to see. I had pictured how this old mission would look converted into a big fort with lots of buildings around the wall. What a shock! We walked into the entrance of this small structure and read what had happened on March 6, 1836. The Texans were fighting Mexico for independence. Inside the fort were 155 men, notables being Davy Crocket and Jim Bowie. Surrounding the site were 4,000 Mexicans led by Santa Anna. The walls eventually were climbed and hand-to-hand combat began. All the Texans were killed. One of the favorite mottos for Texans is "Remember the Alamo!" The courage of these fighters as they died to protect freedom will always be remembered.

God does many things for you:

- He enables you to have the courage to confront other religions.
- He involves Himself in the affairs of your daily life.
- He answers the prayers of the faithful.
- He proves trustworthy in testing time.

D—Directed Prayer

Dear God, help me to respond with courage to life challenges.

March 7

Dorcas' Little Stitches

Your acts of ministry serve as a witness for Jesus Christ.
Acts 9:36-43

A—Advice from the Bible

. . . always doing good works and acts of charity.
(Acts 9:36, HCSB)

B—Biblical Example

The Apostle Peter traveled throughout all Judea, Galilee, and Samaria under the direction of the Holy Spirit. His message of salvation through Jesus Christ was preached everywhere. An amazing evidence of God's power occurred in the city of Joppa. Peter was on a mission trip through the coastal regions to visit Christian communities and became involved in the life of Dorcas (Tabitha, Aramaic name). This woman had a reputation for donating a great deal of her time to helping others. Her main concern was for less fortunate people. One day Dorcas became ill and died. The custom of the Jews was to wash the dead body in preparation for burial and lay the body in an upper room. A message was sent to Peter who was about 12 miles away at Lydda. The note ask him to, "Come to Joppa at once." Peter and his delegation departed immediately. The grieving women gathered around the apostle, showing him the garments Dorcas had made for them. Peter's course of action was to be alone with the dead person. He called upon the Lord through prayer and then turned his attention to Dorcas. Peter commanded her to come back to life. The apostle touched her for the first time and presented her alive to the weeping women.

C—Contemporary Application

Giving your time to helping other people can do many things for you. Consider some of these values in sharing the gospel through Christian service:
- You begin to think about others instead of yourself.
- You develop your talents and spiritual gifts.
- You begin to meet new friends.
- You expose yourself to new experiences.

I have known a few women who could be called, "Dorcas." One woman in particular loved to quilt. This talent has been used to bless people around the world. Minnie provided quilts for migrant workers, international missionaries, children's homes, and the homeless. She died of old age, still ministering to others.

What are some things to consider when ministering to others?
- Ministry frequently begins by caring for physical needs.
- Ministry must be done with an attitude of prayer and dependence upon the Lord.
- Ministry in Jesus name can have far-reaching effects.
- Ministry does not always need to be spectacular.

D—Directed Prayer

Lord, teach me to minister effectively.

March 8

A Little Fruit –Love

Christian virtues are produced inwardly by the indwelling Holy Spirit.
Galatians 5:22

A—Advice from the Bible

But the fruit of the Spirit is . . .
(Gal. 5:22 HCSB)

B—Biblical Example

God is so good to His children! Before Jesus ascended back to heaven, He assured the believers that a Comforter would come. Along with His presence would be nine qualities of Christian character to help believers become more like Christ. These inward traits are called The Fruit of the Spirit. For the next nine days, each devotional will feature one of the fruit. These virtues are like a cluster of grapes that find expression in the lives of Spirit-controlled believers.

Love heads the list and is the most Godlike quality. Paul reminded his readers that love is the greatest (1 Cor. 13:13). A one-word-way to describe this trait is "selflessness." All the rest of the fruit is really an outgrowth of love. Divine love is God's gift to us and we must allow this gift to find expression through us. Concern for others is another way of describing this trait. The greatest example of this love is seen at Calvary. A follower of the risen Christ will ask, "What *may* I give?" instead of "What *must* I give?"

C—Contemporary Application

Seminary life is difficult enough without having a baby added to the stress, or so I thought until March 8, 1956. My husband and I were busy students and rarely found time to spend together. However, God had His plan in place for our lives. That special morning began with the usual sign that a birth was about to occur. We drove on our practiced route to the hospital. Later that day, James Mark Harvey was born. Words cannot express the love I instantly felt for this tiny baby. God had given us a perfect child. Jim and I prayed over our little boy, giving him to God and asking the Father to use his life in service for the Kingdom. Little did we know that through the years our love for Mark would continue to grow, even today as he faithfully serves the Lord half-way around the world from his family. The call to missions came when Mark was a 10-year-old boy involved in missionary education in our church. We never doubted that God would use him in a special way. I understood parental love for the first time on March 8, 1956. How God must have loved His own Son!

Consider this attitude check for evidence of the Fruit of the Spirit—love:

- Assisting an elderly person who needs help.
- Refusing to hold a grudge toward someone who offends you.
- Doing more of your share of tasks at home.
- Taking time to visit and encourage someone who is ill or lonely.

D—Directed Prayer

Lord, help me to practice loving all people.

March 9

A Little Fruit –Joy

Christian virtues are produced inwardly by the indwelling Holy Spirit.
Galatians 5:22

A—Advice from the Bible

But the fruit of the Spirit is . . .
(Gal. 5:22 HCSB)

B—Biblical Example

Before Jesus ascended back to heaven, He assured the believers that a Comforter would come. Along with His presence would be nine qualities of Christian character to help believers become more like Christ. Paul lists nine of these ethical principles. Mentioned first is *love,* meaning selflessness. Today, our focus is on the word *joy.* This characteristic always accompanies love. Sometimes people think *joy* and *happiness* are the same words. However, happiness is determined by outward circumstances. Paul's letter to the Philippians is an expression of joy. He wrote to his friends from a prison cell. The Greek word for *joy* comes from the same root as *grace*. A redemptive experience with Christ and the knowledge that a person's sins are forgiven, plus the assurance that a believer is a child of God and has eternal life, produces joy. Paul was an outstanding example of joy (Phil. 1:4). This inward peace and sufficiency is not affected by outward circumstances. You can have joy in the midst of trouble. Read a beautiful expression of this character of God as expressed in Zephaniah 3:17.

C—Contemporary Application

The Middle Ages was a period of history sometimes called "The Dark Ages." Spiritual and moral darkness had invaded the church. The ethical standards of many Christian leaders were characterized by disgrace, shame, and corruption. And yet, God still loved His people. A devotional poem about the Lord was written at this time by Bernard of Clairvaux. In his early 20's, he chose the life of a monk and entered a monastery in France. God used this young man's forceful personality and talents to provide leadership for his generation of believers. This poem became a hymn, titled, "Jesus, the Very Thought of Thee." One phrase is especially interesting when the situations of his day are recalled. He wrote, "Jesus, our only joy be Thou, as Thou our prize wilt be; Jesus, be Thou our glory now and thru eternity." The joy expressed in these words came from an inward dwelling of the Holy Spirit that produced spiritual fruit. "The Dark Ages" weren't dark for Bernard.

Consider this attitude check for evidence of the Fruit of the Spirit—joy:
- I choose to be joyful instead of miserable.
- I choose to be joyful instead of pathetic.
- I choose to be joyful instead of discouraged.
- I choose to be joyful instead of depressed.

D—Directed Prayer

Lord, the hymn refers to "Joy unspeakable and full of glory." I claim that joy in my life.

March 10

A Little Fruit –Peace

Christian virtues are produced inwardly by the indwelling Holy Spirit.
Galatians 5:22

A—Advice from the Bible

But the fruit of the Spirit is . . .
(Gal. 5:22 HCSB)

B—Biblical Example

Peace is the most precious of all gifts and graces of the Holy Spirit. Some scholars have described this kind of peace as being at ease; a calmness under the skin; a quiet assurance which operates in either war or calm. The one legacy left for us by the risen Lord is "Peace I leave with you, My peace I give unto you . . . " Yesterday, the fruit studied was *joy*. Joy may be more exciting, but peace is more comforting. The Apostle Paul experienced this kind of peace when he wrote, "And the peace of God, which surpasses every thought, will guard your hearts and your minds in Christ Jesus" (Phil. 4:7). One person explained this peace as "God's own calm, restful heart possessing ours and filling us with His divine stillness." A peace like Paul describes cannot be understood. No rational explanation exists for this experience. This spiritual fruit saves us from anxious concerns. Another description of this peace is that it crowds out our anxieties and fills us with such satisfaction that nothing really makes us afraid. A life of peace leads to a life of praise and a life of praise leads back to a life of peace.

C—Contemporary Application

I witnessed this kind of peace years ago when my father-in-law died from lung cancer. A family death was new to us. Other friends had lost loved ones, but not us. My mother-in-law was beside herself with grief. Her companion of many years was gone. They had spent much time together. Now, what would she do? We began to pray for her and asked God to give her peace during these trials. And the prayer was answered. When I went into her bedroom where she was resting on the bed, I sensed something different about her and thought perhaps the doctor needed to be called. Wrong assessment! She sat up and said, "Something warm just passed over my body. I felt like I was totally covered in something I can't explain." From that moment on, through the days of mourning and decisions, she remained strong and said, "God washed over me a peace that is wonderful."

Isaiah 43:1-13 tells of God providing peace for His children. Some of the reasons for peace are:
- When you pass through the waters, God will be there.
- When you walk through fire, God will be there.
- When you are afraid, God will be there.
- When you were formed, God was there.

D—Directed Prayer

Help me, Father, to grow in peace by giving myself totally to You.

March 11

A Little Fruit – Patience

Christian virtues are produced inwardly by the indwelling Holy Spirit.
Galatians 5:22

A—Advice from the Bible

But the fruit of the Spirit is . . . .
(Gal. 5:22 HCSB)

B—Biblical Example

The Bible uses two different Greek words for *patience*. One has to do with *things*. The "endurance" mentioned in Romans 5:3-4 is an example of this kind of patience. The other word for *patience* has to do with people and is sometimes translated "longsuffering." This is the word the Apostle Paul uses in Galatians 5:22. A good definition is: being steadfast toward people who can and will aggravate or persecute others. The word suggests a slowness to avenge wrongs suffered or a refusal to get even. When the experiences of the missionary Paul are recalled, he had many opportunities to lose his patience, but biblical descriptions of his life present an example of patience. One of the characteristics of God is described as patience. "*The Lord does not delay His promise, as some understand delay, but is patient with you, not wanting any to perish, but all to come to repentance*" (2 Peter 3:9). Paul also encouraged believers to be patient: "*And we exhort you, brothers: warn those who are lazy, comfort the discouraged, help the weak, be patient with everyone*" (1 Thess. 5:14).

C—Contemporary Application

A woman noticed a small boy looking in her bakery window one morning. He was obviously hungry and poorly clothed for such a cold day. Customers kept her busy and when she did look out the window again, the boy was gone. Each day he returned to the same spot and sometimes stood in the doorway. The owner began to lose her patience with this little nuisance. One cold morning, she went outside to confront him and immediately noticed the boy had no socks and a worn-out pair of sneakers. She invited him into the bakery and gave him some bread and milk, then asked her assistant to watch the shop for a little while. This once impatient woman went to the shoe store and bought the boy a new pair of shoes. He left her immediately, running down the street. Later that day, he returned to the bakery and said, "I forgot to thank you for my shoes. Are you God's wife?" "No," she replied, "but I am one of His children." Her patience had demonstrated the fruit of the Spirit to a little boy who had been a pest.

How can Christians demonstrate this fruit of the Spirit?

- Focus on God's patience toward His children.
- Show patience in practical ways toward difficult people.
- Seek to overcome negative feelings about people.
- Claim the Holy Spirit's work to produce patience in you.

D—Directed Prayer

Help me, Father, to grow in patience by giving myself totally to You.

March 12

A Little Fruit –Kindness

Christian virtues are produced inwardly by the indwelling Holy Spirit.
Galatians 5:22

A—Advice from the Bible

But the fruit of the Spirit is . . . .
(Gal. 5:22 HCSB)

B—Biblical Example

Christian kindness is an action of love that never fails. The Old Testament example of David and Mephibosheth illustrates the attitude we should have toward other people. Following David's victory over Goliath, he became recognized as the leader to command of the armies of King Saul. Continued wars prevailed between their two followers and lasted even after Saul's death. David grew progressively stronger and Saul's house grew weaker. David's success did not cause him to forget his covenant with his good friend, Jonathan. After David finally triumphed over all his enemies, he desired to show kindness to someone from Saul's house. In 2 Samuel 9:1 David asked: "*Is there anyone still left of the house of Saul to whom I can show kindness for Jonathan's sake?*" He issued a command to find a survivor. The king sought not only to keep a personal promise, but also to be a witness of God's care and blessing to humankind. He actively sought ways to be gracious to others.

C—Contemporary Application

The Apostle Paul wrote to the Colossians (3:12) and said, "Therefore, God's chosen ones, holy and loved, put on heartfelt compassion, kindness, humility, gentleness, and patience." Kindness is one of the characteristics of God (Eph. 2:7). Suppose one of the following opportunities for showing kindness occurred in your life, what would you do in each situation?

- A young mother in your neighborhood has the flu. Her small children are cared for by out-of-town family members, but she needs help. What would you do?
- A care-center calls about a forgotten patient who has died. No family members can be located. What would you do to show kindness?
- Thomas, a senior adult in your church, can no longer drive his car. He loves to go for drives and to eat in restaurants. How could you make his life more enjoyable?
- A farm family lost all their possession because of a fire. How could you get involved in helping these people?

How can we eagerly seek to show kindness?

- Look for opportunities to minister.
- Use your material possessions to benefit others.
- Learn to deal fairly with family and friends.
- Respond promptly to needs.

D—Directed Prayer

Father, I ask for help in practicing kindness.

March 13

A Little Fruit – Goodness

Christian virtues are produced inwardly by the indwelling Holy Spirit.
Galatians 5:22

A—Advice from the Bible

But the fruit of the Spirit is . . . .
(Gal. 5:22 HCSB)

B—Biblical Example

The characteristic of "goodness" is to produce the fruit God desires for us. This "fruit" will help the world know that He loves all people and died for their sins. Psalm 107:1-9 reveals this quality of life that all believers possess. God's dealings with Israel are described as "good." Many Bible teachers believe that this psalm was composed after the Israelites returned from 70 years of captivity in Babylon. The former captives were rejoicing in their return to Jerusalem and thanked God for His act of salvation in delivering them from bondage. The whole psalm is a celebration of God's goodness. The writer wanted his people to worship the LORD because of His goodness. While this characteristic is similar to the goodness of humans, God is perfectly and completely good. His goodness leads to truth and righteousness. Goodness and love are two reasons to thank Him.

C—Contemporary Application

An email came to my computer the other day. The attachment included these words,
Good Morning, this is God.
I will be handling
All of your problems today.
I will not need your help,
So have a good day.

After reading these words, I began to wonder just how I would live if I had a "good day."
First, I would begin the day with a quiet time. Reading my Bible and praying would be top priority. Sometimes people wait until evening to have this special time with the Lord. To me, that habit is like going to battle and forgetting to wear your armor!
I would then focus on my family. Expressions of love and concern would be spoken. "What can I do for you today?" would be asked. Responding to their reply would be very important. Throughout the day, I would look for opportunities to demonstrate goodness. Surely by the end of the day, I could say, "I have had a good day."

How can we eagerly seek to show goodness?

- Send a card to a friend who needs encouragement.
- Visit someone in a care center.
- Prepare a meal for a person who is homebound.
- Call a lonely person and ask what you can do for them.

D—Directed Prayer

Father, I ask for help in practicing goodness.

A Little Fruit –Faith

Christian virtues are produced inwardly by the indwelling Holy Spirit.
Galatians 5:22

A—Advice from the Bible

But the fruit of the Spirit is . . . .
(Gal. 5:22 HCSB)

B—Biblical Example

A favorite definition for faith is: a loyalty based upon a firm persuasion about my conviction concerning Christ. This characteristic of God is commanded in Revelation 2:10, *Be faithful until death, and I will give you the crown of life.* One of the great descriptions of God in the Bible is that He is faithful. Therefore, His children should be like Him. *Let us hold on to the confession of our hope without wavering, for He who promised is faithful* (Heb. 10:23). Faith for the believer means dependability. God can count on us. An example of God's faithfulness in action is found in 2 Chronicles 20:1-30. Judah and King Jehoshaphat were threatened by war. This leader showed remarkable faith early in his reign, however, he compromised his political and religious convictions and disobeyed his faithful God. Prayer, prophecy, and praise finally brought the victory from God. The Holy Spirit has produced the fruit of faith and all believers should practice this virtue in daily living.

C—Contemporary Application

Fanny J. Crosby has been called "the queen of hymn writers." Her faithfulness to God was modeled throughout her life, beginning at her birth in 1820, and ending in her homegoing in 1915. An eye infection when she was an infant was mistreated by a doctor, resulting in a lifetime of blindness. Her grandmother encouraged young Fanny to memorize entire books of the Bible. The Institution for the Blind in New York City provided her education and recognition as a poet. Her walk in faithfulness began during a cholera epidemic. The awareness of life after death led her to attend a revival meeting and she committed her life to Jesus Christ. Because of this new faith in God, and her talents, Fanny began to write songs for Him and never stopped. A line from one of the hymns affirms her desire to utilize the fruit of the Spirit, especially faith. *All the way my Savior leads me . . . Here by faith in Him to dwell! For I know, whate'er befall me, Jesus doeth all things well.*

How would our Christian walk be different if we allowed the Holy Spirit to exercise the fruit of faith?

- We would be trustworthy.
- We would be dependable.
- We would be loyal.
- We would be persistent in doing right.

D—Directed Prayer

Father, I ask for help in exercising my faith.

March 15

A Little Fruit--Gentleness

Christian virtues are produced inwardly by the indwelling Holy Spirit.
(Galatians 5:23)

A—Advice from the Bible

But the fruit of the Spirit is . . . .
(Gal. 5:23)

B—Biblical Example

A good definition for gentleness is a quiet sense of adequacy that comes from being controlled by the Holy Spirit. A good example would be a wild horse that has been broken. When Jesus entered Simon Peter's life, this plain fisherman, later nicknamed "the rock," seemed an unlikely person to serve as the Lord's disciple. He often spoke without thinking and was often impatient and impulsive. Most Bible students remember how Peter denied three times that he even knew Jesus. Later in his life, difficulties surfaced over prejudice against the Gentile people. The word *gentleness* would not be used to describe this apostle until later in his life. His brother Andrew would certainly display the fruit of gentleness. However, Peter was changed by the love of Jesus and became a communicator of the gospel to the early church. He is the author of 1 and 2 Peter, letters that sought to comfort the persecuted believers with the message of the hope of eternal life. Read these two letters and notice the gentleness with which Peter addresses the needs of the people. Is this the same man who cursed and denied knowing Jesus?

C—Contemporary Application

Andrew Jackson was born on March 15, 1767. His mother named him Andrew. Later in his life, the nickname "Old Hickory" would become famous. The child was wild, quick-tempered, and disinterested in anything that was not military. This South Carolina rebel fought in the British invasion of the western Carolinas in 1780–81 at the age of thirteen. The battlefield became the stage for Andrew distinguishing himself. In 1802 Jackson had also been elected major general of the Tennessee militia, a position he still held when the War of 1812 opened the door to a command in the field and a hero's role.

He became the nation's seventh president, but still lacked a gentle spirit. However, as he aged, pain and the death of his beloved wife Rachel humbled the proud leader. During the last years of his life, the battle wounds changed the attitude of this once hardened man. He became gentle to the people around as they tried to make his life more pleasant.

Gentleness in a believer is seen as they:
- Encourage other people to become all God has created them to be.
- Share comfort with others during times of sickness or sorrow.
- Minister in ways that bring glory to God.
- Develop a deeper appreciation for God's Word.

D—Directed Prayer

Lord, help me to do what is necessary to produce more good fruit.

March 16

A Little Fruit—Self-Control

Christian virtues are produced inwardly by the indwelling Holy Spirit.
Galatians 5:22

A—Advice from the Bible

But the fruit of the Spirit is . . . .
(Gal. 5:22)

B—Biblical Example

Today's devotional concludes the thoughts on the fruit of the Spirit. Eight different virtues have been considered and now the ninth focus is on having control over thoughts and actions. First Samuel 26 presents a clear example of mastering self-control. David had been driven from Israel by King Saul who was terribly angry and jealous. His goal was to hunt down and kill this person who was threatening his power. David and one companion slipped into Saul's camp and stood over the sleeping ruler. The king's spear and canteen were taken as evidence of David's opportunity to kill Saul. Complete self-control is pictured for us. The word "self-control" is used in two others places. (Read Acts 24:25 and 2 Peter 1:6.) A person having this fruit does not drift with the current of evil practices; he dares to stand up against them. An interesting fact about these devotionals is that Paul begins with love or selflessness, and closes with self-control. These two virtues make possible the other characteristics.

C—Contemporary Application

Read the following situations and decide how self-control would make a difference:
- Tom gets so angry at the ballgame that profanity flies from his mouth.
- Sylvia has participated in diet programs for the last 10 years, but is still obese.
- Jimmy's parents are often called to the school because of his temper related problems.
- Helen can be described as a "road-rage" driver.

Hebrews 12:1 offers this advice, "lay aside very weight and sin that so easily ensnares us . . . ." "Anything that interferes with our spiritual effectiveness should be eliminated. Habits, practices, or attitudes that hinder our spiritual welfare and service for the Lord, must be controlled. The way to achieve this self-control is to place ourselves under the Holy Spirit's leadership and direction

Consider your personal answer to the following questions about self-control:
- What area of your life is most lacking in self-control?
- In what ways does your lack of self-control affect Christians and non-Christians?
- What do all of the fruit of the Spirit have in common?
- Which fruit do you find most difficult to exercise?

D—Directed Prayer

Begin today thanking God for the opportunity to be fruitful.

March 17

Ezekiel's Little History Lesson

God never leaves Himself without a witness.
Ezekiel 34:1-12

A—Advice from the Bible

The word of the LORD came to me.
(Ezk.34:1)

B—Biblical Example

The Babylonian exile continued when Ezekiel received the call of the Lord to be His spokesman. This prophet's message was to keep the Israelites aware of the reason for their exile and prepare them for the eventual return to their homes. The Lord consistently addressed Ezekiel as "son of man." The main focus of the prophecies was God versus the shepherds (false teachers who had ignored the needs of the people). The Scripture presents the prophet giving a history lesson. The blame was laid on Judah's kings for the nation's plight. These leaders had abused their office for personal gain and so deprived their followers. Condemnation and judgment are combined in the solemn pronouncement, "I am against the shepherds." These kings were held accountable by God for their misuse of power. Four centuries had passed without an official ruler. The highest office was that of high priest. The historic fulfillment of this prophecy began some 30 years after the close of Ezekiel's ministry. Ezra describes the return of the Jews to their homeland.

C—Contemporary Application

March 17 is the designated day to celebrate the ministry of St. Patrick, patron saint of Ireland. Born in Roman Britain in the late 4th century, he was responsible for the conversion of the Irish to Christianity. By the time of his death on March 17, 461, he had established monasteries, churches, and schools. Many legends grew up around him—for example, that he drove the snakes out of Ireland and used the shamrock to explain the Trinity. Ireland came to celebrate his day with religious services and feasts. Boston held its first St. Patrick's Day parade in 1737, followed by New York City in 1762. Since 1962 Chicago has colored its river green on March 17th. Irish and non-Irish alike commonly participate in the "wearing of the green"—sporting an item of green clothing or having a shamrock, the Irish national plant, in the lapel. Corned beef and cabbage are associated with the holiday, and even beer is sometimes dyed green to celebrate the day.

The "Hymn of St. Patrick" is learned by all Irish children:

- Christ be with me, Christ within me, Christ behind me, Christ before me.
- Christ beside me, Christ to win me, Christ to comfort and restore me.
- Christ beneath me, Christ above me, Chris in quiet, Christ in danger.
- Christ in hearts of all that love me, Christ in mouth of friend and stranger.

D—Directed Prayer

Lord, may our shepherds remain responsible to their people.

March 18

A Little Advice

We need the timeless, dependable, true wisdom of God.
(Proverbs 3:5-8)

A—Advice from the Bible

Lean not to your own understanding.
(Prov. 3:5)

B—Biblical Example

The Book of Proverbs is about wisdom and contains more than 900 verses. Some people identify the Psalms as the Hebrew's hymnbook; in Proverbs we have God's manual for daily right living. Most of these sayings are attributed to Solomon and are presented as a father talking to his son. He reigned as king in Israel's golden age of prosperity and power. Remember Solomon's dream in which God asked him what his heart desired above everything else and the king asked for wisdom (1 Kings 3:3-14)? The verses for today instruct a person on how to find the secret of life and the result will be authentic success. The road to true victory lies in trusting the Lord with all your heart, whether you seek success in business, international missions, family relationships, or in some other form of ministry. The promise from God is that He will point you in the right direction. Righteous living will improve most circumstances.

C—Contemporary Application

A favorite hymn from the past is, "Trust and Obey." Daniel B Towner was inspired by Proverbs 3:5-6 to write this song. He served as the worship leader in a Methodist church in Binghamton, New York. In the fall of 1885, D.L. Moody, the famous evangelist, enlisted Mr. Towner to sing and do personal work. The words were inspired at an evangelistic meeting when a young man rose and gave his testimony: "I am not sure—but I am going to trust, and I am going to obey." A song was born with the help of Rev. J.H. Sammis, a Presbyterian minister. Years later, Dr. Towner became the head of the Music Department of the Moody Bible Institute of Chicago where hundreds of young people are trained to lead worship and minister to the Lord in music. In his lifetime, he compiled 14 hymnbooks. Some of his other favorite hymns are, "At Calvary" and "Grace Greater Than All Our Sins." This dedicated Christian died at the age of 70 while leading the singing for a spring revival in Longwood, Missouri.

What are some ways we can trust and obey the Lord?
- When we walk with the Lord in the light of His Word.
- When we do His good will.
- When we lay our life on the altar.
- When He sends us, we will go.

D—Directed Prayer

Lord, help us claim Your promise to guide us.

March 19

The Tax Collector's Little Supper

A Christian has the responsibility to take God's message beyond the local church.
(Matthew 9:9-13)

A—Advice from the Bible

While Jesus was having supper at Matthew's house . . . .
(Matt. 9:10)

B—Biblical Example

Jesus recognized and called people who were despised by the respected community. One such outsider was Matthew. His vocation of representing the Roman government by collecting taxes for them caused him to be hated by the other Jews. Jesus must have seen something in this man that the world did not see. One certain fact was that Matthew needed to follow Jesus. To further disturb the pious Jews, Jesus shared a meal with this sinner. This action violated the teaching of the rabbis, who believed that their association with ritually unclean people would cause them to become unclean. When questioned about His actions, Jesus explained that His mission was to those who saw their need for God. The Pharisees were not able to understand why Jesus would associate with people they had spent their lives avoiding. His disciples were questioned, but Jesus responded. In His view, the sick were those individuals who were actually sick with sin because of their separation from God. He had come to help this kind of person, and would not reject them because of some religious laws.

C—Contemporary Application

David Livingstone was born on March 19, 1813, in Scotland. During his medical studies, he attended classes in theology. In 1840, he was ordained and sent as a medical missionary to South Africa. He immediately fell in love with Africa and would go on frequent expeditions into the jungle. Some of his family members pleaded with him not to go into these primitive areas, but he desired to serve the Lord by helping these medically and spiritually neglected African people. He laid the foundation for generations of future missionaries who sought to reach the lost people of Africa with the gospel of Jesus Christ. On the last trip, he disappeared for seven years. Henry Stanley, an Anglo-American journalist, found him and personally found the Lord, when Livingstone kept sharing the call of Jesus, "Leave all and follow Me."

Consider answers to these questions:
- Why should Christians reach out to those people outside the local church?
- Why is accepting people who are different such a challenge?
- What are some risks of associating with people who are different?
- Why must Christians emphasize God's love and acceptance of repentant sinners?

D—Directed Prayer

Father, help me to be aware of and reach out to the outsiders in my community.

March 20

Jacob's Little Gift

You can learn to forgive and accept forgiveness.
(Genesis 33:1-11)

A—Advice from the Bible

"Please accept the gift that was brought to you."
(Gen. 33:11)

B—Biblical Example

Jacob and Esau were twin brothers born to Isaac and Rebecca. Esau was the firstborn. Therefore, by Hebrew law, he was entitled to the birthright and special blessing of his father. But Jacob very cleverly tricked Esau out of those rights. When the older son learned that he had been cheated out of his blessing, he was outraged and angry enough to kill his brother. Warned by his mother of Esau's threats, Jacob fled to the north to live with an uncle named Laban. Twenty years later, Jacob longed to return to his home and family in Canaan. He knew that he faced a tough test in seeking reconciliation with his brother. He must have remembered Esau's threats to kill him. But Jacob decided to do as God instructed him. He sought to explain his long absence from the land and to assure Esau that he was coming peacefully. Jacob moved boldly to the front of the traveling group to meet his brother. The anxiety about the meeting turned out to be without cause. The reunion was a time of tearful joy as the brothers warmly embrace one another. Jacob's gifts were received and forgiveness was experienced.

C—Contemporary Application

The Schmidt family is an interesting contemporary study of the Scripture passage for today. The parents have two sons. Dad favors Sammy; mom favors William. The boys were constant rivals in school and sometimes seemed like enemies rather than family. One day, William took his brother's new car and wrecked the vehicle. Sam was so furious he threatened to kill his younger brother. The solution to the problem was for one of them to leave home. William chose to relocate across the nation with a family member. Years passed without any contact. The father became ill and word was sent for the younger brother to come home. Of course, he was afraid that the threat made 15 years earlier was not forgiven, however, Will went back. The boys met in the front yard. Silence followed. Finally, the "I'm sorry" was spoken. The embrace erased years of hurt.

Forgiveness, what is it?

- Which is easier to forgive a friend or someone in your own family?
- Is it easier to forgive or to ask forgiveness?
- What makes forgiveness hard?
- Can a person ever completely forgive?

D—Directed Prayer

Father, may family reunions be a time of forgiving and forgetting.

March 21

The Pharisee's Little Party

Christ's love enables us to reach out to different kinds of people.
(Luke 7:36-50)

A—Advice from the Bible

> *Now the Pharisee invited Jesus to have dinner with him.*
> (Luke 7:36)

B—Biblical Example

The term *Pharisee* means separated. The members of this separatist group within the Jewish religion existed two centuries before and after the birth and resurrection of Christ. They insisted upon a meticulous observance of the law and the traditions that interpreted the law. As a result, they tended to have a separated attitude toward life. The name of this host Pharisee was Simon. Jesus' previous encounters with this group were usually hostile. However, in this situation, a Pharisee invited a non-Pharisee to dinner. Jesus did not limit His ministry to the lower levels of society, but included the wealthy, educated, and influential. No home was off-limits to Jesus. The dinner was interrupted by an uninvited woman. Her attention to Jesus annoyed the host and caused him to question the credibility of this Man. A teaching session followed with Simon as the major student. The outcome of this lesson is not revealed, but a sinful woman was forgiven and this experience was a witness to all the invited guests.

C—Contemporary Application

John Newton was a social outcast. As a 22-year-old sea captain on a slave ship bound for England, he was dramatically converted to a saving Christian faith during a violent storm at sea. The date of this event was March 21, 1747. He gave up his vocation of slave-trading and the sea, and devoted his life to the work of the clergy in the Anglican Church. During those years he came in contact with the great evangelist, George Whitefield. Hymn writing became his greatest expression of God's love. "Amazing Grace" is his best known hymn, but I like "Though Troubles Assail Us." The first stanza reads, "Though troubles assail us and dangers affright, Though friends should all fail us and foes all unite, Yet one thing secures us, whatever betide, The promise assures us, 'The Lord will provide.'" He preached 28 years and died at age 82, no longer remembered as a socially unacceptable person.

People from all social levels are:
- Loved by God.
- Ministered to by Christ.
- Forgiven of their sins.
- Accepted by Christians.

D—Directed Prayer

Lord, show me how can I reach out to someone considered socially unacceptable?

March 22

Abraham's Little Negotiation

God hears the cry of the oppressed.
(Genesis 18:20-26)

A—Advice from the Bible

I will spare the whole place for their sake
(Gen. 18:26)

B—Biblical Example

When God announced His intention to judge Sodom and Gomorrah, Abraham began to plead for Sodom's forgiveness. His concern was for a small remnant that might be found faithful to God. Negotiations then began between the patriarch and His God. The outcome of this confrontation was that God would spare the city if only a small group of godly people were located. Abraham needed to learn that God punishes wickedness. Two great truths were kept before Abraham. First, God was the reason for every great thing that would come into his life. Secondly, the blessings Abraham would enjoy were due solely to God's grace. However, God's actions brought punishment for the sins of the people of Sodom, Gomorrah, Admah, Zeboim, and Zoar. These people were exceedingly wicked and had total disregard for God and their fellowman. The cities must have been notorious for some time. Remember that God's judgments are based upon justice; and the facts were in about these cities. A remarkable human intercession follows. The highlight of the story for me is the way God graciously displays His sense of mercy, love, and fairness as he agrees to grant Abraham's request, even if there are only ten found in Sodom, who are righteous.

C—Contemporary Application

Our tour group stood at Masada, an ancient fortress on a mountaintop in the desert about 30 miles south-east of Jerusalem Lying off in the distance was the Dead Sea and the former site of Sodom and Gomorrah. The Bible almost invariably speaks of them together. I thought about Abraham and God having a meeting about the sin problem of the cities, later destroyed by brimstone and fire and perhaps accompanied by an earthquake. Their sites now lie under the Dead Sea. Later in the day we went over to the Dead Sea. How different it must have been in Abraham and Lot's time! Now, everything is dead, no grass or living insects. Tourist are the only ones who care about this region.

God constantly works for our good:
- He can always be trusted to do right.
- He honors the prayers of godly people.
- He stays in complete control of His creation.
- He always finds faithful people to carry on His work.

D—Directed Prayer

Thank You that mercy is still in effect today.

March 23

A Little Farewell Address

Believers should be completely loyal to God.
(Joshua 24:14-18)

A—Advice from the Bible

But as for me and my household, we will serve the LORD.
(Josh. 24:15)

B—Biblical Example

The Israelites were victorious; they had won the Promised Land! However, they were tempted to forget how and why they had won. Joshua, their faithful leader, was aware of this fact. The time was coming for him to end his leadership of God's people. The verses in today's passage are part of Joshua's farewell address to Israel and the establishing of a new covenant ceremony at Shechem. Canaan was won and the land was allotted to the tribes. Joshua was old and thus, a final step was necessary. The ceremony at Shechem was not to make a new covenant, but to renew the old one made at Mount Sinai. The challenge to the people was primarily an appeal for loyalty to God through obedience to the covenant. First, Joshua urged the Israelites to obey God. Second, they were to avoid idolaters and their idols. Third, their God was to be their only God. Every person had to choose the object of their worship. Joshua knew the value of example. He was a model for his people to follow. He had made up his mind; his decision was clear.

C—Contemporary Application

Patrick Henry was a brilliant orator and a major leader in the American Revolution. He was independent Virginia's first governor. At the second Virginia Convention, on March 23, 1775, in St. John's Church, Richmond, he delivered the speech that assured his fame as one of the great advocates of liberty. Convinced that war with Great Britain was inevitable, he presented strong resolutions for equipping the Virginia militia to fight against the British and defended them in a passionate speech. The speech concludes with, "Forbid it, Almighty God! I know not what course others may take, but as for me, give me liberty or give me death!" As wartime governor, he gave General George Washington able support. Henry was greatly responsible for the passage of the Bill of Rights. His life typifies a person who made right choices about obedience and concern for the future of his country. Joshua shared the same vision for the Israelites.

The example of one person can influence the decisions of many by:
- Recalling God's help and blessings.
- Becoming aware of God's goodness and our obligation to serve Him.
- Making personal decisions about the object of their worship.
- Ridding their life of all false gods.

D—Directed Prayer

Father, I choose to pledge my total allegiance to You.

March 24

A Little Honest Confession

Conviction makes us sad; confession makes us glad.
(Psalm 51:1-19)

A—Advice from the Bible

Cleanse me from all my sin.
(Ps. 51:2)

B—Biblical Example

This writing is known as the greatest psalm of repentance. King David wrote the words after he was confronted by the prophet Nathan about his sin with Bathsheba. He admitted his sin and was told that God had forgiven him. However, the king needed to make a complete confession from his heart. David knew he could not demand mercy, so he simply begged for God's forgiveness. When he spoke of his sins, he recognized that they were multiple. Therefore, he agreed with God about what he had done. No excuses were offered. Although he committed adultery and murder, he looked to God for cleansing. The king felt deep and heavy conviction about his sin. It had affected his entire body. A *pure heart* was requested. In other words, David was asking for a miracle! He also knew that his praise was dependent upon God's response. The prayer concludes by asking God for the prosperity of Zion. He wanted Jerusalem to be safe. He believed that his testimony and God's mercy would bring both spiritual and material blessing to Jerusalem.

C—Contemporary Application

Julia and I have been friends for years. We enjoy going to lunch once a month and staying in touch over the phone. Her response toward me recently changed. She seemed distant and uneasy in my presence. One day at lunch, I confronted her about a possible problem. She then confessed to an affair with a man at work. Their relationship was becoming more serious. Of course, I was shocked! Their hidden sin was a secret from everyone, but God. She knew that I would try to talk her out of this affair and I did. Praying with her was meaningless on her part. My phone calls were not answered and she avoided me. I kept her secret and prayed "without ceasing" for my friend. Months passed without contact. Then I received a letter from her. She wanted me to know that she had asked God for forgiveness and felt certain God heard and answered her prayer. She wanted to start anew with a "pure heart." Only God can cleanse and make a sinner whole!

Sin is serious, therefore:

- Forgiveness requires complete confession of sin.
- Sin is the result of a sinful nature.
- Sin causes believers to lose the joy of their salvation.
- Repentance is necessary for all sinners.

D—Directed Prayer

Father, lead me to always confess my sins and repent.

March 25

A Little Palm Sunday

People must determine where they stand in response to the King.
Matthew 21:1-11

A—Advice from the Bible

A very large crowd . . . cut branches from the trees and spread them on the road.
(Matt. 21:8)

B—Biblical Example

The next seven devotionals will focus on the last week of Jesus' earthly life. We begin on Sunday. Although Jesus had shunned public demonstrations as the Messiah, He now felt the need to declare His messiahship publicly. The approach to Jerusalem was from the east and arrangements for His entry were already in place. Military conquerors rode white horses when they returned as conquering heroes. Jesus rode a borrowed donkey! The disciples were not aware of what Jesus had planned for this occasion and the Jewish leaders decided that this imposter must be destroyed. The majority of the crowd affirmed their respect by spreading their garments and small branches as a carpet before their King. The Apostle John called them "branches of palm trees." The impact of this royal entry was great. The Passover season brought great crowds, many had never heard of Jesus. The Savior's rejection and death were imminent and He wanted His followers to know His true identity. He really was the King of the Jews. His royal entry was part of the divine plan for His earthly ministry.

C—Contemporary Application

The Holy Week emphasis in the Christian calendar begins the week immediately preceding Easter. Palm Sunday is the first commemoration as the triumphal entry of Jesus into Jerusalem. Some groups refer to the triumphal entry as the beginning of Passion Week. I recall a celebration planned for our small church in Oklahoma. An Easter cantata was being rehearsed several months before the presentation on Palm Sunday. A drama instructor from the local school, had written a pageant to accompany the musical performance. All these plans were BIG time for our little congregation. The working of these plans blessed everyone who attended the event. Children carried construction-paper palms. Bathrobe/towel costumes were supplied. At the close of the worship experience, people seemed to have a greater appreciation for what Jesus did. The King has come!

How do people today respond to the lordship of Christ?
- Some worship Him faithfully every Sunday.
- Some only include worship if nothing else is planned that day.
- Some never think about the King of kings.
- Some want their lifestyle to reflect their love and appreciation for the Savior.

D—Directed Prayer

Jesus, thank You for revealing Your true identity.

March 26

A Little Temple Cleansing

Evil has no respect for people or God.
Mark 11:15-17

A—Advice from the Bible

Jesus entered the temple and began driving out . . . the money changers.
(Mark 11:15)

B—Biblical Example

This devotional continues the focus on the last week of Jesus' earthly life. We begin on Monday. Jesus spent Sunday night in Bethany and returned to the Temple in Jerusalem on Monday. He discovered a most revolting sight. In the court of the Gentiles He saw what was called the "Bazaars of Annas." Annas was a former high priest. What had begun as a service to the worshippers, now was a profiteering scheme. People coming from a great distance needed approval by the priest for their sacrifice of animals or birds. Of course, their offerings were "unacceptable" and more purchases were required, including a Temple tax. All tables were set up where Gentile coins could be exchanged for Jewish coins; of course, an exchange fee was charged. This service had become a criminal racket. Jesus' reaction to this practice was to cleanse the area of abusive Jews and their evil actions. His act incurred the opposition of the Saducean high priests, who were in charge of the Temple. What Jesus did may have precipitated the crucifixion.

C—Contemporary Application

The story is told about a Christian and an agnostic talking about the devil. The agnostic said, "I don't believe in the devil. I've never met him." The Christian replied, "No. You don't meet anyone when you are going the same way he is." Through the years, some churches have chosen methods that seem to follow the world's pattern. Annual bazaars, Harvest festivals, and other approaches to raise money for the church budget are popular in most areas of the nation. A country dance is being held this week at a local community church. The caution from Mark 11 is to examine the reason for the event. and to use the opportunity to promote Christ and the worship of Him in your local church. A church cleansing needs to be done once in a while; a spiritual cleansing needs to be practiced every day. Materialistic or spiritual choices must be made by the congregation and discussed with the leadership of the church.

Reminders about temple/church cleansings:

- God's house is for worship.
- Making a marketplace out of a place set aside for prayer displeases God.
- Maintain a separation from social and civic organizations.
- Select events that will reach unchurched people with the Gospel.

D—Directed Prayer

Thank You, for reminding us to keep Your house, a house of prayer.

March 27

Little Lessons and Warnings

Believers are to be alert and faithful until Jesus returns.
Luke 21:5-38

A—Advice from the Bible

Heaven and earth will pass away, but my words will never pass away.
(Luke 21:33)

B—Biblical Example

On Tuesday, the day after He cleansed the Temple, Jesus returned to the same area and taught the people. The chief priests and elders began to question the Lord about what authority He claimed for this action. Of course, Jesus could have replied that He exercised God's authority, but He refused. After the disciples were alone with Jesus, they began asking questions about the previous encounters. These followers were once more warned about the coming destruction of Jerusalem. The lessons pointed not only to Jerusalem's fall, but beyond that happening. Great assurance was given that redemption and a meaningful life lay beyond the destruction of the Temple. Luke, the author of this Gospel, saw the world under God's control, moving toward a goal of both judgment and redemption. Redemption was not bound up with Jerusalem, the Temple, or the nation of Israel. Such teaching brought great hope during this discourse. The lessons and warnings continued to focus on what the disciples were to turn *to* as well as turn *from*.

C—Contemporary Application

The Mount of Olives is east of the city of Jerusalem, just across a gorge of the Kidron Valley. The second highest summit overlooks the Temple mound, which is directly across the Kidron. From where Jesus sat on the Mount of Olives that day, the huge white stones of the Temple gave the building the appearance of a snow-covered mountain. The afternoon sunlight sparkled from the dome of the edifice. Peter, James, John, and Andrew began to question Jesus about the destruction of the Temple and the end of the age. My husband and I were near that site in the late afternoon. We read the Scripture passages about the Olivet Discourse and imagined how confused His four intimate followers must have felt. Even having Bible knowledge of this event had not prepared me for the emotional experience I felt. What questions might I have asked about the destruction of such a magnificent structure?

How do these teachings of Jesus apply to our lives?

- Disciples are not to be led astray by false messiahs.
- Disciples are to bear their witness in times of rejection and persecution.
- Disciples are to bear witness of a triumphant life.
- Disciples are to watch for the Son of man's return.

D—Directed Prayer

God, I want to be faithful to Your teachings.

March 28

A Little Quiet Day at Bethany

Disciples must seize opportunities to rest and reflect.
Mark 14:1-8

A—Advice from the Bible

While He was in Bethany . . .
(Mark 14:3)

B—Biblical Example

The Bible does not say what Jesus did on Wednesday; however, He probably remained in Bethany with His disciples. Martha, Mary, and Lazarus were his close friends who lived in that village. Frequent visits were made to their home. One event that occurred that day was an anointing. Mary anointed Jesus. When she was criticized for her extravagant gift, Jesus defended her actions. Judas Iscariot was the spokesperson for those who condemned her generous act. While Mary demonstrated love and sympathy, Judas stooped to humanity's lowest expression of depravity. Jesus recognized the motive of true love and devotion behind the anointing. Following this special time, the Lord again stressed the immediacy of His death. Jesus often went away from crowds and spent time alone. Surely during this time, He needed spiritual strength for the remaining days of His earthly life.

C—Contemporary Application

Wednesday was added to the Holy Week activities as the day on which Judas plotted to betray Jesus. In the modern Roman Catholic Church, this day is called Ash Wednesday, the worshiper receives a cross marked on the forehead with the ashes obtained by burning the palms used on the previous Palm Sunday. Worship services also are held on Ash Wednesday in the Anglican, Lutheran, and some other Protestant churches. The personal message I receive from this week day is that even Jesus needed time away from His major purpose and plans. The next few days would be the most critical of His life. Spiritual refreshment is difficult to schedule on our overbooked calendars. To spend some quiet time in a quiet place just recalling what God has done for me and my family has always been a time of blessing. In recent years, these times of withdrawal seem more important than in the past. God does so much for me and I sometimes fail to express my love and thanksgiving to Him.

What can I do to develop a special quiet time for the Lord?

- Choose the best time of the day or week.
- Select a quiet place.
- Collect devotional materials to use as guides.
- Follow a plan.

D—Directed Prayer

Lord, help me to focus my mind on You.

March 29

A Little Memorial

The new Passover commemorated the freeing of people from slavery to sin.
Matthew 26:20-30

A—Advice from the Bible

While they were eating . . .
(Matt. 26:26)

B—Biblical Example

Thursday of Holy Week began with Passover preparations. Finding a place in crowded Jerusalem seemed impossible, but Peter and John followed Jesus' instructions and all things were ready. His last supper with the disciples set the stage for the unfolding drama of His death and resurrection. During the meal a startling announcement was made by Jesus—a betrayer was in their midst! This man was Judas. He fled the gathering and went out into the night. After his departure, Jesus instituted something new, the Lord's Supper. Two elements from the Passover feast were used. The unleavened bread and the cup served as a picture the Lord's own death. A deeper meaning was now conveyed to the participants: the body and blood of Jesus Christ. The Passover pointed ahead to the Lamb of God who would take away the sins of the world. The Lord's Supper announced that this great work was accomplished. According to Luke 22:19 and 1 Corinthians 11:25, the Lord's Supper is a memorial to Jesus, particularly to His sacrificial death. Every time we celebrate the Supper, we pay tribute to His dying on our behalf. He also expressed confidence that He and His followers would enjoy renewed fellowship beyond history.

C—Contemporary Application

Maundy Thursday or Holy Thursday, the Thursday before Easter Sunday is observed by Christians in commemoration of Christ's Last Supper. The name Maundy is derived from *mandatum* (Latin, "commandment"). In Roman Catholic and many Protestant Churches, the Eucharist (Greek, "thanksgiving") is celebrated in an evening liturgy that includes Holy Communion. In England a custom survives of giving alms ("maundy pennies") to the poor. Our Lutheran neighbors once invited us to the Maundy Thursday service at their church. This celebration was a new experience for me. First, the congregation had a "washing of feet." This event was followed by eating cheese and drinking wine. An offering was taken at the conclusion of the service for the poor.

How can church members make the observance of the Lord's Supper more meaningful?

- By_____
- By_____
- By_____
- By_____

D—Directed Prayer

Thank You, Lord for Your memorial to us.

March 30

The King's Little Trial

The sinless Son of God took our sins upon Himself.
Matthew 26:57—27:26

A—Advice from the Bible

All the chief priests and elders came to the decision to put Jesus to death.
(Matt. 27:1)

B—Biblical Example

The combined evidence of the four Gospels indicate that Jesus had six trials or hearings on Friday. Three of the encounters were before the Jewish authorities: Annas (John 18:12-24); Caiaphas (Matt. 26:57-68); and the trial before the Sanhedrin (Matt. 27:1-2). These men accused Jesus of three crimes: (1) misleading the nation; (2) forbidding the paying of taxes; (3) claiming to be a king. All of these charges were political in nature so that the Roman governor could handle the case. Three hearings then followed. The first was before Pontius Pilate, the Roman official (Luke 23:1-5). After questioning Jesus, Pilate stated that no evidence convinced him to put Jesus to death. The mob then went to a hearing before King Herod (Luke 23:6-12), who wanted to see Jesus do a miracle. Jesus was sent back to Pilate for a third and final trial. This Roman procurator declared that Jesus was innocent of any guilt, however, he was persuaded by the mob to crucify the man claiming to be a king. An interesting study of the individuals involved in this mob-mentality reveal that Annas was the high priest and a shrewd politician. Caiaphas was very materialistic and wealthy; he managed the Temple business. Pilate was anti-Semitic and considered the Jews an inferior race, with a pitiful figure for their king.

C—Contemporary Application

The crowds chose Barabbas that terrible day. (I just know I would have chosen Jesus.) George Beverly Shea used a poem written by Mrs. Rhea F. Miller in 1922 to compose one of his famous signature songs, "I'd Rather Have Jesus." He was practicing on the organ for the next Sunday worship when he saw a poem lying by the instrument. The words expressed his aims and ambitions. The appropriate melody came and he began to sing. His mother wept at the beauty of the song. The next day Mr. Shea sang his new composition for the congregation and the rest is history. *I'd rather have Jesus than men's applause. I'd rather have Jesus than worldwide fame.* This gracious man had both.

Some ways believers today dishonor Christ is by:

- Refusing to do anything about injustices.
- Being willing to please the people, rather than God.
- Denying that Jesus is Lord of one's life
- Looking for the easy way to live the Christian life, rather than the right way.

D—Directed Prayer

I'd rather have You, Lord, than anything.

March 31

The Little Empty Tomb

History is just news from the graveyard—except the empty tomb!
John 20:1-18

A—Advice from the Bible

"They have taken the Lord out of the tomb."
(John 20:2)

B—Biblical Example

The crucifixion was over. The Jewish law required that the body of an executed man be buried the same day death occurred. Jesus died about three o'clock on Friday afternoon and His body had to be buried before the Sabbath began at sunset. Joseph of Arimathea asked for the body of Jesus so that he might bury it properly. On receiving permission from Pilate, Joseph wrapped the body in appropriate material and placed it in a burial place. Nicodemus, a secret disciple, assisted in the burial by supplying "a mixture of myrrh and aloes." Early on Sunday morning, Mary Magdalene and the other women came to Jesus' tomb. Their purpose of the visit was to anoint the body of Jesus, however, Joseph and Nicodemus had already prepared the body. The stone at the entrance had been rolled away. Two angels spoke words of assurance to the women. Suddenly the despair of the faithful women turned to hope. The women were then sent on a mission to find Jesus' disciples and tell them the wonderful news of the resurrection.

C—Contemporary Application

A little boy asked his parents why the family went to church every Sunday. They answered, "We go to church to worship." That word was hard for the boy to understand, so he came as close as he could. He explained to his friends that his family went to church every Sunday to "wash up!" The boy was closer to the truth than he knew. Part of the purpose of worship is to confess our sins to the Father and to experience the cleansing of His forgiving love. Part of the purpose of prayer is to confess our sins to the Father and to ask His forgiveness. So, the little boy was right! We go to church, and we pray in order to "wash up" spiritually. Since that first Easter morning, a body of believers has existed who continue to gather to worship the Lord Jesus Christ. Every Sunday, as believers attend church, the celebration of the resurrection of our Lord occurs. In a sense, Easter Sunday arrives every week.

The resurrection of Jesus Christ means:

- Believers have salvation.
- Believers have eternal life.
- Believers have a new lifestyle
- Believers have victory.

D—Directed Prayer

Thank You, Jesus, for the hope I find in Your resurrection.

April 1

Making a Little Joke

Stay aware of some vital truths about the second coming.
2 Peter 3:3-18

A—Advice from the Bible

> ... *beware of this: scoffers will come in the last days* ...
> (2 Pet. 3:3, HCSB)

B—Biblical Example

The Apostle Peter wrote his general epistles to Christians who were going through great persecution. During this time of struggle, false teachers in the church were leading people away from the truth and into lives of sin. The Bible word for these people is *scoffers*. They mocked the Christians who believed that Christ would return again. One joke presented by these people was the idea of "live anyway you want to live, nothing is going to happen to you." Their lifestyle was devoted to gratifying their own lusts. These actions and attitudes confused the new Christians who were seeking to follow Christ and the teachings presented by Peter. The delay in the second coming of Jesus only confirmed what the scoffers were saying. Today, these people might sound like this: "God doesn't intervene in history, so get over it!" Peter did not back-off from their mocking. His description of these false teachers included the charge that they were deliberately ignorant and had overlooked the basic facts of the return.

C—Contemporary Application

April Fool's Day or All Fool's Day is observed in many countries of the world. For centuries, playing harmless jokes and sending individuals on silly errands have been practiced. Newspapers, television, and radio have presented many stories to hoax their audiences. Perhaps the most remembered joke occurred in 1938. Orson Wells caused a major panic by announcing on the radio that an invasion of Martians was taking place on earth. *The War of the Worlds* was so believable, that before Mr. Wells could say "April Fool's" the fear of the unknown caused people who heard his program great alarm. They raced into the streets, screaming and crying. Today, the second coming of Christ is often mocked by the media. Television movies incorrectly present this great Scriptural truth. The real truth is rarely presented.

Beware of people who make fun of the second coming.
- Scoffers fail to understand that to the Lord, time is unlimited.
- Scoffers do not believe God will change the way the world has always been.
- Scoffers think that living holy lives is pointless.
- Scoffers believe that Christ's promise to return is an empty promise.

D—Directed Prayer

Lord, help me to accept the responsibility to warn scoffers that the Lord will keep His promise.

April 2

A Little Cup of Juice

Celebrating the Lord's Supper
1 Corinthians 11:17-34

A—Advice from the Bible

In the same way He also took the cup . . .
(1 Cor. 11:25, HCSB)

B—Biblical Example

The Apostle Paul and the Corinthian Christians had an unusual fellowship. The old spiritual song describes their relationship the best: "Sometimes they are up; sometimes they are down." Lack of maturity seemed to be the biggest problem in the church. For example, the celebration of the Lord's Supper became a divisive issue for the worshippers. Paul heard about the struggles in the church and responded with this letter, written from Ephesus.

The apostle confronted the church members with a description of their behavior during this special time of remembrance. Three cliques had formed in the church and divided the people along class and social lines. These divisions were bad examples for the new believers. Some partakers were hungry; others were drunk.

Paul was not present at the last supper of our Lord. He had heard about the words of Jesus because eyewitnesses had passed them on their fellow Christians. Verse 25 explains the purpose Jesus intended, His sacrifice was based on a new relationship with God, in which our sins are forgiven. The meal is an acted remembrance of Christ's death. Wonder if the Corinthian church ever figured out this beautiful memorial service?

C—Contemporary Application

The Garden of Gethsemane is centered near the heart of Jerusalem. This beautiful place provided me with the greatest celebration of the Lord's Supper I have ever experienced. Our small group of travelers had toured the city all day and now we walked into the garden. A designated spot had been prepared just for our party of Christians. On a small stump sat a tray with the communion elements. The thought that Jesus had possibly been at this site filled me with awe. My husband, Jim, led in the celebration of the remembrance of what Jesus had done for us. Each participant took of the elements. A time of reflection followed and the closing was a beautiful song. Tears of gratitude rolled from our eyes. What a moment in time for me!

The Lord's Supper needs to be:
- A time of reverence.
- A time of self-examination.
- A time of special worship, not just routine actions
- A time of sensitivity to Christ's presence

D—Directed Prayer

Lord, help me to never participate in Your supper in an unworthy manner.

April 4

Philemon's Little Runaway

You demonstrate Christian love when you accept all people..
Philemon 8-20

A—Advice from the Bible

This is why he was separated from you for a brief time.
(Philemon 15)

B—Biblical Example

Philemon was a prominent Christian in Colosse who owned a slave named Onesimus. The slave ran away from Philemon and met Paul in Rome. Because of Paul's witness, Onesimus became a believer in Christ. Paul wrote a letter from prison asking Philemon to forgive the runaway slave. The love Philemon had was demonstrated by his generosity in opening his own home for a church. He helped Christians by putting his love into action. Up until now, in the letter, Paul had been repairing Philemon for the request he was going to make. As an apostle, Paul had the authority to command Philemon to do what was right, so he appealed to Philemon for the sake of the bond that unites all Christians. In order to help his request Paul described his circumstances. Onesimus had been led to Christ by Paul, therefore Paul showed his deep affection for the slave. The man had changed since he became a believer. Roman law showed little mercy toward runaway slaves. Since Philemon was a Christian, too, Paul was asking him to show the same kind of love to the slave as he had shown to other Christians. The result of that love would be forgiveness instead of anger or revenge.

C—Contemporary Application

The time was soon after the Civil War. The place was one of the most aristocratic churches of Richmond, Virginia. The rector had just invited the congregation to come forward to kneel at the altar rail to receive Holy Communion. Suddenly almost a gasp of shock ran through the pews for an elderly Negro, and ex-slave, rose from his seat in the back row. He was coming down the aisle alone. He climbed the chancel steps and knelt. The congregation did not move. To break bread, even the bread of Christ, with colored ex-slaves simply was not done. All eyes were focused on the altar scene. Then a white-haired gentleman, obviously distinguished in appearance, sensed what was happening. He rose walked down the aisle, went up the chancel steps, and knelt beside the kneeling Negro. General Robert E. Lee understood the meaning of freedom.

The key word of Paul's personal letter to Philemon is *service*:
- Christian service is focused on love.
- Christian service is a model of devotion, faithfulness, and consecration.
- Christian service is demonstrating a clear example of ideal Christian living.
- Christian service is doing more than is actually asked.

D—Directed Prayer

Oh, Lord, my God, Your bonds are freedom. Let me serve you more faithfully.

April 5

A Big Meeting on a Little Hill

Learn how to speak to people about God.
Acts 17:22-34

A—Advice from the Bible

Then Paul stood in the middle of the Areopagus and said, "Men of Athens . . . ."
(Acts 17:22, HCSB)

B—Biblical Example

The distinguished Athenian council met on Mars Hill to hear a speech by a man named Paul. This assembly consisted of men who were in charge of overseeing religious and educational matters. The city of Athens practiced idolatry. Because of their superstitious concerns, many shrines and images existed, even one to an "Unknown God." Paul began his speech with a direct description of their idolatry. He was not on trial and only needed to explain what he had been teaching. This approach captured the philosophers' attention. The next focus in his message was about the true God, not one who was contained in shrines. Paul then displayed his knowledge by quoting Greek poets in support of his statements. The theme of the message was the Lord Jesus Christ. As the sermon continued, Paul called for repentance and pointed out that judgment would be administered through Him whom God had raised from the dead. The response of these Athenians to Paul's message is found in verses 32-34.

C—Contemporary Application

Are any men alive today who can stand before philosophers and educators and speak about God? Of course, the first person who comes to mind is William Franklin Graham, Jr., known as Billy Graham. This witness for God is now in his 80's, but continues to hold crusades throughout the world. During his 50 years of preaching, no scandals, either financial or sexual, have ever occurred. His message has remained true to the Word. Presidents, popes, royalty, and philosophers have all invited him into their realm of responsibility. His work to bring peace among nations is recalled in books and articles, especially seeking peace between China and Russia. Time Magazine in 1993 did a feature issue about this evangelist. The editor said, "He preached in person to more people than any human being who has ever lived." Graham's love for the Word and for the followers of the Word remains a great witness to unbelievers and also motivates believers to take seriously their testimony for the Lord.

Paul shared four basic truths about God in his sermon:

- God is the Creator of all things.
- God is good and the great Provider.
- God is our Ruler.
- God is our Savior.

D—Directed Prayer

Lord, what prevents me from being a wise witness?

April 6

Noah's Little Secret

God uses people in special ways who walk with Him.
Genesis 6:8-10

A—Advice from the Bible

He walked with God . . .
(Gen. 6:9, NIV)

B—Biblical Example

The biblical account of the flood tells of man's wickedness and God's judgment. From beginning to end, God was in complete control of this destruction. The actions of men and women were wrong in God's sight. Therefore, His purpose concerning the coming destruction was revealed to an individual. A man who had been just a name in a genealogy was singled out as the recipient of God's grace. The description of Noah is so refreshing after reading through chapters and chapters of wickedness. This man had integrity and had learned the importance of discipline in order to live according to God's expectations. Remember that Noah lived before God's law was revealed to Moses on Mt. Sinai. Yet people seemed to have some understanding of what God expected. The description of Noah suggests that he was morally upright. He stood out from his generation and lived in relationship with God. His godly living did not demand that God rescue him, but the Lord wanted to protect and bless those who walked in righteousness.

C—Contemporary Application

The taller and sturdier a tree, the deeper the roots grow. The portion of a tree that appears above the earth's surface is really deceptive. Hidden from sight in the soil or rocks is the real secret of growth and strength. A Christian who walks with God usually is rooted in the soil of love. Several actions are needed for walking in righteousness. Growth comes from knowledge, therefore, Bible study is an essential. Prayer is significant for the person walking with God. This time alone with the Lord strengthens a "walker." A mature believer should find walking with God on a daily basis a true blessing. Faith in the Word provides the assurance from God's promises that righteous living is available and possible for you. According to the Lord, the earth will never be washed away again by a complete covering of water, but if He decided to use another natural disaster to judge sin, would your life be considered righteous and the example of your life be characterized as "walking with God?"

Many advantages are experienced by a life spent walking with Christ.

- Circumstances cannot sweep your faith away.
- Fortunes and misfortunes of life cannot drown your faith.
- Praise or criticism cannot change the direction of your faith.
- Crises cannot destroy the calmness of your faith.

D—Directed Prayer

Dear, Lord, thank You that "in times like these I have a Savior."

April 7

Tired Little Do-Gooders

Even the strongest Christian gets weary.
Galatians 6:9-10

A—Advice from the Bible

. . . we must not get tired doing good.
(Gal. 6:9, HCSB)

B—Biblical Example

The letter to the Galatians was written by Paul sometime between A.D. 48-49 and was probably addressed to several churches in the area of southern Galatia. Paul and Barnabas had visited these towns during their first missionary journey. Today's verses encouraged the weary Christians to keep-on-keeping-on. The enemies of the church kept insisting that more of the gospel existed than was being preached by Paul. Therefore, he suggested an example of a farmer toiling in the fields and despairing that the crops would ever mature. He urged the Galatians not to give up or to neglect to do what was good. Although the timing of the harvest was not in the control of believers, the harvest would come in due season. Just as a farmer had a growing season for his crops, the Christian had been granted a season or opportunity to do good. The idea that believers should help all people is rooted in the example of Jesus, who always met the needs of people regardless of their social or economic status. If the Galatians could not treat each other in a Christlike way, then they would never be able to express His love to those outside the church. Keep working!

C—Contemporary Application

The small congregation was asked to turn to page 50 in their hymnals. The pianist played an introduction and the people began to sing, "We'll work 'til Jesus comes, we'll work 'til Jesus comes." The fervor of singing these words seemed to take on an urgency to get out of the building and get busy for the Lord. This gospel song was first sung in 1836 and contained six stanzas. An English hymnist Elizabeth Mills (1805-1829) wrote the words to the present song. The first known publication, with a shortened version, appeared seven years after her death. Through the years, I have heard many congregations sing Mrs. Mill's version and one thing is always consistent—the excitement of serving the Lord. Some Christians give up too soon and settle for a routine Christian life. Someone once said, "They are in a rut . . . a grave with both ends knocked out."

Don't grow weary:
- Serving others through love.
- Living by the Spirit.
- Knowing that those who live a life of sin will reap the consequences of sin.
- Believing that living in faithfulness to Christ will harvest eternal life.

D—Directed Prayer

Father, I want to keep "working 'til Jesus comes."

April 8

A Little Duet

Focus on God's redemptive work throughout history.
Judges 5:1-11

A—Advice from the Bible

On that day Deborah and Barak . . . sang.
(Judg. 5:1, NIV)

B—Biblical Example

Deborah, a prophetess, judge, and song writer, and Barak, a military leader, were involved in a final phase of the conquest of Canaan. Their great victory over Sisera, a captain in the enemy army, was celebrated with a war song. Looking back over Israel's history, Deborah reviewed the significant happenings at Sinai and Seir. She maintained hope and named six tribes who helped in this war. According to Numbers 20:14-21, the king of Edom refused to allow passage through his kingdom. However, that did not stop God's children from progressing. Still continuing to recall recent history, Deborah came to the time of the Judges, to which of course, she belonged. Shamgar, Othniel, and Ehud were leaders whom God raised up for the deliverance of His people. Their history of faithfulness and repentance are included in this recounting of the past. Deborah and Barak had to fight to secure freedom for Israel. Their song included an invitation to others, who were rich or poor, to join in this offering of praise.

C—Contemporary Application

Poetry is always a beautiful way to record a historical event. Singing ballads about pioneer heroes is a favorite way of recalling the past. In high school chorus, I was introduced to the history of the western United States through the lyrics we sang. A favorite ballad of mine is "The Ballad of Davy Crockett." Our small son had a coon skin hat and play-rifle as a result of this song. Remember these words, "Born on a mountain top in Tennessee . . ."? Crockett (1786—1836) was an American frontiersman and pioneer. He served as a member of the Tennessee state legislature. Many oral legends have been recorded about Crockett and his fellow contemporaries, Daniel Boone and Kit Carson. These men fought Indian wars, settled wilderness areas, and taught other pioneers how to survive in difficult regions. Our history books are more colorful in words and pictures because of these men and their experiences. Deborah and Barak sang about their past and what God had done for them. Our heroes have done the same thing.

Deborah's story contains truths for today.
- Opposition to a godly life is real, but God is more real.
- God sent a Deliverer.
- Repentance for sin and faith in God are necessary for survival.
- Victory won with God's help can be lasting.

D—Directed Prayer

Lord, help the history of my life to magnify You.

April 9

A Little Fishing Net

Our call to follow Jesus is also a call to serve Him.
Mark 1:16-20

A—Advice from the Bible

They were casting nets into the sea . . .
(Mark 1:16, HCSB)

B—Biblical Example

Shortly after Jesus returned to Galilee He was rejected by His hometown of Nazareth. Thereafter, He established headquarters at Capernaum, a city located on the northwest shore of the Sea of Galilee. He began to choose the men who would be closely associated with Him in that ministry. One day as Jesus walked along the seashore, He saw two fishermen, Simon and his brother Andrew, busy at work casting a net into the sea and He began preaching His good news to this congregation of two. In New Testament times two kinds of nets were in common use. One was a large trawling net and the other was a small circular net. The net was thrown into the water by hand. The fish were enclosed in the round net being pulled through the water. Jesus said to them, "Follow Me, and I will make you into fishers of men." *To become* means to make them something that they were not at that time. Their present vocation was fishers of fish; Jesus would make them into fishers of men. Before Jesus called them, they were simple folk, just doing their day's work. They followed Jesus, not only because of what He said, but most of all because of who He was.

C—Contemporary Application

A commitment to follow Christ is a demanding task. The television programs sometimes visualize for us a preacher in an air-conditioned sanctuary, decorated lavishly with stained glass, mahogany, and marble. That image may be true most of the time, however, a call to Christian service also includes dirty hands from helping build a church building; broken finger nails from carrying boxes of food and clothing to needy people; blisters on your feet from taking a census or going on a prayer-walk in a neighborhood; sore backs from lifting children who attend a backyard Bible study or are living in overseas orphanages; or weary eyes from long airplane trips to help distribute Bibles and food to lost people. Jesus calls His people to work. Sometimes the pretty clothes need to be replaced with leather gloves and work boots!

Some facts about these "fishers of men" are:

- Simon and Andrew knew about the Lord, but had not followed Him.
- Knowing about Christ and serving Him are not the same.
- The invitation to follow Christ is extended to everyone.
- A major responsibility is included in accepting the call to follow Jesus.

D—Directed Prayer

Lord, I want to be faithful in following You and serving You.

April 10

A Little Serious Worship

We are not to enter into worship without preparation.
Leviticus 8:6-9

A—Advice from the Bible

Then Moses had Aaron and his sons come near and washed them with water.
(Lev. 8:6, NIV)

B—Biblical Example

Leviticus 8—10 addresses the eight-day consecration of the priests, their functions, and priestly failures. Moses called all the congregation of Israel to a meeting at the tabernacle to witness a public ordination. The men involved in this induction were Aaron and his four sons. They were being presented to God to fulfill their spiritual role. The washing with water signified the need for purity and separation. An outward, physical action represented the need for inward spiritual cleansing. Following the ritual, the men were dressed in priestly garments. This attire became like a uniform. Only the priests were qualified to wear these impressive garments. The process for dressing followed a clear pattern. Each piece was placed on the men at a certain time. Leading worship and participating in worship was a serious matter. The people needed to observe the setting apart of those who would be their spiritual leaders. Priests were then made ready to offer sacrifices for the sins of the people. Such a process reminds us of our responsibility in preparation for worship. Serious worship must include preparation.

C—Contemporary Application

The believers began to arrive for the worship service. A serious quietness settled over the small congregation. Then a psalm was recited and a leader read an invocation of praise. The members followed with a confession of faith. One of the men then led in prayer. The Scripture reading, considered the most serious aspect of worship, was next. The leader appointed someone to preach the sermon. The service closed with the leader pronouncing the blessing. This worship describes the synagogue service in Antioch of Pisidia. The Apostle Paul participated with the congregation (Acts 13:15-16). Today, churches offer all kinds of worship services—traditional, contemporary, praise, high-church, corporate, and private. However, what must be the common thread of all forms of worship? Each group must seek to encounter the holy God. The danger of any kind of worship is taking the experience lightly or without preparation.

Think about these suggestions for worship preparation:

- Actively prepare to experience God's presence.
- Worship God with reverence and honor.
- Respond with joy mixed with genuine humility.
- Practice living a godly, holy life.

D—Directed Prayer

Lord, forgive me for taking You for granted or presuming on Your grace.

April 11

Little Priceless Letters

Learn the value of New Testament letters.
Ephesians 3:1-13

A—Advice from the Bible

> *By reading this you are able to understand my insight about . . . the Messiah.*
> (Eph. 3:4, HCSB)

B—Biblical Example

The Apostle Paul was a letter writer. He liked to communicate with people in other areas of the land, people who had become participants in churches that were established on his missionary journeys. The letters were used to explain doctrine, Christian behavior, and other issues necessary to live the Christian life. Paul was confident that his readers had some awareness of his unique mission in the work of the gospel. Yet, he often felt that a reminder was necessary about his ministry and an explanation in some detail was appropriate. This letter is an example of his concern. He wrote about three subjects in these verses: stewardship (vv.2-6), service (v. 7), and suffering (v. 13). The stewardship involved a great "mystery" of redemption. Paul then explained his understanding of this mystery and that it did not come through the instructions of others but by an immediate revelation from God. Paul's own stewardship was carried out in the service of the gospel. He also knew that the way of service was not always easy. Suffering must be expected. In fact, as he wrote this letter, he was chained to a Roman soldier.

C—Contemporary Application

If you had a letter from Mark Twain in your attic, some antique dealer would offer you a large sum of money. For example, a personal, 9-page letter written to his daughter in 1875 sold for $33,000 in 1991. Ordinary correspondence from Twain usually brings $1,200 a page. Expects say that even though Mark Twain, author of *Tom Sawyer*, wrote 50,000 letters during his lifetime, demand is still strong for these personal notes from one of America's favorite authors. I have a personal letter that is worth nothing to anyone but me. The letter is addressed to my Grandmother Poore, dated April 11, 1944. On that day I accepted Jesus as my personal Savior and I wanted to share the good news with this favorite person in my life. Childish words were used to communicate this great event. The letter was returned to me when my grandmother passed. She had kept the letter all those years. What a priceless treasure! I was special to her.

The value of New Testament letters today is:
- Reading about God's special revelation to us.
- Reading about God's wisdom in dealing with people.
- Reading about problems in the early churches.
- Reading about the lives of great men and women.

D—Directed Prayer

Father, thank You for the letters from the New Testament.

April 12

Moses' Little Funeral
God keeps His word.
Deuteronomy 34:1-12

A—Advice from the Bible

Moses the servant of the LORD died there in Moab.
(Deut. 34:5)

B—Biblical Example

The final section of Deuteronomy is an account of Moses' last days. This leader had urged the Israelites to obey the Lord and to remember God's past goodness to them. He had reinterpreted the Law in terms of their need for guidance in Canaan, and had challenged the people to renew their covenant as God's people. Now the end of his life had come. Moses had accomplished many things during his servant years. Joshua was to be his capable successor. God promised Moses that he would see the Promised Land, but from Mt. Nebo. Moses was allowed an expansive view of the territory, but could not go in because of disobedience at Meribah. God did not change His mind. The nation could face the future knowing that the Lord would be faithful to His promises. To the Hebrews, the burial of a body was an important matter. No man was present to bury Moses' body; God did the burying. The people could trust God to care for their needs. Moses' last acts and messages encouraged the people to obey God. These wanderers could face the future with the same calm faith as their mentor, Moses.

C—Contemporary Application

Franklin Delano Roosevelt experienced many things similar to Moses. This 32nd president of the United States led our nation through the Great Depression and World War II. He was stricken with polio in 1921 and spent most of his remaining years in a wheelchair. He was famous for his programs to help poor people during the depression. His campaign promise was "A new deal for the American people." When the Japanese bombed Pearl Harbor, this leader made the decision to declare war against that nation. His desire for world peace was evident as heads-of-state were invited to many conferences and peace talks. This remembered leader/politician did not live to see the end of the war and his nation's return to peace-time prosperity. He died from a brain hemorrhage on April 12, 1945. Moses did not see the Promised Land and the president did not see his nation at rest.

Bible truths from Moses' experience:

- God can and does forgive, but we have to suffer the consequences of our sin.
- Believers are encouraged to seek God's guidance in daily living.
- When God retires one leader, He provides another.
- The opportunity for us to have spiritual fellowship with God is available today.

D—Directed Prayer

Lord, help me to realize that a right relationship with You is the key to spiritual success.

The Little Hebrew Passover

God gives His people instructions for deliverance.
Exodus 12:1-28

A—Advice from the Bible

It is the LORD'S Passover.
(Ex. 12:11, NIV)

B—Biblical Example

April is designated National Anxiety Month. Stress and worries were certainly being experienced by the Hebrew slaves in bondage in Egypt. The Lord was going to send one more plague on Egypt. After that tenth plague Pharaoh would be willing to allow Israel to depart. In preparation for demonstrating His power to deliver, the Lord gave instructions for observing the first Passover and for celebrating it as a memorial. Moses and Aaron were the instructors for this experience. The people were to begin the celebration in their month of Nisan. On our calendar that date would fall in March and April. Tensions were running high following the previous nine plagues on Egypt. The families were told to select a lamb for the Passover observance. Specific ways of selecting, preparing, and eating the sacrificial animals were provided. The Israelites were to eat quickly and be ready for travel. God concluded all His instruction by assuring the Hebrews that He was the LORD.

C—Contemporary Application

A man who played a major role in delivering the early American people from dominance by a powerful nation was Thomas Jefferson. He was born April 13, 1743 and was the principle writer of the Declaration of Independence. The American Colonists were seeking their political freedom from British rule. Jefferson addressed the issue by proclaiming that the "tyrannical" acts of the British government gave the colonists the right to seek independence and freedom. This great statesman did many fine things during his lifetime, but he wanted only three of them mentioned at his grave for future generations to remember. One remembrance was the authorship of the Declaration of Independence. Israel's Declaration of Independence was the Passover. This ceremony meant life, liberty, and the pursuit of happiness—life because those protected by the blood were not slain; liberty because Israel was delivered from bondage; and the pursuit of happiness because deliverance meant they were on their way to the Promised Land.

Bible truths about deliverance:
- Everyone experiences oppressive situations from which deliverance is needed.
- Everyone needs deliverance from sin.
- Everyone needs to follow God's instructions for deliverance.
- Everyone needs to share the good news about deliverance.

D—Directed Prayer

Thank You, that Christ is my Passover Lamb, who has given His life for me.

April 14

Just a Little Comfort, Please

Christians are to share in suffering and comfort.
2 Corinthians 1:1-11

A—Advice from the Bible

He comforts us in all our affliction.
(2 Cor. 1:4)

B—Biblical Example

Paul expressed the greatness of God's comfort in 2 Corinthians and encouraged his readers to find that same comfort. The letter was addressed to a group larger than the Corinthian church. He wanted all Christians in the province of Achaia to discover this reassurance. The memories of God's mercies led Paul to begin this section with words of praise. Two facts are presented about this subject. First, God provides the strength and determination to go forward. Second, His comfort protects us from our self-pity or resentment. All Christians face circumstances of economic, physical, or psychological needs that demand comfort. God can satisfy those needs. The result of receiving this comfort is so that we can pass on His care to others. The Corinthians, because of their commitment to Christ, experienced added difficulties in the form of persecution and misunderstanding. God calls believers to be partners in Christ's suffering and united with one another. This part of the letter concludes with a personal prayer request.

C—Contemporary Application

The British luxury liner advertised the elegance and comfort of their new ship. Twenty-two hundred passengers boarded for the maiden voyage from Southhampton, England to New York City. This great liner was advertised to be unsinkable. Just before midnight on April 14, 1912, the liner became the worst maritime disaster in history. Fifteen hundred and thirteen people perished as the Titanic struck an iceberg near Newfoundland, causing the ship to sink in less than three hours. In 1998 the story of this crisis became a Hollywood blockbuster. Personal stories revealed how passengers attempted to comfort one another. Lack of adequate lifeboats created problems for families. Some members had to stay on board; others, like children, were loaded into the boats. All the comforts and sophistication developed and designed by humans became meaningless. The Apostle Paul's desire was that the believers in Corinth find help from the true Comforter in times of crises.

What methods does God use to bring comfort to Christians?
- The Scriptures (Rom. 15:4).
- The word and deeds of other believers (2 Cor. 2:7).
- Our knowledge of His own actions and promises (1 Thess. 4:18).
- Our need to seek and help other suffering Christians (2 Cor. 1:4).

D—Directed Prayer

Lord, use me to comfort one suffering person this week.

April 15

A Little Tax Collector

Salvation changes people.
(Luke 19:1-10)

A—Advice from the Bible

> . . . *a man named Zacchaeus who was a chief tax collector.*
> (Luke 19:2)

B—Biblical Example

The time of Jesus' death was approaching and He determined to go to Jerusalem for the Passover. A local citizen from Jericho named Zacchaeus wanted to see this miracle man. What caused him to be so interested? He was a rich man who had contracted with the Roman government to collect certain taxes in the town. Under Roman law he was entitled to exact a profit from those he taxed. His vocation was hated by the people. Zacchaeus was considered a traitor and national disgrace. This short man climbed a sycamore (fig) tree to be able to see Jesus come by. The Lord recognized the tax man and began to converse with him. His acceptance of the man was unconditional. Fellowship with a man like this was considered a sacrilege. The citizens of Jericho were shocked that Jesus also was going to eat at this unclean man's house. That experience transformed Zacchaeus' life. Jesus gave assurance to the man that he had been saved through his faith and he would enjoy the fullness of the kingdom of God.

C—Contemporary Application

Today is the last acceptable opportunity to file your personal income tax. Many people resent this taxation and argue with the tax collectors about this assessment. The Zacchaeus hatred still exists. Where did this program begin? During the Civil War the United States enacted an income tax that remained in effect from 1862 to 1872. An income tax was again enacted in 1894, after President Grover Cleveland had been elected on a platform that promised lower tariffs and other reforms sought by the farmers in the West and South. However, this law was held to be unconstitutional by the Supreme Court, which forced its backers to seek an amendment to the Constitution that would give Congress the right to impose income taxes without apportionment among the states. In 1913 the 16th Amendment was ratified, and a new individual income tax was voted by Congress. Jesus can change your attitude about this legal requirement just as the little Jewish man in the tree was changed.

Consider some basic truths about Zacchaeus' salvation experience:

- Salvation is available to everyone, not just a special race.
- Salvation changes a person's attitude about life.
- Salvation is for all people who believe in Jesus.
- Salvation is always preceded by conviction.

D—Directed Prayer

Thank You, Lord, that You still seek and save the lost.

April 16

Ezra's Little Doxology

Thank God for opportunities to serve Him.
(Ezra 7:25-28)

A—Advice from the Bible

Blessed be the Lord God of our fathers.
(Ezra 7:27)

B—Biblical Example

The Jews had lived in exile in Babylon for a long time. Their homeland, Judah, was experiencing a national disaster. Now, God was about to reveal His greatness by delivering His people from exile, providing for the rebuilding of the Temple, and making possible the rebuilding of the wall of Jerusalem. Ezra had asked King Artaxerxes for permission to return to Judah and his request was granted. The king believed Ezra had a unique wisdom that was of a divine origin and had a full understanding of God's law. Certain political authority also was granted by the king. This priest and scribe praised God for making the return home possible. His doxology reveals that a person cannot do the Lord's work without the Lords' help. The Lord often enables a person to outdo themselves. Ezra had God's help and he also had select persons who went with him.

C—Contemporary Application

The word *doxology* means "word of glory." This term is not found in the Bible, but many doxologies occur in the Old and New Testament. The main function of this practice seems to have been as a conclusion to songs (Ex. 15:18), psalms (Ps. 146:10), and prayer (Matt. 6:13). Several New Testament books contain a doxology. Read the following references and notice how each "word of glory" is expressed.

- Romans 16:27
- Philippians 4:20
- 1 Timothy 6:16
- 2 Timothy 4:18
- Hebrews 13:21
- 1 Peter 5:11
- 2 Peter 3:18
- Jude 25

Truths discovered from this Scripture passage:

- God has a unique mission for each one of us.
- We must be sensitive to His call and leadership.
- God can use us best when we prepare our hearts through consecration to Him.
- We must respond quickly to opportunities for service that God provides.

D—Directed Prayer

Begin today thanking God for reasons to praise Him.

April 17

A Little Cry for Help

We must respond to the leadership of the Holy Spirit.
(Acts 16:9-12)

A—Advice from the Bible

"Cross over to Macedonia and help us."
(Acts 16:9)

B—Biblical Example

Luke placed special emphasis on the work of the Holy Spirit. Paul, the Apostle, was sensitive to the leadership of the Spirit. Two times in his ministry, distinct situations occurred that caused him to change his plans. How the Spirit communicated with Paul is not revealed, however, the missionary faithfully responded. This new change of plans led this itinerant Jewish Christian missionary to the Roman colony of Troas, a port on the Aegean Sea. He must have been impressed by the people he saw, people who had never heard the gospel. That night Paul learned what God wanted him to do. In a vision, the missionary had received a commission from God to open up new territories. Instead of being disappointed that God prevented him from going in the area of Asia, a sense of eagerness, assurance, and anticipation was displayed. Paul and his companions traveled two days to reach Macedonia and then headed straight for Philippi. Do you remember what happened next? Lydia became the first convert in Europe.

C—Contemporary Application

A few years ago, my husband was invited to Uganda, Africa, to preach and teach. His assignment was the bush country where people lived in huts with dirt floors. Each day he shared the gospel with these willing listeners. A lantern served as the light for the evening Bible study. One day a canoe was spotted coming across Lake Victoria. Two men were rowing the small, homemade means of transportation. Through an interpreter, these men wanted Jim to come over to their side of the lake and tell them about Jesus. This experience was not a vision, but the actual calling by people who wanted the good news. Jim and his translator squeezed into the little canoe and soon reached their shore. Africans gathered to hear him tell the Jesus story. Many accepted Jesus as their personal Savior. A favorite picture in our house is all-white Jim baptizing these really black people in the lake. Their smiles and display of happiness are still precious memories.

How can we respond when "the call comes ringing—send the Light?"

- Let us pray that grace may everywhere abound.
- There are souls to rescue, there are souls to save.
- Let us not grow weary in the work of love.
- Let a Christ-like spirit everywhere be found.

D—Directed Prayer

Father, help believers to commit and respond to Your directions.

April 18

Some Little Mistaken Beliefs

God's people sometimes lose sight of what is expected.
(Micah 6:1-8)

A—Advice from the Bible

What does the LORD require of you?
(Micah 6:8)

B—Biblical Example

Micah was primarily a prophet to the Southern Kingdom of Judah, however, his message was addressed to both Judah and Israel. The people had lost sight of what God had expected of them. Outside pressures mounted. Doubts and deception invaded their lives. Suddenly God's people stopped responding to Him as they should. The book reads like a courtroom scene, with Micah, the prophet, declaring God's case against His people. The prophet clearly wanted his audience to visualize a judgment scene. The Lord accused His people of failing to respond appropriately to His revelation of Himself. He wanted to know what He had done to make His people weary of Him, so they were invited to testify. The people were facing difficult times and had either forgotten or ignored their history. Events that had occurred in the past were recalled in order to know His faithfulness. These backsliders misunderstood how to please God. They thought that all God required was for them to make more offerings. This assumption led to a mistaken belief that God wanted things when He really wanted them. The people had the information about what God wanted, but they lacked dedication.

C—Contemporary Application

The famous midnight ride of April 18, 1775, was made by Paul Revere (1735-1818) and two others from Boston to Concord to warn of the approach of British troops. I remember memorizing the famous poem by Henry Wadsworth Longfellow entitled, "Paul Revere's Ride." This American silversmith, engraver, and patriot was a hero. His vocation did not require him to be a soldier. However, problems with the British developed that necessitated a patriotic belief in America. The conflict started for him when, he took part in the Boston Tea Party in 1773. When the fighting began, he carried messages for the revolutionaries of the area. His actions helped prevent the British from destroying what the patriots had established. This man displayed dedication to a cause.

How does God expect His people to respond to Him?

- Act justly.
- Love mercy.
- Walk humbly with God.
- Obey Him.

D—Directed Prayer

Heavenly Father, what do You require of me?

April 19

A Couple of Little Tentmakers

God uses people of varying abilities to teach and witness.
(Acts 18:1-17)

A—Advice from the Bible

He was a tentmaker as they were.
(Acts 18:3)

B—Biblical Example

Corinth had the reputation for wickedness and immorality. Paul had been with the philosophers in Athens and now he had to contend with another ignorant and superstitious population. He supported himself by working as a tentmaker. A couple named, Aquila and Priscilla joined him in this vocation. They, too, were tentmakers, who cut and sewed the woven cloth of goat's hair into tents. A strong friendship developed between these three individuals and the apostle lived with them and worked at their craft. However during his second missionary journey, the opposing Jewish element finally drove Paul away from Corinth. His coworkers went with him and assisted him in his travels. In Romans 16:3-4, Paul greeted Priscilla and Aquila as those "who risked their lives for me." This couple were successful colaborers and used their hospitality to spread the gospel.

C—Contemporary Application

This famous Bible couple had learned a secret about serving Christ in all kinds of circumstances. They are an example of workers who don't give up. The story is told about two boys approaching a man shoveling snow from his driveway. They offered to do the job for $2. The man responded, "Can't you see I'm doing it myself?" The enterprising boys replied, "Yes, sir, that is why we asked. We get most of our business from people who are half through and feel like quitting."

John and Darla are a married couple who love serving the Lord. Their personal motto is "anywhere, anytime." However, a negative pattern developed in their lives. After a short time of serving in a local church or mission, they quit and sometimes moved away. People were so impressed by the dedication of this pair, but their testimony was not lasting. From the Scripture we learn that Aquila and Priscilla stayed focused in their ministry of teaching and witnessing.

What are some personal abilities that believers can use for God?

- Sandy is gifted in a kitchen. Cooking and serving are her favorite things to do.
- Bert enjoys working with minor building projects.
- Tracy finds preschoolers a delight. She is involved in this ministry
- Doug loves to sing and faithfully participates in the choir program.

D—Directed Prayer

Lord, help me to see that I have abilities that can be used by You.

April 20

Little Excuse Making

Temptation to sin is due to Satan, the tempter.
(Genesis 3:8-13)

A—Advice from the Bible

"The woman you put here with me . . . and I ate it."
(Gen. 3:12)

B—Biblical Example

One of the clearest pictures of temptation and sin in the Old Testament was when Adam and Eve began questioning their relationship with God. The result of their actions was that sin separated them from God and made life harder. Adam and Eve had walked with God and known God. But things now had changed; the couple had disobeyed their Creator. The man blamed the woman and the woman blamed the serpent. Several things were lost because of their choice. Innocence was replaced by guilt. Strife developed between the couple and each began making excuses for their behavior. Fear also was an obvious consequence of the sin. After eating the fruit, they were ashamed and sought to cover their naked bodies from one another. No one can hide from God, so He began an interrogation. Adam's answer to God's question did not deal with what he had done, but with the one who influenced him. His excuse at the time seemed good. Everyone was to blame but him! Temptation is strong and sin is attractive.

C—Contemporary Application

Connie and Sandy were college roommates. A question about this relationship was always, "How can this be?" These girls were as opposite as night and day. Here are some examples to explain that question:
- Connie's motto in life should be, "Always late." For example, a class agenda listed all the assignments at the beginning of the year. When the time came for something to be presented, her excuse was "I didn't know it was due already." Or she might blame the professor for not reminding her.
- Sandy is just the opposite. A description of her life could be, "Always early." Therefore, she did not make excuses or spend time blaming someone else.

The girls roomed together until graduation. Sandy thanked the people who had influenced her life; Connie could have won the "Best Excuse Giver of the Year" at graduation.

A person does not sin until they give in to the temptation, therefore:
- Pray for strength to resist.
- Run, sometimes literally.
- Say "no" when confronted with what you know is wrong.
- Avoid the desire for worldly living.

D—Directed Prayer

Lord, forgive me for the excuses I make about my sins.

April 21

A Little Sound Doctrine

Believers are to properly relate to the local church.
(1 Timothy 1:1-11)

A—Advice from the Bible

Some have wandered away and don't know what they are talking about.
(1 Tim. 1:7)

B—Biblical Example

Timothy was one of Paul's special associates. This young man, born of mixed parentage, along with Titus, dealt with some of the tough assignments in the churches Paul had established. Like many servants of the Lord, Timothy became discouraged in the work and Paul would write to encourage him to stay on the job. Ephesus was not the easiest place to pastor a church. The city was devoted to the worship of Diana, who promoted sexual immorality of all kinds. This letter was written to explain how a local church should be managed. The people giving Timothy trouble needed to remember that their pastor was there because he was sent by the Lord Jesus Christ. One reason the leaders were told to stay with the work was that false teachers were busy trying to capture the Christians. Their message was not good news for sinners! These false teachers were raising questions, but not providing answers. In these early churches, the believers were taught the Word of God and the meanings of basic Christian doctrines. God had committed the truth of the Word to Paul, who was passing on this message to Timothy.

C—Contemporary Application

This advertisement appeared in a city newspaper:
Men wanted for hazardous journey, small wages, bitter cold, long months of complete darkness, constant danger, safe return doubtful. Honor and recognition in case of success. Thousands of men responded to Sir Ernest Shackleton's search for his Artic expedition. If Jesus had advertised for workers in the Ephesus church, with a priority assignment of teaching sound doctrine, how many individuals would respond? *The conditions of being misunderstood exist. A constant attack from an invisible enemy will occur. A full reward will not come until after your work is completed. The job may cost you your home, ambitions, and even life.* How many people do you think would volunteer? God needs church leadership who will be faithful to His Word.

Things to watch for in the local church:
- Curriculum with an unsound doctrinal message.
- People who join the church with different doctrinal ideas.
- Para-church groups that pull member loyalty away.
- Worship styles that praise self, rather than God.

D—Directed Prayer

Father, protect us from false teachers who are seeking to destroy the local church.

April 22

A Little House for a Great God

God enables people to face challenging obstacles with courage.
(Ezra 5:1-11)

A—Advice from the Bible

"We are rebuilding the temple that was built years ago.
(Ezra 5:11)

B—Biblical Example

Some of the Jews whom Cyrus allowed to go home from the Babylonian exile, returned to Jerusalem and the temple area. They offered to help the resident Jewish leaders rebuild the temple, but were rudely rejected. Discouraged and harassed, the "outsiders" waited more than a decade to proceed with the restoration project. Strong leadership finally came. Haggai and Zechariah, two prophets, began to encourage the people to complete the task. The people began to remove the brush and debris from the foundation. Interruptions continued to plague the builders, but evidences of God's presence and power kept the project going. Persian investigators came to inspect and question the builders. The Jews explained they simply were rebuilding the temple that Solomon had built long years before. The first great temple was lost to the Jews because of God's anger on them for their sin. His wrath was expressed through Nebuchadnezzar and the Babylonian invasion, which destroyed the temple. Now the construction was begun and the vessels of gold and silver were placed back in their original temple site.

C—Contemporary Application

Oklahoma is known as the "Boomer Sooner" state. When the railroads began their construction, revenue was needed, so the companies were anxious to move into the coveted Indian's land. The white man also wanted more land to establish new farms and ranches. By 1879 organized bands, the Boomers, were moving in despite federal law. Finally Congress opened some 2,000,000 acres of western Indian Territory, bringing on the famous land run beginning at noon on April 22, 1889. Known as Oklahoma Territory, these pioneers built and rebuilt their lives due to conflicts and obstacles, such as Indian raids and weather. The settlers, many called Sooners for entering the area before official permission, sought prime land. My great-grandfather was a Sooner and claimed farm land in Washita, County, where he helped build a church and home for his family.

Lessons from this Scripture passage.

- The Lord's work is done best by people who are His faithful servants.
- Believers must expect opposition from nonbelievers.
- God's people must not allow difficulties to discourage them in the work.
- God gives spiritual leaders to encourage us.

D—Directed Prayer

Thank You, for the joy found through faithful service.

April 23

A Little Battle against Evil

Christians are to prepare for battle against evil.
(Ephesians 6:10-18)

A—Advice from the Bible

Put on the full armor of God so that you can take your stand against the devil's schemes.
(Eph. 6:11)

B—Biblical Example

The apostle Paul began the letter to the Christians in Ephesus with a description of redemption through the grace of God. Realizing that carrying out the duties and responsibilities of the new life would require a strength that they did not possess. To clarify the previous chapters, he reminded his readers of the source of that power. The message of this passage is one of warfare. He warned the believer to put on the full armor of God. The devil is well organized, and he employs cunning plans. Therefore, the battle is against a very powerful enemy and is with the invisible forces of evil. Verse 12 lists the spiritual descriptions of wickedness. To overcome the evil one, Christians must stand firm in their faith. The pieces of the spiritual armor are then compared to a Roman soldier. These items help keep a soldier alive during warfare. A new believer must learn that personal strength will not be adequate to fight spiritual battles. Our strength for combating evil comes from God.

C—Contemporary Application

Jack became a Christian at summer camp when he was 12-years-old. However, he never took seriously his faith in Jesus. He was satisfied with God's Word based on scriptural truths from his childhood. Many spiritual battles occurred in his growing years. Each time the warfare began, he went back to church, only to discover that occasional preparation would not be successful. For example, Jack married and had a happy home life until he met an attractive woman at work. At first he resisted the temptation to take her to lunch, but before long an affair developed. His wife discovered the problem and threatened divorce. Jack called the pastor for "armor" to use in the warfare going on in his life. He did not win this attack from the evil one and lost his family, house, friends, and even the woman involved in the battle. Later, his pastor suggested the idea of "putting on the whole armor of God." This man still did not see the need for this practice.

Your battle against the evil one requires the following:
- Being covered with truth and displaying integrity, holiness, and purity of life.
- Being balanced during the battle with a foundation based on truth.
- Being able to use the shield of faith.
- Being protected with a helmet of salvation and applying the Word of God.

D—Directed Prayer

Thank You, Father, that praying for victory is effective.

April 24

A Little Meaningless Life

Our world idolizes physical and social pleasures.
(Ecclesiastes 2:1-11)

A—Advice from the Bible

Everything was meaningless.
(Eccl. 2:11)

B—Biblical Example

Psalms, Proverbs, and Ecclesiastes are classified in the Bible as wisdom books. A philosopher usually shares observations, reflections, reasonings, and conclusions with his readers. About 3,000 years ago, the *Preacher* of Ecclesiastes made an observation. This son of David believed in God and that God had a purpose for his life. He also searched diligently to discover the purpose. Solomon records in chapter 2 about the emptiness of living according to human values. He tried to live by whatever means the world offered. Personal satisfaction was sought by busying himself with building houses and planting vineyards. But then as he thought about the work he had accomplished, he realized it was full of emptiness. This fact is usually realized when a person totally drains the world's cup of all kinds of pleasure. The sad testimony is the feeling of emptiness. Pleasure, enjoyment, laughter, and wine were not enough to bring fulfillment in life. A summary of Solomon's life could be this: He had wealth, fame, wisdom, and many servants, but he made the mistake of leaving God out of his pursuits.

C—Contemporary Application

Benjamin Franklin (1706-1790) was an American printer, author, diplomat, philosopher, and scientist. He is ranked among the country's greatest statesmen. In 1731 he founded what was probably the first public library in America, chartered in 1742 as the Philadelphia Library. As a philosopher, he first published *Poor Richard's Almanack* in 1732, under the pen name Richard Saunders. This modest volume quickly gained a wide audience. The homespun, practical wisdom of Franklin influenced American character. In addition to his common sense, wisdom, and wit, he discovered great determination of purpose, unique tact, and broad acceptance of other ideas. He was a sympathetic listener, who counseled other people in living a meaningful life. He and Solomon would have enjoyed sharing their experiences about life.

Selected thoughts about Solomon's life:
- Chasing fulfillment in life is as impossible as taming a tornado.
- The more we learn the more we realize how little we know.
- How can you feel empty with a full stomach?
- Trying to find fulfillment without God is like trying to play golf with clubs.

D—Directed Prayer

Lord, thank You that life's ultimate purpose is never found through human investigation.

April 25

Little Memories of Malta

Christians need to claim the secret of Paul's service and success.
Acts 28:1-10

A—Advice from the Bible

They honored us in many ways.
(Acts 28:10)

B—Biblical Example

A man on his way to Rome for trial became the benefactor of all who sailed with him and of the people on the island of Malta. The ship transporting Paul on his journey to Rome encountered strong winds and forced the crew to depart from their original plan. The ship began to disintegrate but all 276 passengers safely reached the shore. The island people welcomed the shipwrecked crew by lighting a fire and seeking to make the survivors comfortable. Paul was immediately offered opportunities to serve the people and God. He helped gather wood and experienced a snake bite, but did not die. Paul did his share of the work. News of the snake experience spread quickly, and he became involved in a great ministry among the sick. The father of a local dignitary was restored from a great fever. Crowds soon gathered to the scene for additional healing. The people of Malta (Melita) honored the apostle and his associates during their three month stay on the island. Many gifts were presented and all the necessities for their continued journey to Rome were provided. Paul obviously shared the gospel with anybody who would listen

C—Contemporary Application

A famous English soldier and statesman was born on April 25, 1599. His name was Oliver Cromwell. He was the most successful general of the English Civil War. During his tenure in the British administration, a shortage of silver occurred and the government needed this metal for coins. Lord Cromwell sent his men on an investigation of the local cathedral to see if they could find any precious metal. After the men returned, they reported, "The only silver we could find is the statues of the saints standing in the corners." To which the radical soldier and statesman of England replied, "Good! We'll melt down the saints and put them into circulation." A practical goal for authentic Christianity is to serve God outside the familiar comforts of padded pews and dimmed lights. Paul taught this principle everywhere he went.

Lesson learned from Paul's experience:
- A faithful Christian will be admired by many people.
- A faithful Christian can keep his courage.
- A faithful Christian can always find someone to help.
- A faithful Christian can overcome a bad situation.

D—Directed Prayer

Father, lead me to serve You in all kinds of circumstances.

April 26

Little Leftover Grain

A common way God provides for believers is through personal contacts.
Ruth 2:1-12

A—Advice from the Bible

She began to glean in the fields.
(Ruth 2:3)

B—Biblical Example

Ten years had passed since Naomi had been home to Bethlehem. She and Ruth were now threatened with economic destitution and were still grieving over the loss of their husbands when they returned from Moab. A sense of financial insecurity was a great burden for the women. The work ethic of widows allowed very little assistance. The barley harvest was about to begin and a job might be available for Ruth during this short gleaning season. The women asked permission to work behind the regular laborers. Some grain was left behind and Ruth would gather all she could find. The land owner was Boaz, a relative of Naomi. He was generous with Ruth and provided for her safety and extra barley. The grain would be processed into flour, assuring bread for the following months. The hand of the Lord was definitely at work. Individuals often try various manipulations to bring about this kind of Ruth/Boaz encounter. But God has already made the preparations for our needs according to His time.

C—Contemporary Application

A favorite American naturalist of mine is John James Audubon (1785-1851). However, discovering facts about his life made this artist, noted for his realistic portrayals of American wildlife more believable. Insecurities and struggles plagued his life. The National Audubon Society was founded in his honor on his birthday, April 26, in Les Cayes, Santo Domingo. At the age of 18, Audubon returned to America and settled on a farm near Philadelphia. He devoted himself to a study of natural history, especially to making drawings of American birds. The next project was establishing a general store in Louisville, Kentucky, and later in Henderson, Kentucky. Neither venture was successful. Several friends came to his rescue in the following years. His drawings of American birds became masterpieces. Because of people who recognized his talent, James was able to support his family without being involved in common labor.

When faced with extreme needs, how can we act boldly in accordance with God's Word?

- Let God know about your problems.
- Read Scripture that focuses on God's love in times of need.
- Share your insecurities with a Christian friend.
- Trust God to hear and answer your requests.

D—Directed Prayer

Lord, You are faithful to meet my needs.

April 27

A Little Tower in Siloam

What makes an accident a tragedy?
Luke 13:1-5

A—Advice from the Bible

You too will all perish.
(Luke 13:3)

B—Biblical Example

The Pharisees created rules for the Hebrews. Unacceptable individuals who did not follow these rules were considered lost sinners or Galileans. Some of these people were wicked. Terrorist cells planned armed revolts against Rome. On this day, they were offering their sacrifices in the Temple, so Pilate issued orders for their slaughter. About eighteen other people were witnessing this interruption by the Roman soldiers from a tower. The weight on the tower probably caused a collapse of the structure and all the people were killed. Pilate was guilty of mass murders ever since he became the procurator in A.D. 26. Another kind of accident was also occurring. Pilate had financed an aqueduct from the Jerusalem tax money and the Jews were preparing to fight Rome.

C—Contemporary Application

A terrible accident happened at the Chernobyl nuclear power plant in the Ukrainian republic of the Union of Soviet Socialist Republics (USSR). A plume of radioactive debris drifted over parts of the western Soviet Union, Eastern Europe, and Scandinavia. The accident, which took place on April 27, 1986, was the worst nuclear power accident in history. Roughly 200,000 people had to be resettled. The accident raised concerns about the safety of the Soviet nuclear power industry, slowing its expansion for a number of years, while forcing the Soviet government to become less secretive. Slavic is a young man from Russia who is our friend. His father and older brothers worked at the power plant. When the time came to clean the affected area, Slavic's brothers were "volunteered." However, their father insisted that he, as the father, go in their place. Their father died three years later from thyroid cancer. Lives have been sacrificed throughout history. The main reason for such slaughters is the sin of greed. The answer to the problem is repentance. Jesus had come to show the way from sin to salvation. He delivered His message.

Why do the following people need to repent?
- Some church members falsely blame innocent people.
- Some deacons are included in worldly schemes.
- Certain family members are unkind to extended family members.
- Some people of different races are unwelcome at school meetings.

D—Directed Prayer

Father, use me to call people to repent.

April 28

Little Servants of the Lord

Every believer needs to be a servant.
2 Kings 2:2-16

A—Advice from the Bible

"Look, we your servants have . . . ."
(2 Kings 2:16)

B—Biblical Example

The great prophet Elijah realized that his ministry had come to an end, and the time to anoint Elisha as his successor was approaching. But first, he wanted to visit the three main centers where the prophets received their training—Gilgal, Bethel, and Jericho. Interesting events happened at each school. With the great prophet's departure, Elisha was now ready to assume his next assignment. He was loyal to God, his friend, and mentor, Elijah. The future prophet realized that his ministry would be fruitless without the power of God and so he made a bold request. He desired to serve God with spiritual boldness. This sentence summarizes Elijah's departure from earth—walking, talking, a chariot of fire, horses of fire, and a whirlwind. The younger prophet was now all alone except for God's continuing presence and Elijah's mantle. This wool garment was a symbol of the prophet's calling and of God's anointing. The power for his ministry was available from God. This strength was present for his lifetime of service.

C—Contemporary Application

Each believer has a unique service for God. When Thomas A. Edison died in 1931, President Herbert Hoover suggested that every light in American be extinguished for one minute. This action was to honor Edison for his invention of the incandescent lamp. However, responsible leaders pointed out the risk of putting out the lights, even for one minute. Mr. Edison, at age 32, had designed a product that the world could not get along without for 60 seconds. Each of us is called to be a servant in special ways and the promise of boldness and strength are always present. Therefore, a believer must be a devoted servant of God and must never forget total dependence upon Him. The success of a servant's ministry centers on the word, *faith*. Elisha had witnessed the definition of a servant/leader and he selected more prophets to assist in his leadership role. Today, a new idea is a good testimony of a person who serves God.

Live your faith with:
- loyalty.
- boldness.
- self-confidence.
- leadership.

D—Directed Prayer

Father, thank You for biblical examples of faithful servants.

April 29

A Little Roman Governor of Judea

Believers must respond to Jesus' death on the cross.
Mark 15:1-15

A—Advice from the Bible

"Are you the king of the Jews?" asked Pilate
(Mark 15:2)

B—Biblical Example

The crucifixion of Christ was the final development in a series of failed attempts on Jesus' life. The Jewish trials during the night revealed growing opposition to His ministry. Early one morning Pilate found a crowd at his door demanding a man's death. The crowds were incited to violence and determined that Jesus must die. However, Roman law prevented His enemies from applying the death penalty. Pontius Pilate had ruled Judea since A.D. 26, but his term of office was marred by constant strife with the Jewish people. He repeatedly insulted the citizens concerning their customs and religion. Jesus' silence at His trial amazed the Roman governor. Prisoners usually begged for mercy. Pilate did not seem to want to punish Jesus. He found little truth in the charges against Him and viewed this mob-mentality as an opportunity to do his rebellious subjects a favor. The governor resented the way Jews treated Rome and so he sought ways to mistreat the Jews. Pilate's response to the Savior was a big mistake!

C—Contemporary Application

Pretend that four adults are confronted by the Savior in various situations. How could you offer advice during these uneasy moments?

- Elmo never went to church unless his mother escorted him. His attitude toward Christians has grown more ill-mannered through the years. He writes letters to the hometown editor complaining about "whatever." One day he responds to the Lord
- Georgia ignores Christ and local Christian events. She thinks Jesus is dead and the resurrection never happened. One day she responds to the Lord and . . . .
- Sherry models her love for the Savior everyday. She responds to His Word through Bible study classes. One day she responds to Jesus . . .
- Dennis is married to a non-Christian. However, he refuses to allow her threats to get a divorce keep him from responding to God.

When people are confronted by the Savior, some will respond

- With a disrespectful attitude
- By ignoring Him
- By loving Him.
- With courage

D—Directed Prayer

Thank You, Lord, that people are responding to You with faith.

April 30

The Little Meeting in Sinai

God's people need to know their strengths and abilities.
Numbers 1:1-3

A—Advice from the Bible

The LORD spoke in the Tent of Meeting.
(Num. 1:1)

B—Biblical Example

The Israelites were now camped in front of Mount Sinai. The first year anniversary of the departure from Egypt was remembered. God established His covenant with them and the Scripture in today's devotional reveals some final things these people did before leaving this location for Canaan. Each tribe was to organize for war and the Levites were organized for worship. The Lord instructed Moses to take a census of the congregation of Israelites. The meeting spot was a portable sanctuary where God met with His people. Every adult male was to be counted head by head. Previous census taking was for two reasons—taxation purposes and for determining the potential size of a fighting force. God knew that the Israelites needed to be aware of their military capability as they journeyed toward Canaan. The wanderers needed to know how to best serve God during the unknown days ahead. Strengths and abilities were now a priority.

C—Contemporary Application

The citizens in my town and county received a letter advising them of a census in the area. Then a packet of material was sent with a questionnaire about the family. The response to the questions was to be returned to the Census Bureau. If these instructions were ignored, a representative would visit your home. The United States made history when it took its first census in 1790, not only because of the size of the area enumerated and the effort to obtain data on characteristics of the population but also because of the political purpose for which it was undertaken—namely, representation in Congress on the basis of population. Churches will canvas the neighborhoods around them to identify families who are unchurched or in-house methods are used to discover ways members can use their abilities and gifts in service for God. Numbers are important in the Kingdom work. Discovering people, through "counting noses," helps find workers who can use their abilities for Him.

Take a census of your family, but count only Christians.

- How many of your family are equipped to serve in God's army?
- What are some spiritual gifts used by your family to serve in God's church?
- What areas of Christian service are lacking in your family's abilities?
- Why do families need to be morally and spiritually pure?

D—Directed Prayer

Lord, is a self-inventory necessary in my Christian service?

May 1

A Little Command

An obedient response to God's command saves lives.
Genesis 7:1-5

A—Advice from the Bible

"Go into the ark . . . "
(Gen. 7:1, NIV)

B—Biblical Example

Noah is first introduced in the Bible as a man who *found favor in the eyes of God* (Gen. 6:8). The Lord's tolerance for the sinfulness of His people would last no longer. The total depravity that covered Noah's world was unacceptable to the Creator. However, an exceptional man was chosen to survive the disaster that was coming. Three words are used to identify Noah. He was righteous, blameless, and walked with God. *Righteous* means he treated people right. *Blameless* means he was uninfected by the sin-diseased environment. The fact that he *walked with God* reveals that a special communication with God was possible in such an evil world. The writer of Hebrews adds a little more insight, *By faith Noah after being warned about what was not yet seen, in reverence built an ark to deliver his family* (Heb. 11:7, HCSB). The directive from God to build an ark was followed to completion (6:22) and now a new opportunity for obedience was given. This **little** four-word command would save Noah and his family from the devastation of the coming flood.

C—Contemporary Application

How can family siblings be so different? For example, Bill and Betty are twins, born into a fine Christian family. These children were expected to attend church each Sunday. This practice was not an option and participation in a daily family worship time was required. However, the teen-years brought changes. Betty forgot the commands she had been taught; Bill drew closer to God and his church. The family watched as Betty drifted away from the Lord. Undesirable friends became a part of her life and seemed more important than her family. Her chosen lifestyle was offensive to those who loved her and surely to God. However, Bill centered his life and later his family around the teachings of God's Word and chose to obey the commands of God. His choice to serve God brought much happiness to his life. What happened to these twins?

Think about these truths:

- God wants to protect and bless those who live according to His expectations.
- We can live godly lives in the midst of ungodliness.
- Obedience to God is a lifetime commitment.
- Nothing can change God's ultimate purposes for humankind.

D—Directed Prayer

Lord, guide me to understand and be obedient to Your commands.

May 2

Some Little Deceivers

Learn to live from the inside out.
2 John 1-13

A—Advice from the Bible

Many deceivers have gone out into the world.
(2 John 7, HCSB)

B—Biblical Example

James, John's brother is dead; Peter is dead; Paul is dead; Thomas, Andrew, and Philip, are dead. A lonely old man, living in Ephesus, is the only survivor of the first apostles of Jesus (Mark 3:13-19). The Apostle John knew the truth about the Lord Jesus Christ as no other person on earth. The church is now into the third generation of believers. At this time, no temple exists. No capital city is available for worship. The homeland is under control of Rome, and no king, but Caesar is on the throne.

The Elder writes his letter to a senior person worthy of respect. The subject is false teachers also called false messiahs and false prophets (Mark 13:22-23). The writer was warning the church about individuals who offered something the people didn't have, when in reality they took away what was already possessed. The church was admonished not to go backwards. Any teaching that goes beyond the clear message of Scripture should immediately put us on alert. Progressive theology that denies Christ is not progressive at all; it is regressive—all the way back to Genesis 3:1.

C—Contemporary Application

Frances lives alone now as a widow. Making friends has always been difficult for this 60ish woman. She did move her church letter when she came to live near her daughter, but getting involved in a class of "old women" just didn't appeal to her.

One day she answered a knock on her door and discovered two women had come to visit her. An invitation was extended to come inside. The conversation soon led to the reason for the visit. These women were part of a group known for false teaching. Frances loved the personal interest they expressed. Soon, she began attending meetings at their Kingdom Hall. Months passed and Frances became uneasy about some of the teaching especially the refusal to salute the flag, to vote, and to serve in the military forces. Other teachings began to confuse her and before long, her daughter had to free her mother from their influence.

Be aware of false teachers today:
- They compromise the truth.
- They do not remain true to the basic doctrines of the Christian faith.
- They deny the incarnation (when God became flesh).
- They need to know that you will **not** accept their doctrine as truth.

D—Directed Prayer

Lord, help me understand better, that love and truth originate in God.

May 3

On Little Eagles' Wings

The Lord will bear you up when you feel to weary to fly.
Exodus 19:1-6

A—Advice from the Bible

. . . and how I carried you on eagles' wings . . .
(Ex. 19:4, NIV)

B—Biblical Example

Exodus 19 begins the second major section of Exodus. The focus is on God's covenant and plans for Israel beginning at Mount Sinai. The people of Israel had begun the long hard trek to Canaan. This desolate, dry place would be their home for about a year. Before the covenant could be revealed, God wanted the people to look back once more at past events. These witnesses were to recall how God had rescued them from slavery in Egypt. Witnesses cannot deny what they had seen! The whole experience of deliverance is beautifully phrased using an eagle as an example. The picture of the eagle speaks of God's power which He demonstrated when He brought the people out of captivity with a mighty hand and outstretched arms, and led them into the Promised Land. The people were now freed from bondage and oppression and had become an independent nation. However, God was redeeming them for Himself. They were to find their purpose and satisfaction in Him, not in earthly freedom and independence. God concluded His plan to Moses with the statement that each person was to be holy.

C—Contemporary Application

My family and I were watching a lumberjack show in Ketchikan, Alaska. Suddenly the crowd focused on something in the sky. The performers stopped the show as a baldhead eagle perched on a pole near the entertainment area. At first we thought this exciting incident was part of the show. However, we were told that the eagle liked to fish for salmon in a nearby creek and just paid a visit to the crowd. The bird was huge and beautiful and I wanted to know more about them. Here are some things I discovered:

The baldhead eagle became the national bird in 1782. They are birds of prey and can identify food by soaring in the air. Some eagles have a wing span of 7 feet. Movies, poem, songs, and books have been written about the giant raptors. The verse about God carrying His people on eagle's wings and bringing them to Himself became very meaningful to me.

Despite your past or present actions,

- God loves you.
- God will never leave you nor forsake you.
- God accepts you when other people won't.
- God will love you always.

D—Directed Prayer

God, thank You for Your guidance and power today.

May 4

A Little Game of Endurance

Believers should maintain their courage and hope.
Hebrews 10:35-39

A—Advice from the Bible

For you need endurance . . .
(Heb. 10:36, HCSB)

B—Biblical Example

The Book of Hebrews is anonymous and the date is unknown. However, the fact that some Christians were living in a time of limited persecution is obvious. This special group of people seemed to have been born again and raised in the Jewish culture. They were a fellowship of faithful followers of Christ. Nevertheless, these believers had suffered many things such as the loss of material possessions. Their joyful attitude during this time was a witness to the unbelieving community. There previous compassion for the prisoners motivated them to help meet the needs of these Christian friends. The need expressed by the writer was for perseverance. This action was not an optional choice, but necessary. The encouragement to wait patiently for Christ's second coming must have inspired these Hebrews to continue on day-by-day, living the Christian life

C—Contemporary Application

Communism had forced the Christian missionaries out of South Vietnam. Sam James left the area with a broken heart. Years later after some freedom had been restored, he decided to return for a visit. A message had been sent to his Vietnamese Christian friends that he was coming, but he doubted if any of these believers would be available. Years of prison suffering, "re-education" camps, and persecution for following Christ had cost many lives. A message was pressed into his hand as he left his hotel in Ho Chi Minh City. Written on the note were these words. "Meet us at the park at 2 o'clock." When he arrived, a man led him through a jungle of overgrown weeds to a tiny clearing. Seven of his former seminary students waited there, seated around an old wrought-iron table. They embraced him with tears and laughter and spoke of the trials they had faced under communism. From a brown paper bag, an aluminum tray appeared and was set on the table. Next came a loaf of bread and a small bunch of grapes. The bread was broken and passed around. Each person took a grape. Nobody said anything about the Lord's Supper, but each believer knew what was happening. They had maintained their courage and hope during times of great trials. A way to endure in their faith was found.

What can we learn from these Hebrew Christians?

- God's people live by faith.
- God's people remain true to their identity.
- God's people take advantage of the resources God provides in Christ.
- God's people will find strength to endure present crises.

D—Directed Prayer

Lord, may I always maintain courage and hope in my daily walk with You.

May 5

Five Little Poems

To disobey God is to invite disaster.
Lamentations 1:15-20

A—Advice from the Bible

... My children are destitute because the enemy has prevailed
(Lam. 1:16, NIV)

B—Biblical Example

The prophet, Jeremiah, wrote two books. The destruction of Jerusalem by the Babylonians is the focus of both pieces—one book predicts the disaster of the city and the other book looks back on the crisis. Lamentations is known as the book of tears or a dirge (a funeral song.) How does a person deal with grief? Jeremiah deals with the subject and expresses his emotional feelings toward Jerusalem's fall and the temple's destruction. The book is entirely in poetry form. The desolation of the Holy City is portrayed in moving detail. The once great international city had disappeared completely. No nation came to her support. The first poem details Jerusalem's great sorrow. The second poem reveals the Lord's anger at the city. The third poem is about the experience of personal faith and community confession. The fourth poem communicates the Lord's judgment because of the sins of the prophets and priests. The fifth poem concludes the book with a prayer for restoration. The poems were written in a specific form to help individuals memorize the important material.

C—Contemporary Application

Mattie was sitting on the porch of her assisted living residence. My visits with her were very important to both of us. Today, however, I noticed a sadness in her countenance. Tears began to fall on her cheeks as we identified the source of her sorrow. Her small church was dying. Family quarrels, political positioning, and untrained leaders resulted in a small group of older worshipers left to attend the services. This dear saint grieved over the loss of her church. Sin problems had infiltrated the congregation about 40 years earlier. New members became fewer and fewer. Conflict between the preachers and the deacons was an ongoing issue. The good news of the gospel was rarely shared with the believers. Most sermons were about dealing with conflicts. And so I listened to this wonderful Christian woman share her broken heart. Could God intervene in this crisis and punish the sins of some of the members?

Lessons learned from Lamentations:

- God is serious about sin.
- God can send judgment on a nation, a city, and a church.
- God punishes sin.
- God is merciful.

D—Directed Prayer

Thank You, Lord, that you allow me to grieve for past mistakes.

May 6

Little Clouds

Beware of teachers who prey instead of pray.
Jude 1-25

A—Advice from the Bible

They are waterless clouds . . .
(Jude 12, HCSB)

B—Biblical Example

The Book of Jude contains one of the most vivid and interesting descriptions of false teachers. The writer, who identifies himself as a servant of Jesus Christ and the brother of James, wanted his readers to understand what being a Christian means. Confusion about this subject had occurred because of individuals who claimed to be heavenly messengers with superior knowledge or power. These apostates offered no standard of truth because they were constantly changing their position. They were divided into cliques and made a mockery of the meal of fellowship held on the Lord's Day. This meal became a drunken travesty, much like that of the Corinthian church mentioned by Paul in his letter. These meals or feasts were a time for showing love for one another; however, the kiss of peace was used as an opportunity for perversion to gratify their own lusts. A leader who feels no responsibility for the welfare of anyone except himself stands condemned. These false teachers stockpiled the severe and certain judgment of God. Jude compares them to clouds <u>without</u> water.

C—Contemporary Application

Cults and isms have occurred throughout history. People are attracted to something about these false teachers and choose to follow their leadership. One of the saddest examples of this kind of cult-worship was The People's Temple lead by James Warren Jones. This man deceived 900 people into following him to Jonestown, Guyana. He proclaimed his evil teachings to these worshipers. Most of his followers were citizens of the United States. In 1978 Jones ordered his cult to take poison. This mass suicide shocked the normal world. Another example of a group of people blindly believing false leaders happened in Waco, Texas in 1993. A 51-day stand-off ended in the death of 87 commune members of the Branch Davidian cult. Once again, the media covered this event in disgust. Religious broadcasters tried to explain the madness of this kind of thing. What do you think needs to be done about false teachers?

Why do people become involved with false teachers and cults?

- They are sometimes victims of prejudice.
- They are from dysfunctional families.
- They are living in poverty.
- They are non-conformists.

D—Directed Prayer

O, heavenly Father, help me keep myself in Your love.

A Little Sneak Preview

God gives us wisdom, promise, and hope.
Deuteronomy 34:1-7

A—Advice from the Bible

The LORD showed him the whole land . . .
(Deut. 34:1, NIV)

B—Biblical Example

Moses was the only Old Testament person who ever spoke with the Lord face to face (Ex. 33:11) and now, during the last hours of his life, he would spend in communion with God. He is called Israel's greatest prophet. However, disobedience prevented him from entering the promised land. God's discipline for this leader's sin was to keep Moses from his dream of completing the exodus. This 120-year-old prophet pronounced blessings on the Israelites and ascended to the top of Mount Pisgah, which is called Nebo. The splendor of the covenant land was viewed from north to south. God had promised Abraham, Isaac, Jacob, and their descendants this land to which Moses had led the Hebrew people. Standing at the border of the land of hope, Moses lay down the burden of leadership which he had carried for 40 years and the responsibility for leading God's people was passed to Joshua. The death and burial of this servant of the Lord would occur on a Moabite plain.

C—Contemporary Application

The covered wagons began to assemble in Independence, Missouri. The year was 1842 and the first wagon train to the Western frontier was about to move out. The wagon master and his scout informed the pioneers of the dangers they would face on this journey. Many would die from illness, weather, or Indians. The opportunity to change their minds was still available. Some of the people chose to remain in familiar areas; others would go as far as Nebraska. The eager families were now ready to board or walk beside their wagons. Hope for a better future impelled many of these early adventurers to leave everything and head to the promised land of the Northwest. The journey would take about five or six months with rest stops at Fort Laramie and along the Snake River. Oregon was the final destination. The wagon master was a trusted, experienced leader. His goal was to get the people safely to the Columbia River. Then, he would turn the leadership over to someone else who would help the pioneers get settled.

Lessons learned from this biblical experience:

- God is the true leader of His people.
- God keeps His promise no matter what may come.
- God can be counted on to be consistent with His plans and purposes.
- God will always be with us and lead us onward.

D—Directed Prayer

Thank you, Father, for giving me a vision and a hope through Your promises.

May 8

A Little Riot in the Temple

God can work in all our circumstances to accomplish His purposes.
Acts 21:26-39

A—Advice from the Bible

> *The Jews . . . saw Paul in the temple . . . and stirred up the whole crowd.*
> (Acts 21:27, HCSB)

B—Biblical Example

The Apostle Paul's experiences can provide guidance on how to face personal crises. Despite various warnings that sure danger lay before him, Paul insisted on completing the trip to Jerusalem. His arrival completed the third missionary journey. The Jewish Christians continued to practice Jewish laws, so Paul and four men participated in the purifying rite. Seven days were required for the purification and when the vows were completed the Jews from the Roman province of Asia started trouble. They recognized Paul and began to incite the people into a mob mentality. He was seized and charged with abandoning the Jewish laws. Paul was accused of desecrating the temple by taking Gentiles into a forbidden area. The riot began! The mob would have beaten Paul to death had not the Roman military commander intervened. The whole city was in turmoil. The mob wanted to kill Paul. The apostle finally identified himself to the Roman officer and asked for permission to explain what had happened. Paul gave his personal testimony.

C—Contemporary Application

The opening statement in a biography I was reading raised my curiosity. "Roger Williams was a gentle and loveable man, but he stirred up trouble wherever he went." His vision and determination made a profound impact on our world. Without his courageous vision, many personal freedoms might never have come to Americans. Roger Williams was born in England in 1603 and belonged to the Church of England. This church was the only one allowed to assemble for worship. People who refused to participate were punished, imprisoned, or put to death. Williams became quite outspoken and critical of the Church of England. The Bishop gave him a choice of either banishment or jail, so he sailed to Boston. Williams was later banished from the colonies because he believed that every person should be free to worship as he saw fit. His revolutionary ideas finally were achieved in Providence, Rhode Island. His suffering had made a difference!

When a personal crisis comes, remember:

- That the Lord will comfort and encourage you.
- That your honest and sincere efforts to explain the problem may fail.
- That God can fulfill His purposes in your life.
- That your actions express your Christian testimony.

D—Directed Prayer

Lord, thank You for your promised presence in times of trouble.

May 9

A Little Song by a Little Mother

Identify feelings of personal joy during Mother's Day
1 Samuel 2:1-10

A—Advice from the Bible

"My heart rejoices in the LORD . . ."
(1 Sam . 2:1, NIV)

B—Biblical Example

Elkanah, father of Samuel, was probably a Levite and had two wives. Hannah was her husband's favorite companion, but she was barren while his other wife had children. Not providing a son for her husband was a grief for a Hebrew woman. Hannah sought God through prayer as a possible answer to her problem. She also promised to dedicate the child to His service. God heard and answered her prayer. She named her son Samuel, which means "heard by God." Hannah expressed her gratitude in song. The first part of her song is praise to God for who He is and what He does. The second stanza extends to others as God is praised for His actions of judgment and justice. A truly grateful person focuses attention on the Giver, not the gift. Of course, she was thankful for Samuel, but she was more grateful for God, who provided her with a son. Hannah took comfort in the fact that God was all-knowing. He recognized who was arrogant and who was humble. He knew those who pretend to be faithful and those who sincerely were faithful. Becoming a mother brought true joy for this little Jewish wife.

C—Contemporary Application

The first recorded formal celebration of mothers began in the spring in ancient Greece. The people honored Rhea, mother of the gods. This pagan practice came to America in 1872 when Julia Ward Howe (who wrote *Battle Hymn of the Republic*) suggested a day dedicated to peace and motherhood. Ana Jarvis took up the cause following her mother's death. She began a campaign in her home church in Grafton, West Virginia in 1907 to honor her mother's passing. By 1911 Mother's Day was celebrated in nearly every state in the United States. The joy of setting aside one day a year to honor mothers became a national tradition. Finally, in 1914 President Woodrow Wilson declared the second Sunday of May as the official national Mother's Day. Women today come in all kinds of mother-roles. Some are step-mothers, foster mothers, aunts, grandmothers, and adopted moms. These caring individuals should be recognized for their love and care.

How should we honor our mothers both past and present?
- We should rejoice because of God's goodness in providing us with a mother.
- We should honor our mother by our character and conduct.
- We should tell our children about their grandmothers.
- We should become all that our mother hoped we would be.

D—Directed Prayer

Father, I praise You for making motherhood so important to my life.

May 10

John the Baptist's Little Mother

Do not doubt God's ability to fulfill His promises.
Luke 1:5-80

A—Advice from the Bible

"The Lord has done this for me."
(Luke 1:25, HSCB)

B—Biblical Example

Many mothers are featured in the Bible. Some of them are well-known, others are recognized for having special or famous children. Elisabeth is first introduced in Luke 1:5 along with her husband, Zechariah. He served as a Jewish priest, who had the responsibility for managing the temple, teaching the people the Scriptures, and directing the worship services. The priests rotated their times of serving in Jerusalem and then returned home after two weeks. This couple had the reputation of being devoted to God. However, one thing was missing from their life. Elizabeth was barren and as an aging woman she faced personal hardship and public shame. But God had other plans for this couple. Zechariah had an experience with an angel that left him speechless. The good news was that a son would be born to prepare the way for the Messiah. Trying to understand the emotions of this aging, pregnant woman would be impossible. God did what He promised. The baby was named John.

C—Contemporary Application

Paul and Kathleen married right out of high school. Common interests in farming and cattle brought them together. After the wedding, they moved on to a family farm and began their life together. Their tenth wedding anniversary was celebrated as usual—dining out in a nearby town and coming home to watch television. The existing problem was no children. Both longed for a big family, but Kathleen couldn't conceive. The process of finding the cause of barrenness began. Doctors, tests, and hospitals became new factors. Adoption was finally discussed. About that time, Kathy began to experience unusual abdominal pains. Yes, their miracle baby was going to be born. Through the years this mother learned how to be effective in her son's life. One day John, Jr. came home from college and shared his desire to become an international missionary. His testimony of his mother's life was, "She taught me about the world and the lost people and now I want to go to and share the good news that the Messiah has come."

What lessons can be learned from this mother's experience?

- God's faithfulness to His servants is an encouragement to His followers.
- God's timetable is not the same as ours.
- God's ability to fulfill His promises should not be doubted.
- God's plans are often better than anything we can schedule.

D—Directed Prayer

Thank you, God, for providing an example of a special mother.

May 11

Jacob's Little Mother

Parental favoritism hurts a family.
Genesis 25:19-28

A—Advice from the Bible

. . . but Rebekah loved Jacob.
(Gen. 25:28, NIV)

B—Biblical Example

The marriage of Isaac, who was God's chosen vessel, and Rebekah is a beautiful story. The process of finding a wife for him is recorded in Genesis 24. After 20 years of marriage, Rebekah was still without a child. In those days such infertility was looked upon as being punishment from God. Isaac prayed and his wife conceived. The conflict between her twins began before birth. (The Bible records only two accounts of the birth of twins—this passage about Jacob and Esau and in Genesis 38:27-30 Judah and Tamar.) Rebekah was concerned about her difficult pregnancy, but her faith in God was revealed as she prayed. God gave her a brief glimpse of what her boy's lives would mean in the future. He had great plans for them. The boys were born and were completely different from each other. Daddy loved Esau; Mommie loved Jacob. This experience leaves a sad picture of the heartache that parents can easily bring upon themselves and their children by playing favorites.

C—Contemporary Application

Charles and Betty were so excited to learn that their invitro-fertilization had been successful this time. Now they could proceed with plans to begin the longed-for family. The good news about twins being born came on their tenth wedding anniversary. However, the story does not have a happy ending. Charles loves sports and soon recognized that Billy was more athletic than his brother. Betty enjoyed reading to Bobby, who liked the quiet times with his mother. The teen years finally revealed the family favorites. Both boys were good sons, but one was an athlete and the other was a scholar. Family time was divided as each son participated in things they enjoyed. Charles felt that Bobby was a "weakling." Betty accused Billy of being a "bully." Only one solution seemed practical for this alienated family. The father and his favorite would get an apartment; the mother and her favorite would keep the house. Parental favoritism destroyed the unity of this family.

What lessons can be learned from this family unit?

- Showing favoritism toward other family members often provokes jealousy.
- God may sometimes delay the answers to our prayer to test our faith.
- Prayer is important for both parents.
- Family sins grieve God and bring painful consequences into their lives.

D—Directed Prayer

Father, guide parents to love each child equally.

May 12

A Little Scab

Miracles are events that God uses to reveal Himself to people.
Matthew 8:1-4

A—Advice from the Bible

Immediately his leprosy was cleansed.
(Matt. 8:3, NIV)

B—Biblical Example

In Matthew's Gospel we read that Jesus worked miracles. Miracles of healing were used to reveal the nature of Jesus, to show His care for people, and to validate His message. The first miracle in this chapter relates to the healing of a leper. Lepers in biblical days were considered contagious, hopeless and suffered exclusion. The leper, who came to Jesus, had no hope until this miracle. Jesus had finished His Sermon on the Mount when a man smitten by the disease ignored the Jewish law and came out of isolation to seek Jesus. The dreaded skin disease was identified when small scabs began to form on the skin. The Mosaic Law treated leprosy as highly defiling. The infected ones were required to live in isolation. This man appeared to have no doubt of the Savior's power to heal. The Law forbade touching a leper, however, Jesus showed His willingness to help by touching the man. The cleansed one was sent the priest and make the offering required by a recovered leper. This experience of healing shows Jesus' power over disease. Because of Jesus, hope lives eternally.

C—Contemporary Application

The most extraordinary nurse in history was named Florence Nightingale. She was born on May 12, 1820 in Florence, Italy. Her ideas revolutionized hospital methods in England and throughout the world. She served in the first field hospital ever tended by women. Schools were established to train nurses, and she introduced procedures that have been benefiting people ever since. Suffering always challenged her. She even set up a system for extending nursing care to the poor and the criminal underworld in the slums of English cities. She did not think of herself as deeply religious, but on February 7, 1837, when she was scarcely 17-years-old, she felt that God spoke to her, calling her to future "service." From that time on her life was changed. She wrote, "I am 30, the age at which Christ began His mission. Now no more childish things, no more vain things, no more love, no more marriage. Now, Lord, let me only think of thy will."

Jesus demonstrated for us that:
- He has the power to overcome disease.
- His love reaches out to all people in need.
- His concern knows no social or cultural boundaries.
- His kingdom is intended to reach all people and nations.

D—Directed Prayer

Lord, thank You for the supernatural events that are happening today.

May 13

A Little Pure Worship

God expects purity of worship from His people.
Zephaniah 3:9-13

A—Advice from the Bible

Then I will purify the lips of the peoples.
(Zeph. 3:9, NIV)

B—Biblical Example

The study of this minor prophet reveals God's announcement of judgment on Judah and the nations for their treatment of God. Zephaniah called for repentance and hope for the Hebrews and the other nations, if they would purify their worship and their lives. Years of evil leadership and idol worship had prevailed when Josiah came to the throne in 640 B.C. at the age of 8. Changes for Judah occurred when this young king began to seek the Lord. He destroyed the places and altars of idol worship, driving out the priests who led in such worship. Zephaniah received his call from God during the days of this good king. He proclaimed to the people that their worship was totally unacceptable to God. Zephaniah was to prophesy about coming judgment. He described the day of the Lord and called on Judah to repent. The promise from God was that the day would come when the people would again be united in their worship and service to the Lord. God would bring about personal change. Only the humble and submissive would remain to worship and serve Him. These "afflicted and poor people" would trust the Lord. Their worship would be pure. The prophet's message ended in a song of joy. God offered hope to Jerusalem.

C—Contemporary Application

Someone has said that a preacher has two responsibilities: to comfort the afflicted and to afflict the comfortable. Sometimes preachers lean toward the first of those responsibilities and neglect the second. John Newton desired to preach to both kinds of people. This converted slave trader's testimony is sung in some church every week in the hymn "Amazing Grace." He wrote that the point of his preaching was "to break a hard heart and to heal a broken heart." A word of judgment and then a word of comfort are both a part of true prophetic preaching. Because the "afflicting-the-comfortable" side of preaching had been neglected in his day, the prophet Zephaniah focused on that subject. However, his message also included a word of comfort.

Truths to be learned from this minor prophet:
- People are condemned for not seeking the Lord.
- Judgment will come on political and religious leaders for their sinful practices.
- God promised a pure speech for all nations.
- God calls His people to gather before the Lord prior to the day of His anger.

D—Directed Prayer

Father, help me to identify any impure practices in my worship.

May 14

A Little Lower than the Angels

Jesus died for all people.
Hebrews 2:1-18

A—Advice from the Bible

But we do see Jesus, made a little lower than the angels.
(Heb. 2:9)

B—Biblical Example

The Book of Hebrews reminds us that God expects complete loyalty from His people. Chapter 2 involves a person's response to Christ and includes both an exhortation and a warning. The warning is against showing indifference to Christ by people who hear the gospel for the first time. Because Jesus is better than the angels, the readers must pay careful attention to react to the gospel message. God's ultimate will that all creation be in submission to humankind has not yet been accomplished. However, through Jesus, people can become what God intended His creation to be. Jesus voluntarily came to earth, became human, and experienced every temptation, disappointment, opposition, and difficulty. Because of His coming and His suffering, Jesus was crowned with glory and honor. He took on Himself the entire curse of sin for everyone. No person is excluded from God's offer of salvation. Jesus did not become an angel; He became a man. Since He suffered, Jesus can help those who, in the course of life, must also suffer.

C—Contemporary Application

Samuel was a successful farmer in southwestern Oklahoma. His family was active in our small church, but he was not! Every year during revival time, efforts were made to lead Sam to the Lord. His reply was always the same, "I don't need to be a Christian." Prayers were offered on his behalf year after year. Accepting the gospel message and what Jesus had done for all people did not interest this unsaved man. One time in late spring, he almost became a believer. A tractor accident left him with a broken leg. The wheat needed to be harvested. One day as he looked out the door, 10 combines with grain-hauling trucks were in his field. The harvesting continued until dark. Food was brought to the working crews. The witness of these Christian men and women almost persuaded him to learn about Jesus. His family noticed a change in his attitude about going to church and praying. However, Sam remained a lost sinner all of his life.

What are some things Jesus did for us?

- He is the only way to God for all humanity.
- All individuals should respond to His offer of salvation.
- His death provides for the salvation of all who trust Him.
- He is able to free us from the fear of death and the power of Satan.

D—Directed Prayer

Lord, I pray for people who deliberately shut their ears to the gospel's commands, warnings, or invitations.

May 15

Tekoa's Little Prophet

No one can escape the certainty of God's judgment.
(Amos 2:1-16)

A—Advice from the Bible

I will send fire upon the land.
(Amos 2:2)

B—Biblical Example

Amos was a prophet to the people of Israel for a short time. In his past he was a shepherd and keeper of sycamore or fig trees. A man with a simple life—until God called. The Hebrew nation was divided at this time into two parts, the Northern Kingdom and the Southern Kingdom. Amos was sent to preach to the Northern Kingdom. God was going to pronounce judgment against a people guilty of corruption, immoral conduct, and superficial faith. The prophet's strategy for delivering his message was unique. He drew a circle around Israel pointing out the failures of the neighboring nations. Most of the regions had a total disregard for human life. Fire (v. 2) in the Old Testament suggests the desolation of war. The message from God then focused on Israel's horrible sin. This nation had rejected God's revealed will. Judgment was now pronounced by God through Amos. No one would escape God's condemnation. The prophecies of the prophets would come to pass.

C—Contemporary Application

World War II is appropriately called "Hitler's War." The German leader was principally responsible for starting World War II. Germany was so extraordinarily successful in the first two years that this man came close to realizing his aim of establishing control of Europe. But his triumphs would not secure victory in the long run. My only remembrance of this dictator was on the newsreels during a Saturday movie matinee. His appearance always frightened me and I wondered why people would follow his leadership. In mid-January of 1945 he withdrew into his underground bunker in Berlin where he remained until his suicide on April 30, 1945. By that time Soviet soldiers were streaming into Berlin. His guilt for the Holocaust will forever be remembered. He changed German policy from the expulsion to the extermination of a race of people. Upon Germany's defeat, Hitler's suicide, and the Allied occupation of the country in 1945 at the end of World War II, the Nazi Party was banned, and its top leaders were convicted of crimes.

How would you respond if someone like Amos spoke a message like this to you?

- You have sinned again and again.
- You cannot escape God's judgment.
- You disregard the need of the poor and hungry.
- You are disobedient to the teachings of God's Word.

D—Directed Prayer

Father, help me to hear what You are saying through Your messengers.

May 16

A Little Growing Faith

Discover the promises God has for you today.
(Hebrews 11:8-12)

A—Advice from the Bible

He went out, not knowing where he was going.
(Heb. 11:8)

B—Biblical Example

Abraham's choices influenced numerous generations. He responded to God's promises and was willing to change his life in order to follow God. The writer of Hebrews looked back upon this Old Testament patriarch's pilgrimage and determined how those ancient events related to his place in time. Faith is one of the most important words in the Christian's vocabulary. Living by faith means believing God's promises enough to do something about this belief. Think about some of the things experienced by this great man. He left his homeland, gave up his citizenship, and moved to a country where he had no legal rights. Abraham was looking for a city that existed only in the mind of God, the architect and builder. This patriarch lived with the expectation that the promise of God would become reality. The occupation of the Promised Land by other settlers was a minor problem when compared with the other part of God's promise. Abraham would be the father of multitudes, yet Sarah remained childless! We know how this story ended. God was faithful to this huge task of relocating His people.

C—Contemporary Application

Joseph B. Strauss died on May 16, 1938, in Los Angeles, California. This name may not be familiar, but when associated with the Golden Gate Bridge, we see the connection. In the early 1920s, when public opinion in San Francisco was beginning to encourage a bridge over the Golden Gate (the entrance to San Francisco Bay), Strauss submitted a design proposal that was received with cautious enthusiasm. The construction of this bridge, under the supervision of Mr. Strauss, involved many difficulties: rapidly running tides, frequent storms and fogs, and the problem of blasting rock under deep water to plant earthquake-proof foundations that would challenge any builder/designer's faith. Being a man of action, he made wise decisions about building this suspension bridge. His courage and determination made life much easier for the people in Marin County, CA.

Think of some biblical people who could have responded to this Want Ad:
- Seeking: World traveler. Serving attitude required.
- Seeking: Experienced leader with courage and strength.
- Wanted: Someone with faith. Must leave family and friends and relocate.
- Needed: Valiant warrior to deal with conflict. Will train.

D—Directed Prayer

Begin today thanking God for faith to believe what you cannot see.

May 17

A Little Bow of Hope

God's bow of hope is our assurance that He is sovereign and in control.
(Genesis 9:8-17)

A—Advice from the Bible

I will place My bow in the clouds.
(Gen. 9:13)

B—Biblical Example

The biblical account of the great flood is not about the ark or the animals, not even Noah. Nothing is reported of his thoughts or feelings. His family is brought into the ark, but then ignored until the events described in chapter 9. God is presented as the central character. His plans and purposes form the background of the account. God made a covenant with Noah and his family that they would escape the flood. The agreement declared that God would never again destroy all life with a flood. Covenants often involved symbols or signs. This time the sign was a bow in the cloud. As though the faithful word of God were not enough, He sealed His covenant of hope with the rainbow. The sign seems so natural to us since we see rainbows as the sun breaks through at the end of a rain storm, but this might have been the first time any person had witnessed this phenomenon. God's grace is still at work, "not willing that any should perish, but that all men should come to repentance" (2 Peter 3:9).

C—Contemporary Application

Las Vegas, Nevada is a Spanish word for "the meadows." Early Spanish explorers noticed the grassland along spring-fed desert streams. The area was home to the Paiute Indians, who hunted, fished, and gathered roots, piñon nuts, and other foods. The first white settlers were Mormons, who maintained a colony on the site from 1855 to 1857. Fort Baker was built here by the United States Army in 1864 to guard a route to California, and the modern community was established in 1905 with the coming of the railway. However, floods came to this new pioneer area in 1907 and 1910 and washed out all signs of progress. Many people perished in the rapidly flowing water. When Hoover Dam was built in 1931, just 30 miles away on the Colorado River, the floods ceased. The most beautiful rainbow I have ever viewed was across the desert near Las Vegas. I thought about God's patience with human sins and His covenant even today.

When you see a rainbow, remember these words:
- God never forgets His promises.
- We must never doubt God faithfulness.
- God's redemptive plan includes all people.
- God's grace renews us daily.

D—Directed Prayer

Thank You, God, for Your willingness to make a covenant with humankind.

May 18

A Little Needed Encouragement

We can trust God based on His past actions and His fulfilled promises.
(2 Thessalonians 1:2-12)

A—Advice from the Bible

We boast about your perseverance and faith.
(2 Thess. 1:4)

B—Biblical Example

Paul's second letter to the Thessalonians provided the church with needed encouragement. He began by encouraging them to continue their work in spite of difficult circumstances. Trusting God in spite of any circumstance is the mark of a mature believer. The apostle shared with them how thankful he was to God for their growing faith and mutual love. Paul's thankfulness extended to the work of God in the lives of the Thessalonians. These believers had a Christlike love that was increasing all the time. The missionary also was able to boast to other churches about their perseverance and faith. The boasting was in the Lord's achievements at Thessalonica. He referred to their faith in a general sense, but in verse 4 a specific faith is mentioned. They had endured and grown spiritually in the midst of difficulties. Persecutions and trials did not affect their survival. When problems surface, remember that God is not an umpire or referee subject to an argument. What God has planned for Christians and unbelievers is just. We can, however, trust God based on His past actions and His fulfilled promises. To accept God's will, no matter how painful or difficult, is to trust in the wisdom of God.

C—Contemporary Application

Justin Martyr was killed in Rome in about A.D. 167. His last name is a result of the way he died. He was brought before the city ruler who said, "You who think that you possess true insight, answer this question: "If you should be scourged and beheaded, do you believe you will ascent into heaven?" Justin answered, "I believe that if I endure these things I shall have what Jesus promises." He, then, was asked, "Do you suppose then that you will ascend into heaven and receive some reward there?" Justin replied, "I do not suppose it. I know it. I am certain of it." This man had learned how to survive in the midst of extremely difficult circumstances. This same statement could be made about the Thessalonians in their persecutions.

Consider some answers to the following questions:

- Has your church ever suffered any persecution and trials? When?
- Do you think it is okay for a Christian to ask God why?
- Would Paul be able to thank God for the growing faith of your church?
- Do you constantly pray for anyone like Paul did? Who?

D—Directed Prayer

Dear Lord, trusting You allows us to grow spiritually in difficult times. Thank, You.

May 19

Little gods

This commandment gives basic guidance in relating properly to God.
(Exodus 20:1-6)

A—Advice from the Bible

"You shall have no other gods before me."
(Ex. 20:3)

B—Biblical Example

Israel arrived at Mount Sinai three months after departing from Egypt. Immediately Moses went up the mountain to speak with the Lord, and there God offered to enter into the covenant with Israel. The Law was given only to Israel at that time to mark them as God's chosen people. The key to understanding the first commandment is the phrase "no other gods before me." These commands are not merely good advice or tips on etiquette, but what people must do for God. The Egyptians had numerous deities, but God claimed Israel for His own. The Hebrews were to worship Him and Him alone with all their hearts. God would allow no other god to stand or sit beside Him on the throne of their hearts. Since God was greater than all creation, idols carved from wood or stone were unacceptable. The Lord also forbade the Israelites to bow down before any image or to serve any god represented by an image. God's love for His people is rooted in His steadfast and righteous love.

C—Contemporary Application

Our day in Hong Kong was planned to include a visit to the Temple of a Thousand Buddhas. The temple was located on a beautiful hillside overlooking the city. Every wall was covered with these idols, except for a huge 274,428 pound, manmade statue, sitting inn the middle of the room. A question to myself was, "Why would anyone worship this ugly image?" I decided to read some material about Buddha and found that he was born near Nepal on the Indian border. The historical details of the Buddha's life are hard to establish. According to tradition, the Buddha began his search for enlightenment at the age of 29. After a lifetime of missionary activity, the Buddha died in Kusinagara, Nepal, as a result of eating contaminated food. He was 80 years old and his body was cremated. Today, Buddhism is a major world religion centered in India and based on the teachings of Siddhartha Gautama, who is known as the Buddha, or Enlightened One.

Truths about the Commandments:

- A right relationship with God is the foundation of all other relationships.
- God's redemptive actions gave Him the right to set His covenant requirements.
- Even good things can become gods.
- Obeying the commandments comes from a living, active, faith in God.

D—Directed Prayer

Lord, I pray for wisdom to know the difference between good things and gods.

May 20

Little Roots

Christians experience a new life through faith in Jesus Christ.
(Colossians 2:6-15)

A—Advice from the Bible

Continue to live in him, rooted and built up in him.
(Col. 2:6)

B—Biblical Example

Paul had never visited Colosse or the church established in that city. Timothy and Epaphras were among the founders of the church. Now in Roman captivity, the apostle received word that false teachers were working among the believers. This epistle was written to warn the church about those false doctrines and the urgency of deepening their loyalty to Christ. The main message of the letter is a challenge to demonstrate their profession of faith. They were to live in vital union with Christ. The lesson is presented that as a person walks, they are on their way to a destination. Terms were used to describe the Christian's walk with the Lord. One illustration is "rooted." This word is an agricultural metaphor that suggests a once-for-all experience. Believers are permanently fixed in Him. This step was the beginning and implies continuous development. A great tree has massive roots, which provide nourishment and support. The Colossian Christians needed to trust in the care of the true and living God.

C—Contemporary Application

One thing you can count on in January is seed catalogs. The companies know that people are bored with cold weather and ready to think about seed planning and spring time. Every year, we order beautiful veggies and fruits for our garden. Then in May, we plant and wait. Somehow the produce never looks as good as the catalog cover, but the taste is what matters. Our earliest vegetable is asparagus. This plant is so deceiving. The roots are deep and thick; then a spear comes from the ground. Next, very fine branches grow to feed the roots. What an amazing process! The best part of this process is the harvesting and eating of the veggie. Deep roots make this garden product possible. Deep roots continue to grow year after year, even when covered with ice and snow. God indeed has a plan for roots in His creation. Therefore, I want my life to be rooted in Him, so that no matter what happens to me, I will survive, because I am nourished by His love.

We demonstrate our new life in Christ by:
- Growing in our relationship with Him.
- Learning more about Him.
- Expressing gratitude for our blessings.
- Rejecting false ideas and teachings.

D—Directed Prayer

Father, help me to maintain a strong root system.

My Little Light

Don't stumble in the darkness of the world.
(John 1:1-14)

A—Advice from the Bible

The true Light gives light to every person.
(John 1:9)

B—Biblical Example

The opening verses of this chapter introduce Jesus as "the Word." His uniqueness is described first. He has lived for all eternity. Before the Lord came, people had a limited understanding of what God was like. Now, through Jesus, God has been revealed to the world. Many times in the Gospel of John the word "life" refers to the spiritual realm. Jesus brings spiritual life to a person. He redeems us from sin and gives us life in its fullest meaning. "Darkness" symbolizes evil in our world. That darkness is unbelief and the sin of the human race. Sin darkens the lives of many believers. Most places that practice evil do so in the dark. Walk past a bar or nightclub and you will discover that very little light shines in that place. The world was like that at one time. Then, someone or something had to light the way to righteousness. Experimenting with the lights of false teachers and doctrines always ends up in darkness. Only Christ can provide the eternal life and light we need in a difficult world. He can point the way so that we do not make a wreck of our lives.

C—Contemporary Application

Many people will be planning summer vacations during this month. A motel chain once had a series of radio/TV commercials with the reassuring word, "We'll leave the light on for you." What a relief to see the lights of a place to rest at the end of a long traveling day. When I was young, my mother would sometimes say, "I'll leave the light on for you." Sure enough the porch light was always shining in the darkness. This light seemed to say, "This is where you belong. Someone loves you here. You are home." In the same way, our lives and words can be beams of warm light piercing the cold darkness of this world. Perhaps a member of your family is still in the dark. During your vacation, use this opportunity to reflect the love of Jesus in your life. Be a witness about the true Light of the world to individuals who are losing their way because of personal sins.

Light and darkness are recurring themes in John's Gospel. Read also:
- John 8:12.
- 1 John 1:5.
- John 3:16-19.
- John 12:35-36.

D—Directed Prayer

Thank You, Lord, that Your coming was the dawning of a new day.

May 24

A Little Cleft in the Rock

God is not limited to a personal body like a human.
(Exodus 33:19-23)

A—Advice from the Bible

I will put you in a cleft in the rock.
(33:22)

B—Biblical Example

Moses prayed and God promised His continued presence with Israel. What events led to this point in Moses' life? He came down from the mountain a second time and broke the sacred tablets, because of the sins of the Israelites. Next, God rejected Moses' plea and promised judgment in the form of a plague. Now, this leader wanted God to go up in their midst into Canaan. The Lord, however, refused, but promised to send an angel with the people. Moses put a tent outside the camp so that the Israelites would personally seek God's face in order to be forgiven and restored. Encouraged by God's promise of continued presence, Moses asked God for additional assurance and to show him His glory, that is, His total self without any reservations. God refused, but did promise him rest. Moses was assured that the holiness of God was such that no one could really see Him and live. Humankind can only see where God has been. The loving God explained what He would do in response to Moses' request. He would pass before him in a space in the rock and let His servant know His name, His mercy, and compassion. God's great hand would shield Moses as God Himself passed by.

C—Contemporary Application

Augustus Montague Toplady was born in 1740 in England. He became interested in the Lord at age 11. These words were later found on a card he had written to himself: "I praise God I can remember no dreadful crime; to the Lord be the glory." A year later he was preaching sermons and began writing hymns. Father Toplady later became an Anglican priest. He wrote an article about God's forgiveness that ended with these words:

Rock of Ages, cleft for me,
Let me hide myself in Thee;

This poem has been called the best known, best loved, and most widely used hymn in the English language.

Humans can only see where God has been:

- In the hospital room of a sick child.
- In the beauty of the mountains and oceans.
- In the comfort of a caring friend.
- In the birth of babies and animals.

D—Directed Prayer

Father, I can see where You have been and I am reassured.

May 25

A Little Mutual Submission

The Christian home is the best place to begin submitting to each other.
Ephesians 5:21-33

A—Advice from the Bible

Submit to one another out of reverence for Christ.
(Eph. 5:21)

B—Biblical Example

A Christian home is almost on the world's endangered list. The idea of submitting to one another in the marriage relationship is not always acceptable to a man and woman. The thought behind submission is to abandon one's rights to another. The role of the wife is introduced first. For the home to have unity, order and leadership must be practiced. The Lord is the one who assigned the husband the task of being the head of the family. A woman will submit to her husband when she fully understands that her husband cares about her needs and her welfare. His actions are patterned after the sacrificial interest of Christ for His church. An interesting observation about these verses is that Paul wrote three verses about the wife's responsibilities and nine verses on the husband's tasks. A truly loving husband does not use his wife for his own self-gratification. The greatest prize to the husband is that he loves his wife as Christ loved the church. He also desires that she become all that God has created her to be. Mutual submission will make both partners happy.

C—Contemporary Application

A pet-peeve of mine is to see a sign that reads, "Home for Sale." Of course, I know what the realtor means, but a house doesn't make a home. Someone felt sorry for a youth from a military family because they moved so many times. The boy replied, "Oh, we have a home—we just don't have a house to put it in!" American families are one the move and this affects our culture. Once upon a time families stayed rooted to their hometown and state. Circumstances, such as job relocations, military assignments, and vocation changes have altered that policy. Families are on the move today, but they can still provide their children with love and a sense of security even though they don't put down roots like their grandparents once did. Local churches often benefit from this mobile family lifestyle. New people moving into their area bring fresh, new ideas for ministry.

The love of a husband and wife is *agape* love. This means:

- Sacrificing love.
- Sanctifying love.
- Caring love.
- Lasting love.

D—Directed Prayer

Lord, I pray for Your strength and guidance in building a Christian home.

May 26

Little Strengthened Hearts

God fulfills His purposes and keeps His promises
Ezra 1:1-11

A—Advice from the Bible

The LORD moved the heart of Cyrus.
(Num. 1:1)

B—Biblical Example

God is at work in history. The proclamation of Cyrus was made before the return of the exiles from Babylon and provided good publicity for the treatment of captives. This Persian ruler was an instrument in the hands of the Lord God concerning the return of the people of Judah and the restoration of the Temple. During the 70 year exile, the people of Jerusalem and Judah were without a place to worship. The yearning was strong for the return of Temple worship. This homecoming from Babylon parallels the Exodus from Egypt when the liberated Hebrews took most of the Egyptian riches for a future time. The people believed God's promises concerning the rebuilding of the Temple. To insure that the best work was done on the temple objects, Cyrus even sent his most talented men to work on the endeavor. All the priceless vessels were adorned for the Temple. The skills of these artisans returned all the treasures into their former splendor. The fact that God is the sovereign power, who controls the world, is clearly seen in the historical moment.

C—Contemporary Application

God prepares all kinds of people to be leaders in history. At some point in time, their heart was stirred by God and desires were uncovered that would affect the future. For example: Jean Henri Dunant (1828-1910), was a Swiss philanthropist and founder of the Red Cross. He was born in Geneva. Dunant was appalled by the conditions of the wounded he saw near the battlefield during the Franco-Prussian War. He suggested that neutral organizations be established to aid wounded soldiers in time of war. In 1863 an international conference was held in Geneva, and the Geneva Convention of 1864 established the permanent International Red Cross. In 1901 Dunant shared the very first Nobel Peace Prize. These two historical events continue to work in our world. Recent television reports focus on the International Red Cross. Rescue efforts usually succeed when God is in charge of our victories as well as our defeats.

Use words that describe how God is working to strengthen our world.

- He
- He
- He
- He

D—Directed Prayer

Lord, thank You for stirring my heart and hands.

A Little Quote from Moses

We need to tell everyone about Someone who can save anyone
Romans 10:5-17

A—Advice from the Bible

Moses describes in this way the righteousness that is by the Law.
(Rom 10:5)

B—Biblical Example

Paul was identified as the apostle to the Gentiles, however, he never gave up concern for his own people, the Jews. He continued focusing on the theme of righteousness. The nation of Israel should have eagerly awaited the arrival of their Messiah. Old Testament prophecies were used to prepare the nation, but when Jesus Christ came, they rejected Him. Instead of letting the Law bring them to Christ, they worshiped their Law and rejected their Savior. Moses' quote was used to prove that they did not even understand their own Law. Several reasons are given for why Israel rejected their Messiah. The nation did not feel a need for personal, spiritual salvation. Even Paul at one time considered Jesus Christ an imposter. Some of the Jewish leaders were trying to gain righteousness by something they could do. Paul called this interpretation of the Word misguided and unnecessary. The fact that "there is no difference" between people was especially hard for a Jew to accept. The main emphasis is that all persons, rich or poor, high or low, Jews or Gentiles, are in need of a Savior.

C—Contemporary Application

The local Bible study class was planning a three-month outreach emphasis. One night was spent in presenting personal testimonies. This opportunity was a first time challenge for some of the newer Christians and so was overcoming fear. Ralph was excited about this prospect and requested the pastor as his partner. Packets had been prepared and distributed to interested individuals. The pastor had prayed that Ralph would have a good experience, but he looked up and saw the "community troublemaker." She came up to Ralph and said, "Sir, you must not know who I am." Ralph looked her in the face and said, "A judgment day is coming and it will not make any difference who you are." The woman quickly left the scene and Ralph said, "Now what do I do!" Paul gave a spiritual understanding that the gospel is available and accessible to all people.

Consider these four missions imperatives from this passage:

- Sending missionaries is no substitute for your own witness.
- Christians have the joy and responsibility of sending missionaries.
- We are to go and share Christ as far as we can.
- Jesus' authority is not limited racially.

D—Directed Prayer

Father, I thank You for giving all people salvation who trust in You.

May 28

The Little Finished Wall

Many distractions keep us from doing the Lord's work.
Nehemiah 6:1-16

A—Advice from the Bible

"I had rebuilt the wall."
(Neh. 6:1)

B—Biblical Example

The wall of Jerusalem was finished because the man in charge, by personal courage and trust in God, resisted all enemy efforts to distract him from his task. Nehemiah was subjected as a leader to threats and pressures. An alliance of opposition to the building was formed. Several of their attempts to get Nehemiah away from the city failed. This determined builder refused to be entrapped by the powers of evil. Four different times pressure was placed on him and four times he refused to be distracted from his purpose. The enemy then resorted to a rumor that Nehemiah and his companions were planning a revolt against Persia. Of course the rumors were totally false. Instead of reducing him to fear, the opposition and intrigue only served to strengthen his hand and to cause him to rely more heavily on the help of God. The wall was completed in 52 days. However, they were using materials from the previously destroyed wall. They were rebuilding the existing walls. Nehemiah had refused to be stopped from his well-organized plan and the power of Israel's God once more revealed His ability to aid His people.

C—Contemporary Application

Nehemiah was one of the most successful men in the Old Testament. He set a goal to rebuild the walls of Jerusalem and he carried through until the job was done.

- Glen signed up to help rebuild the playground at church. All week he had considered what tools to bring for this project. However, a Saturday morning phone call distracted him and a game of golf became his priority.
- Sarah invited a new member of her Bible class to lunch on Tuesday. She made the reservations but a distraction changed her plans. Her mother came by for an unannounced visit. Sarah's good intentions never came to pass.
- The boss decided to give each employee and extra day of vacation. Families made plans for the beach or some theme park. Later, the boss changed his mind!

How can you stay focused on the things that are most important to you?

- Prioritize the every day events of your life.
- Eliminate "things" that prevent you from completing your tasks.
- Avoid people who "drop by" and claim valuable time.
- Rely on God's promises when facing demanding challenges.

D—Directed Prayer

Lord, thank You that victory over distractions is possible.

A Little Disagreement

God works even through conflicts and disagreements.
Acts 15:36-41

A—Advice from the Bible

They had a sharp disagreement.
(Acts 15:39)

B—Biblical Example

In the days following the Jerusalem Council, Paul and Barnabas continued to teach and preach in Antioch. However Paul must have wondered about the new believers in those cities where he and Barnabas had ministered. These men agreed it would be good to revisit these churches established on their first missionary journey and see how they were doing. Barnabas suggested they take John Mark again, but Paul refused because of their first experience with him, when Mark failed to endure the rigors of the tour. It was an unfortunate experience and caused a separation between these two men that lasted for many years. They resolved the difficulty by going their separate ways. Barnabas and Mark went to Cyprus. Paul and Silas went to visit the new churches. Later Paul came to appreciate John Mark and referred to Barnabas as his missionary partner. God worked through this crisis for His good. Now, instead of work being done in one area of the world, the good news was spread to Europe. Years ago a motto was used in Sunday school classes called, "To multiply, we must divide." Old classes were divided and new units were started and Bible study attendance increased.

C—Contemporary Application

Disagreements still exist in the Appalachian Mountains of Tennessee. Some of these feuds began over a hundred years ago. Usually the fathers of the groups would disagree over some issue and peace was never restored. Two such men were named Jacob and Thomas. They inherited their hatred for the people who lived on the other side of the mountain. The problem began over land boundaries, then over charges of animal rustling. Occasionally some of the young people would fall in love with a forbidden clan member and shootings would cause further hate. One day a home missionary moved into the "holler" and sought to begin a church. The work of the Holy Spirit changed the hearts of both of the clan families and several years later a little mountain church was established.

What causes disagreements among Christian people?
- Lack of good communication.
- Attitudes that are opposite in handling a situation.
- Strong-willed individuals with too much pride.
- Leaving God out of the conflicts.

D—Directed Prayer

Disagreements hurt Your work. Forgive us, Lord.

May 30

Little Clumps of Clay

The Potter of the Universe continues to reshape broken lives.
Jeremiah 18:1-12

A—Advice from the Bible

Like clay in the hands of the potter.
(Jer. 18:6)

B—Biblical Example

Jeremiah labored for the Lord for 40 years, during the darkest, most difficult, and most dangerous period in the history of Judah. Several influences helped prepare him for his life work. He was blessed with a godly Hebrew home and the preaching of the great prophets of his time such as Hosea. The truth that Jeremiah communicated through his writing was obvious for anyone to understand.God would give Judah a second opportunity. As this prophet watched a potter at work on his wheel, he was given divine insight into the ways of God with men. Several lessons were learned by this man of God. The potter had a purpose for the clay. Before a person is conceived, God has a plan. No good potter would design a poor vessel. When the clay is flawed, the artisan is not to be blamed. Some stubborn spots often develop. However, the potter does not immediately destroy or discard the clay. He forms another vessel. God's first plan for us may not be the same, but He will make us into a useful container.

C—Contemporary Application

The Lincoln Memorial located in Potomac Park, Washington, D.C., honors Abraham Lincoln, the 16th president of the United States. When Mr. Henry Bacon was selected as the architect, he chose marble, granite, and limestone for the structure. Certain flaws were present in the materials, but the builder knew how to make the stones usable. Begun on February 12, 1914, the memorial was dedicated on May 30, 1922. The famous white marble statue of Lincoln inspired me the most on our visit to Washington. Daniel French had created a masterpiece of Mr. Lincoln. He started the project with clay! As I stood by this beautiful work of art, I was reminded about God, the Potter, and how He has a plan for each person. Wouldn't it be great if a person could see the finished statute of their life as God intended it to be? Would any flaws show? Would we feel honored by God's workmanship in our life?

God is a God of second opportunities when a person has:

- Neglected prayer and Bible study.
- Created problems in family life.
- Disobeyed God's ideals for living a Christian lifestyle.
- Departed from the fellowship of other believers.

D—Directed Prayer

Lord, thank You for Your patience in reshaping broken lives.

May 31

Little Letters of Christ

The more closely we follow Christ the more we will be like Him.
2 Corinthians 3:1-18

A—Advice from the Bible

You show that you are a letter from Christ.
(2 Cor. 3:3)

B—Biblical Example

Chapter 3 begins with Paul describing the work of the Spirit in a Christian's life. Once again false teachers had infiltrated the church in Corinth and the apostle again stressed the work of the Holy Spirit to prove how God was accomplishing all things. Traveling preachers and teachers often carried letters of recommendation to insure they would be received by the believers. Paul followed this practice, but because he founded the church in Corinth, he felt that no letter was needed to prove his authenticity as an apostle. Their salvation proved beyond doubt the divine source of his ministry. The church was the recipient of Paul's love and devotion. The believers were a letter *known and read by all men*. He owed the evangelistic success he experienced at Corinth and elsewhere to God. The false teachers at Corinth had arrogantly appointed themselves as ministers. In contrast, Paul humbly described himself as appointed by Christ to serve.

C—Contemporary Application

The need for daily guidance is a major concern of a serious believer and many great hymns have been written about the subject. During the 18th century, a great revival movement started in Wales. A 24-year-old Welsh preacher, Howell Harris, stirred the land with his evangelistic preaching. Many lives were transformed during this Holy Spirit-led revival and became letters of recommendation for Christ. William Williams was 20-years-old, and preparing to become a medical doctor. The Holy Spirit challenged him through Evangelist Harris. For the next 43 years William traveled on horseback preaching and singing the gospel. He became known as the "sweet singer of Wales." One of my favorite Williams' hymns is, *Guide me, O Thou great Jehovah, pilgrim thru this barren land; I am weak, but Thou art mighty—Hold me with Thy pow'rful hand. Bread of Heaven feed me till I want no more.* The congregation sang these great words during the funeral of Princess Diana of Wales.

We give evidence that our lives are letters of recommendation for Christ by:

- Relying on God's Spirit in ministry.
- Taking the message of Christ to spiritually needy people.
- Praising God for His work of setting us free from bondage to sin and death.
- Being transformed by the Spirit into the image of Jesus Christ.

D—Directed Prayer

Lord, I pray that people will know and follow the guidance of the Holy Spirit.

June 1

A Little Praise Hymn

The greatness of God is seen in His creation.
Psalm 8:1-4

A—Advice from the Bible

O LORD, our Lord, how majestic you your name in all the earth!
(Psalm 8:1, NIV)

B—Biblical Example

Psalm 8 reflects the thoughts of someone who loved the outdoors. This person is identified in the superscription as David. He didn't know all about the solar facts, but he still marveled as he gazed at the sky. He was worshipping in the world God had created. No complaints or requests are mentioned in these verses. The total focus is on God and His mighty works.

Perhaps David, the shepherd boy, had marveled at the thousands of stars as he gazed into the clear Judean night sky. This hymn of praise was probably a result of those days out on the hillside near Bethlehem. Two words are used to address God. The translation means "Jehovah our Lord" (*Adonai*). The expressions from the heart of this worshiper are so sincere. The thought must have entered his mind as to why God would choose such insignificant creatures as humans to be the object of His love. The prophet Isaiah shared similar thoughts from God in his writings, "*I have put my words in your mouth and covered you with the shadow of my hand—I who set the heavens in place, who laid the foundations of the earth, and who say to Zion, 'You are my people'*" (Isa. 51:16 NIV).

C—Contemporary Application

A poem was written in 1885 called "O Mighty God." Carl Boberg, a 26-year-old Swedish minister published the words, but they were soon forgotten. Several years later, the poet heard his words being sung to a familiar Swedish melody. An English missionary heard the hymn sung in Russian and was so inspired by the words that Stuart Hine did his own arrangement adding a few verses. Still later, Dr. J. Edwin Orr heard "How Great Thou Art" being sung in India. The song was brought back to the United States, published, and copyrighted. During the 1954 Billy Graham Crusade in London, George Beverly Shea was given a leaflet containing the hymn and the rest is history.

This **little** praise hymn teaches us that:
- All of God's creation bears testimony to God and calls forth praise and worship.
- The appropriate response to God's power and majesty is worship.
- We need to create a personal praise hymn to God.
- God involves Himself intimately with every stage of human life, from infants to senior adults.

D—Directed Prayer

Help me today, Lord, to rediscover Your greatness in this beautiful world.

June 2

Jonah's Little Temper Tantrum

Show compassion for people who are different from you.
Jonah 3—4

A—Advice from the Bible

But Jonah was greatly displeased and became angry.
(Jonah 4:1, NIV)

B—Biblical Example

Jonah served as a reluctant prophet to Israel and Assyria from 793-753 B.C. God had given this man a mission to accomplish. His challenge was to preach to the great Assyrian city of Nineveh. However, Jonah hated the idea of going to these heathen people. He did not want them to receive God's mercy. Can you imagine a spokesperson of God not wanting to warn lost people to repent before judgment came?

This minor-prophet of the Old Testament made a choice. He decided to run from God and the opposite direction led to the cities of Tarshish and Joppa. The familiar experience of Jonah and the great fish have been taught since early childhood. However, God gave Jonah a second chance. The prophet obeyed God this time and went to Nineveh. A great revival occurred among these pagan people. Even the king became involved in the repentance event. Jonah would surely celebrate the compassion God had shown these Gentiles. Wrong! This man-on-mission from God had a temper fit!

C—Contemporary Application

Anger is included in the Seven Deadly Sins. This concept is not biblical, but comes from the writings of great theologians. These religious thinkers did not list these sins because of their severity, but the sins inevitably became the source of other sins.

Suppose God called you to show compassion to people you do not particularly like. Complete the following statements regarding ways you might respond to God's assignment:

1. A time when I tried to run from God's presence and calling was when I _____ _____.
2. A time when I became angry with God because of the way something turned out was__ _____.
3. I am like Jonah in that I did not show compassion when_____ _____.

Four basic truths about anger from New Testament teachings are:

- We should realize that anger demonstrates the same negative attitude as murder.
- We should know that hating people is inconsistent with loving God.
- We should treat others well, even when they mistreat us.
- We should love and pray for our enemies.

D—Directed Prayer

Lord, help me to become reconciled quickly with my enemies.

June 3

A Little Gold Ring

People come in all sizes, colors, and conditions.
James 2:1-13

A—Advice from the Bible

Suppose a man comes into your meeting wearing a gold ring . . .
(James 2:2, HCSB)

B—Biblical Example

The Letter of James is considered a how-to book on Christian living. The writer was the leader in the Jerusalem church. At this time, the Jewish Christians had been scattered around the Mediterranean world because of persecution. These believers needed help in living their faith in a hostile environment. James wanted his readers to not only hear the truth but to do what they had learned. Chapter 2 gets right to the subject of honoring people of wealth or high positions in the community. Showing partiality to the rich was wrong. The genuineness of personal faith is demonstrated by our good actions to all people. James illustrates his concern using an assembly or synagogue of believers at a meeting. These followers of Christ gathered to read the law, recite the Scriptures, and secure some ruling on the issues of the day. The rich man in this experience wore a gold ring, indicating he was of political rank or a Roman nobleman. The actions of honoring this guest are compared to the poorly dressed individual who was overlooked by the worshippers. In today's language, James might have said, "Shame on you."

C—Contemporary Application

The first time I saw her picture I thought, "How can this frail woman make such a difference in this world?" The year was 1979 and Mother Teresa had just been honored with the Nobel Peace Prize. Books and television began to reveal her background. Mother Teresa of Calcutta (1910-1997) was a Roman Catholic nun. The presence of the sick and dying on the Calcutta streets grieved her. A home for the dying and destitute was opened in 1952. This work spread to five continents. A unique thing about her ministry was the lack of favoritism among people whether in palaces, governments, or homes of the wealthy. Her love for all people remained the same. One picture that touched my heart was Mother Teresa holding a sick baby in her arms. Standing next to this scene was a well-dressed woman with tears streaming down her face. Love was working in the hearts of both people. You are to love all persons without favoritism.

Consider these hindrances:

- The problem of feelings or attitudes regarding getting along with others.
- The problem of pride and jealousy.
- The problem of showing partiality toward those who have possessions.
- The problem of the "in-crowd" and the "outsiders."

D—Directed Prayer

Thank You, Lord, for teaching me how to treat all persons in a Christ-like manner.

June 4

The Poor Little Rich Man

We always want more than we have.
Ecclesiastes 5:8-12

A—Advice from the Bible

Whoever loves money never has enough . . .
(Ecc. 5:10, NIV)

B—Biblical Example

The personal name of the author of Ecclesiastes is not revealed, but he is identified as "the son of David, king of Jerusalem." Solomon is considered to be that son. A good subtitle for the book could be "The Things That Won't Work." Solomon speaks from personal experiences about living for riches and how he ended in disappointment. He explains that money will not satisfy, for money does not leave you enjoying life. From experience, he points out that a rich person will attract a crowd of "clingers" who will gather round you to spend your money. These people will mean nothing to you except expense. Another disadvantage to being rich is worry and sleepless nights. Questions like, "How much money do I need to make to keep all my possessions?" cause stress and prevents living a peaceful life. He continues his thoughts by pointing out that you cannot take anything away with you when you die. Companionship, popularity, and fame will not bring lasting happiness. Solomon's final answer to what really matters was knowing the living God and believing that He controls what comes into your life.

C—Contemporary Application

Rick and Becky were high school sweethearts. His poverty-level background and her wealthy background seemed incompatible, however, their relationship continued to last. Rick worked hard after school and promised himself that someday he would be rich. A benefactor provided a college scholarship for him. He continued to work and save money until at last, he could support Becky as his wife. Their married years began with many material comforts. He continued to work harder and became the president of his company. Nothing seemed to stop their financial progress. Nothing, that is, except quality time with his family. Becky and the children seemed to live one life and he worked at another. Their 25th wedding anniversary came and the marriage seemed to go. One night Rick finally sought guidance from God. He called a family counsel meeting. Decisions were made to reunite the family. The quality of life is not measured in material terms.

Consider these life-lessons this family learned:

- God is in charge of life, so let Him be in charge of your riches.
- We never learn to enjoy anything by complaining.
- God sees all of life from beginning to end.
- God never plays games with us.

D—Directed Prayer

God, help me to know the Author of true values.

June 5

A Little Loneliness

When you feel lonely, meditate on God's love.
Psalm 42:1-11

A—Advice from the Bible

Why are you so downcast, O my soul?
(Ps. 42:5, NIV)

B—Biblical Example

The word "lonely" means a deeply-felt emotion that comes from sorrow or regret. The psalmist was experiencing such a time in his life. Being an exile away from Jerusalem and among ungodly, hostile people caused him to long for the place of God's dwelling. He describes his feelings as an intense thirst and a yearning for communion with God. Loneliness came because he did not feel a sense of God's nearness. The writer was probably surrounded by dead and lifeless idols. He longed for the living God. The depths of his despair are expressed by "tears." Former pleasant days were remembered, when he was involved in the procession to the house of God. Verse 5 reveals a personal seeking to find the resources for encouragement. He continues to hope for a refreshing experience of God's loving kindness. A prayer of thanksgiving to God indicates his persistent desire to seek God's favor and proceed on his spiritual journey.

C—Contemporary Application

Three times in my life can be expressed as lonely occasions:
- My daddy's death, a personal illness, and an airport.

Daddy died suddenly at the age of 42. I was 14-years-old and a baby Christian. The traditional funeral service was held, the cemetery parade was over, and now people filled the house, seeking to comfort and feed us. Everyone finally departed and Mother and I sat alone at the kitchen table. I have never experienced such loneliness in all my life. We did not know how to seek comfort from God.

In my 30's, serious surgery was required. One night, I woke from the blur of medication and a sense of loneliness swept over me. The hospital room seemed like a threat. However, at this time, I was a growing Christian and began to think on Him.

I sat in an airport late one night in a small city. A snowstorm had canceled all flights home. Though surrounded by people, I felt loneliness overcome me, but this time I took out my Bible and began to read Psalm 42. God's presence was comforting to me.

Sorrow and the expression of sorrow is a fact of life, so what can you do?

- Crying may help.
- Remembering former times of happiness may help.
- Relying on patience and hope may help.
- Praying may help.

D—Directed Prayer

Lord, help me to seek You during times of loneliness.

June 6

Little Doves and Dealers

Expose and confront evil.
Mark 11:15-18

A—Advice from the Bible

He began to throw out those buying and selling in the temple.
(Mark 11:15, HCSB)

B—Biblical Example

Jesus confronted evil wherever He was. His confrontations certainly did not please the individuals who were sinning. Many enemies were formed by the Lord's unyielding stance against deliberate wrongdoing. His righteous actions provoked the people against Christ to seek ways to punish Him. The scribes, chief priests, and Pharisees of Jerusalem were the main groups who appointed themselves as self-righteous tormentors. The trip to the Temple was a repeat visit from the day before. Jesus inspected the transactions and noted the secular atmosphere in which the workings of God's house were conducted. The rich were exploiting the poor. The court of the Gentiles (outer area) was a disgusting sight. Merchants sold the sacrificial animals and oils at unbelievable prices. A dove bought for sacrifice outside the Temple might cost one day's pay. A fee was charged for a special coin needed by the worshipers. Money passed from hand to hand. Jesus boldly confronted these evil circumstances. The exclusiveness against the Gentiles was unacceptable. Action was taken to cleanse the Temple and restore godly behavior among the Jews.

C—Contemporary Application

My husband and I were pastoring a church in a small southwestern Oklahoma town when legalized gambling became an issue. Immediate actions were planned by a group of interdenominational Christians. The media became involved and names of people against gambling were printed. Mean things began happening after that news release. One night a bullet struck the side of our parsonage. Some pastors' tires were sliced with knives; windows were broken out of churches; and anonymous letters were mailed to the anti-gambling coalition. The citizens of this small country town did not like what was happening to their Christian friends. These acts of vandalism worked against the enemy trying to bring gambling to the county. On election day, special protection was provided by the state law enforcement agencies. The votes were counted and the right prevailed!

Some lessons learned from Jesus' anger at the temple carnival are:

- Do not take advantage of poor people who want to worship God.
- Do not let the church become a money-making venture.
- Do not let the place of prayer be defiled.
- Do not be afraid to confront evil.

D—Directed Prayer

Lord, help me to stand up and speak out against any form of evil.

June 7

A Little Request for a King

Don't think you always know what is best.
1 Samuel 8:1-9

A—Advice from the Bible

Now appoint a king to lead us . . .
(1 Sam. 8:5, NIV)

B—Biblical Example

The dark years of the Judges was coming to an end and God brightened the scene with the arrival of Samuel. He was the link between the days of anarchy and the monarchy. God called this prophet to service during the young boy's days with Eli, the priest. This distinguished man led the nation in repentance and cleansing. However, the elders of Israel desired a change in government. Samuel's age, his dishonest sons, and the governments of other nations was the reason for their request. These facts provided the elders of Israel an excuse to demand a king. From the political standpoint, the desire for a king was a reasonable one. Disunity and jealousy between the tribes caused a lack of stability and the elders took action. Samuel was upset by their demand. He knew the people would easily forsake the living God. However, this aged leader did not fight back, but prayed. God heard his prayers and told him to do what the people wanted. The Lord's answer helped Samuel put the matter in the right perspective. Israel had forsaken the Lord to serve other gods; now the leaders were forsaking the Lord to have a king. God said, "Make them a king." So the issue was settled and the people got what they wanted.

C—Contemporary Application

Life is a series of changes. Consider some of these examples:
- Fred and Julia had just built a new house. Then the company president offered Fred a big promotion on condition that his family relocate to another city.
- Janet wants to complete her college education at the state university, but her financial situation is not adequate. A community college must be chosen.
- Single-by-choice Jack has met a young woman at his club who has two small children. Their future plans will require many changes.
- Velma cannot live alone anymore. Her children must decide on an assisted care facility for her near their home. Their mother is very unhappy with the choice the family has made about her future.

What are some principles of changes that will help a growing Christian?

- In times of change, do not yield to fear.
- In times of change, listen for God's instruction.
- In times of change, examine new ideas and their strengths and consequences.
- In times of change, determine to cooperate with God's plans.

D—Directed Prayer

Lord, guide me to follow Your will as I face personal changes in the days ahead.

June 8

A Little Beatitude

Sure and lasting happiness can be found only in fellowship with God.
Psalm 1:1-6

A—Advice from the Bible

Blessed is the man . . .
(Ps.1:6, NIV)

B—Biblical Example

Psalm 1 contrasts the way of the righteous person with the way of the wicked person. To be righteous is to be in right relationship with God. This psalm offers helpful insight for living. Therefore, some teachers refer to these words as the "wisdom psalm." Verse 1 begins with the word "blessed" and is sometimes called a beatitude. The psalmist emphasized the happiness and blessedness of the person who orders his life according to God's Word. That individual demonstrates wisdom and the result is blessing and joy. The way of the righteous person results from faithful obedience to God's Word. A righteous person does not pay attention to the advice of evil people as his guide for living. He does not stand with people who are habitually immoral. He does not sit in the presence of people who despise what is holy and ridicule obedience to God. The righteous person is like a tree planted beside a stream of water and is deeply rooted in God's truth and constantly nourished by God's living water. He is always fruitful. The righteous person will prosper in his attempts to be a blessing to God. A warning is given concerning the two ways to travel in life. Every person must choose a way to go.

C—Contemporary Application

Two identical apple trees grow in our orchard. Both were planted several years ago and look about the same. However, one tree produced fruit and the other tree did nothing. The good tree has lush green leaves; the bad tree had leaves that curled up and dropped off early in the summer. The reason for the difference became evident during a spring wind storm. The good tree survived and the bad tree was uprooted and lay on the ground. The roots made the difference. Shallow roots depend on uncertain rains. Perhaps underground rocks prevented the roots from growing. Certainly some obstacle got in the way. Sometimes people are like trees. Their roots go deep into the underground streams of God's Word. Other people live shallow lives occasionally reading a devotional. Decide that you want to produce abundant spiritual fruit.

The following truths support this beatitude:
- Happy is the person who reads God's Word daily.
- Happy is the person who is a blessing to others.
- Happy is the person who determines righteousness by God's standards.
- Happy is the person who finds guidance and direction from God's Word.

D—Directed Prayer

Dear God, please help me see the importance of living a righteous life.

June 9

A Little R and R

Learn to balance Christian service, prayer, and rest.
Mark 6:30-33

A—Advice from the Bible

"Come away by yourselves to a remote place and rest a little."
(Mark 6:31, HCSB)

B—Biblical Example

Instead of remaining in Nazareth, Jesus departed and made another circuit of the towns and villages in Galilee. What he saw broke his heart, so He decided to send out His disciples to minister with His authority and power. When the weary, excited apostles returned from their first tour of ministry apart from Jesus, they shared with Him what they had learned. Mark wrote that all twelve disciples reported to Jesus. When He noted the physical and emotional toll Christian service had taken among them, He prescribed a remedy—"rest." Resting is an important aspect of active Christian living. The Lord went on to discuss the ministry of these disciples and prepare them for their next mission. Growing opposition of both the political and the religious leaders was another factor in meeting and resting with His apostles. Prayer, service, and rest are all proper ingredients of the active Christian life, but they cannot be mixed out of proportion. Vance Havner once said, "If you don't come apart and rest, you will come apart."

C—Contemporary Application

Many people plan vacations, retreats, or camps in the summer. These learning opportunities should be carefully planned to provide for physical rest. One year our family went to a popular theme park and then on to see the sights in the area. When we returned home, everyone was exhausted. All of the playing and traveling was not what we really wanted to do. One year we chose to go to the mountains, stay in a cabin, fish, and relax. That experience is one of our favorite memories. The opportunity to teach at our Baptist conference centers became an annual summer event. The family enjoyed these weeks more than any other "away-from-home" times. After thinking about those summer weeks, I concluded that all the family needs were met including physical rest, social activities, mental stimulation, and spiritual refreshing. We found a way to strengthen our total being. The trip home was spent recalling the fun times and looking forward to the next summer.

Consider these suggestions for a little R and R in your life:

- Plan well in advance a time for absolute physical rest.
- Occasionally, decide to go somewhere that requires no major preparations.
- Plan a vacation at home. This "staycation" includes doing local things.
- Sometimes, include friends or family who enjoy your lifestyle.

D—Directed Prayer

Help me, Lord, not to burn-out in my service for You.

June 10

Nahum's Little Doomed City

God will punish evil and provide lasting protection for His people.
Nahum 1:1—3:19

A—Advice from the Bible

The Lord is slow to anger and great in power.
(Nahum 1:3, NIV)

B—Biblical Example

The Book of Nahum, written by a minor prophet, is a prophecy regarding the destruction of Nineveh. This capital city of Assyria was doomed to destruction because former kings had made fun of any attempt to trust in the Lord for help. They bragged that no god had been able to stand against Assyria, not even Judah's God. The prophet had warned earlier that plans against God were futile. The city was guilty of shedding blood, lies, robbery, sexual sins, witchcraft, destruction of nations, and destruction of families. Therefore, God planned three punishments for this wicked city. First, they would be stripped of all previous defense and military power. Second, the city would be humiliated in public view by all kinds of filth being thrown on the people. Finally, the once proud, haughty, and cruel nation would be brought to its knees in judgment by God. Nineveh would cause all enemy nations to dread falling into the hands of God.

C—Contemporary Application

Hisoshima, Japan was founded in 1594. This beautiful city soon became recognized as a commercial center for all southeast Asia. Beautiful cherry trees and gardens were planned for the people to enjoy. Diligent workers maintained the attractive parks and lakes. In 1868 the city was designated as a military base. World War II was the result of some of the plans created there. Emperor Hirohito believed that all Japan's imperial rulers were divine. Therefore, world conquest would be successful. However, August 6, 1945 introduced the first atomic bombing of Japan. The blast flattened 60% of the city and killed thousands of people. President Harry Truman and his military staff had warned the imperial rulers not to proceed with their plans of conquest, but the words went unheeded. World War II spread throughout southeast Asia. After the war the Japanese government dedicated a Peace Memorial Park that stands on the epicenter of the bombing. Tourists visit this peace shrine and express deep emotions in tears and prayers. They are reminded of the destruction that can come to a city that follows ungodly rulers.

Lessons learned from Nahum:
- Stand against evil and for righteousness in your community.
- Believe that God will judge evil.
- Stand for the truths of God in governmental elections.
- Believe that God is long suffering toward sinful America.

D—Directed Prayer

God, help me to avoid Your punishment and enjoy Your protection.

June 11

Paul's Little Thorn

Christians can boast about Christ's power in times of personal weakness.
2 Corinthians 12:1-10

A—Advice from the Bible

"A thorn in the flesh was given to me."
(2 Cor. 12:7, HCSB)

B—Biblical Example

The Apostle Paul continued to defend his apostleship. He responded to accusations made against him by these believers, but he did so reluctantly. The Corinthians had been listening to other leaders who enjoyed boasting about their good works and also deceiving these young Christians. Paul described himself as "weak" because he had not abused the Corinthians. He described an unusual spiritual experience in the third person. He was concerned that some people might exalt him because of this occurrence. He went on to share a different kind of spiritual experience that God gave him 14 years earlier in order to keep him humble. God permitted Satan's messenger to buffet Paul by giving him a "thorn in the flesh." The apostle begged God three times to remove the thorn. Some people think this handicap was weak eyes, or his personal appearance, or his lack of eloquence. Whatever happened served a needed purpose. Paul wrote that God had promised His grace would be sufficient in all situations, even to the Corinthians

C—Contemporary Application

Fanny Crosby was six weeks old when her parents realized that something was wrong with her eyes. The local doctor was away, but her parents found a man who claimed to be a physician. He put hot poultice on the baby's inflamed eyes, insisting this treatment would draw out the problem. The infection did clear up, but white scars appeared causing this baby to lose much of her vision. The result was major vision problems. Fanny was not totally blind. Even in old age she could discern day from night, but most of her vision was gone. Later in life, this remarkable woman said, "My blindness is a special gift from God and equipped me for a special work." Her "thorn" enabled Fanny to write hundreds of songs—many are among our favorites.

What do these experiences teach us?

- Christians should recognize the importance of their accomplishments, but give God the credit for what happens.
- Christians should discover that the Lord's strength becomes most real through weaknesses.
- Christians must sometimes realize that God's answers to our prayers are not what we expected.
- Christians should respect and speak well of their Christian leaders.

D—Directed Prayer

Father, help me realize that sometimes my weakness is a blessing.

June 12

A Little True Worship

Because God is God, and man is man, worship is necessary.
Exodus 33:9-16

A—Advice from the Bible

They all stood and worshiped.
(Ex. 33:10, NIV)

B—Biblical Example

The wandering Israelites needed to learn how to effectively worship God. They had worshiped him before, for example during their joyous celebration of Pharaoh's defeat and victory at the crossing of the Red Sea. However, no prescribed method of worship had been given to them by God. Idolatry was an ever present problem, especially while Moses was away on Mount Sinai receiving the laws from God. He began a pattern of personal worship that soon affected the people. He sought direction and encouragement from the Lord. No tabernacle or system of ritual worship and sacrifice existed at that time, so Moses simply pitched an ordinary tent away from the main camp. The site was called the "tent of meeting." The pillar of cloud, signifying God's presence came to rest at the tent door, and the people also worshiped at their own tents. True worship occurs when people stand in the presence of God and praise Him for His mercy and forgiveness. Worship cannot be forced, but must begin from within. True worship grows out of an awareness of who God is and what He has done for us.

C—Contemporary Application

People have different concepts of worship. Suppose you are enlisted to plan a meaningful worship service for your church. Complete the suggested outline. What items would you include to make the experience more worshipful? How can you include the worship needs of all the people?

Call to Worship—
Hymns of Praise—
Tithes and Offerings—
Hymns of Victory—
Sermon—
Hymn of Commitment—
Invitation--

Some guidelines for effective worship:

- Affirm God's presence with confidence.
- Claim God's promises.
- Express thankfulness to God for His protection and provisions.
- Consistently participate in personal, family, and public worship.

D—Directed Prayer

LORD, I worship and adore You.

June 13

Little Interruptions

Christians are to serve faithfully even in demanding situations.
Mark 5:22-42

A—Advice from the Bible

A large crowd followed and pressed around him.
(Mark 5:24, HCSB)

B—Biblical Example

Most people today can relate to Mark, chapter 5. Jesus experienced a full day of demanding situations and interruptions. His daily schedule is not revealed in the Bible, however, the day began with a man in the region of Gerasenes, on the east side of the Sea of Galilee, being healed from unclean spirits. The local residents were frightened by this event and asked Jesus to leave. He returned to Capernaum and a great crowd gathered around Him by the seaside. An opportunity to teach all these people was available until an interruption came. Jesus and his traveling companions finally headed down the road, when another disturbance came. A woman with a long-term illness was healed. Next, Jairus, one of the synagogue rulers, had a sick daughter. This ruler took a great risk by kneeling down publicly in front of Jesus. His reason was concern for a loved one. Jesus left behind His plans and immediately departed with this grieving father. The Lord had established His priorities—people are more important than anything else.

C—Contemporary Application

Consider the following situations and how you would deal with each interruption:
- You are on your way to church and running a little late. Important responsibilities are waiting for your presence. An old car with a woman and two children is stopped on the roadside. The day is cold and the little family is poorly dressed. You are under no obligation to stop and assist these people. But you are under obligation to bring the opening devotional in your Bible study department. How would you respond to this situation?
- Your dinner guests have arrived when a phone call comes from a distressed church member who needs help and is upset and frustrated. How would you handle this situation?

Jesus' actions provide an example of how to deal with demanding situations and interruptions:
- We often serve the Lord by serving people.
- We need to understand that when people are in great need, they seek help.
- We need to be aware that the more we help people, the more interruptions we will experience.
- We need to experience being used by God to lessen human suffering.

D—Directed Prayer

Father, help me to be a blessing to people who are suffering and sorrowing.

June 14

Little Banners

God has specific words of assurance for His people.
(Psalm 20:1-5)

A—Advice from the Bible

We will lift up our banners in the name of our God.
(Psalm 20:5)

B—Biblical Example

The setting of this psalm was a royal worship service offered on behalf of an unidentified king in the dynasty of David. Some Bible teachers believe the king may have been preparing to lead his armies into battle. The presence of God, at this time, was important to the people. They were looking to Him for both protection and deliverance. Since Israel was almost constantly at war while David was king, certain preparations were necessary before a king went to battle. He would bring offerings to the temple to be used a burnt sacrifice to the Lord. These meat and meal offerings, accompanied by drink offerings assured the king of divine help in the coming conflict. Banners or flags also were prepared for some of the soldiers to carry at the procession of the military forces. The people anticipated cheering the success of their leader by waving banners in the triumphal parade. The symbols played a significant role in Old Testament history such as with the Twelve Tribes, who were identified by certain banners that always preceded the movement of the people.

C—Contemporary Application

Banner or flags are always present at celebrations of the American people. Congress officially adopted the United States flag on June 14, 1777 and the nation still proudly lifts this symbol of freedom. At the request of George Washington, Betsy Ross (the legendary person who designed and made the US flag) was enlisted to provide a banner for the new nation. She chose 13 stars and 13 alternating white and red stripes. The flag has become identified with a grateful nation. Christians, too, have reasons to celebrate. The Arizona Baptist Convention was preparing to observe their jubilee year. Each local church had been asked to prepare a banner for the "Parade of Churches" pageant. What an exciting moment! Down the aisles came banner-bearers joyfully celebrating the established local churches. The banners were displayed along the front of the worship center as a reminder that God's people would have assurance and victory against evil by working together in the spiritual war.

Consider these reasons to celebrate.
- God must be offered praise and thanksgiving for the ways in which He blesses us.
- God will keep His promises to lead His people to victory.
- God's presence in daily life is a fact.

D—Directed Prayer

Thank you God for banners to remind us of Your assurance of victory in life.

June 15

Little Living Stones

Live by high moral standards.
(1 Peter 2:5-12)

A—Advice from the Bible

You yourselves as living stones are being built . . .
(1 Peter 2:5)

B—Biblical Example

Peter wrote from Rome to Christians living in Asia Minor. These believers were undergoing some degree of opposition and threat. His letter for tough times was meant to inspire, instruct, exhort, and encourage his Christian friends. Peter challenged these followers to live the committed Christian lifestyle. He used the imagery of building a house of worship. The Apostle was affirming that Christ is the essential foundation for life. Notice that Jesus is called, "the living Stone." The writer then urged the Christians to become *living stones* which were to be built into a spiritual house. The foundation of our lives is Christ. The church was not primarily thought of as bricks and mortar, but the church is first of all people. God's people were to accomplish two tasks: (1) all Christians were to have ready access to God and (2) believers were to offer their work and their worship as expressions of love and obedience to the Builder. God's graciousness provides a way for all people to be in His special family. However, a warning was issued concerning the danger of self-righteousness as opposed to the righteousness of God.

C—Contemporary Application

His parents would not allow a Bible in their house, but somehow their son heard the gospel as a teenager and came to Christ. Edward Mote was born into a poor family on January 21, 1797. This skilled carpenter and owner of a cabinet shop had an unusual experience one morning. The words, "On Christ the solid Rock I stand/All other ground is sinking sand" came to his mind. That day he completed four verses of this future hymn. In 1852 Edward became the pastor of the Baptist church in Horsham, Sussex. A member called requesting prayer for his dying wife. Pastor Edward went to their house and sang his new song for her. The last verse of The Solid Rock was experienced when Mr. Mote passed away at age 77. "When He shall come with trumpet sound, O may I then in Him be found! Dressed in His righteousness alone, Faultless to stand before the throne!" This man was special to God because of his faithfulness as a living stone.

What makes people special to God?

- We make a choice to be the people of faith who worship God.
- We adopt qualities for our lives which have been given us by Christ's power.
- We are special to God because God is gracious.
- We live out His Word by loving Him and loving each other.

D—Directed Prayer

On Christ the solid Rock I stand, all other ground is sinking sand.

June 16

The Little Ephraimite Father

Every child needs a worshipping parent.
(1 Samuel 1)

A—Advice from the Bible

This man would go every year to worship and sacrifice.
(1 Sam. 1:3)

B—Biblical Example

The story about Israel's monarchy begins with Samuel. He served as Israel's last judge and one of her earliest prophets. From his book we learn about a man named Elkanah. He was a devout man who lived during the time after the Israelites moved into the Promised Land and before a king had been crowned. At this time the tabernacle was located at Shiloh and still was the center of worship. Elkanah went there every year with his two wives, Peninnah and Hannah, and Peninnah's children. Two wives in one family usually presented difficulties, so this father had to make adjustments for the conflict. Peninnah had children; Hannah was barren. Jealousy surfaced when this husband paid more attention to Hannah. His kindness to her problem is evident in the scripture passage. After returning home from worshiping at Shiloh, Hannah experienced an answer to her prayer for a child. This father's love and patience are obvious in his treatment to his favored wife. She was allowed to remain at home the next year and care for her new-born son, named Samuel.

C—Contemporary Application

A day commemorating all mothers was begun in 1914 in the United States, but nothing was done to honor fathers. Credit for originating the holiday is generally given to Sonora Smart Dodd of Spokane, Washington, whose father, a Civil War veteran, raised her and her five siblings after their mother died in childbirth. She is said to have had the idea in 1909 while listening to a sermon on Mother's Day, which at the time was becoming established as a holiday. Local religious leaders supported her idea, and the first Father's Day was celebrated on June 19, 1910, the month of the birthday of Dodd's father. In 1924 President Calvin Coolidge gave his approval to the observance, and in 1966 President Lyndon B. Johnson officially proclaimed it a national holiday. Observance on the third Sunday of June was decreed by law in 1972.

Consider these godly characteristics of fathers:
- They know how to express love to their family.
- They know how to support their family.
- They are leaders by Christian example to their family.
- They know how to encourage their family to be all God created them to be.

D—Directed Prayer

Begin today thanking God for your father.

June 17

A Little Son for Boaz

The only place for God's people is in His will.
(Ruth 4:13-17)

A—Advice from the Bible

And she gave birth to a son.
(Ruth 4:13)

B—Biblical Example

The Book of Ruth begins with a funeral and ends with a wedding. A brief review of this story finds Ruth moving from Moab to Judah with her mother-in-law, Naomi. These women arrived in Bethlehem at the beginning of the harvest. Harvest time meant gleaning time for the poor and these women would need help. Ruth's first meeting with Boaz occurred in the field where she was to glean. He became a hero to these family members. He did the right thing at the right time. Boaz was always sensitive to the needs of others. Several characteristics are revealed about this man. He kept his word and cared for his field hands. Dependability and integrity would describe him as a land owner. This wealthy farmer expressed kindness to this non-Jewish woman. When he discovered that she was living with Naomi, the traditional kinsman-redeemer responsibility took place. The couple married and before long a son was born. This birth fulfilled a Hebrew law about carrying on Naomi's husband's name. The grandmother named this child Obed.

C—Contemporary Application

Marilyn and Ryan married right after high school graduation. They lived on a farm owned by Ryan's father. However, Ryan's National Guard Unit was called up for military duty. The couple was saddened by this interruption. After Ryan reported for duty, Marilyn discovered she was expecting a baby. The young soldier never got to see his son. An enemy ambush destroyed his life. Years passed and Marilyn finished her college education and worked at a nearby hospital. The thought of meeting a man who would become her husband never occurred to her, but God had special plans. Dr. Ben soon noticed this beautiful woman and discovered that she was a widow, raising a son. As time passed their affection for each other grew. The wedding was a joyous celebration for both families. Ben became a wonderful father to little Ryan and a faithful husband to Marilyn. The loss of the past was replaced by the wonderful events of the present.

Some examples of being a good father are:

- Being sensitive to the needs of his family.
- Doing what is right for other people.
- Establishing a reputation of integrity.
- Displaying kindness to all people.

D—Directed Prayer

Lord, may all fathers seek to follow Your ideal for their life.

June 18

A Little Watchfulness

Believers should be alert to the presence of those who oppose Christ.
(2 John 8-9)

A—Advice from the Bible

Watch yourselves, that you do not lose what we have accomplished.
(2 John 8)

B—Biblical Example

Second John consists of only one chapter and is one of the shortest books in the New Testament. This epistle is a pastoral letter from John to believers. The term "the elder" designates an older gentleman, a senior person worthy of respect, or a senior official in a local church. The apostle was concerned about false teaching. He feared that his missionary and pastoral efforts would prove to be in vain. The seriousness of false teaching is outlined. A warning is issued when any teaching goes beyond the clear message of Scripture. That idea should immediately put a Christian on the alert before it contradicts the truth revealed in the Bible. One primary acknowledgement is fundamental to the faith—Jesus Christ has come in the flesh. To deny this revelation is to have a false understanding of God and the way to God. John warned the believers to be alert to the false teachers who proudly claimed to have advanced or superior teachings. He surmised that these deceivers had advanced so far they left God behind. A caution light serves as a reminder that we are going to either stop or go. John wanted the Christians to "watch for the signs."

C—Contemporary Application

I married into a family of outdoor enthusiasts. Camping trips were planned early in the winter for the summer months. The big focus of the campsite was the fire pit. Wood was gathered (or brought from home) and chairs were arranged around the soon-to-be fire.
Those evenings were times of special family sharing, especially tales from the past. One story I always remember is about a camper who sat by a big fire one evening. A hiker came by the campsite and asked why the fire was needed on such as warm evening. The hiker assumed the camper wanted to scare away wild animals. To his surprise the camper responded that the fire was not to keep away animals; it was to allow him to see the animals coming. Stay alert! Deceivers can lead believers away from the truth.

Think of some ways believers today can reject deceivers:

- Believers can—
- Believers can—
- Believers can—
- Believers can—

D—Directed Prayer

Father, help us to be aware of opportunities.

June 19

Obed-Edom's Little Responsibility

To please God, we must do His work, His way.
(1 Chronicles 13:1-14)

A—Advice from the Bible

> *The ark of God remained with the family of Obed-Edom for three months.*
> (1 Chron. 13:14)

B—Biblical Example

King David defeated the Philistines and captured Jerusalem. Now he desired to make this city his capital and the center of Hebrew worship. One thing was missing—the Ark of the Covenant. This special item had been lost some 80 years earlier. When Samuel died, no one else in Israel probably knew much about the ark and the rituals involved in caring for this furnishing. During the reign of King Saul, the ark was never used. So David was serious in his longing to serve God. Since the ark had been unused for so long, much had been forgotten concerning God's commands about handling this piece of furniture. The moving did not go as planned and one man died in the process. David became angry and fearful of God. Therefore, he allowed the ark to rest temporarily at the house of Obed-Edom. Nothing is known about this family except that God blessed them during this time of housing one of Israel's national treasures.

C—Contemporary Application

James I of England was born on June 19, 1566, in Edinburgh Castle. He was the only son of Mary, Queen of Scots, and her second husband, Henry Stewart. Although James was a Protestant, he was not as radical as some of his Protestant subjects in Scotland and England. The king preferred the Church of England, of which he was the head. But some of his English subjects wanted the English Church to become more like the Scottish Church. So in 1604 James called a conference to answer Puritan demands for church reform. At this time he authorized a new English translation of the Bible, generally called the King James Version of 1611. He desired that his subjects be able to read God's Word in a language common at that time. This translation has remained a favorite Bible through the generations. Some churches today will not allow any newer translations to be read in their church. I remember an old deacon in our church who claimed that the Apostle Paul was the writer of this Holy Bible!

Here are some situations when we might do His work, **our** way:

- A new worship center is planned. You want a center aisle.
- The communion table is the wrong kind of wood. You fuss.
- Your class room is just like you want it. Keep out everyone else!
- The pulpit is too small for the leaders. You want a new one.

D—Directed Prayer

Lord, help me not to push through my opinions without Your guidance.

June 20

A Little Fellowship with God

Jesus doesn't need lawyers; He needs witnesses.
(1 John 1:3-7)

A—Advice from the Bible

Our fellowship is with the Father and His Son, Jesus Christ.
(1 John 1:3)

B—Biblical Example

The Apostle John was one of the earliest disciples of the Lord and remained with Jesus during His earthly ministry. For three years or more, he had fellowship with the Son of God. For that reason, John and his fellow disciples could testify that they came to know the Son of God through physical senses—sight and hearing. The truth and realities they had experienced were shared as good news, the gospel of salvation. The first evidence of real faith in the risen Christ was a person becoming a part of a unique fellowship of people. A believer will share and care about all people. John wanted the readers of his sermon, who had in common a confession of the Father and the Son, to keep having that kind of fellowship with him and other believers. These followers had a unique relationship since it was a direct contact with God. Verse 4 shows the positive purpose of God's good news. John sought to give a solid base for having pure joy. The message that brings good news to the world is simple and life-changing. The life of the Christian is bound up in fellowship—fellowship with God in Christ and with one another.

C—Contemporary Application

Family reunions are usually planned a year in advance. Many groups gather during June for this special time of fellowship. As the years pass, more relatives are added to the gathering. A friend of mine told about their recent family get-together. A retreat setting in the Smokey Mountains of Tennessee was the chosen location. This year the meal was catered by a local restaurant. The crowd began arriving on Friday evening. The older members sat around in folding chairs recalling the past and showing pictures of the way things used to be. The next generation gathered and discussed the successes of their children, showing pictures of awards and achievements. The youth bunch went off to listen to their music. However, every member present would exclaim, "This is the best reunion we have ever had." Why? Because they were family and they loved each other.

We enjoy fellowship with God when we:

- Live in obedience to His will.
- Learn to communicate with Him through prayer.
- Love to worship Him.
- Like being with the fellowship of believers.

D—Directed Prayer

Lord, show me ways to improve my fellowship with You.

June 21

This Little Day

Individuals may choose between life and death.
(Deuteronomy 30:11-20)

A—Advice from the Bible

The LORD your God, will bless you in the land you are entering to possess.
(Deut. 30:16)

B—Biblical Example

The third of Moses' speeches in Deuteronomy begins in chapter 29 and continues in chapter 30. This speech urged the people to choose the way of life and blessing. God's requirements were given in a language all the people could understand. Moses did not use the technical terminology of professional theologians. His words were clear and simple and God's Words were to be obeyed. The children of Israel were in position to enter the Promised Land. The law had been given, the people reminded of the history of God's dealings with them, and the possibilities of the future had been set before them. Two possibilities were given, life and prosperity or death and destruction. If life and prosperity were chosen, three requirements were involved. The first was *to love the Lord your God*. The second condition was *to walk in his ways*. And finally, *to keep his commands, decrees, and laws*. The choice was more than a basic, one-time decision; it was a way of life. Rejecting God and His commands would lead to false worship and death.

C—Contemporary Application

Sanford Fillmore Bennett, 31, was a local pharmacist in Elkhorn, Wisconsin. His friend, Joseph Webster, came by the store each day. He was the local musician, vocalist, and violinist. However, he also suffered from periods of deep depressions. Sanford cared about his friend, especially one day when he came by looking very sad. "What's the matter now?" asked the pharmacist. "Not much, but it will be all right by and by." The idea for a hymn hit Sanford's mind. He sat at his desk and began to write, "In the sweet by and by, we shall meet on that beautiful shore." The word and accompaniment were completed in thirty minutes in a drugstore. For over 100 years, this song has been a favorite of Christian churches. One of these days, God's people will "meet on a beautiful shore" and be greeted by "the Father who waits over the way." However, only individuals who have made the right choice will be included in this promise.

Choosing a godly life includes:

- Loving the Lord your God.
- Listening to His voice.
- Clinging to Him through obedience.
- Blessings from understanding God's promises.

D—Directed Prayer

Dear Lord, I choose this day to serve You with my remaining years.

June 22

A Sick Little Son

Christians need to be used by God to meet human needs.
(Mark 9:17-29)

A—Advice from the Bible

"Teacher, I brought you my son . . .
(Mark 9:17)

B—Biblical Example

Jesus and three of His disciples, Peter, James, and John, had just experienced the Transfiguration. God's power was evident. However, back in the valley, the scene was different. The other nine disciples were trying to meet human needs. They lacked the spiritual power to heal a father's son. The crowds began to doubt these followers of Jesus. Then, the Lord approached the frustrated father. The diagnosis of the son's condition was "possessed by a spirit." The lad had apparently suffered this problem for most of his life. Walking and talking were impossible. Going to school and playing with other children would be limited. Eating meals would have been a challenge. The father used the world "if" which reveals his limited faith. Jesus, however, proved that all things are possible to the one who truly believes. The demon of disease was confronted and conquered. Jesus took the boy's hand and lifted him up to a life of wholeness.

C—Contemporary Application

Parents with physically challenged children, often miss out on everyday activities of childhood. The little sayings and gestures are absent from their lifestyle. The story is told about Johnny, who came home from Sunday school and his mother asked him what he had learned. The boy said, "The teacher told the story about Moses and the Hebrews escaping from Egypt." The mother asked more questions. Johnny continued, "The Hebrews were trying to get away from the Egyptians when all of a sudden they came up to this big body of water. So Moses called his engineers, and they constructed a pontoon bridge across that sea. The Hebrews crossed over the other side. But then here came the Egyptians. They were crossing over the pontoon bridge when Moses called his explosion experts; they set some dynamite and blew up that pontoon bridge and all the Egyptians were killed." The Mother asked, "Are you sure the teacher told this story?" "No, but you wouldn't have believed it the way she told it."

Jesus brings to us in times of crisis:
- Confidence.
- Hope.
- Healing.
- Authority and power.

D—Directed Prayer

Father, I am so grateful that I can experience the fullness of Your presence and power.

June 23

Little Sacrifices

Christians will work toward a new goal of oneness with Christ.
(Philippians 3:1-11)

A—Advice from the Bible

I want to know Christ . . . becoming like Him.
(Phil. 3:10)

B—Biblical Example

Several of Paul's epistles contain references to Judaizers. These persons of Jewish faith had professed belief in Christ, but were using their influence in the churches to promote a doctrine of works. To correct these false teachings, Paul offered himself as an example of the difference Christ should make. He had come to consider that his former life offered self-satisfaction, status, influence, and security, but that wasn't enough! When Paul met Jesus, his values changed. What was once gain to him suddenly became loss. As a result of his new calling to follow Christ, he was now a prisoner in Rome, writing to his fellow Christians at Philippi. His purpose was not to exalt himself as a meticulous Jew, but to contrast past and present choices. The basic change for Paul was the rejection of works as a means to salvation and acceptance of Christ as sufficient Savior. He still had objectives, not for gaining personal merit, but for expressing his love and devotion to his Savior.

C—Contemporary Application

A favorite invitational hymn of mine is "I Surrender All." The message of this song touched my heart during a spring revival in my home town. At that point in my walk with Christ, I was still holding on to the past. Someone once said, "Only in the Christian life does surrender bring victory." A man named Judson Wheeler Van De Venter helped me discover this truth. He, too, had learned that fact about sacrifice. Judson was born in Michigan, in 1855, and converted to Christ at age 17. He became a school teacher. The choir of his local Methodist Episcopal Church inspired him to become involved in church music. His friends encouraged him to resign from the school system to enter fulltime music evangelism. He struggled with this decision for five years. Then during a revival, he "surrendered all" to Jesus and wrote the words to this invitation, recalling his personal submitting to full-time ministry.

The knowledge of Christ begins with:
- Learning who He is.
- Learning what He thinks.
- Learning what He says and does.
- Learning what He desires.

D—Directed Prayer

Lord, help me to live a life that indicates knowing You is a priority.

June 24

Moses' Little Wooden Stick

God equips people He calls to leadership positions.
(Exodus 4:1-17)

A—Advice from the Bible

Take this staff in your hand.
(Ex. 4:17)

B—Biblical Example

When Moses thought about his inadequacies for the work God called him to do, he was overwhelmed with fear. Many reasons were offered to God about why he could not lead the Israelites out of Egyptian bondage. Moses then offered a third excuse—no one would believe him! God responded by giving a sign to demonstrate God's power. A question is asked; the answer to the question that God asked Moses seems obvious. Moses was holding a plain wooden stick. Moses would soon learn that this ordinary shepherd's rod would become a symbol of power and authority to deliver Israel from bondage. Moses must have felt reluctant to cast down this object when God commanded him to do so. What happened next persuaded Moses that his life was about to change. The staff turned into a serpent and Moses ran in fear. Next, God commanded Moses to reach out his hand and grasp the serpent's tail. God turned the snake into a staff again. This sign would help convince the Israelites to believe that God was in control of their life. Moses was hard to convince and needed more reassurance from God. The power of God is unlimited as more signs and wonders were performed. However, poor Moses had God's Word, the miraculous signs, and the assistance of his brother, Aaron; yet he still was not ready to walk by faith.

C—Contemporary Application

He was born the son of a country pastor in Caldwell, New Jersey. The family eventually moved to New York, where nine children struggled to survive on their father's modest salary. One of the sons was Grover Cleveland (1837-1908). He became the 22nd and 24th president of the United States (1885-1889, 1893-1897). He worked as a clerk for a law firm and was admitted to the bar in 1859. He used the "wooden sticks" of his life to become a leading political figure. In 1897, Cleveland returned with his family to Princeton, New Jersey, and died at Princeton on June 24, 1908.

Awareness of our weaknesses can be a blessing when:

- We depend on God for strength.
- We pray to God for guidance.
- When we obey God.
- When we commit to God's challenge.

D—Directed Prayer

Lord, thank You, that leadership opportunities provoke us to walk by faith.

June 25

Little Fears

God offers help and hope for the future.
Psalm 27:1-7

A—Advice from the Bible

Whom shall I fear?
(Ps. 27:1)

B—Biblical Example

David expressed enthusiastic confidence in the Lord's protection and triumph over people who wanted to destroy him. Perhaps an army of enemies were about to attack him. David reasoned in this psalm that he should not fear anyone. God was his light and salvation. Notice the use of the personal pronoun "my." Light seemed to be the answer to fear and to the evil forces that threatened him. David had an understanding that God was the One who gives life and joy by illuminating the darkness of danger. The enemies were compared to a pack of wild, hunting animals that if given the chance would eat his body. The perils of war often led to despair. The adversary would set up camp just across the way, preparing for the fight and possibly killing David. A request was made to God that he might live continually in intimate fellowship with Him. The psalmist felt secure under God's protection, however, his tone changed dramatically in verse 7. Instead of singing a song of faith, he pled anxiously with God. His desire was to spend his time with God, mediating on God, and learning about God. Personal fear would prevent this kind of relationship. The final verses of this psalm summarize what the writer learned. It is enough to wait for God, because God is worth waiting for!

C—Contemporary Application

The great-nephew of General George Custer was a member of our church. His name was Jack Custer and he possessed much memorabilia about his famous great-uncle. The most tragic event of this general's life happened on June 25, 1876, in what is now Montana. History records that event as the Battle of the Little Bighorn. The chiefs of the Sioux and Cheyenne Indians were Sitting Bull and Crazy Horse. White settlers were moving into Indian Territory and the tribes were attacking them. The Little Bighorn River became the site of the battle. Custer and his men were all killed. Evidence of great fear is recorded in the history books. David's fear was controlled by faith in God's guidance.

God helps us overcome our fears by:
- Providing for our needs.
- Guiding us along our paths.
- Hosting us in fellowship with Him
- Teaching us to wait on Him.

D—Directed Prayer

Father, when I am overwhelmed with concerns and fears, teach me to depend on You.

June 26

My Little Service to God

Mission involvement is not an option for Christians.
Romans 15:15-24

A—Advice from the Bible

I glory in Christ Jesus in my service to God.
(Rom. 15:17)

B—Biblical Example

Paul was not proud of his attainments, but he was proud of his work in Christ. However, he was a man on mission. His wonderful conversion experience not only freed him from the burden of his sin, but gave him a burdened heart for a lost world. Remember the intensity of Paul's racial and spiritual commitment as a Jew and the severity of his persecution of Christians? And now, Paul had become God's international missionary, proclaiming the gospel to people he once despised. Jesus Christ became the center of his life, and from that center he launched a lifetime of missions service. His efforts prospered as Christ worked in him. Paul was empowered by the Holy Spirit to do miracles that confirmed the reality and truth of the gospel. He intended to go to places where Christ was not known and where others had not labored. He was a true pioneer and saw himself as God's messenger. He would not speak of anything except what Christ was doing through him to bring the gentiles to faith in God.

C—Contemporary Application

Women have served God in mission situations for years. Sometimes the mission field was primitive and unsafe. Let's meet some of these remarkable women:
- "Ma" Slessor was on the continent of Africa before David Livingston arrived.
- Lillian Carter, who sobbed by a roadside in India as she fed with her own hands a leper whose body was deteriorating from the disease.
- Ann Judson, though desperately ill, poured out her tears, love, and devotion on the pages of a diary that still throbs with love for Jesus. She longed for the people in Burma to hear the name Jesus and to know His story of salvation.
- Lottie Moon was a woman on mission in China. She died of malnutrition after sharing her food with starving Chinese women and children.

Are you a servant of God on mission to do His will?

God calls every Christian to be on mission:
- Your mission field may be a local ministry.
- Your mission field may be part-time volunteer missions service in your state.
- Your mission field may include international mission trips each year.
- Your mission field may call for support through prayer and finances.

D—Directed Prayer

Father, I pray for missionaries who are in dangerous situations today.

June 27

A Little Confidence

Eternal life is not based on feelings, but on facts.
1 John 5:13-21

A—Advice from the Bible

This is the confidence we have.
(1 John 5:14)

B—Biblical Example

John closed his letter by stating his purpose in writing—to assure those who believe in Jesus as the Son of God, that they possess eternal life. False teachers continued to confuse the believers by making them unsure of their spiritual state. (The same thing is happening today.) This epistle was written to strengthen Christians who are tempted to doubt the reality of their faith or their new-birth experience. Included in his writing are doctrinal, moral, and social tests by which readers could determine their true status before God. Verse 14 offers confidence in answered prayer. God listens carefully to the prayers of His people and also acts powerfully to answer them. A Christian must also pray for others. This practice is called intercessory prayer. This type of praying is one of our highest privileges as believers. As God's children we may be confident that God will answer prayers made in accordance with His will. One assurance that offers confidence is that those born of God remain God's children with permanent privileges and responsibilities.

C—Contemporary Application

My favorite musical is *The Sound of Music* and the score contains a song titled, "I Have Confidence." A challenging job as governess to seven motherless children confronts the main female character, Maria. To boost her courage, Maria sings about the confidence she has in herself to care for these mischievous children. At first, lack of confidence is evident in the words and actions of the former abbey girl. However, as she sings, her confidence grows and before the song ends, I believe in her! Many times when I am faced with a challenge and my confidence is lacking, I stop and remember that I am not doing things by myself. Confidence is gained when God is included in daily living. I never doubt my salvation, because Bible study offers all the confidence needed to serve Him. Eternal life is mine; I belong to Jesus; He will keep His promises to me.

As believers we should:

- Affirm our faith in Christ.
- Know that He alone is sufficient for salvation.
- Pray according to God's will.
- Follow Christ's guidance.

D—Directed Prayer

Father, help me to celebrate my confidence in You

June 28

Little Meaningless Offerings

It is possible to do the right thing the wrong way.
Isaiah 1:1-20

A—Advice from the Bible

Stop bringing meaningless offerings.
(Isa. 1:13)

B—Biblical Example

The book of Isaiah follows the twofold theme common to most of the Old Testament prophets—judgment and blessing. A major function of the prophet was to call the people and the nation back to the covenant relationship with God, and Isaiah is an example of these actions. Three other prophets were serving God at this time, Amos and Hosea in the Northern Kingdom and Micah in the Southern Kingdom. Isaiah appealed to stubborn Judah to listen to God's message. The problem in Judah was not lack of religion. The problem was feverish religious activity without a heart Because of Judah's violence, God rejected every effort of the nation to approach Him, including prayer. The voice of the prophet thundered against carrying out mere religious forms. God had ordered no more vain offerings be brought before Him. These offerings were empty of meaning and contained no sense of true worship.

C—Contemporary Application

Our church decided to have a Vacation Bible School on the Navajo reservation. The tribes live on reservations in northeastern Arizona and contiguous parts of New Mexico and Utah. The week was spent meeting some of the Navajo Christians who had a small adobe church near a cluster of typical houses. I asked how most of the Indians worshipped. The women shared that traditional Navajo religion included the worship of the winds and watercourses, and of a number of gods who are believed to intervene occasionally in human affairs. These gods are frequently invoked; offerings are made to them, and ceremonial dances are performed in which they are represented by painted and masked men. Songs, chants, prayers, and sand paintings also form part of the complicated religious rituals, and a large body of mythology exists. She compared her Christian offering with the "old way" and said, "The rituals are fun and the ceremonial dances are exciting, but they do not provide worship from my heart."

How does worship result in service?
- Relates to other people's needs.
- Inspires a deeper Bible study.
- Leads to more financial giving.
- Promotes a desire to share the Gospel.

D—Directed Prayer

Thank You God, that You still call people to proclaim Your message of grace and power.

June 29

Little Criticisms

Believers will encounter opposition when doing ministry.
Mark 3:21-26

A—Advice from the Bible

He is out of his mind.
(Mark 3:21)

B—Biblical Example

After choosing the twelve men to help Him, Jesus returned home, which was probably the home of Simon and Andrew in Capernaum (1:29). Again the crowds came to Him in such numbers that they prevented a simple activity like eating. The people probably wanted to touch Him to be healed from a disease. Others were attracted by His words and wanted to hear more from Him. When His friends and family heard about the crowds, the excitement, and the constant pressure on Jesus, they came to rescue to Him. They tried to seize Him and accused Him of being out of his mind. This kind of criticism must have hurt the Lord. His family, according to their understanding of life, just wanted to protect Him. The scribes had already arrived from Jerusalem and were accusing Jesus of being possessed by Satan. Criticism became a weapon used against the ministry of Jesus. This time He summoned the slanderers into His presence. He wanted to refute their false accusations and to defend Himself in their presence. Their criticism was ridiculous, but it never stopped.

C—Contemporary Application

A great American statesman died 154 years ago in Washington, D.C. His name was Henry Clay, (1777-1852), He was one of the most popular and influential political leaders in American history. His genius in the art of compromise resolved bitter political conflicts three times that threatened to tear apart the nation. These rescues won him the title the Great Pacificator. He faced more criticism during his lifetime than most other government related individuals. Perhaps the most heartbreaking event of Clay's career was caused by criticism. The presidential contest of 1844 was his dream. However his resistance to the annexation of Texas cost him support in the South. Many believe that his greatest service to the nation came when, in spite of enemy opposition, he delayed the threat of civil war over the issue of slavery.

What are some ways you can overcome criticism?

- Confront your critics.
- Keep serving the Lord.
- Pray for people who hurt others.
- Remain faithful.

D—Directed Prayer

Father, help me to be brave when I encounter opposition.

June 30

Search for a Little Queen

Opportunities arise for devotion to duty and meaningful personal actions.
Esther 1:1-21

A—Advice from the Bible

Let a search be made for beautiful young virgins for the king.
(Esther 2:2)

B—Biblical Example

The object of this book is to give us a historical record of the wonderful deliverance of God's people from their total extermination as planned by Haman. The Persian Empire dominated the world scene at this time. In order to show off his kingdom, Ahasuerus decided to plan a celebration that would last for six months. The final seven days would become a drunken orgy, including banquets, entertainment, and other sinful acts. The tragic figure in this story is Vashti. After days of celebration, she was ordered to come before the king so she might display her beauty to his male guests. The queen chose not to follow orders. Total chaos occurred because the Persian regime was based on law and order. The Council asked the king to dispose of the queen immediately. She was to be cut off forever from royal privileges and a new queen had to be found. The choice would take weeks. The aim was to select the most beautiful girl in the world to be the queen. And God had Esther ready "for such a time as this" (4:14).

C—Contemporary Application

Purim is one of the most joyful of all Jewish holidays and is one of the later Jewish festivals. Jews celebrate the downfall of the villain Haman, who was introduced in the book of Esther. The event commemorates the deliverance of the Persian Jews from destruction during the reign of the Persian king Ahasuerus. Temples and synagogues throughout the world focus on family services during which the story of Purim is read. Great happiness and noise accompanies the reading of the story. Purim is the only time that behavior of this kind is allowed in the sanctuary. The Jews include feasting, alms-giving, sending food to neighbors and friends, and chanting the text of Esther. It is perhaps the most joyous day of the Jewish year, with masquerades, plays, and drinking of wine even in the synagogue. Esther's beauty, both inner and outer, made the difference in life or death for her people.

God is more concerned about our inner beauty. Read:

- 1 Samuel 16:7.
- Proverbs 31:30.
- 1 Peter 3:3-4.
- 2 Corinthians 2:14-15.

D—Directed Prayer

Lord, help me to seek divine guidance in times of difficulty.

July 1

Little Stumbling Blocks

Every Christian must guard his conduct to keep from hurting someone else.
Romans 14:13-15

A—Advice from the Bible

Therefore, decide not to put a stumbling block or pitfall in your brother's way.
(Romans 14:13, HCSB)

B—Biblical Example

Roman visitors, who had gone to Jerusalem for the Passover and were converted during Pentecost, began the Roman church. These new believers returned home to eagerly follow the teachings of Jesus. Now, twenty-eight-years later, the Apostle Paul longed to visit this group of worshippers. While in Corinth he wrote a letter encouraging them about some matters that had developed in the church. The congregation of strong and weak Christians had become divided over special diets and special days. Criticizing and judging one another was disrupting the fellowship. The strong Christians felt their faith in Christ completely liberated them from all religious regulations. What mattered most was loving Jesus and telling others about Him. The weaker Christians were stumbling over these attitudes and problems. Paul admonished the strong believers to guard their freedom in Christ and be better stewards of their influence. He introduced his principles for dealing with these gray areas of Christian life.

C—Contemporary Application

A stumbling block is any hindrance or difficulty standing in the way of progress or understanding. These obstacles are sometimes very **little.** Consider these two examples:
Frank is a devout Christian. Serving Christ through numerous ministries has been his passion for years. The teachings from God's Word have brought freedom to his lifestyle. Every Sunday, after worship, he hurries to a tee-time at the local golf course. Occasionally, he and his golfing buddies will place a small bet on each green.

George is a new Christian and church member. He wants to "do things right" and "make-up for lost time" so following every rule and regulation from God's Word is very important to him. An invitation to join the Sunday golfing foursome was extended to him. His reaction was one of shock! The Lord's Day was established for worshipping and resting only!

How can these "gray-areas" divide Christians?
- Drinking wine with meals
- Playing cards
- Smoking
- Attending movies on Sunday

D—Directed Prayer

Lord, make me aware of my stumbling blocks.

July 2

Little Chains

One positive route to freedom is to serve God with all your heart.
Psalm 2

A—Advice from the Bible

"Let us break their chains . . . "
(Psalm 2:3, NIV)

B—Biblical Example

Israel gave their kings a unique place in national life. Some of the psalms are called Songs of Royalty and include Psalm 2; 20; 45; and 110. Psalm 2 was written when a new king, anointed by a priest or prophet, came to the throne. This time of celebration also provided the enemies of Israel an opportunity to attack the incoming monarch.

The enemies apparently made their plans in their own strength. The psalmist warned that when someone took action against God's chosen person, they were attacking God Himself. Verse 3 suggests a picture of people who resent discipline and desire to set goals based on personal ambitions. The new king, however, modeled courageous defiance. The assurance of the presence of God offered protection and deliverance from the enemies. He knew that God was in control of the circumstances and ultimate victory was certain. Throughout history, heroes have surfaced to help break the chains of bondage to certain sins.

C—Contemporary Application

July 2, 1979 was a significant day for the United States Mint. For the first time in history, a woman's picture was featured on currency. This person was a reformer and dedicated believer in God. She fought to break the chains of human slavery. Witnessing the sale of Africans in the market place stayed in her mind. From the fight against slavery to the use of alcohol became her next project. Drunks appeared on the streets using vulgar language for women and children to hear. Fighting the enemies of evil and unfairness became her role in life. Many wives were being abused and treated like property. These issues only angered this young crusader even more. Woman Suffrage became a 50 year struggle. She and her coworkers longed to see women given the freedom to vote. This liberal Quaker lived from 1820—1906 and was named Susan B. Anthony. Death prevented her from seeing the great celebration of victory as women were given the right to influence government for good.

Beware of the chains of sin that:

- Keep you from serving God faithfully.
- Keep you from preserving the freedom of all people.
- Keep you from displaying courage against present evils.
- Keep you from convictions that honor God's will and work.

D—Directed Prayer

Lord, make me aware of my weaknesses in understanding social issues.

A Little Christian Unity

We grow in Christian unity when we live in a worthy manner.
Ephesians 4:1-16

A—Advice from the Bible

Diligently keeping the unity of the Spirit . . .
(Eph. 4:3 HCSB)

B—Biblical Example

The Ephesian letter probably was intended for a group of churches. The strong emphasis on the appeal for unity indicates that divisions were widespread in the Christian community. Paul focused on three truths about unity: one Lord, Jesus Christ; one faith; and one baptism. The same Spirit indwells all Christians and binds us together in oneness and unity. Paul was in a Roman prison at this time and yet his concern was about these early believers and their struggles to get along with each other.

For several decades attempts were made to unite all Christians in a common body. *Ecumenism* was a popular subject. This endeavor to cross denominational lines has weakened because of different opinions on specific doctrines. Denominations disagree on certain Scripture interpretations. However, in verses 4-6, Paul outlined seven commonalities among the community of faith. Each one can produce true unity among God's people by the power of the Holy Spirit.

C—Contemporary Application

Excitement was building in Philadelphia on July 3, 1776. The Second Continental Congress was going to convene the next day. Thirteen representatives from the British colonies were meeting to form a unity apart from Britain. People like Thomas Jefferson, John Adams, and Benjamin Franklin were present. The manuscript to be considered was called The Declaration of Independence. Unity among these early leaders was challenged by different ideas. Most of the members were strong men with specific ideas about how this independence from Britain should be expressed. Some leaders wanted the grievances of the colonies against the crown to be more specific. Thomas Jefferson finally drafted an acceptable document.

Christian unity is often hampered by little things that some people consider big issues. Some churches never reach their potential of Christian unity because of in-house fighting over insignificant matters.

Here are some ways members can build unity:

- Allowing new people to find a home in your church.
- Overlooking the faults of fellow believers.
- Allowing for differences of opinion, interest, and ability.
- Overlooking each other's thoughtless words.

D—Directed Prayer

Lord, help me understand the importance of Christian unity.

July 4

Cyrus' Little Proclamation

Following God ultimately leads to freedom.
Ezra 1:1-7

A—Advice from the Bible

Let him go up to Jerusalem and build the temple of the Lord.
(Ezra 1:3, NIV)

B—Biblical Example

God is always at work in history. Jeremiah had prophesied that the exiles would return to Jerusalem and now the return was a reality, because "the Lord moved the heart" of Cyrus, king of the Persian Empire. This leader had created the largest kingdom in the world. The overthrow of Babylon and thus taking control of the Jewish captives was the beginning of his success. These Hebrews had been in captivity for over 50 years. Cyrus had the reputation for showing respect for the religions of the conquered nations. As a result he gave permission for exiled Jews to return to their homeland. His motive was to win their loyalty and provide safety zones around his borders. His reverent references to the God of the exiles could cause us to think of him as a convert, but he was not. He remained a devotee of the god Marduk, (Bel) the god of thunderstorms, light, and life.

The proclamation of freedom allowed the exiles to return to Judah. He also provided protection, money, and temple articles taken by Nebuchadnezzar. Freedom had finally come!

C—Contemporary Application

The men of the Continental Congress finally met in a smoke-filled room in Philadelphia, Pennsylvania. Their purpose was to adopt the Declaration of Independence. The date was July 4, 1776. This document of freedom had been a struggle to write—so many opinions; so many disagreements. The colonists were now free from British rule. This event is celebrated annually in the United States. Parades, patriotic speeches, and fireworks appear in every town and city. Family picnics and reunions have become a special time of gathering. Freedom is wonderful!

My favorite part of the declaration are these words: *We hold these truths to be self-evident that all men are created equal, that they are endowed by their Creator with certain unalienable Rights, that among these are Life, Liberty, and the pursuit of happiness.* Thomas Jefferson had the right idea when he penned these words.

Freedom is:

- Having a doorknob on the inside of the room.
- Worshipping God according to your preferences.
- Being able to vote for leaders.
- Being able to sing "God Bless America."

D—Directed Prayer

"America, America, God shed His grace on thee." Thank You.

July 5

A Little Reminder

A believer's commitment and loyalty must be continually renewed.
John 18:15-27

A—Advice from the Bible

Immediately a rooster crowed.
(John 18:27, HCSB)

B—Biblical Example

All four gospels record Peter's denial experience of Christ. This apostle repeatedly displayed his emotional, erratic, and unstable character. Jesus knew this fault about him and warned His follower about his disloyalty (13:38). The gospel writers did not try to conceal Peter's weakness. The culmination of his human problems surfaced during the arrest and trial of Jesus. The Lord was first taken to the palace of Annas. Peter's first denial of Jesus occurred when a girl at the gate was suspicious of him and challenged his association with the band of disciples. He denied his relationship with Jesus and gained admittance. Peter's second denial came as he warmed himself by the fire with the enemy. His relationship to Jesus was questioned and he denied all knowledge of him. The third denial happened when Peter was betrayed by his Galilean dialect. He denied his discipleship. At that time, the reminder of his denials happened just as Jesus had predicted. The rooster crowed (Matt. 26:34). John's gospel stops the story at this point.

C—Contemporary Application

A colossal statue sits on Liberty Island in New York harbor. This monument is a reminder of liberty. The tall woman in a long robe is holding two things. In her right hand is a torch; in her left hand is a book inscribed, *July 4, 1776*. This beautiful symbol was given by France in 1876 to celebrate the centennial of the United States independence. Originally the structure was considered a gesture of friendship. Through the years, Miss Liberty became a global symbol of freedom. When immigrants entered the harbor and saw this statue, they were reminded that freedom was now in their possession. Our government designated the site as a national monument in 1924.
Emma Lazarus wrote a beautiful poem about her experience at the site. Her thoughts are inscribed at the main entrance. Remember this verse, "Give me your tired, your poor, your huddled masses, yearning to breathe free . . ." What a great reminder to stay loyal and committed to our country!

We need reminders in our Christian walk because:

- We sometimes stumble when least expected.
- We sometimes deny Christ.
- We sometimes have a loyalty failure.
- We sometimes have problems keeping our commitments.

D—Directed Prayer

Lord, how many times have I denied You?

July 6

Sing A Little Song

We have reasons to praise God in songs.
Exodus 15:1-10,13

A—Advice from the Bible

In your strength you will guide them . . .
(Ex. 15:13, NIV)

B—Biblical Example

This song of victory and praise expressed the feelings of Moses and the Israelites when God freed them from Egyptian bondage. These liberated people needed to celebrate their new freedom from idolatry in Egypt. From now on they would be identified as the children of God. The surrounding nations would know the miracle of the Red Sea crossing. The journey toward the promised land of Canaan was about to begin. A victory celebration honoring God was planned. He provided the victory and He would be honored by His followers. The celebration began with a hymn. Moses apparently composed the words at that moment. From this time on, music became a central part of worship. These travelers had no background for singing together, so Moses became the song leader. Singing to the Lord means praising Him for His greatness. God's strength and salvation were celebrated. The soon-to-be nation had witnessed His power and deliverance. The hearts of the Israelites were worshiping with spiritual freedom.

C—Contemporary Application

A young theological student named Samuel Francis Smith (1808-1895) desired to write a national hymn that would allow Americans an opportunity to offer praise to God for our wonderful land. On a scrap of paper in less then 30 minutes, he wrote the words to "My Country, 'Tis of Thee." Many Americans consider this song their favorite patriotic hymn. The tributes to our fatherland in the first three stanzas lead to a worshipful climax of gratefulness to God and a prayer for His continued guidance. Following his education, Samuel became an outstanding minister in several Baptist churches in the East. He composed 150 hymns during his 87 years of life and was instrumental in compiling the leading Baptist hymnal of his day. Think about these words from his song, *Our father's God, to Thee, author of liberty, to Thee we sing. Long may our land be bright with freedom's holy light; protect us by Thy might, great God our King!*

Consider answers to these questions about heart-songs:
- What experiences with Christ have resulted in special inspiration?
- What would you write in your praise song to God?
- What elements of God's work would you like to celebrate?
- What favorite hymn can you sing as a celebration to God?

D—Directed Prayer

I want to have a disciplined mind and heart to continually praise You.

July 7

A Little Stretcher

We must somehow get through to the physically and spiritually sick.
Luke 5:18-24

A—Advice from the Bible

. . . carrying on a stretcher a man . . .
(Luke 5:18, HCSB)

B—Biblical Example

Jesus was teaching in a house. His presence had attracted a crowd, and not all of them were friendly. For the first time, Luke records hostility on the part of the Jewish leaders. Certain Pharisees and doctors of the law were sitting in the crowd observing and listening to Jesus. Suddenly a shocking interruption occurred. The roof over the house where they were sitting was broken through. As Jesus was talking, dust and chunks of clay began to fall about Him. Then a paralyzed man on a stretcher began to be lowered through the opening of the roof. His friends were determined to bring the sick man to this Healer. Notice the first reaction of Jesus. He did not heal the man physically, but forgave his sins. The words spoken by the Lord caused an outburst of criticism. The religious authorities now had a case against this Man. They had witnessed a theological flaw. Their question was, "Who can forgive sins, but God alone?" Without giving an answer, Jesus did what only God could do. He told the man to take up his bed and walk. The Savior had made His point very clear. God forgives sins and God heals.

C--Contemporary Application

Marion would have died in childbirth had her friends not come to her rescue. Pete and Marion were pioneers by heart. Wilderness living always appealed to this couple. The pressures of the corporate world increased and the time to live their dream had come. A small acreage was purchased in remote Alaska. Specific plans were made for survival. Two trips "out" a year were scheduled. An extensive system of radios and two-way receivers was their only connection with the outside world. However, the advance plans did not include an unexpected pregnancy. Marion decided to stay in the wilderness until the last month before delivery. The baby had other plans and wanted to come earlier. Alaskan medical doctors were available in extreme situations. Their response by plane helped save Marion and the baby's life. An organization of Flying Doctors is available in many remote areas of the world to provide help for missionaries and other people.

Every Christian should feel:

- The need to help bear another's burdens.
- That miracles start when Christians begin helping others.
- The need to bring hope and confidence to sick friends.
- That the healing touch of Jesus is for all people.

D—Directed Prayer

Lord, help me to care enough to carry others to You.

July 8

Jonah's Little Vine

Show compassion for all people even if they are different from you.
Jonah 4:1-11

A—Advice from the Bible

Then the LORD God provided a vine . . .
(Jonah 4:6, NIV)

B—Biblical Example

The Book of Jonah teaches the tenderness of God toward a repentant nation and His rebuke of the false exclusiveness of Israel. God called this minor prophet to go to Nineveh, a great Assyrian city, to pronounce God's judgment because of the peoples' wickedness. But Jonah did not want these people to experience God's mercy and forgiveness. Remember the extreme effort he made to flee from the presence of God? However, he did make his way to the city, not because he wanted to see these heathen saved, but because he was willing to obey God and go where God told him to go. Jonah walked through the streets of Nineveh proclaiming the message that God had given him. The result was that the people did repent, causing Jonah to became angry "enough to die." His problem was caused by the fact that he cared more for a vine that perished than about the people of Nineveh. Perhaps God said something like this to the prophet, "Jonah, it's fine to be concerned about the vine; it shaded you when you needed it. But you didn't tend to it; you didn't even plant the vine. It was provided for you. Should I not pity 120,000 people? Surely you can see there is no comparison. I am a God of mercy and I must heed all who cry out to Me."

C--Contemporary Application

One man's generous giving helped raise the standard of education for the poor children in the South. Philanthropy and Christian stewardship characterized the life of John David Rockefeller who was born July 8, 1839. He was raised in a strict Baptist family in Cleveland, Ohio. After a business course, Mr. Rockefeller became involved in the oil industry. His success according to the world was measured in billions of dollars. His success in God's sight was the huge amount of his fortune used for humanitarian needs. People of all kinds benefited from his generosity. Although he was a dedicated businessman, he realized that wealth was no substitute for religious faith and personal virtue. Rockefeller and his wife cared for people who were less fortunate.

How do you compare to Jonah's call to show compassion to "other" people?

- A time I tried to run from God's presence was when I _____
- A time I became angry with God was when _____
- A time I was like Jonah was when _____
- A time I showed compassion to "other" people was _____

D—Directed Prayer

Father, help me to be concerned for the welfare of all kinds of people.

July 9

A Little Test Question

If we have a right relationship with God, we can handle the test questions.
Matthew 22:34-40

A—Advice from the Bible

An expert in the law asked a question to test Him.
(Matt. 22:35, HCSB)

B—Biblical Example

Jesus entered Jerusalem and was immediately confronted by the religious leaders. Their agenda included many questions, primarily about the source of Jesus' authority. The two power groups, the Pharisees and the Sadducees, rarely agreed on any subject, but in this case, Jesus was declared their enemy and they decided that He must be stopped. A series of questions were involved in the discourse, with the purpose of discrediting Jesus. The question and answer time continued with Jesus' pointing out the errors of His enemies. These religious leaders were concerned about taxes, the resurrection, and the Law. Finally, a person experienced in the Law asked one more question, "Teacher, which commandment in the law is the greatest?" Jesus now answered all three difficult questions. He had clarified the relationship between religion and government. The meaning of this life and the next life were clarified and most important He responded to the significance between God and a neighbor. The bottom-line to these questions is that the love commandment was the essence of both the Law and the Prophets. If a person has a right relationship with God, the problems with His commandments won't exist.

C--Contemporary Application

Thomas lived next door to a Christian couple. They were great neighbors until the subject of religion came up. The answers provided by this couple to his questions always seemed to make sense. However, Thomas wanted "all" the answers! Year after year he would say, "Well, I have another question for you." One day this unbeliever died. He waited too long to get all the answers about God, the Bible, and Christian living. A simple faith in Jesus would have ultimately provided help with his "need to know all" problem. What a shame that Thomas never experienced God's saving power!

 Suppose a non-Christian friend or neighbor asked you one of the following questions. What answers would you give?

- Why do you go to church so often? _____
- Who do you really think Jesus was? _____
- How can anyone keep all the commandments? _____
- Why do you think the Bible is so important? It's just another book._____
_____

D—Directed Prayer

Lord, when I have questions about You, lead me to Your answers.

July 10

A Little Plumb Line

Stand firm for truth.
Amos 7:8-17

A—Advice from the Bible

"Look, I am setting a plumb line among my people Israel."
(Amos 7:8)

B—Biblical Example

King Jehu's dynasty proved to be no better than past kings. Yet, God refused to give up on His people. He continued to send His prophets with a message of coming consequences for their rebellion against Him. During the closing days of the nation, two prophets represented God. About 760 B.C., God called a shepherd from Tekoa named Amos. He lived in a small village south of Jerusalem and was directed to leave his home and journey to the Northern Kingdom to proclaim Israel's downfall. The economy was good; the people were happy, and so this message of doom was not accepted. Amos and his confrontation with the political and religious leaders became a major point of attention. God used visions to enforce Amos' message. The prophet pleaded with God for mercy. Instead he saw a plumb line as an instrument of judgment. This construction tool was placed beside a wall being erected to determine if it was out of line vertically. A wall that leaned was torn down and rebuilt. In a similar manner, God measured His people by His standard of righteousness and they failed. Judgment would not be postponed.

C--Contemporary Application

A serious tourist to Europe will include a trip to Pisa, Italy, to see the famous leaning tower of Pisa. This central Italian city has capitalized on the fame of a building constructed without a plumb line. Active work on the site began in 1174 and after six stages of construction, the tower was completed in 1350. Pictures reveal a stone structure 180 feet tall and 52 feet in diameter. However, the magnificent architecture and decorations are overlooked because the building leans 13 feet from the foundation. Why would the builders continue the erection of such a heavy facility on a shallow foundation of soft soil? History books do not record the answer, but people were not allowed to worship there after 1996 for safety reasons. The prophet Amos warned God's people about staying on course in life and following God's requirements. If these standards are overlooked, a person's relationship with God is meaningless.

What is the plumb line for your life?

- God has a standard for me in His Word.
- God wants me to uphold His moral precepts.
- God has the right to measure His people.
- God desires true worship from His people.

D—Directed Prayer

Thank you, Lord, for continuing to be the Builder of my life.

July 11

Israel's Little Anniversary Banquet

Pass on to future generations the stories of God's dealings throughout history.
Psalm 78:1-16

A—Advice from the Bible

We will tell the next generation . . . .
(Ps. 78:4, NIV)

B—Biblical Example

Psalm 78 is a hymn of history. The opening words command the people to listen to what the composer, Asaph, has to say. The words begin to recall the unhappy days of disobedience which characterized the Jews during their rebellion and wandering. The psalm contrasts God's faithfulness and patience with Israel's failure and unbelief. Verse 9 provides an insight into a strange situation. The men of Ephraim were skilled in the art of archery. They had sufficient weapons to handle any enemy attack. However, on the day of battle, they "turned back" and ran for cover. The sound of battle made them nervous. Although well-armed and capable with their weapons, they lacked steadfastness. Underneath the polished armor they were cowards. Asaph felt a need to retell this situation to the next generations. The future listeners needed to refuse to retreat. Instead they should look to God for power. Psalm 78 is also called Israel's "anniversary banquet," a review of what God has done in and through and for His people—not a time for reminiscing, but an obligation to share the past with the present generation.

C--Contemporary Application

Today is the birthday of John Quincy Adams, the sixth president of the United States. He was born in 1767 at Braintree, Massachusetts. This man was a brilliant statesman and fought many battles for freedom. Some historians have said that he was the leading defender of freedom of speech. He also was the primary spokesman for the antislavery cause. Many battles were carried out in large, smoke-filled meeting rooms. Shaping a new nation was not an easy task and required leaders who would fight for the causes of freedom. President Adams trained himself through studying war tactics. He was similar to the Ephraimites at this point. However, while the early Israelites would run from the battle, Adams met the conflicts head-on. At the time of his death, his son found a detailed diary of the many years of history and experience. This journal provides insight into our nation's past that is recalled in no other way.

Many stories in your life have now become part of history. Respond to the following by completing the event you want others to remember.

- Remember when . . .
- Remember when . . .
- Remember when . . .
- Remember when . . .

D—Directed Prayer

Lord, remind me to pass on to future generations what I know about You.

July 12

Solomon's Little Queen of Sheba

A wise and good king is a blessing to his people.
1 Kings 10:1-13

A—Advice from the Bible

King Solomon gave the queen of Sheba all she desired and asked for.
(1 Kings 10:13, NIV)

B—Biblical Example

Solomon was the son of David and Bathsheba. Early in his life he sensed the need for wisdom. God granted wisdom to Solomon, but wisdom did not mean he couldn't make mistakes. His royalty and riches made him famous throughout many kingdoms, including Sheba, in southwest Arabia (present-day Yemen). The queen of that area was interested enough in Solomon's success to discover the truth of the report about the king. She came to Jerusalem with a large caravan of camels carrying the trade goods for which Sheba was noted. Her presentation to the court finally arrived and she met the king. All the questions on her mind were asked and she was not disappointed in his ability nor in the wisdom he displayed. The splendor of the court and the manner of the temple ceremonies overwhelmed her. The queen freely confessed that his fame had not even begun to do him justice. When this interesting visit concluded, she returned to her kingdom, carrying the generous gifts from the king. God's choice of Solomon as king was a mark of his love and favor for Israel throughout the region.

C--Contemporary Application

Another noted king was born in 1566 in Edinburg Castle in Scotland. He name was James Charles Stuart. He was crowned King James VI at the age of 13 months. His rule in his native Scotland began when he was 19 years old. He believed in the Divine Right of Kings and the monarch's duty to reign according to God's law and the public good. King James kept his kingdom out of war. Peace ruled during his reign. He was an evangelist of the true gospel, which automatically made him an enemy of Rome. His crowning achievement was the greatest piece of religious and literary work in the world. He gave his subjects the Holy Bible, so they could be saved and nourished from the Word of God. For many Christians the King James Bible of 1611 is the Word of God and is the first English translation of the Bible they can remember.

An interesting parallel exists between 1 Kings 10:13 and Ephesians 3:20. Consider what these verses have in common:

- Solomon gave whatever the queen asked.
- Solomon gave all she desired.
- Solomon gave of his royal riches.
- Our biggest asking is never too big for God.

D—Directed Prayer

King of my life, I desire all of Your best for me.

July 13

Anania's Little Vision

Is there a risk you need to take in order to obey God?
Acts 9:1-19

A—Advice from the Bible

The Lord said to him in a vision, "Ananias!"
(Acts 9:10)

B—Biblical Example

Ananias, a Christian from Damascus, was called by God to minister to a man named Saul. This faithful follower of Christ did not immediately jump at the opportunity to share Christ. He expressed some very strong reservations about doing what God wanted him to do. Saul's reputation among the believers as a persecutor of Christians prevented people from confronting him. Ananias had no way of knowing that a change had taken place in the life of this very dangerous Pharisee. The Lord assured him that Saul was aware of this mission through a vision. The fact that Saul was praying indicated the seriousness he felt about his conversion. The Lord did not get angry with Ananias for having doubts or asking questions. He spoke freely and permitted Ananias to speak freely in return. God revealed that He planned to use Saul to change history. With information and directions from God, this believer went to the house where Saul was staying. From a practical standpoint the risk was still there, but God had revealed the truth that enabled Ananias to obey. He went to Saul, accepted him as a believer, and explained why he had come.

C--Contemporary Application

Risk is facing the possibility that a loss will occur if a certain thing is attempted. However, sometimes the only way to achieve a goal is to take risks. Christians live in a world where taking some risks are necessary. Certain people must have an opportunity to hear the gospel message. To decide not to take the risk of getting involved in ministry to others means a certain spiritual loss. The joy and fulfillment of seeing an individual become a follower of Christ is exciting. Of course, what lies ahead in the unknown may appear risky to you, but the only way to be obedient to this ministry is to accept the risk. Fear can be immobilizing. God is the guide for a risk-taker who is acting in obedience to Him. Ananias was willing to face danger in order to respond to God's command.

Consider the following examples about taking a risk for the right reasons. How would you handle your fear?

- If I share Christ, my friends may reject me.
- If I give my life to God, He may want me to be a missionary.
- If I really follow God, I may not like His plans for my future.
- If I help someone, I may miss out on personal fulfillment.

D—Directed Prayer

Lord, Your call to minister may involve personal risk. Help me to be brave.

July 14

A Little Plug for Purity

Be committed to a godly course of action.
Daniel 1:1-8

A—Advice from the Bible

But Daniel resolved not to defile himself with . . . .
(Daniel 1:8)

B—Biblical Example

Nebuchadnezzar was the crown prince and general of the Babylonian army at this period of history. He led a siege of Jerusalem and took not only people into exile, but also vessels of worship from the temple in that holy city. These sacred items were then apparently converted to the worship of the Babylonian gods in their temples. Several Jewish young men also were chosen for service to the king. Physical development came first. Then they were to grow intellectually by receiving the best education.

One of the three young captives decided not to eat the king's food or drink the wine. He believed that such a practice would be personally defiling. These foods had possibly been associated with idolatrous worship. Daniel did not want to come into the presence of his God ritually unclean. A request was made to the chief officer that he not be forced to participate in these kinds of meals. This young captive had a goal to remain pure in spirit and body. He purposely turned from that which he believed would harm his body or damage his relationship to God. Spiritual intervention led the steward to grant compassion to Daniel and his friends.

C—Contemporary Application

Jennifer could hardly wait for August and her official enrollment at the state university. She had set personal goals for the next four years. Daily Bible study and prayer were at the top of her list. The practices had been a apart of her life for as long as she could remember. The new roommate arrived! Not exactly what Jen was expecting. Within days, Jen was introduced to worldly activities and ideas that shocked her. The "roomie" kept insisting that this Christian young woman go with her to some of these off-campus activities. The temptation became very great for Jennifer, however, she felt like her relationship to God was more important than pleasing her roommate. She remained committed to her godly course of action.

How can we maintain God's ideal of purity?

- Christians should willingly separate themselves from alcohol and other drugs.
- Christians should turn away from whatever harms the body or spirit.
- Christians should know that wise living promotes health.
- Christians should do God's will under the control of the Holy Spirit.

D—Directed Prayer

Father, lead me to be ready to say "no."

July 15

A Little Pursuit of Happiness

Happiness depends on what you are, not what you have.
Matthew 5:1-10

A—Advice from the Bible

Blessed are the poor in spirit.
(Matt. 5:3)

B—Biblical Example

The next eight devotionals will focus on the Beatitudes found in the Sermon on the Mount (Matt. 5—7). The Scripture passage contains important statements Jesus made to His followers about the qualities that should characterize their lives. Each beatitude begins with an affirmation and ends with a promise. At this time Jesus was ministering in the Galilean region and great crowds of ordinary people were following Him.

The first blessing begins with Jesus congratulating kingdom citizens for being *poor in spirit*. This means that Christians recognize their absolute helplessness in making themselves right with God. The personal awareness that we are spiritually nothing in ourselves becomes a reality. (Read Romans 3:23 which speaks of our need.) However, when this need is discovered, God has the answer for His people. For a believer to take pride in his spiritual wealth is to turn his back on God's blessing. How can this attitude be eliminated in the life of a follower of Jesus? Self-interests and self-centeredness have to be conquered. Welcome to the kingdom of heaven!

C—Contemporary Application

Robert was the wealthiest man in our church. His material accumulations were vast in number. New cars, condos on the beach, airplanes, and houses were part of his lifestyle. And yet, this man was an example of *poor in spirit*. His love for and faithfulness to the Lord were witnessed by the community as he served in places of leadership. Several truths had been discovered in his 50-years of living. He recognized his absolute helplessness in making himself right with God. He became sensitive to his sinful condition as a young adult. He placed his strength under God's control and he had an intense desire to live in a right relationship to God and other people. Robert, though a leader in our town, practiced submission, trust, and faithfulness toward God. This citizen continues to study God's Word and stays in touch with God through prayer. Welcome to the kingdom of heaven, Robert!

The person who is *poor in spirit*:

- Regards himself as nothing in the sight of God.
- Understands that the fear of the Lord is the beginning of wisdom.
- Manages life-experiences similar to the Old Testament Job.
- Places trust completely in Jesus.

D—Directed Prayer

Father, help me to recognize my spiritual helplessness.

July 16

A Little Pursuit of Happiness

Happiness depends on what you are, not what you have.
Matthew 5:1-10

A—Advice from the Bible

Blessed are those who mourn.
(Matt. 5:4)

B—Biblical Example

Jesus became very popular as He ministered throughout the Galilean region. On one occasion He led the crowds up to a mountain. His disciples came closer and He taught them about being kingdom citizens. This experience is called the Sermon on the Mount. The second beatitude sounds shocking! A question is asked, "What possible blessing could there be in sorrow?" One answer could be that the people were grieving over their need for Christ. Sorrow can teach us what really matters most in life. Since Christianity is about caring, we feel the sin, pain, grief, and sorrow of others. This beatitude speaks of godly sorrow for sin. A broken and penitent heart God will not despise. The closer we get to God, the more aware we become of our sins and imperfections. Therefore, the reward for those who mourn is that "they shall be comforted." The comfort and joy of forgiveness will be celebrated.

C—Contemporary Application

Sorrow has the potential to make us bitter or better. An old story relates how a woman went to Buddha and asked that her son be restored to life. Buddha agreed to her request, provided she could bring him a bowl of peppercorns from homes where the family unit was still intact—no death of a family member. The woman went out confidently, but returned with an empty bowl. Sooner or later sorrow comes to all of us. Myra is a bitter old woman. Her husband passed 40 years ago and she is still angry at God. The comfort of the Holy Spirit has not been claimed in her bitterness. She refuses to mourn over things she has done in the past that were wrong. On the other hand, Nell became a widow at age 42. Years have passed since that great personal loss. However, this Christian woman has been comforted through the years by Christian friends and the Holy Spirit. She grieved over her sins and the sins of her family. What comfort it is to know that the Comforter lives in us! Nell's radiance is a testimony to the forgiveness of God.

A person whose life is characterized by the qualities in the Beatitudes demonstrates:
- Submissiveness to God. How?
- Trust in God. How?
- Faithfulness toward God. How?
- Spiritual helplessness without God. How?

D—Directed Prayer

Father, help us to realize the awfulness of sin.

July 17

A Little Pursuit of Happiness

Happiness depends on what you are, not what you have.
Matthew 5:1-10

A—Advice from the Bible

Blessed are the gentle.
(Matt. 5:5)

B—Biblical Example

The third Beatitude contradicts what the world teaches. The world's message, that only people who are aggressive will succeed, is void of truth in the light of what Jesus said. The Lord congratulated the gentle. Gentleness or meekness is a kingdom quality that is often misunderstood. Meekness is not weakness! The word picture is of a strong animal that has been tamed. Gentleness must have sounded strange to the people of Jesus' day. This Beatitude means placing your strength under God's control to be used in the kingdom service. A promise is made to this kind of believer. Jesus said that all who practice gentleness will inherit the earth. Only two men in the Bible are called meek or gentle: Moses, the mighty lawgiver, and Jesus, the Son of God. Neither person would be described as weak. Another characteristic of the meek is that they are authentically humble. Pride is the opposite of this attitude. A final thought about gentleness is that such persons live in submission to God and His will.

C—Contemporary Application

A hymn that has been meaningful to me through my Christian life is, "Take My Life and Let It Be." The hymnist Frances Havergal felt that something was missing from her Christian experience. She read a little book called "All for Jesus," which stressed the importance of making Christ the King of every part of your life. On December 2, 1873, she wrote this great hymn. For the rest of her life, she used these words as part of her devotional life. The message of the song reminds me of the third Beatitude. Only a person who seriously makes this commitment to Christ can expect to find the real happiness that Jesus spoke about on the Sermon on the Mount. A complete consecration to the Lord and His service must be experienced. This attitude of surrender usually comes through personal prayer times with the Lord and the ultimate victory will come when Christ returns.

Blessed is a gentle person who says:

- Take my life and let it be consecrated, Lord, to Thee.
- Take my feet and let them be swift and beautiful for Thee.
- Take my voice and let me sing always, only, for my King.
- Take myself and I will be ever, only, all for Thee.

D—Directed Prayer

O how happy are the God-controlled: heaven and earth are theirs.

July 18

A Little Pursuit of Happiness

Happiness depends on what you are, not what you have.
Matthew 5:1-10

A—Advice from the Bible

Blessed are those who hunger and thirst.
(Matt. 5:6)

B—Biblical Example

The fourth Beatitude describes a longing for God. In Jesus' day, religion was largely an external matter. Worship consisted of rules to be kept and performance of ceremonial rituals. This method of adulation seemed to please men, but not God. Imagine that you are starving to death. Your body craves food and water. You can think of nothing else. You would do anything in your power to get the food and liquid you need to survive. This example illustrates what Jesus meant by *hunger* and *thirst*. However, a follower of Jesus needs more than food and water. Spiritual nourishment is needed and we cannot provide that for ourselves. Remember how Jesus experienced physical hunger and thirst during the 40 days in the wilderness? His spiritual thirst was to do God's will. That desire should be the same for us. Kingdom citizens desire the true righteousness that comes from being right with God on His terms. Our self-righteousness leaves us spiritually faint. Jesus offers His congratulations to the believers who are earnestly desiring God's righteousness. We will find total satisfaction in what He imparts to all who trust Him.

C—Contemporary Application

Some of life's lessons are learned through reading books or hearing stories from ancient times. These illustrations tend to place the Scripture in real-life settings. For example, an old story is told of a seeker who went to a wise philosopher, asking the way to God. The thinker seized the man, thrust his head beneath water, and held him there! The seeker almost drowned. When he finally came up, he was struggling for air. The wise man told him that when he wanted God as desperately as he wanted air, he would find Him. When we are satisfied, we have an intense desire to live righteously in our relationships to God and others. Our spiritual development does not happen at a certain time on the calendar. God's Spirit has to guide us and strengthen us in our desire to be righteous. Growth for the blessed person goes on all the days of our life.

What are the promises from this fourth Beatitude?

- The hungry body can be fed.
- The inquiring mind can learn.
- The seeking spirit can worship.
- The obedient will find satisfaction.

D—Directed Prayer

Think on this: O how happy are those who hunger for God for they shall be satisfied.

July 19

A Little Pursuit of Happiness

Happiness depends on what you are, not what you have.
Matthew 5:1-10

A—Advice from the Bible

Blessed are the merciful, for they shall receive mercy.
(Matt. 5:7)

B—Biblical Example

The fifth Beatitude is more easily understood than some of the others. *Mercy* describes God's kindness and unwavering love for His people. Some Old Testament examples of this mercy are Lot, Joseph, Moses, and David. In the New Testament, mercy is seen as sympathy and comfort. This beatitude means that we do more than feel pity for people in need. We express mercy in acts of kindness and grace that flows from a sympathetic heart. Merciful people place themselves in the shoes of other people in need and act accordingly. These words of Jesus were radical in His day. The Jews were taught to show no mercy to Gentiles. Romans and Greeks did not have a reputation for mercy. They despised other races as senseless barbarians. All people believed that suffering was a direct result of a specific sin. Therefore, this teaching was difficult for His disciples to practice. The reward for showing mercy to others is to receive this same mercy. The old saying is true, "We get what we give."

C—Contemporary Application

Frank and Anna Mae don't have much in the way of material wealth. Their farm house is nice and meets this senior adult couple's comforts. However, to describe them in spiritual terms is another subject. Marilee stood at their backdoor one night, knocking and crying. This young teen was pregnant and her parents had "kicked" her out of the house. She had no where to go except to this couple who were known to care about other people. The young, expectant mother moved into a guest bedroom, helped with the chores around the farm, learned to cook, and also how to worship. Months passed and a baby boy was born. Frank and Anna Mae became the grandparents. This new mother and her son experienced the mercy of a loving, caring couple. The young son went to college, studying medicine. At this point the old farm couple received their reward. They were blessed when Dr. Frank opened a local practice and cared for their health the rest of their lives.

What are some principles of this fifth Beatitude?

- We must believe the best about people.
- We must seek opportunities to help people.
- We must show mercy rather than justice.
- We must think brothers instead of "those other people."

D—Directed Prayer

Thank You, for loving the merciful.

July 20

A Little Pursuit of Happiness

Happiness depends on what you are, not what you have.
Matthew 5:1-10

A—Advice from the Bible

Blessed are pure in heart, for they will see God.
(Matt. 5:8)

B—Biblical Example

The sixth Beatitude is about purifying your motives in serving God. When Jesus congratulated the *pure in heart*, He meant to have one's motives purged of anything that does not please God. He emphasized the importance of inward purity. People who meet this standard of behavior will exhibit a single-minded purpose in seeking to honor and please the Lord in everything they do and say. Later in the Sermon on the Mount, Jesus said, "Seek first His kingdom and His righteousness" (6:33). These qualities of life will bring blessings to individuals. This most demanding beatitude offers the richest reward. The promise of this verse is that people with a pure heart *will see God*. A believer's heart is purified by faith in the Lord Jesus Christ. Living with devotion to the Lord allows us to be aware of His presence in our lives each day. If evil motives persist, evil will be seen in almost everything. If pure motives persist, we will see God at work in everything we experience.

C—Contemporary Application

An Englishman finished his first travel tour of the United States. He was interviewed by a reporter about his impressions of our great nation. The visitor commented, "The trouble with you Americans is that you are concerned about being so confoundly happy. Surely, there are more important things in life than just being happy." Most Americans do seem concerned about happiness. In the Declaration of Independence, Thomas Jefferson expressed this idea when he wrote that the rights of man are "life, liberty, and the pursuit of happiness." Remember the old story about a little boy being shown saints depicted in stained-glass windows? He said, "I know what saints are. They're the people the light shines through." Purity is a pathway to happiness in a person's choice to live in the unpolluted world. Two prisoners looked through the jail windows. One saw mud; the other saw stars. What made the difference?

Elizabeth Barrett Browning wrote,

- "Earth's crammed with heaven,
- And every common bush afire with God;
- But only he who sees, takes off his shoes."
- Be aware of God's presence in the world about you

D—Directed Prayer

Father, lead me to be a single-minded, pure-in-heart believer, so I may see You.

July 21

A Little Pursuit of Happiness

Happiness depends on what you are, not what you have.
Matthew 5:1-10

A—Advice from the Bible

> *Blessed are the peacemakers for they will be called the sons of God.*
> (Matt. 5:9)

B—Biblical Example

The seventh Beatitude is about a person who has peace with God through faith in Jesus Christ and seeks to live at peace with all people. The noun *peacemaker* appears only here in the Bible. Understanding what Jesus meant in this Beatitude requires a definition of the word "peace." The key factor to this attitude is having a right relationship with God. He is the One who gives us true spiritual peace. This way of thinking is a gift from God, a fruit of the Holy Spirit (Gal. 5:22). Peace is not simply the absence of strife. Peace is not gained through compromise with evil, nor is peace at any price worth the cost. The local condition at the time of this teaching was marred with hatred between the Jews and Romans. A state of revolution was about to happen. A person speaking about peace would be considered unpatriotic and yet, Jesus dared to assert that God considers those who make peace His children. The promise of this Beatitude is that we will resemble our Father in attitude and actions, and share His nature. We belong to God!

C—Contemporary Application

James Earl Carter, Jr. was born in Plains, Georgia, on October 1, 1924 and became the 39th President of the United States (1977-1981). His major concern was for peace in the world. Carter initiated a foreign policy based on respect for human rights. His greatest triumph in foreign affairs came in 1978, when he provided the outline for the historic peace treaty between Egyptian president Muhammad Anwar al-Sadat and Israeli Prime Minister Menachem Begin, paving the way for a peace treaty signed in 1979. The memories I have of this president are not in the area of foreign affairs, but his love for a small, local church in Georgia. He taught a men's Bible study class for years and evidence from his life indicates he knew how to be a peacemaker. Today, he helps build houses for needy people and still travels to warring nations seeking to solve the problems with peaceful negotiations, rather than war.

A peacemaker:

- Has peace with God.
- Seeks to live at peace with other people.
- Helps others find peace with God.
- Encourages kingdom citizens to recognize the ownership of God.

D—Directed Prayer

Thank You, that a believer can be filled with Your peace.

A Little Pursuit of Happiness

Happiness depends on what you are, not what you have.
Matthew 5:1-10

A—Advice from the Bible

Blessed are those persecuted for righteousness for theirs is the kingdom of heaven.
(Matt. 5:10)

B—Biblical Example

The eighth and last Beatitude is about a person who accepts the consequences of living by Christian values. You would think that the world would like to have citizens who live by the beatitudes of Jesus, but don't count on it! This individual knew from the beginning that persecution for commitment to righteousness would attract enemies. However, Jesus congratulates these believers. Insults, persecution, and false accusations will happen because of faithfulness to Him. Secular society does not interest this disciple. During the first century, Christians found their religion declared illegal and their faith considered revolutionary because they refused to say, "Caesar is lord" and worship him as divine. They lost their jobs, were imprisoned, and often martyred for their faith. The promise attached to this beatitude is that a person who remains part of God's kingdom will receive a reward of a relationship with Christ that awaits us in heaven.

C—Contemporary Application

Near our town is a settlement of Amish people. This North American Protestant group is of Mennonite origin. They have maintained a distinctive and conservative agricultural way of life and are often persecuted for their chosen lifestyle. The name Amish came from Jakob Amman, a Swiss Mennonite bishop. He insisted that discipline within the church be maintained by excommunication. The Amish, subject to persecution in Europe, migrated in the 18th century to Pennsylvania, where their descendants are called Pennsylvania Dutch. They dress in a severely plain style, using hooks and eyes instead of buttons. They ride in horse-drawn buggys instead of cars. Discipline is enforced by shunning; and marriage with outsiders is condemned. Every summer, my husband and I go to the Amish community and buy strawberries and homemade breads. The women were very shy at first, but now a relationship had been established. I admire their dedication even though I don't understand their "ways."

A pattern for living according to the Beatitudes includes:
- Studying God's Word to know His Will.
- Staying in touch with God through prayer.
- Trusting God.
- Being faithful to God in every aspect of our lives.

D—Directed Prayer

Father, I want Your Beatitudes to be reflected in my life.

July 23

The Little Wise Woman from Tekoa

A Christian needs to overcome the bitterness of a broken relationship.
2 Samuel 14:1-19

A—Advice from the Bible

Joab sent to Tekoa and had a wise woman brought from there.
(2 Sam. 14:1)

B—Biblical Example

King David and his son, Absalom, needed to be reconciled after a three-year absence. Joab, David's friend and servant, realized that his king's heart would not be at peace and life in the kingdom would not be normal unless this family feud was resolved. To make possible reconciliation, he devised a plan to confront David and convince him to bring Absalom back to Jerusalem. The village of Tekoa lay just 10 miles south of Jerusalem. Joab chose the perfect person, a wise woman, to carryout his plan. He gave the woman a script and then relied on her acting ability to drive the point home. Act I focuses on a grieving widow telling a fictitious story reminiscent of Cain and Abel. David agreed to protect her surviving son from the vengeance sought by relatives. He swore to protect her son so he could carry on the name of his father. The woman's story paralleled David's family situation and he suspected someone had coached her. She confessed Joab was behind her performance. The king accepted Joab's plan to confront him with his wrong.

C—Contemporary Application

Two American Appalachian mountaineer families engaged in a legendary feud that attracted nationwide attention in the 1880s and '90s. The Hatfields were headed by William Hatfield (1839–1921), and the McCoys by Randolph McCoy (1839–1921), each of whom fathered 13 children. The families lived on opposite sides of a stream in West Virginia. The origins of the feud are unclear. Some attribute it to hostilities formed during the American Civil War, in which the McCoys were Unionists and the Hatfields were Confederates. The first major bloodshed did not occur until 1882, when Ellison Hatfield was mortally shot in a brawl with McCoys and, in revenge, the Hatfields kidnapped and executed three McCoy brothers. These murders began the backwoods warfare, and thereafter Hatfields and McCoys repeatedly ambushed and killed one another. The feuding gradually abated and had ended by the second decade of the 20th century.

Questions about reconciliation:
- To whom do I need to show mercy rather than vengeance?
- What is needed to heal the wounds of bitterness?
- Why is full reconciliation difficult?
- What bitterness still plagues my life?

D—Directed Prayer

Thank You, Lord, that forgiveness can remove bitterness and bring about peace.

July 24

A Little True Freedom

The worst bondage is to think you are free, and yet really be a slave.
John 8:31-41

A—Advice from the Bible

So if the Son sets you free, you will be free indeed.
(John 8:36)

B—Biblical Example

Chapter 8 of John's Gospel is about a series of contrasts that reveal the kindness of Jesus and the wickedness of humankind. The writer dwells on the disputes between Jesus and the Jews. The Feast of Tabernacles was over and Jesus used the remaining time to minister to the people in the temple. Word quickly spread that Jesus was giving testimony about Himself, so crowds began to gather around Him. The result of the meeting was that many people believed (v. 30). He emphasized the proof of discipleship in a simple sentence, "If you continue in my word, you are truly my disciples." Someone once said, "Life leads to learning, and learning leads to liberty." The unbelieving Jewish leaders did not understand His message. Jesus was speaking about spiritual freedom, freedom from sin. These men were interpreting what the Lord was saying as a part of political freedom. In fact, they denied that Abraham's descendants had ever been in bondage. Apparently the leaders had forgotten that in the Old Testament, they had been enslaved seven times. The Pharisees and other religious leaders thought they were free, but they were actually enslaved in terrible spiritual bondage to sin and Satan.

C—Contemporary Application

Patriotic displays are featured in July. One reminder of American's freedom is the Liberty Bell. This symbol of freedom is located in Philadelphia, Pennsylvania, at Independence Hall. The history of the bell is interesting. It was commissioned in 1751 by the Pennsylvania Provincial Assembly. The bell was cast in London and delivered to the U.S. in August 1752. It was cracked by a stroke of the clapper, recast twice, and hidden from British forces. The motto, "Proclaim liberty throughout all the land unto all the inhabitants thereof" (Leviticus 25:10), still remains as a reminder of our responsibility. The last ringing was for George Washington's birthday in 1846. On January 1, 1976, the bell was moved to a new pavilion near Independence Hall.

Jesus calls no temporary followers:

- We are to be faithful to the end.
- We are to stay active in the life of His church.
- We are to show proof of true salvation.
- We are to avoid bondage to sin.

D—Directed Prayer

Father, You provide spiritual freedom for Your children and we are thankful.

July 25

Little Paths

Life can never be fully understood except through a relationship with God.
Proverbs 4:14-27

A—Advice from the Bible

Do not set foot on the path of the wicked.
(Prov. 4:14)

B—Biblical Example

When David's son, Solomon, became king he had a vision in which God asked him what his heart desired above everything else. The young man asked for wisdom. Because he asked for the treasure of wisdom instead of riches or fame, God gave him all three. Therefore, these proverbs are from the wisest of all the kings of Israel. Verse 14 begins with the two ways of life: the way of righteousness and integrity, or the path of the wicked. The readers are admonished to walk in the straight and narrow way (Matt. 7:13-14). The result of this command is that no cause for fear will exist and no reason to stumble will occur. Trouble always comes when an individual decides to explore the ways of wickedness. A lesson to be learned from these verses is: watch where you are going and don't swerve to the right or left. Keep your eye on the road and drive on the right side, and you will be doing what you should do. Someone once said, "We stumble over pebbles, not mountains." This proverb advises believers to go to God for help in maintaining their life course.

C—Contemporary Application

I still remember the day we watched our television screens as the first man to the moon "took a walk." Neil Alden Armstrong, (1930-   ) was his name. On July 25, 1969, as commander of the Apollo 11 lunar mission, he became the first person to set foot on the moon's surface. He had served as a civilian test pilot at Edwards Air Force Base, Lancaster, California, before becoming an astronaut. His companions on the mission were Edwin E. Aldrin, Jr., and Michael Collins. Years of training were necessary before that first step was taken. Manuals and guidance materials were studied. The Book of Proverbs is similar as an instruction book for a Christian. The wisdom and assistance offered by these words provide direction down life's pathways and help us not to compromise the way of righteousness.

Advice from Proverbs 3:5-6:

- Trust in the LORD with all you heart
- Lean not to your own understand
- In all your ways acknowledge Him
- He will make your paths straight.

D—Directed Prayer

The complexities of life are too hard for me to handle, but You show me the way.

July 26

A Little Towel and Basin

The love of God needs to be expressed through believers.
John 13:1-17

A—Advice from the Bible

Jesus poured water into a basin and . . . drying them with a towel.
(John 13:5)

B—Biblical Example

The Jewish Passover provides the background for these verses. Jesus assembled His disciples in an upper room for the purpose of observing the feast and to provide opportunity for the final instruction of these men. The Passover commemorated Israel's deliverance from Egypt. A common courtesy of the East was for a host to make provision for washing the guest's feet. Dirt roads and hot weather caused discomfort for visitors, so a bowl of water would be available for washing. Normally this service would be rendered by a slave as the guests arrived. When no one moved, Jesus assumed the role of a servant by removing His outer garment, wrapping a towel around Him, pouring water, and proceeded from disciple to disciple, washing their feet. His primary motivation was His love for them. Peter protested that Jesus would never wash his feet. Jesus asked the group if they understood what had happened. Their Teacher had humbled Himself by taking the place of a slave. Jesus' followers needed to learn to be servants, not masters. He expected His disciples to act on what He taught them.

C—Contemporary Application

Dr. Wilfred Grenfell (1865-1940) spent a large part of his life in service for Christ in Labrador. To raise funds for the mission work there he traveled extensively and told of his work. Speaking one night on the early years in Labrador, the doctor told of the struggle and hardship he endured. Afterward a woman praised him profusely for his sacrifices. Grenfell responded quickly, "Oh, you completely misunderstood me. I was having the time of my life." He had found his greatest joy and fulfillment in serving others. Christ provided the model on that last night of His life when He washed the feet of His disciples. Too often we know the right thing to do, but fail to do it! Opportunities can pass so quickly and may not return. A Christian will find the same joy and satisfaction in meeting the needs of other people as Dr. Grenfell.

Focusing on serving attitudes: Yes? No?

- I can do certain things to serve other people.
- I can serve people that nobody else cares about.
- A servant attitude is demonstrated in something like . . . .
- Jesus' followers should have a limit in their serving others.

D—Directed Prayer

Father, help me to be willing to serve others.

July 27

A Little Unconditional Compassion

God promises forgiveness and restoration.
Micah 7:7-20

A—Advice from the Bible

You will again have compassion on us.
(Micah. 7:19)

B—Biblical Example

Micah delivered some tough messages from God to the Israelites. But as he closed out his book of prophecy, this country prophet presented a message of hope. He offered assurance to the remnant, the Israelites who faithfully trusted God. The Lord would provide a Savior to rescue His people from the corruption and desperation of this world. He quickly cautioned those who opposed the True God. Even though Israel had been through some tough times and would possibly face difficult circumstances in the future, the prophet knew that ultimately, God's faithful people would triumph. God would bring them from the darkness of sin and rebellion into the light of His love and forgiveness. Once again God's chosen nation would enjoy a prominent place in the world. He concluded his prophecy with a prayer. He asked God to safeguard His people for He alone was able to forgive sins. Compassion is a major theme throughout this closing chapter of Micah. God had lovingly offered complete forgiveness to His chosen people. The prophet presented the facts to the Israelites: their sin and rebellion had separated them from God. Now He offered unconditional compassion and forgiveness.

C—Contemporary Application

Charles and Molly are parents who struggle with a disobedient daughter. How often have they asked themselves, "Why? Where did we go wrong?" The guilty feeling often prevents them from experiencing the joy of their salvation. Becky was pregnant at 15 and chose adoption rather than motherhood. She asked her parents to forgive her and they did. At 16, Becky quit school and ran away from home. Finally at 20, she contacted the family and begged to come home. Her life on the streets was a total disaster. Her parents did not hesitate for a minute to bring her home. Becky repented from her sinful life and responded to the unconditional compassion of loving parents. What kept Charles and Molly going all these years? Hope! God's promises! And the Savior.

Examine God's offer of unconditional compassion:

- He loves you.
- He forgives sinners.
- You must decide to turn from sin and trust Christ.
- You can receive Christ by believing that Jesus died and rose again for you

D—Directed Prayer

Lord, thank You, that Your offer of forgiveness and love is available today.

July 28

Two Little Copper Coins

Christians are to be generous givers
Luke 21:1-4

A—Advice from the Bible

A poor widow put in two very small copper coins.
(Lk. 21:2)

B—Biblical Example

Giving was apparently a public event in Jesus' time. In an area of the Temple stood thirteen offering chests with a horn-like receptacle mounted on each. Each of the thirteen collection boxes was designated for a specific use in some area of the Temple expenses. The giver chose the area or areas he wanted to support and dropped his offering into the appropriate box. Jesus spent at least a portion of a day observing people as they brought their offering to the Temple. He watched as the rich walked by and deposited their gifts in the offering chests. They probably made rather substantial gifts to the treasury. The widow stood in stark contrast to these rich contributors. In monetary value, her gift was two of the smallest coins in circulation. The Jewish law of that day required that two offerings by made. Her two copper coins represented all that she had. Out of her love, the poor woman was willing to sacrifice herself and yet, Jesus placed superior value on her gift. The fact is she gave all she had. Jesus praised her giving. He noted how much she had left, not how much she gave.

C—Contemporary Application

On a trip to Salt Lake City, Utah, we toured the city's Temple Square. This great area is the contemporary center of the Mormon Church, officially the Church of Jesus Christ of Latter-Day Saints. The majestic temple was completed on July 28, 1893 after 40 years of construction. Six towers rise 220 ft in the air. The facility is not open to visitors, but pictures provide a look at the interior. This building was created from the offerings of Mormon people. They desired a place to worship and they believed God had given them this site. Through the generations, worshippers have provided the money to build great places for God. I am sure many people gave sacrificially to these causes. Generous givers continue to provide buildings for serving God and in turn reaching people for Jesus Christ. Would Jesus have praised you for your giving?

Generous giving enables a person to meet many needs:

- Giving for world missions.
- Giving for construction of worship buildings.
- Giving for medical treatments.
- Giving for educational facilities.

D—Directed Prayer

Thank You for blessing a generous giver.

July 29

Lot's Little Weakness

God cares about the spiritual needs of people in urban areas
Genesis 19:20-25

A—Advice from the Bible

Look, here is a town near enough to run to.
(Gen. 19:20)

B—Biblical Example

Lot, his wife, and his daughters loved the world too much. When he chose to move to the cities of Sodom and Gomorrah, instead of living on the plains, things went from bad to worse. All kinds of sexual abuses were present in Sodom. Lot was even willing to sacrifice his daughters to the wicked men in order to spare the guests God had sent. Then the men of the city threatened Lot himself. His guests announced the coming destruction of the city, urging Lot and his family to leave quickly. However, he had become so sinful that he had lost his influence with almost everyone in Sodom. Heavenly visitors were convinced of the hopelessly evil condition of the area. Destruction was imminent, and they gave Lot his evacuation orders. Apparently Lot's two daughters were engaged to be married to two men of the city, for Lot found them and told them of the impending disaster. They refused to heed his warning. The next morning, when time came to leave, Lot still wanted to stay. Finally the angels had to take Lot and his family by the hand and lead them out of the city, as an adult might lead a child away from a favorite playground. The weakness of Lot's faith is revealed as he continued to find reasons to stay in the sinful city of Sodom.

C—Contemporary Application

Cindy hated living in a small town. She was constantly bored with the lifestyle of her parents. She often would tell them, "The minute I graduate from high school, I am out of here." And so she graduated, packed her bags, and headed for Dallas. The money she had saved for the last three years would keep her supplied with needs. However, she realized how much she missed relationships. Attending church was not in her plans, so Cindy continued to exist in her eat, sleep, and work routine. A crisis forced her to return to the small town. Before long she discovered the love and personal support of friends. Her faith was strengthened by Christian examples. She never returned to the city.

Biblical truths from Lot's experience:
- God knows humans.
- God honors the presence of righteous people.
- God is long-suffering.
- God has methods for destroying wickedness.

D—Directed Prayer

Father, help me to pray for others who need to experience the love of God.

July 30

Little Apostles of Christ

Believers must demonstrate sincerity of motive.
1 Thessalonians 2:3-12

A—Advice from the Bible

As apostles of Christ . . . we were gentle among you.
(1 Thess. 2:6)

B—Biblical Example

Acts 17:1-10 describe how the people in Thessalonica responded to the gospel. Some rejected the good news and become enemies of Paul. The apostles had to leave the area for safety reasons. His opponents tried to discredit him with a number of accusations and so Paul wrote this letter to defend himself against these charges. He proclaimed God's gospel, not theirs. Silvanus and Timothy were traveling companions at this time. This team was not seeking personal glory, even though they were recognized as apostles of Christ. These men did not act as rulers over the Thessalonians. They displayed gentleness and applied no pressure to make the people become believers. Paul always held himself accountable to God and he wanted all people to know that fact. He claimed that he and his friends had behaved themselves with holiness and without blame. The goal for the Thessalonians was that they have a lifestyle which was God's way for them. By God's salvation, they were His church, His redeemed people.

C—Contemporary Application

William Penn (1644-1718) died on July 30, 1718. He was an English Quaker and the founder of the colony of Pennsylvania. His conflicts in dealing with people reminds me of the Apostle Paul. His religious convictions brought him into discord with the authorities, and he was imprisoned (much like Paul.) He returned to England in order to aid persecuted Quakers. This religious group consisted of nonviolent people and William would not fight his enemies. He was twice accused of treason and of corresponding with the exiled James II, but he was acquitted. Though often accused of various offenses, he was never found guilty. In 1699 Penn paid a second visit to Pennsylvania, where his presence was required to restore peace and order. This man's accomplishments during this visit included a guarantee of religious freedom. Crippled by a stroke in 1712, Penn died in Buckinghamshire on July 30, 1718.

Consider these reasons for being gentle apostles of Christ:

- People need to know you care about them.
- People fail to respond to Christ when being treated harshly.
- People need to be aware of the opponents of the gospel.
- People need to trust you.

D—Directed Prayer

Thank You for Paul's example of being an apostle of Christ.

July 31

King Solomon's Little Women

Other loyalties can distract you from God's plan for your life.
1 Kings 11:1-11

A—Advice from the Bible

Solomon loved many foreign women.
(1 Kings 11:1)

B—Biblical Example

Solomon, son of King David, was a sincere and loving believer. He wanted to follow his father's spiritual example by obeying God. He asked the Lord to give him an understanding mind with which to govern the people. The Lord was delighted with Solomon's request and He not only gave Solomon a wise and discerning mind, but He also blessed Solomon with riches and honor. Tragically, the young king became distracted from God's design for his life by his massive building projects and the pagan influences of his foreign wives. His sin finally led to open rebellion and brought forth God's judgment upon him and his family. Polygamy was common in the ancient world. Most monarchs had many wives and very large harems. Most of the marriages were the result of political treaties made to boost trade or to provide military security. Such marriages inevitably brought pagan influences into the nation. God had frequently warned the children of Israel about the dangers of intermarriage with people from alien nations. The greatest danger was that of idolatry. Distractions of evil usually drive people away from God and Solomon was no exception. God's intervention would soon occur.

C—Contemporary Application

Twice in our newspaper this week, men were caught in pornographic incidents. This sinful practice happens often, but these men were pastors of local churches. During an interview, the man said he didn't realize how deep this sin affected him. The other man was older. He explained that his fascination with this subject started out of curiosity. A magazine featured many sexually explicit pictures and "I just wanted to see more." His family has suffered great embarrassment; his church lost some of its witness in the community; and the pastor lost his influence in his church and state. Each man was distracted from God's plan for his life. King Solomon also made bad choices and suffered spiritually. These activities lead good people away from God's power and guidance.

How can the following areas of life become a distraction from God's plans?
- Friends.
- Activities.
- Work.
- Family.

D—Directed Prayer

Lord, lead me to keep focused on Your plan for my life.

August 1

Tired Little Muscles

Growth is necessary to a true Christian experience.
Philippians 3:12-16

A—Advice from the Bible

I pursue as my goal the prize promised by God's heavenly called Christ Jesus.
(Philippians 3:14, HCSB)

B—Biblical Example

Paul wrote this letter from a Roman prison. The church at Philippi had been established about 10 years earlier during Paul's second missionary journey (Acts 16:12-40). One continuous theme in the letter is the joy a believer finds in Christ. However, conversion is not an end, but a beginning. Paul was concerned that these Christians were not growing up in Christ. He used a sports metaphor as an example of growth. A runner is pictured as straining every little muscle to win the prize. The competitor in the Roman races longed to receive the laurel wreath of success. All of the runner's energy was focused on the goal. Paul wanted the Philippian believers to be more like Jesus. He obviously did not believe in instant Christian maturity. Personal experiences revealed progress in his Christian life. God used him to accomplish great things for the gospel, but he needed to persevere like an athlete practices regular training and self-discipline. A competing athlete does not look back, but keeps focused on the goal. Perhaps the reward is suggested when Jesus said, "Well done, good and faithful servant" (Matt. 25:21).

C—Contemporary Application

Several years ago, the hit movie of the season was the film "Chariots of Fire." The journey of two distinct runners and their heroic efforts to become the best Olympic runners in the world was portrayed. Years of struggle and training brought eventual success. I can still picture the athlete straining to gain a few more seconds. Remember how his special coach encouraged him to keep working? The result was the thrill of victory.

To live the Christian life effectively, we must identify the standards and goals for measuring our growth. Learn to appreciate the importance of Christian training. Decide to keep spiritually healthy. Don't stop growing too soon. You will miss so much in life.

Think about these statements:

- Spiritual development is vital to a healthy life as physical growth is to your body.
- Spiritual growth is part of God's plan for you. He wants you to be the best you can be.
- Spiritual maturity is not the result of "luck," but Christian growth in daily living.
- Spiritually starved individuals neglect prayer and Bible study.

D—Directed Prayer

O Lord, my God, may I never get to a point where I am satisfied with past attainments.

August 2

A Little Lesson on Success

Believers are to follow spiritual leaders.
Joshua 1:1-17

A—Advice from the Bible

". . . that you may be successful . . ."
(Joshua 1:7, NIV)

B—Biblical Example

Israel had followed the leadership of Moses from the time he arrived in Egypt until his death. The time had come for God's people to accept someone new. God's choice for leadership was Joshua. The assignment was to complete the work Moses had begun by leading Israel into the land of promise. God's expectations for Joshua were expressed in the familiar laws from Mt. Sinai. God gave a charge to His new leader to keep these commandments. A comforting promise follows. God would be with Joshua. Two
words stressed the success or failure of the next assignment from God. *Strength* and *courage* were necessary for the difficult times ahead in the journey. Two other words are used to identify the result of faithfulness to God's calling. The words are *prosperous* and *successful*. This promise is about spiritual blessing, not material things.

C—Contemporary Application

Harrold had started his church with a blank piece of paper—no members, no place to meet, no leaders. However, he did have a calling from God to build a church in an area of town that lacked a place for worshipping God. Thirty-one years later, he stood before a large congregation and announced that retirement time had come. During his leadership, the church had grown in size, built new buildings, sent missionaries around the world, and gave faithful financial support to local, state, and international missions.

Of course the church members knew this day would come, but fear began to surface. "Who could possibly replace Brother Harrold?" "He has played a major role in our family for three generations." "What do we do now?" The members soon learned that God had already prepared a new leader. The older pastor wrote a letter to the new pastor and encouraged him. Advice and help were offered during the days of adjusting to the new congregation. Just like Joshua, Pastor Jay continues to lead faithfully and successfully a growing church dedicated to God's will and work

Ways to be a successful leader:
- Christian leaders must always be learners.
- Christian leaders must have a clear sense of mission.
- Christian leaders must claim victory daily.
- Christian leaders must be servants to the Lord and His people.

D—Directed Prayer

Lord, I pray today for Christian leaders.

August 3

A Little Boat

The storms will come.
Matthew 8:23-27

A—Advice from the Bible

As He got into the boat . . .
(Matt. 8:23, HCSB)

B—Biblical Example

Matthew begins to summarize Jesus' ministry of teaching, preaching, and healing. Ten miracles are listed in chapters 8 and 9. These miracles were sermons in action. The Lord did not use His power to gather crowds, because some people would trust Him simply because of the amazing performance rather than faith in Him. This miracle took place in the evening after a day of teaching. Jesus and His followers went to the other side of the Sea of Galilee to escape the crowds and have time for some rest. The boat Jesus used was probably a small fishing craft without a sail. These kinds of fishing boats were popular on the lake.
The Sea of Galilee is a fresh-water lake that is fed by the Jordan River. The area around the lake is enclosed by hills. This body of water is 13 miles in length and about 8 miles wide. Sudden and violent storms often occur without warning. The disciples were scared by the storm and believed the boat was sinking. Where was Jesus? He was peacefully sleeping in the midst of the storm. The troubled disciples soon discovered that God is always available to see His people through such storms and to meet their needs.

C—Contemporary Application

Hugh and Carolyn bought a large pontoon boat. These friends often invited us to go with them to the lake. A picnic supper was prepared and several couples would take turns planning a worship time at sunset. For several years, our little "clique" enjoyed these times of peaceful boating around Percy Priest Lake. However, one afternoon we had gone to the far side of the lake and a storm suddenly came across the water. Hugh thought we could make it back to the dock, so we headed for shore. Rain began to fall and the water became very rough. Each person privately began praying for our safety. Jesus had calmed the storm before, why not now? After about 15 minutes, a calm settled over the lake and us. The fear was real; the Savior was sufficient. As the sunset began, our little group had a wonderful worship time, praising our great Lord.

Some truths about the storms of life that only faith can overcome:
- Some Christians are overwhelmed when the storms come.
- Some Christians believe they are immune from difficulties and fear.
- Some Christians feel that all hope is gone when an unexpected crisis occurs.
- Some Christians must learn that God is always available.

D—Directed Prayer

"When the storms of life are raging, stand by Me."

August 4

Poor Little Gomer

The meaning of forgiveness
Hosea 1:1-9; 3:1-3

A—Advice from the Bible

Love her as the LORD loves the Israelites . . .
(Hosea 3:1, NIV)

B—Biblical Example

The foremost theme of the Book of Hosea is the love of God and the compassionate appeal of God to His defiant people. The only source of personal information concerning Hosea is found in this writing. The example of Hosea's love for and marriage to Gomer is a story of heartbreak and rejoicing. Among the eighth century prophets, Hosea served as God's spokesperson to the Northern Kingdom. He prophesied primarily the destruction of the Northern Kingdom. However, Hosea magnified God's redeeming love that would lead to salvation under the house of David. God began His relationship with Hosea by commanding him to marry a prostitute! Gomer became an unfaithful wife, who broke Hosea's heart. Through this tragic union, God enabled Hosea to understand His heartbreak over Israel's unfaithfulness to Him. Three commands from God were obeyed by the prophet. First, Hosea was commanded to take a wife. Next, God commanded Hosea to name the three children of Gomer with words that pictured the tragic consequences of Israel's sin. The final command to Hosea was to redeem Gomer and create a disciplined lifestyle necessary to change her life from prostitution to faithful love for her husband.

C—Contemporary Application

The old saying that "marriage is the union of two forgivers" is probably true. Many problems surface in family life today. Sometimes your friends seem to go from one crisis to another, especially involving husbands and wives. What are some practical ways to survive in a marriage that is under attack? Consider these principles:

1. Recognize the feelings that your spouse is experiencing during a difficult time. Learn to express fears, doubts, and distrust to one another.
2. Express your needs to your companion—some people like to be alone; others need to be held.
3. Pray together. The source of strength is usually found during a prayer time.

Lessons to learn from Hosea:

- Sin is the rejection of love and grieves God's heart.
- Sin destroys family life.
- God's message provides the power of redeeming love.
- God's message provides unity that leads to love for one another.

D—Directed Prayer

Lord, help me to be a good forgiver and forgetter.

August 5

A Little Career Woman

Career people can find time to worship.
Acts 16:11-15

A—Advice from the Bible

A woman named Lydia, a dealer in purple cloth . . .
(Acts 16:14, HCSB)

B—Biblical Example

Sometimes the Scripture does not provide all the background information on an interesting subject. For example, a woman named Lydia. Questions such as, "How did she become a worshiper of God?" or "Who motivated her to make a public confession of her faith?" However, some information about this "seeker" is available. She lived in Thyatira, one of the Macedonian colonies. The chief object of worship was Apollo, a sun-god. An established Jewish group in this city maintained faith in God. Selling purple cloth was her vocation. The dye for this fabric was unique and found only in this area. Philippi became her business headquarters for selling her merchandise. She represented the "new woman" of her day. Business people are often consumed in their secular obligations, but she daily made her way to the riverside to pray with other women. Lydia was sincerely religious, but not a Christian until she met the Apostle Paul. As a Christian woman, she was baptized following her confession of faith. Paul paid a special tribute to her in Philippians 4:1, as his "joy and crown."

C—Contemporary Application

Ruthie married right out of high school. The Korean War was beginning and her childhood sweetheart was being sent to that war. A brief time of marriage secured their love. Going to college was out of the question. Money was not available, so she worked at various jobs, saving her money, and longing to see Bill come home. The war finally ceased and the soldiers returned. The young couple began life together once more. The church had always played a major role in their family life, so Sundays were spent in worship. Two sons were born and later desired to become doctors. Ruthie knew the financial responsibilities that kind of education would bring. As a Christian woman, she prayed for God's leadership, studied to be a realtor, and together this couple provided each son the necessary education to have successful careers as physicians. Today, Ruthie is recognized as the most successful seller of property in her area and still worships God.

Lydia's transformed life provides a model for Christian example.

- She expressed her faith in God.
- She led her servants to a faith in God.
- She provided gracious hospitality to other believers.
- She cared for Paul and Silas during their recovery from prison.

D—Directed Prayer

Father, may I always provide an "open house" for the saints of God.

August 6

Broken Little Landmarks

Count the cost before entering God's service.
Nehemiah 2:11-18

A—Advice from the Bible

Examining the walls of Jerusalem . . . destroyed by fire.
(Neh. 2:13, NIV)

B—Biblical Example

The second chapter of the Book of Nehemiah reveals some essential principles for Christian service. Nehemiah is a good example of a person serving the Lord. At this time of writing, he had just completed a three-month journey from Persia with building supplies from the foreign king. His assignment from God was to return to Jerusalem and begin a construction project. Information was needed regarding the extent of the work that needed to be accomplished. Nehemiah took an inspection tour on horseback, at night, to see first-hand his mission. God had called him to the task of rebuilding this once mighty fortress and he was obedient to this assignment. The site was surveyed and Nehemiah realized the necessity of securing other people to help him. The motivating factor in the planning was not just the burden felt by the people, but the realization of the dishonor this disaster brought to the name of God. The enemies' actions in destroying Jerusalem appeared complete. The rubble was evidence of their success. However, God was involved in this desolation and He had prepared a leader to complete the task of restoration.

C—Contemporary Application

Wars have always been part of history. Greed and ambition by men and women have caused countries to rise against other countries. The result of this unholy attitude is devastation and disaster. I remember the day the Japanese bombed Pearl Harbor. Our nation was shocked. President Franklin Roosevelt called the United States to action. War raged for years, and men and women sacrificed their lives for peace. Finally on August 6, 1945, the atomic bomb was dropped on the city of Hiroshima, Japan by a B-29 Superfortress. What happened to that city cannot be described. The death of 100,000 citizens became front-page news. A Peace Museum is now erected on the bomb site to remind the sane world that love is the most important deterrent for world peace. Christians need to be challenged like Nehemiah, to help make the world a better place.

Some question to answer before entering God's service:

- Is your heart ever stirred by the lack of spiritual concern?
- Have you ever wept over the millions of unevangelized people?
- Do wars and rumor of wars encourage a stronger prayer life?
- Do you endorse helping countries rebuild after being destroyed by conflicts?

D—Directed Prayer

Dear Lord, lead me to faithfully complete Your tasks.

August 7

Little White Lies

Never be trapped by a lie.
Proverbs 12:17-22

A—Advice from the Bible

The LORD detests lying lips.
(Prov.12:22, NIV)

B—Biblical Example

The Book of Proverbs is an inspired collection of Hebrew wisdom. The Psalms are recognized as the Hebrew's hymnbook while the Proverbs serve as a manual for daily righteousness. Practical and ethical guidelines for a pure and undefiled godly life are provided for the reader. Traditionally, the Psalms are ascribed to David and the Proverbs are mostly identified with Solomon. These six verses from chapter 12 focus on the theme of lips of truth contrasted with a lying tongue. God delights in the truth. Lying is a disgrace to Him who is the Truth. Honest speech reveals integrity of a person's heart. Pain and sorrow are deliberately spread by a liar. No respect is shown regarding the place, people, or time of telling lies. The words of a prevaricator pierce like a sword into the hearts of sensitive and gentle people. However, a day is coming when the lips of truth will be established forever and the lying lips will be punished.

C—Contemporary Application

The Japanese Ambassador to the United States and his delegation were meeting in Washington to continue discussing international peace. However, these men knew that at that very time the Japanese military was preparing to bomb Pearl Harbor. What deceit! What lies! President Roosevelt addressed the nation the next day after the attack and said, "The United States was at peace with that nation . . . our meeting with the ambassador contained no threat or hint of war . . . the attack deceived the United States by false statements . . ." We had been lied to! The battles in the Pacific raged as our military forces sought to stop the war. The battle of Guadalcanal began on August 7, 1942. Our marines landed on the island and a powerful air and sea assault followed. The jungle fighting made victory difficult. Many men and women perished in the conflict. Admiral William Halsey successfully regained control of the island months later. The Pacific conflict involved in World War II was basically begun with lying lips. The president warned our nation to never allow deceit and lying to harm the United States again.

Why do some people lie?

- They carry deceit in their hearts.
- They like to see friends "put in their place."
- They cannot stand for the truth to prevail.
- They enjoy spreading rumors about people.

D—Directed Prayer

Father, lead me to abhor that which is false and love that which is true.

August 8

James' Little Mirror

The person in the mirror needs to practice God's Word.
James 1

A—Advice from the Bible

> *... a man who looks at his own face in a mirror ...*
> (James 1:23, HCSB)

B—Biblical Example

The devotionals for the next five days will be from the Letter of James. These words were written to Christians who had problems and questions. They had become believers and now were uncertain about how to live this new life. The writer of this book was James, the half-brother of Jesus. He was not a believer during the life and ministry of Christ (John 7:5). Later, however, he became a follower of Christ and the leader of the Jerusalem church. His letter encouraged believers to endure the coming trials with positive attitudes. James pointed out that Christianity was not only a truth to believe, but a life to be lived. The summary statement of James' message is "Be doers of the word and not hearers only." Hearing the word without doing anything about it is compared to a person who sees himself in a mirror. Mirrors in biblical times were often a piece of metal polished to give a reflection. Haven't you ever glanced at yourself in a mirror and soon forgot what you saw? The person who merely hears the Word soon forgets and remains unchanged.

C—Contemporary Application

The County Fair in my hometown was always planned in the fall after harvest. I remember as a child the excitement of seeing the carnival taking shape in the city parking lot. My friends and I would plan which rides and which tent shows to see. Of course, the scariest ones were our favorites. However, the most laughter came from a tent that was full of mirrors. My reflection changed in each of the mirrors. Sometimes I would be 10' tall or 10' wide. The more I moved around in the room, the more ridiculous my shape became. After much laughter and teasing, we returned to the outside world and guess what? We looked like who we really were, just growing young girls. Now, in later years, I reflect on those moments from a spiritual perspective. Do I see myself as God sees me? Am I reflecting all the knowledge I have about His Word in a positive way? Have I been deceived into thinking I am someone else in His Kingdom work?

Some mistakes people make when they look into the mirror of God's Word:

- They fail to examine themselves when they read the Word.
- They forget what they feel deep in their hearts.
- They fail to obey what God's Word tells them to do.
- They are afraid of what they might see in this mirror.

D—Directed Prayer

Heavenly Father, lead me to put my knowledge of Your Word into action.

August 9

James' Little Royal Law

The characteristic of people who are members of God's kingdom is love.
James 2:1-13

A—Advice from the Bible

If you really carry out the royal law . . .
(James 2:8, HCSB)

B—Biblical Example

Sometimes when reading the Book of James, I think more about the present than about Christians in the first century. The first part of chapter 2 focuses on the issue of favoritism in the church. The fact that some people are cruel and unloving to each other is seen on a daily basis. The media enjoys reporting stories about conflict and heartache. Everyone has special friends or individuals they enjoy being with more than others. James the Jerusalem pastor, however, writes that such attitudes have no place in the church. He challenged the body of Christ to be different. To show partiality to one person over another is inexcusable for the Christian. The Pharisees practiced religion on the basis of a complicated system of laws. James, however, condensed all the laws of human relationships into one. He got to the heart of what God intends for human relations by writing, "You shall love your neighbor as yourself."

C—Contemporary Application

Most people are members of a group. A group may be nothing more than a collection of friends or it may be a carefully structured organization with certain requirements for membership. Adults often seek to find persons of similar convictions with whom they can perform deeds of Christian service. They recognize the value of combined strength and mutual inspiration for additional insight into opportunities for helping others, that is, until someone of a different background seeks to be included in their clique. For example, one adult Bible study group enjoyed fellowship together. They promoted outreach and set goals for finding new members. One Sunday a woman entered the room. One look at her shabby clothes and unstyled hair sent out a message of "poor, uneducated woman." She stood just inside the room for a few minutes, waiting to be recognized. Nothing happened, so she left. One member finally spoke and said, "Didn't that look like Eloise? She used to be one of us."

The love of God extends to all people. Describe one way you can show acceptance and love for one of the following:

- A person who is old and homeless.
- A person of a different race.
- A person with a different lifestyle.
- A person who is rude and unkind.

D—Directed Prayer

Lord, help me to show Christian love without any regard for appearance or status.

August 10

James' Little Tongue Taming

You show God's control of your life by using your speech for good.
James 3:1-12

A—Advice from the Bible

. . . but no man can tame the tongue.
(James 3:8, HCSB)

B—Biblical Example

The Book of James was written to Christians and is sometimes called, "The Handbook for Christian Living." Because his readers were far from perfect, this pastor wrote a to-the-point letter. A problem had surfaced when immature teachers began to teach false doctrine. From that subject, the writer moved on to the dangers of the human tongue. The discovery of fire was a great achievement for the human race. Gone was the darkness and cold. When under control, fire could benefit all humankind. For James, human speech was like fire. Self-control was the essential way to deal with human speech. Two other comparisons are used, guiding a horse and controlling a ship. However, he devoted more attention to fire. He declared that if a believer could control what he says, that person could manage all areas of his life. The difficulty in controlling the tongue was compared to taming wild animals. However, animals can be tamed, but the tongue cannot.

C—Contemporary Application

Greek mythology contains many traditional tales of gods and goddesses. These creatures were considered divine and worshipped. Since the Greek religion was polytheistic, nothing was equivalent to our Bible. Each god had a special story that usually included fearful behavior. Perhaps you have seen a picture of the statue named Typhoeus. This hideous monster has broad shoulders out of which grow a hundred heads with dark, flickering tongues. What a terrible way to look! And yet, some Christians have tongues that create as much fear and heartache. Gloria's face could be attached to Typhoeus' body. She was constantly saying cruel things to people. Her tongue "wagged" all day long. The tragedy of her life is that this woman claimed to be Christian and attended church regularly (every time the door opened). One day the pastor confronted her about her actions that created sorrow for people. Gloria denied that she had any problem. "I keep my tongue in my mouth and my lips closed." Do you know anyone like this?

The love of God extends to all people. Describe one way you can show acceptance and love for one of the following:

- A person who is dying from an incurable disease.
- A person of another culture.
- A person with a terrible handicap.
- A person who hates the church.

D—Directed Prayer

Lord, help me to show Christian love every day.

August 11

James' Little Advice about the World

Devotion to God outweighs devotion to self-indulgence.
James 4:1-15

A—Advice from the Bible

God resists the proud . . . .
(James 4:6, HCSB)

B—Biblical Example

James, the writer, was a practical person. He liked to ask basic questions, such as, "Is your aim in life to submit to the will of God or to gratify your own desires for the pleasures of this world?" The New Testament clearly states that the overwhelming desire for the pleasures of this world is always a threatening danger to the spiritual life. A person can become a slave to passions and pleasures, and when he yields to these things, wickedness, envy, and hatred enter into life. The ultimate choice lies between pleasing oneself or pleasing God. And, if we choose our own desires, we have thereby separated ourselves from our Christian friends and from God. James warned that loving the world causes a person to be an enemy of God. When an individual realizes his own ignorance, he will ask for God's guidance. Only when a person realizes his own poverty in the things that matter will he pray for the riches of God's grace. Only when a person realizes his weakness will he come to call upon God's strength. Only when a person realizes his own sins will he appreciate his need for a Savior.

C—Contemporary Application

Gerald and Ray grew up in the same town. Gerald's parents are hard working, proud people. Their small salary barely took care of their family. No money was available for the "fun" things of life. A big event for the family was getting hamburgers on Friday night. The work schedules of each family member provided the excuse to avoid becoming a Christian.
Ray's parents were wealthy and loved worldly pleasures. Sundays were spent on the lake in their cabin-cruiser. Therefore neither of these young men cared about becoming a Christian or attending church. How could these men become aware of the dangers of pride and worldly pleasures? How would you tell them that God resists the proud?

Warnings for the believer:

- A person may either use the world as a servant for God or be used by the world.
- The world can become the controller and dictator of your life.
- A Christian must be pure inwardly and outwardly, for only the pure in heart see God (Matt. 5:8).
- A person who thinks himself as independent of God is on the way to ultimate collapse and defeat.

D—Directed Prayer

Father, help my choices to always include You and not the world.

August 12

James' Little Prayer Advice

God hears and answers the prayers of His children.
James 5:13-20

A—Advice from the Bible

The intense prayer of the righteous is very powerful.
(James 5:16, HCSB)

B—Biblical Example

The scripture passage for today deals with the lifeline of the Christian life—the importance and power of prayer. James has spent the greater part of his letter in instructions and warnings concerning the Christian life. He has been specific in his treatment of various questions and possible snares. Now he sums up his whole letter with a discussion of the ways we can achieve through prayer the things he has set forth. When Christians find themselves in trouble, prayer seems to be the most natural response. Sometimes Christians feel a little guilty about asking God for assistance when trouble comes. James said that even though you are not in trouble, be faithful in prayer .The Lord is the Creator of the body so it is right for us to pray to Him concerning bodily needs. However, God's choice to heal a person may not be His will. Praying about a physical need is good, but remember to thank God for whatever answer He gives. Instead of a general request, ask for specific things for certain people. Let Him give you what you should have; and than thank Him for what He does or does not give you.

C—Contemporary Application

Phillip Brooks, a native of Boston, entered the Episcopalian ministry. He pastored with great power in Philadelphia and in Boston. His sermons were often topical rather than expositional, so he was criticized for the shallowness of his doctrine. However, Brooks is considered one of America's greatest preachers. He also is recognized as the writer of the Christmas hymn, "O Little Town of Bethlehem." His thoughts on prayer are sometimes overlooked. One special statement about the subject of prayer is so meaningful that it is quoted by many writers and pastors. Philip Brooks once stated that we are not to pray for easy lives, but to pray for stronger men! He suggested to pray for tasks equal to your powers. Pray for powers equal to your tasks. Nothing is too small or insignificant for you to talk over with the Lord. So, pray earnestly—but only if you are interested in powerful results.

A self-evaluation about prayer. Do I—

- Pray simply?
- Pray specifically?
- Pray often?
- Pray about everything?

D—Directed Prayer

Lord, teach me to pray effectively.

August 13

Elijah Meets a Little Widow

God often uses other people to express His care for you.
1 Kings 17:7-16

A—Advice from the Bible

"I have commanded a widow in that place to supply you with food."
(1 Kings 17:9, NIV)

B—Biblical Example

1 Kings 17 recounts a series of events from the life of the prophet Elijah. In the first recorded public act of Elijah, he announced that a drought was coming. This event was so sever that not even dew would fall until he spoke the word from God. However, the Lord made provision for Elijah's welfare by sending him to the city of Zarephath. A widow would provide for him. A great display of faith by Elijah and the widow was required for them to care for each other during the famine. The woman recognized the prophet as an Israelite and Elijah promised that his God would provide for the woman's need for food. She responded by being obedient to the command of God. She looked beyond her own need to that of another person and fed Elijah from the last of her flour and oil. She did not have the luxury of helping another person at her own convenience. She had to give out of her poverty. God rewarded her compassion by miraculously providing all the food she and her son needed to survive a famine. God performed a miracle for this caring widow.

C—Contemporary Application

Care and concern are expressions that most people desire to receive. We all want other people to be concerned for our needs, but we may not always think about the needs of others. However, meet Hank and Sue, who became involved in the life of Virginia through a class mission project. This aging woman was in a care center because her family lived in a distant state and could not provide for her needs. Visits from her family were often years apart. She really did not need to be in this facility, but no one provided for her—until this Christian couple came into her life. A relationship developed over a series of weekly visits and Hank and Sue decided to invite Virginia to live in their home. Permission was grated from her uncaring family and so these people became a new family. All three individuals cared for each other. Virginia replaced a mother who had died years before; Hank and Sue became the children she had never had. Together, a more meaningful life was experienced.

How would you respond to these questions?
- Why does God care about what happens to me?
- How does God care for me through people in my life?
- How do I know that God cares for me?
- What conflict in my life may be an opportunity for caring?

D—Directed Prayer

Father, help me not to take for granted the care shown to me by others.

August 14

A Little Puzzling Phrase

The Holy Spirit leads people to understand truth.
John 16:12-18

A—Advice from the Bible

"What does he mean by saying . . . ?"
(John 16:17)

B—Biblical Example

This chapter is part of a lengthy discourse recorded only in the Gospel of John. The teaching occurs in an upper room. This experience is sometimes referred to as "our Lord's farewell message." Chapter 16 contains our Lord's last words of encouragement, counsel, and instruction for His disciples. He recognized that their learning was limited by their prejudices and lack of wisdom. The Master Teacher was especially concerned for them to understand the functions of the Holy Spirit, who would take His place among them and within them. The followers were naturally grieved over Jesus' announcement of His impending departure. The silence of the believers indicated an inability to receive what Jesus was teaching. However, the Holy Spirit would take up where Jesus left off. This present encounter created confusion among both friends and enemies.

C—Contemporary Application

Craig regularly attended a local church. He studied his Bible and was a faithful follower of a famous television preacher. However, Craig could not grow in Christ because of the many questions that perplexed him. Unless a reasonable answer was provided to his questions, he would withdraw from participation in the church activities. Each week he would call the pastor with another confusing passage of scripture or some statement that conflicted with what he wanted to believe about the Bible. A famous response from Craig was, "What does this mean?" Instead of seeking answers through a Bible study class or interacting with other believers, he sought to answer his own questions. Of course, this plan of action only led to more confusion and frustration.

One day the pastor encouraged this disturbed seeker to begin a study of the work of the Holy Spirit. Books were provided for him, but Craig only made more questions on a notepad as he read the books! If you were given the opportunity to increase this man's understanding of biblical truth, what method would you choose?

How can we better understand the nature of the Spirit's work?

- The Spirit brings about new insights and changed attitudes.
- The Spirit leads us to an increased understanding of a biblical truth.
- The Spirit helps us recognize the spiritual nature of His work.
- The Spirit helps us to grow spiritually.

D—Directed Prayer

Dear Lord, help me as I continue to search for biblical truth.

August 15

Little Pharaoh's Last Chance

Consider the consequences of resisting God's will.
Exodus 11:1-10

A—Advice from the Bible

Pharaoh would not let the Israelites go.
(Exod. 11:10)

B—Biblical Example

Israel had been in bondage in Egypt for 430 years. God intervened and changed the oppressors' feelings by a series of remarkable miracles, called the ten plagues on Egypt. Moses demanded that the Pharaoh free God's people, but the Egyptian ruler refused. These slaves were his major work force in building great cities along the rivers. Remember how Moses was reluctant to accept this call from the Lord (Read Exodus 4)? God revealed to Moses and Aaron what the tenth and final plague would be and Moses gave the warning to Pharaoh. The Scripture records that the Egyptian's heart was hardened each time a plague occurred. The tenth plague was distinct from all the others; it was the first and only one that brought death home to the Egyptians. The first-born son of every family would die. The most terrible sorrowing the country had ever or would ever experience resulted. This tragedy resulted in the deliverance of Israel.

C—Contemporary Application

Benito Mussolini was the Italian prime minister (1922–43) and the first of 20th-century Europe's fascist dictators. Mussolini's obvious pride in his achievement at becoming (October 31, 1922) the youngest prime minister in Italian history was not misplaced. In 1924 Mussolini's henchmen kidnapped and murdered people who were outspoken critics. Mussolini's government passed shameful anti-Semitic laws in Italy that discriminated against Jews in all sectors of public and private life and prepared the way for the deportation of some 20 percent of Italy's Jews to German death camps during the war. His reputation was much like the Egyptian Pharaoh. No information exists regarding his relationship with God. His last chance to regroup failed. He tried to cross the frontier disguised as a German soldier but was recognized and, together with his mistress he was shot and killed on April 28, 1945. Jubilant crowds celebrated the fall of the dictator and the end of the war.

Truths from this experience about Pharaoh and the Italian dictator:
- God is powerfully at work in the world today.
- God has a plan for us and we need to discover His will.
- God's judgments can be drastic as we harden our hearts against Him.
- God delivers believers from spiritual death and gives them eternal life.

D—Directed Prayer

Thank You for Your power to deliver people from the oppression of sin.

August 16

Little Foolish Stunts

Sin weakens our capacity for service.
Judges 16:19-31

A—Advice from the Bible

"Bring Samson here to entertain us."
(Judges 16:25)

B—Biblical Example

Samson, the last of the 12 Old Testament judges, is remembered in history as a "what might have been." This man had talent, but he lacked the discipline to do what was right. He simply wasted his abilities because he would not practice self-control. His story begins when God announced to the wife of Manoah that she would have a son, who would deliver Israel from the Philistines. His mother was instructed to lead her son to observe some of the Nazirite precautions pertaining to food and drink. Judges 14 and 15 reveal the exploits of Samson. Certain facts are presented about this judge: (1) He was given supernatural strength to overcome men and beasts. (2) The Holy Spirit stirred him to provoke the Philistines. (3) He developed a reputation as a hero of God's people. However, he yielded to temptation and had an illicit affair with a woman. He fell in love with a Philistine named Delilah. This evil woman finally discovered the secret of Samson's strength and the great warrior was blinded, bound, and made to entertain at pagan festivals. His strength was gone and he did not know that "the Lord had left him."

C—Contemporary Application

A popular American entertainer died Aug. 16, 1977, in Memphis, Tennessee. Elvis Aaron Presley was widely known as "the King of Rock and Roll" and one of rock music's dominant performers from the mid-1950s until his death. From 1956 through 1958 he completely controlled the best-seller charts and ushered in the age of rock and roll. His films also were box office hits. However, Presley developed a lethal lifestyle, spending almost all his time, when not on the road, in Graceland, his Memphis estate. Presley lived nocturnally, surrounded by people-users and stuffed with greasy foods and a variety of prescription drugs. His shows deteriorated in the final two years of his life, until he lived in the world of an addict and recluse. Finally, in the summer of 1977, he died of a heart attack brought on largely by drug abuse. He was 42 years old.

Pressures face God's people today that are similar to Samson's:
- We are surrounded by all kinds of temptations.
- Resistance comes through building godly habits.
- We are helped by Christian leaders who stand for what is right.
- The Holy Spirit is available today for strength in times of need.

D—Directed Prayer

Father, forbid that we ever allow desires and wishes to weaken our relationship to You.

August 17

Even Little Things

Joy and peace should not depend on possessions or prosperity.
Philippians 4:11-14

A—Advice from the Bible

I am able to do all things through Him who strengthens me.
(Phil. 4:13)

B—Biblical Example

The Apostle Paul returned again and again to his basic themes: love, joy, and peace. The generosity of his Philippian friends made him very happy. These believers were the only ones who provided financial support for his ministry. However, he was not dependent on their gifts. With God's help he had learned to be content in every circumstance of life. Now, Paul wanted to share with this church the lessons he had learned in the discipline of contentment. His philosophy of contentment was based on Christ's sufficiency. The apostle is our best model of someone who discovered the secret of a satisfied life. An observation from these verses reveals that Paul did not deny that needs had existed, but he refused to complain about his needs.

C—Contemporary Application

Six decades of my life have been lived learning the lessons of Philippians 4:13. The following experiences are personal, but appropriate for this devotional.

I—The 20's decade was one of self-discovery. The main focus was me.
I can—The 30's decade was one of relational discovery. Circumstances required that I learn to do many things. Personal time seemed to disappear.
I can do everything—The 40's decade entered with the self-assurance that I really could do everything. Been there! Done that! Spiritual progress was evaluated.
I can do everything through Christ—The 50's decade began with the revelation that life is too complicated for one individual. "Through Christ" was really the only way to joy and peace.
I can do everything through Christ who gives me strength—The 60's decade taught me that Christ has been providing the strength I needed to accomplish all things for Him.
I can continue to do everything through Christ who gives me strength—The 70's decade is becoming the best time of my life. (To be continued.)

The way to be independent of circumstances and dependent on Christ:
- Contented people are usually happy people.
- Contented people will distinguish between their wants and needs.
- Contented people know how much it takes to make them happy.
- Contented people refuse to be on a materialistic treadmill.

D—Directed Prayer

Father, lead me to accept the challenge of life's circumstances.

August 18

Esther's Little Uncle

Trust God through life's ups and downs.
Esther 2:5-23

A—Advice from the Bible

Now there was in the citadel of Susa a Jew named Mordecai.
(Esther 2:5)

B—Biblical Example

Chapter 2 of Esther introduces us to Mordecai. He was a Jew who lived in Susa, the capital of Persia, since the Hebrews had been exiled from Israel. This man had many ups and downs as he lived as an alien among pagan people. He apparently was well aware of the palace affairs and was a government official in the house of King Ahasuerus. An opportunity surfaced when the present queen, Vashti, was banished from the throne. A beauty contest was held and Mordecai entered Esther in the competition. Perhaps this man sensed a storm of persecution brewing and knew the value of having a family member close to the king. What a difference this position made to the welfare of the exiled Jews! Esther was given instructions by her uncle not to reveal her origin as his adopted ward entered the king's domain. Every day Mordecai inquired about how she was doing in this new role. The king finally summoned Esther and she was selected to be the queen. Her uncle must have been overjoyed. His presence at the palace gate helped him to discover a plot to assassinate the king. Esther reported this plot and Mordecai was given more privileges in the palace compound.

C—Contemporary Application

A call to serve on a jury is the responsibility of every U.S. citizen. When my summons came, I wasn't sure this opportunity would be a privilege or a nightmare! Picture this scene. The courtroom is packed with spectators and officials. Everyone is waiting for the verdict of the jury. Finally this group of 12 men and women enters and is seated. The judge asks, "Have you reached a verdict?" "Yes," the foreman replies. "And what is your verdict?" the judge asked. The foreman said, "We the jury have decided not to get involved!" What? How ridiculous! However, some Christians make that choice when they lose sight of their responsibilities. More Mordecais are needed today to deal with the many challenges that face our nation. Courage and commitment are required.

God still calls people to be like Mordecai in times of crisis.

- People who are courageous.
- People who are committed.
- People who are equal to the challenges of life.
- People who are not concerned about popularity.

D—Directed Prayer

Lord, may my lifestyle reflect my commitment to You as Lord and Savior.

August 19

A Little Insight

A Christian keeps going because of the thought of victory.
2 Timothy 2:1-7

A—Advice from the Bible

The Lord will give you insight into all this.
(2 Tim. 2:7)

B—Biblical Example

The Apostle Paul was widely known as a leader of Christians. When the Roman Emperor Nero decided to destroy all the believers in Christ, Paul's days were numbered. He used his prison time to remember his associates and friends in prayer. Timothy became his main focus. Paul told Timothy to find his strength by abiding in God's grace. This young man had remained true to the teachings of his mother, grandmother, and Paul. Their insight into Christian behavior led him to make a personal commitment to God. Now, he was to become a link in the chain of Christian tradition that he had received and to pass it on to others. Regardless of what circumstances that would come into his life, he would never disappoint Paul. With the imprisoned apostle facing execution, Paul turned his thoughts to his beloved colleague and the churches to which he ministered. This young pastor is a good example of how a person should grow spiritually and improve his own Christian service. Second Timothy contains Paul's last words to Timothy.

C—Contemporary Application

The first time I heard Dr. Hershel Hobbs speak was in seminary chapel. His presence seemed to exude humility, and yet, this biblical scholar shared insights into the Gospel of John that were foreign to me. At that time, he was pastor of the great First Baptist Church of Oklahoma City, a prolific author of Christian books, and a curriculum writer for the Baptist Sunday School Board (now LifeWay Christian Resources). His message was scholarly, yet we seminary students were able to understand the teachings he was presenting. Years later, I was privileged to meet this wonderful Christian teacher. Even in his senior years, he was "sharp" in Scripture interpretation. His use of the Greek language made the chapters of John come to life. The words of our English translations did not express the meaning as well he was able to do. When he passed at an old age, I purchased all the books he had written to be placed in my library for my children.

Some interesting facts addressed from Paul's letter:

- An unsaved sinner cannot become a great Christian.
- Many Christians dream of mighty things, but neglect the little things.
- A life that is bound by itself is limited to itself.
- Nothing must be allowed to interfere with our devotion to Christ.

D—Directed Prayer

Father, help me to rely on the spiritual insights You provide in Your Word.

August 20

The Prophet's Little Calling

What God asks us to do; He equips us to do.
Jeremiah 1:1-19

A—Advice from the Bible

"The word of the LORD came to me."
(Jer. 1:4)

B—Biblical Example

Jeremiah, a major prophet of the Old Testament, lived during the reigns of five kings in Judah. God called him to warn His people against coming judgment. He has been called the weeping prophet because he lived in a time of great turmoil, which should have caused all people to weep. According to Scripture, his call from God came about 627—626 B.C. The LORD was active during this historical turmoil of the day. He spoke, and Jeremiah was the recipient of the word. God's first words about him were unique. The prophet was formed and selected to be the Lord's spokesman before his birth. Jeremiah was the object and beneficiary of God's knowledge. His ministry was to be international. Of course, when he heard this challenge, the response was in the form of flimsy excuses. The awareness that he lacked the experience to fulfill God's calling for him brought uncertainty. God then assured him that His presence would strengthen him. God touched Jeremiah's mouth as a symbol of instilling His word to the prophet. This action would be needed in the days and years to follow. Jeremiah, called messenger for God, would be over nations and kingdoms in the sense of delivering God's all-powerful Word to Judah and all the other nations of the world.

C—Contemporary Application

Vance Havner once described the characteristics of a preacher as having the mind of a scholar, the heart of a child, and the hide of a rhinoceros. He also suggested that a called person of God should realize that the primary problem is how to toughen his hide without hardening his heart. My husband was called by God during a summer break as a student at the University of Oklahoma. A series of events led to his encounter with God. Some guys in his dorm had a Bible study. He was invited. Noon-day worship at the Baptist Student Union became part of his daily routine. The pastoral guidance of "Preacher" E.F.Hallock kept him near enough to hear the call.

What can you expect when God calls you to a special ministry?

- His abiding presence.
- His promises.
- His Word will come to pass.
- His strength will be sufficient.

D—Directed Prayer

LORD, help me to be an enduring messenger for You.

August 21

A Little Rest

God's invitation is open to all who are exhausted and burdened down.
Matthew 11:25-30

A—Advice from the Bible

Come to me . . . and I will give you rest.
(Matt. 11:28)

B—Biblical Example

Jesus had been speaking to a large crowd about John the Baptist. He wanted them to appreciate John's courage and the importance of his work in God's plan. At the time of this teaching experience, John was in prison and his voice had been silenced. Now, the Lord thanked His Father that the truths about Himself and the kingdom were revealed. He declared that His Father had delivered all things in life to Him. God, then, was the source of His authority. An invitation was extended to people who were burdened by trying to win God's favor by keeping the law and all the elaborate interpretations of this restriction. The Pharisees said, "Do!" and tried to make people follow Moses and the traditions. Jesus promised relief and referred to the law as a yoke. His disciples were to follow Him and His way of life, the way of total dependence upon God. Jesus' earthly life had seen hard work, disappointments, and defeats. The rest He offered came from the security of a person knowing acceptance by God. The meaning was peace in the midst of life's trials and struggles.

C—Contemporary Application

Our family was in Alaska during the famous salmon run. This phenomenon was familiar to us because of TV programs and books we had read. Now, we were seeing the real thing! Each August these fish make their weary way through the last stages of their spawning run to the sandbars along the rivers and creeks. Some months earlier, they leave the Pacific Ocean and begin the long journey. Driven by instinct, they swim against currents, up waterfalls, and around hydroelectric dams. Despite eagles, bears, and other predators, they struggle to reach their ancestral spawning grounds to lay their eggs. No time for rest! Finally they arrive, lay their eggs, and die. The journey of humankind also is remarkable. A natural instinct to know and love God is within us. He is our source of life and our hearts are restless until we come to Him. Then, rest is found!

When we come to Jesus by faith:

- He gives us rest.
- He provides a way to learn.
- He wants us to submit to God.
- He wants us to trust Him more each day.

D—Directed Prayer

Thank You for the peace with God and the peace of God that provides rest.

August 22

A Little Help for the Hostile

Christians can serve God by helping the hostile experience His power.
2 Kings 6:11-22

A—Advice from the Bible

"Those who are with us are more than those who are with them."
(2 Kings 6:16)

B—Biblical Example

Most people are familiar with the problem of hostility. Elisha is a good example for us to study. He was experiencing hostility from the king of Syria. This king planned several ambushes designed to capture the king of Israel, but each attempt failed. He accused some of his men of being disloyal and informing the Israelite army. Some soldier then told the king that Elisha, the prophet, was warning his king. The prophet was in Dothan at this time, so horses, chariots, and a great army of men were sent to capture him. This great prophet of God was in trouble and surrounded by a powerful, pagan army. His panic-strickened servant cried in desperation, but Elisha was confident that greater strength was present in the unseen hosts of heaven than in the visible reality of the Syrian forces. In the face of hostility, Elisha prayed for his servant and his enemies. The prayer was not about destroying those against him, but blinding them temporarily. He wanted to use their blindness to teach them about God. The prophet's acts of kindness made such an impact upon the Syrian army and the Syrian king that their troops withdrew and Syria ceased warring with Israel. Love had accomplished what hostility had failed to achieve!

C—Contemporary Application

Some local people can remember when Betty was friendly to them. She would greet them in public places. After a series of personal disappointments, she seemed to withdraw into her small world. Groceries were delivered to her back door. No one came by the house, because of her harsh words, "Leave me alone!" She was hostile. However, her neighbor continued to watch Betty's house for evidence that she was okay. For three days, this friend saw nothing. Two women began knocking on Betty's door and looked through the bedroom window. Betty was lying on the floor. She was rushed to the hospital, suffering from a stroke. The loving actions that followed helped Betty to rediscover life and joy. Hostility was gone!

Hostility takes many forms:

- Political hostility causes wars and conflicts among nations.
- Domestic hostility causes homes to become battlefields.
- Emotional hostility causes resentment, bitterness, and hatred.
- Spiritual hostility causes Satan to attack and assault believers.

D—Directed Prayer

Lord, help me to offer love and kindness to hostile people

Final Little Greeting

Believers can enrich their relationships by showing concern to other Christians.
Colossians 4:7-18

A—Advice from the Bible

Give my greeting to the brothers and the church.
(Col. 4:15)

B—Biblical Example

Paul did not disclose to the Colossian church the kind of life he was experiencing in prison. Instead he sent a fellow worker named Tychicus to report what was happening in Rome. This friend was a delegate from the Gentile churches, who accompanied Paul on his last visit to Jerusalem. The purpose of Tychicus's assignment was to bring encouragement to the Colossian believers. Onesimus, a runaway slave, also made the trip back to Colosse. The apostle desired that reconciliation be accomplished between Philemon and his former slave. The farewell letter then continues to six fellow Christians in the church. Not wanting to leave anyone out of his greeting, he showed his concern for them with a challenge. The believers were to encourage the church at Laodicea. Perhaps the letter would be carried to this congregation and read to them. A brief plea for continued prayer for the apostle was issued. Paul urged these readers to give attention to his teachings and not yield to the false teachings in Colosse. The closing words from Paul expressed his confidence that God's grace would sustain and defend His church.

C—Contemporary Application

"I will never make close friends like this again," I said as we followed the moving van to another church ministry. Our first pastorate out of seminary was a small town in southwest Oklahoma. Jim and I were young and totally inexperienced. This loving congregation taught us how to pastor. Older adults became my mentors. A bonding occurred with many people in this community. Kindnesses were often expressed through love gifts. Leaving this group of fellow believers was very painful for me. Years later, the names of people who influenced my life continue to bless me. Paul had friends in many churches. He relied on their prayers and ministry. I understand his greeting. (Of course, I did become close to the remaining four congregations in our years of ministry, but none ever "had my heart" like First Baptist Church, Roosevelt, Oklahoma.

A letter of encouragement or challenge to someone you know might include:

- Words of thanksgiving for their friendship.
- Words of advice about personal problems.
- Words of concern for their spiritual growth.
- Words of prayer for their daily needs.

D—Directed Prayer

Lord, how thankful we are for the gift of friendship.

August 24

Five Little Poems

God is serious about sin because it is deadly.
Lamentations 1:1-22

A—Advice from the Bible

The LORD has brought her grief because of her many sins.
(Lam. 1:5)

B—Biblical Example

Lamentations is a series of five poems, each a funeral song, grieving over the fall of Jerusalem. Jeremiah wrote about how to deal with such sorrow. The book opens to reveal the deplorable condition of fallen Jerusalem. The city had become like a widow; no one could defend her. What happened to cause such grief to the writer? Jerusalem had once been like a princess, but sin ruined that image and the Lord had removed her. Judah belonged to God and when the people sinned, they experienced God's judgment—He brought destruction on them. When this terrible tragedy occurred, Jeremiah expressed his feeling by writing poetry. Sin caused the physical and spiritual suffering of God's people. The writer also wanted to reveal God's character and purpose. He chose to write about a nation and a city that was defenseless against aggression. The walls were broken down and the army was defeated. Many righteous people suffered when Jerusalem fell. The Babylonians destroyed the Holy City in 587 B.C. and now these people could only grieve and wait for God's forgiveness.

C—Contemporary Application

Poetry has always been my choice of reading material. A high school English teacher first introduced me to this medium of expression. I still remember the words I memorized from Henry Wadsworth Longfellow's poem, "Tales of a Wayside Inn." He was an American (1807-1882), who was one of the most admired and celebrated poets of his time. One reason for his success is the use of familiar themes, easily grasped ideas, and clear, simple, language of the people. The writer of Lamentations used subject material that expressed grief and sorrow. Wadsworth used everyday experiences. He still remains one of the most popular of American poets, primarily for his descriptions and recounting of the historical events of our nation. On one occasion I recited my favorite poem while staying at the Wayside Inn, the place where the words were penned.

The consequences of sin affect nations and families by:
- Causing wars.
- Causing marital issues and divorce.
- Causing congregational misunderstandings.
- Causing friendships to cease.

D—Directed Prayer

You are serious about sin, Lord, and You desire for us to live obedient lives.

August 25

A Little Charge

Christians are to choose eternal, spiritual values.
1 Timothy 6:11-19

A—Advice from the Bible

I charge you to keep this command.
(1 Tim. 6:13)

B—Biblical Example

The apostle Paul finished warning Timothy about the false teachers in Ephesus and now he gives his last exhortation to this "man of God." Timothy is urged to flee from people who are devoted to material values. Different doctrines and divisive controversies were characteristic of these teachers. The challenge is given to Timothy to pursue Christian virtues. Six values are listed. Paul then moved to another set of imperatives. The pursuit of godliness would require perseverance and discipline. These words are defined as having an athletic or military meaning. A disciplined struggle against false teaching would be a constant challenge. Timothy was congratulated for his previous profession of faith in Jesus Christ before many witnesses. Then Paul returned to the subject of riches, emphasizing the importance of using what a believer has for God's purposes. The wealthy Christians were to avoid an attitude of arrogance. A warning was issued not to depend on wealth; fortune is deceptive. The apostle knew from experience that satisfying things don't have a price-tag attached. The summary statement of this Scripture passage to Timothy is that no matter how little we may possess, we can choose to share with other people.

C—Contemporary Application

A newspaper article told about a burned car found on a country road. A body, the car, and most of the contents in and around the vehicle were burned beyond recognition. However, the police did find a torn checkbook sub that revealed when, to whom, and for how much checks had been written. The name of a church in a nearby town appeared repeatedly in the material. The police called the pastor of the church with the details and the young woman's identity was confirmed. This information revealed how the woman had invested her money and showed other people what was most important to her. She now enjoys the presence of the Lord.

How can we determine our values? Examine your:

- Checkbooks
- Credit card statements
- Daily calendar
- Church giving.

D—Directed Prayer

Lord, lead me to make personal changes in order to establish spiritual values.

August 26

Job's Little Plea

Our pain often lures us to feeling sorry for ourselves.
Job 10:1-12

A—Advice from the Bible

Do not condemn me.
(Job 10:2)

B—Biblical Example

At this point in Job's life, he tries to discover some secret in God's mind that would explain why He has sent such terrible suffering to him. Several questions needed answering such as:
1. Does God really enjoy punishing innocent people?
2. Does God mistake the innocent for the guilty?
3. Does God think His victim will escape before the punishment is completed?
4. Does God create people so he can punish them?

God graciously guided Job and protected him in past years. Now, it seemed He had turned against him. Job expresses the universal need of man for a mediator between himself and God. He knows that a great gulf has separated him from his creator. God is all-powerful; man is weak. Job is asking for an umpire or a mediator who can bring reconciliation. Several times he asked to die. He was suffering great physical affliction; his friends and neighbors were abusing him; and now God had abandoned him. The bottom line to this chapter is that when we cannot understand, we still can trust God.

C—Contemporary Application

This poem was pressed between the pages of my grandmother's Bible. I don't know the source, but when I think about Job, he could have been the writer.

I cannot see the end,
The hidden meaning of each trial sent,
The pattern into which each tangled thread is bent.
I cannot see the end;
But I can trust,
And in God's changeless love I am content.

At the end of the Book of Job, a more blessed restoration occurs.
If you find yourself doubting God:

- Pray for understanding.
- Search the Scriptures.
- Talk to a Christian friend.
- Consider that trials are sometimes steps to Christian maturity.

D—Directed Prayer

Father, help me to avoid feeling self-righteous when I am suffering trials.

August 27

Little Rules for Holy Living

Christians are to behave like they belong to God.
Colossians 3:5-16

A—Advice from the Bible

God's chosen people are holy and dearly loved.
(Col. 3:12)

B—Biblical Example

Paul explains true Christian behavior in Chapter 3. A believer is to take on a new identity. They were urged to seek the things from above. Death to the old way of life had occurred and now they have been raised to a new life in Christ. Certain evil practices that indicated a loss of self-control are included in a list. The Colossians had a conversion, a radical, life-changing experience. The full, available knowledge of God in Christ contrasted to the false teachers at Colosse who taught a distorted, imperfect knowledge. Since the Christians had already put on the new self; the apostle appealed to them with urgency to clothe themselves with the garments appropriate to this nature. Some descriptive terms from the Old Testament are used to emphasize the favored position now enjoyed by Christians as the heirs of Israel's privileges. The last article of Christian clothing believers should put on is love (*agape*). This caring love results in all of the qualities Paul mentioned in earlier verses. Believers must show love toward each other.

C—Contemporary Application

When Sherry moved into our neighborhood, something seemed wrong. Several men unloaded her small trailer. She disappeared inside the house with a small child and did not appear for several days. I finally saw her one morning and walked over "just to be friendly." Sherry looked terrified at me and dropped her trash and ran back inside the house. I went home and prayed for this frightened woman and asked God how I could help her. Weeks passed and a limo pulled up in her drive. Sherry and her little girl looked over at me, smiled and waved. Several more weeks passed and I received a note from her. She was part of the Witness Protection Program and was being protected by the FBI. One year later a car pulled into my driveway and Sherry got out. She was like a new person. The people, who were seeking to hurt her, were in prison and now she was free. Isn't that similar to the old way of life compared to the new way of living?

Evaluate the extent to which your behavior shows you belong to God:
- Are you guilty of covetousness?
- What comes out of your mouth—anger, malice, slander, abusive speech?
- Have you stopped lying?
- Do you show favoritism or prejudice along racial lines?

D—Directed Prayer

Lord, help me obey Your rules for holy living.

August 28

The Little Armless Hand

The world will attempt to destroy distinctions between the sacred and the secular.
Daniel 5:1-12

A—Advice from the Bible

The king watched the hand as it wrote.
(Dan. 5:5)

B—Biblical Example

This chapter records Belshazzar's celebrating a sacrilegious feast and the fall of the Babylonian empire. The event occurred about 23 years after the death of Nebuchadnezzar. The ruling degenerate king, at the height of his intoxication, made a very serious mistake. His servants were ordered to bring in the vessels of gold and silver taken from the temple in Jerusalem. The holy vessels were used to toast the gods of the Babylonians. A mysterious hand suddenly began to write on the wall. The court wizards were called to help solve the mystery, but failed to interpret the writing. The queen (probably the king's mother) informed the king about Daniel's ability to interpret dreams. He was immediately summoned to translate the words. The message was about the destructiveness of pride. A great blasphemy was committed by Belshazzar's drinking from the sacred temple vessels. The proclamation of the obvious end of the Babylonian empire had finally come. Once again Daniel remained true to his decision to be faithful to God. He never wavered from his commitment, and truthfully interpreted the handwriting.

C—Contemporary Application

Down through the ages, evil rulers used their power to punish innocent people. Adolph Hitler was a German political and government leader and one of the 20th century's most powerful dictators. He converted Germany into a fully militarized society and launched World War II. For a time he dominated most of Europe and North Africa. He caused the slaughter of millions of Jews and others whom he considered inferior human beings. Once in power Hitler quickly established himself as a dictator. The movie reels focused on his evil lifestyle and dishonesty. His actions reflect some of the Babylonian king's habits. World War II brought total destruction to Hitler's world. His mockery of people who loved and worshiped God came to an end by his own hands.

Name some ways the world attempts to destroy the sacred things of God.

- by.
- by.
- by.
- by.

D—Directed Prayer

Father, help me to survive the daily oppositions to my faith.

August 29

A Little Heart Problem

Don't lose heart.
2 Corinthians 4:1-15

A—Advice from the Bible

We do not lose heart.
(2 Cor. 4:1)

B—Biblical Example

Paul had confidence through knowing that his ministry was assigned by God who showed him mercy. He magnified Christ, not himself, because God had brought Christ's light into his life. All kinds of trials occurred in Paul's life—beatings, stoned and left for dead, shipwrecked, was without food or water, and at times had been naked and cold. However, he did not complain about what he did not have, but rejoiced in what he did have. He believed that his calling would help others find life in Christ. His attitude kept him from being a promoter of himself; he practiced genuine humility. This fact made Paul's hardships worthwhile. The afflictions of his ministry were temporary but the results and reward would be permanent. Therefore, Paul labored patiently and confidently that God would transfer him to his eternal home when his mission was completed. One constant feature of his writing was life and death. The time would come for him to leave. The apostle's sufferings had brought the gospel across many barriers to bring life to the Corinthians. Paul paid the price so that others might have life in Christ.

C—Contemporary Application

Here are two examples that show how a person does not lose heart during a time of conflict. Only a few TV cameras focused on Linda Downs as she came across the finish line at the New York marathon. By this time, most of the spectators had gone home. People shouted, "This is incredible!" Later the president called to congratulate her. Why? She crossed the finish line for the 26-mile marathon on crutches. Her courage was an encouragement to many people. The other athletic event happened during the 1992 summer Olympics. Derck Redmond was entered in the 400-meters track race. As the crowd watched, they gave a gasp at once. Derck had torn a hamstring and fell to the track. Tears came to my eyes as his father ran out on the path and helped his son stand up. Together, they finished the challenge with Derck leaning on his dad's arm.

When something seems to be working against you, how do you deal with:

- fear
- discouragement
- doubt
- resentment

D—Directed Prayer

Lord, thank You that my afflictions can work for me.

August 30

God's Special Little Helpers

The Bible is our authority for the truth about angels.
Psalm 148:2-5

A—Advice from the Bible

Praise him, all his angels.
(Ps. 148:2)

B—Biblical Example

The images of angels are popular in our culture. Books, jewelry, and songs about angels interest shoppers. The internet provides all kinds of angel paraphernalia. A question that concerns many people today is, "Are angels real?" According to the Bible, the answer is "yes." Jesus the Son of God obviously believed in angels and taught His followers that these celestial creatures are real. Psalm 148 is a call for all God's creation to praise Him and celebrate Him as the Creator of everything. The LORD established and controls the entire universe. Apparently verse 2 refers to the angelic hosts that surround the throne of God. One clear statement about angels is that they are created beings. Angels are mentioned many times from Genesis to Revelation. Angels are messengers for God. Humans will never become angels. This psalm also is called the Hallelujah Psalm. Notice how the writer's jubilant mood is expressed. Joy fills his heart and praise graces his lips. Can you imagine the sounds coming from heaven as all the heavenly beings praise God?

C—Contemporary Application

St. Francis of Assisi was the son of a rich merchant and studied about heavenly beings. He accepted Christ as his Savior after returning from a war and also renounced his wealth. His ministry began as he traveled about central Italy, preaching the gospel, living simply, and seeking to make Christ real to everyone he met. According to legend, when Francis of Assisi preached the Word of God, even the birds and animals enjoyed his sermons so much that afterward they flew off rejoicing. Whether this is true or not, Saint Francis enjoyed all of God's handiwork. He wrote sixty hymns of praise and worship, often mentioning how the angels praised the Lord. One composition, just before his death in 1225, is called "Song of Brother Sun." Today we sing the same words in the song titled, "All Creatures of our God and King." Psalm 148 was the inspiration for the lyrics.

The angels praise God and we, too, can praise Him more effectively by:
- Expressing thanks for what He has done for us.
- Getting better acquainted with God.
- Thanking Him for life itself.
- Fellowshipping with God daily.

D—Directed Prayer

Father, what an honor to praise You along with the holy angels.

August 31

Little Rolling Things

God has a way of suddenly dealing with the enemies of God and His people.
Isaiah 17:9-14

A—Advice from the Bible

Like a tumbleweed (rolling thing, KJV) before a gale.
(Isa. 17:13)

B—Biblical Example

In this passage, the prophet Isaiah of Judah was foretelling the doom of the enemies of God's people. The alliance between Syria and Israel, that occurred late in the eighth century B.C., had no hope of standing against the mighty strength of the Assyrians. Isaiah was explicit in describing the destruction of Damascus at the hands of the Assyrian emperor. The devastation would be as thorough as a harvest. Only the gleanings would be left of these people. The enemy was confident of conquering God's people, but God would intercede for Judah. The prophet believed in his God and His invisible power that could overpower the enemy, who would become like chaff before the wind, and like a rolling thing before the whirlwind. Assyria also would feel the rebuking power of God. They made all kinds of noise, but God would soon quiet them. The good news from this prophecy is that all people who made mistakes, would turn again to their true Creator and no longer worship the things which their own hands formed.

C—Contemporary Application

Tumbleweeds are a common sight in southwest Oklahoma where I once lived. Some years the fences along the highways would be covered with this round, dry plant. Creative people would take three of these weeds, stack them, spray white, and decorate them like a snowman. In the book of Isaiah this plant is associated with wickedness. Perhaps certain characteristics of tumbleweeds remind people of sinners. For example, the plant has a taproot to which are attached many slender branches. As the weed matures and dries, it forms a kind of ball, circular in appearance. When the root is under pressure from the wind, the plant breaks loose and begins to roll over and over. How are tumbleweeds similar to some people? Persons without strong roots are easily upset by the storms of life. Like tumbleweeds they roll with the winds of temptation or other kinds of trials.

God's people can learn from the mistakes of other people:

- who refuse to worship God.
- who fight against the things that are right.
- who live beyond their financial means.
- who neglect their relationship with God.

D—Directed Prayer

Lord, help me to learn from mistakes that are made by unstable persons.

September 1

A Little Piece of Coal

The significance of a life that says "yes" to God.
Isaiah 6:2-8

A—Advice from the Bible

Then one of the seraphs flew to me with a live coal in his hand, which he had taken with tongs from the altar.
(Isaiah 6:6, NIV)

B—Biblical Example

Isaiah was called and commissioned by God for a very difficult ministry. Jerusalem and Judah had broken their relationship with God and participated in false worship much like their idol-worshipping neighbors. Their apostasy was so severe that God referred to them as *Sodom* and *Gomorrah*. Isaiah's call to ministry was a vision of the Lord. This experience changed his life forever. At first the awesome presence of God caused the prophet to feel doomed to die. He was made aware of his own sinfulness. Isaiah needed cleansing and God cleansed him. The contact of the hot stone from a seraphim with Isaiah's unclean mouth, was symbolic of the divine act of purification. Touching the mouth symbolized the transfer of God's holiness to Isaiah's mouth. Only after Isaiah experienced forgiveness did he hear the sovereign Lord speak. God sends those who are willing to say "yes." The influence of the great prophet lasted for 60 years.

C—Contemporary Application

Cyrus was raised in a Christian home. His parents were devoted to God and faithful church worshippers. However, their young son did not care for the Bible. Other great writings impressed him more. After college, he became a respected and influential lawyer. An amazing thing happened one day in his office. A friend came by and ask this question, "Why aren't you a Christian?" God used this conversation to lead Cyrus to faith in Jesus Christ. The fact of his ignorance of the Bible led this 36-year-old man to desire to know the Word. Thirty years later, in 1909, *The Scofield Reference Bible* was published. The significance of the life of Cyrus Ingerson Scofield can never be measured in this lifetime.

Consider these truths from today's Scripture:
- Once we enter into a right relationship with God, He opens doors of service for us wherever we are.
- As we accept Christ as our Savior and are filled with His presence, we will understand His will for our lives and His service.
- Sometimes we feel like an unworthy servant taking on a difficult task.
- Our knowledge is always limited. We do not know the whole story.

D—Directed Prayer

Thank You, Lord, for still calling people to proclaim You Word.

September 2

Just a Little Light

The surest way to drive out darkness is to bring in the light.
Matthew 5:14-16

A—Advice from the Bible

You are the light of the world. A city situated on a hill cannot be hidden.
(Matt. 5:14, HCSB)

B—Biblical Example

The hillside on the northern end of the Sea of Galilee was bustling with people from all over Galilee, Judea, Decapolis, and Tyre and Sidon. Miracles had been witnessed by some of these individuals and now from a boat on the lake, Miracle Worker was teaching. However, the sermon was directed to His disciples, not the gathered crowd. The Teacher knew that His followers must learn fast His worldwide challenge before He would leave them.

I wonder what these faithful men thought when Jesus called them lights? And then, Jesus set a boundary for the use of their new name, *the world*. Where were they to let their light shine? What did Jesus mean by *world*? These followers must have asked other questions.

Jesus would later identify Himself as *the Light of the world* (John 8:12; 9:5) and His witnesses would understand the importance of reflecting the Light. To emphasize the new name, Jesus reminded the listeners that a lighted lamp is not covered up with some object, but displayed for the purpose of pushing away darkness.

C—Contemporary Application

The sight was unforgettable that warm desert night as my husband and I were driving back to Phoenix, Arizona from a retreat near Flagstaff. Out of our car window, a light seemed to be suspended from the sky. At first, we thought maybe an airplane was in the area, but as we drove on down the mountain, the lighted town of Jerome, Arizona came into view. This mile-high, copper mining village once thrived with miners and prospectors. Now the nearly vacated little community provided a sight that demonstrates a light set on a stand. Suspended in space between dark and dark, these lights were reminders of how powerful just a little lamp can be. The feeling of personal accountability for being a light in the world became very real to me.

To be the *light of the world* you need to:

- Warn unbelieving friends or family about the dangers of life without the Light
- Develop a compassionate attitude that attracts other people to the Light.
- Plan some helpful actions that show you care about people in darkness.
- Deal with any personal doubt about not having a Light that is bright enough.

D—Directed Prayer

Lord, help me to discover areas of spiritual darkness where my light might shine for Your glory.

September 3

Little Hands
Working with our Father
1 Thessalonians 4:9-12

A—Advice from the Bible

. . . and work with your own hands . . . .
(1 Thess. 4:11, HCSB)

B—Biblical Example

This brief letter to the church at Thessalonica is a gentle reminder of truths already known by the believers. Paul gives encouragement to live blameless lives. An interesting fact is that each chapter tells of Jesus' second advent. The city of Thessalonica was the capital of the Roman province of Macedonia. Paul traveled to this area on his second missionary journey. This prosperous, commercial center offered many opportunities for people to work. However, the Greeks despised manual labor. Slaves did most of the work. In this pagan environment, some of the church members had quit working and were living from the church's benevolence. Strong words were written to these individual's who were waiting the Lord's return. The apostle emphasized the physical work he and Silas had done. Paul, then, admonished them to get back in the work force and become faithful laborers using their hands to provide for a living.

C—Contemporary Application

My parents were middle-class workers. The 1920's depression and drought had created major problems for southwest Oklahoma. Long working hours were involved in order to make a decent living for our family. Daddy worked with his hands. He was a baker. Mother worked with her hands. She checked groceries. My family responsibility was to prepare supper. As a 10-year-old child, I learned to work with my hands. Our family survived those tough years and then World War II by appreciating the value of honest labor. I am grateful for hard working parents.
The first Monday of September is celebrated by honoring the working class people. This designated Labor Day was introduced by the Knights of Labor in 1882. An annual parade is held in New York City to serve as a reminder that middle-class people provide much of the services to make our life easier. A summary of the Scripture for today would be, work strengthens our testimony. Work done in Christ's name makes us workers with our Father.

Some of Paul's practical advice on living to please God is:

- Continue to improve your lifestyle by working.
- Continue to live by being an example to unbelievers.
- Continue to live pure, holy lives.
- Continue to stand firm in your beliefs.

D—Directed Prayer

Thank You, Lord, for the privilege of work!

September 4

The Little Shema

We are to express sincere love for God by the way we live.
Deuteronomy 6:4-9

A—Advice from the Bible

Hear, O Israel; The LORD our God, the LORD is one.
(Deut. 6:4, NIV)

B—Biblical Example

One day a scribe approached Jesus. He had heard the debate going on with the Sadducees and liked the way Jesus answered these wealthy Jewish men. This scribe had his own question in mind when he asked Jesus which commandment was the greatest (Mark 12:29). Jesus responded with words from the Shema. Every Jew knew this confession of faith. The words were recited every morning and every evening. Moses received God's commandments and then was responsible to teach them to the people. The result would be life-long reverence for God. Moses wanted the second generation of wilderness wanderers to pay close attention to what was about to be said. The Shema provided a means for validating this relationship from generation to generation. God alone was to be the object of Israel's allegiance and worship. Monotheism was to be the practice for the Hebrews unlike the numerous gods of the Egyptians. The Shema became the confessional point to prove their faith in God. Love for God was a way to express loyalty. The command to love God was based on God's prior love for His people. Loving Him was to become the integral part of every day life.

C—Contemporary Application

Our tour guide had taken us to the ancient city of Jerusalem. The Wailing Wall, a remnant of the temple built by Herod in the first century BC, was our next point of interest. I noticed a small bracelet on the guide's wrist as we departed the bus. Later that day I learned that the bracelet was a phylactery and inside the little box were the words of the Shema. Many Jews were praying and reading from the Shema as they faced the wall and nodded up and down. I felt transported to the Old Testament and times of Moses' instruction. For many of these Hebrews, a special pilgrimage to this site was a life-time goal. A vacant place opened along the wall and I chose to take my place among the praying Jews. My prayer of thanksgiving began with the good news that the Messiah had come. Then I prayed that these people around me would know the Truth and be free.

Some truths about your love for God:

- Love God by giving Him your total existence.
- Love God by making His commands the focus of your family life.
- Love God by remembering His blessings and provision.
- Love God by making His commands an integral part of your lifestyle.

D—Directed Prayer

Lord, help me express my love for You everyday this week.

September 5

My Little Ways

Your whole manner of life is to be consistent with God's Word.
Psalm 119:1-8

A—Advice from the Bible

Oh, that my ways were . . .
(Ps. 119:5, HCSB)

B—Biblical Example

Psalm 119 is the longest psalm in the Bible. The focus of the chapter is a celebration of God's laws. One reason for feeling thankful as you read these words is that God has set out His requirements for our lives. Some basic principles are provided to guide us in doing His will. Sometimes the word "precepts" is used. The words do not change the message. The personal application of these truths to life's experiences are invaluable. Careless behavior regarding following His laws is unacceptable. Attentiveness is needed to fully obey. Verse 5 indicates that the way to true happiness will lead to prayer. The psalmist wanted his whole manner of life to be compatible with God's Word. No disgrace or disappointments will occur in a life that is lived according to His precepts. A command is given that cautions the reader to keep *all* the teachings. Progress in learning God's Word is a cause for praise. A blessing on the obedient follower is promised. In concluding this stanza of testimony to God's Word, the psalmist states his intention to observe all God has required. An awareness of God's presence is the delight of life.

C—Contemporary Application

Franklin was born into a wonderful Christian family. His salvation experience occurred at a summer camp for children. His parents adored their obedient son. Then, Frankie became a teenager! His choices in friends, clothes, and entertainment were just opposite from his parents desire for his life. These teen years were a struggle for the family. Coping with his disobedience was handled by "grounding" for weeks at a time.

Questions surfaced about the need to continue Frankie's education after high school graduation. However, his parent made the financial sacrifice and allowed him to enroll in a local college. The freshman year was predictable, but the parents continued to pray "without ceasing" for him. Their son soon changed from an angry teen to a 20-year-old blessing. What happened? A serious, Christian girlfriend came into his life. Her desire was to follow God and her influence on Franklin changed his life.

How does God want us to follow His ways?
- Keep His commandments carefully.
- Search for Him.
- Walk only in His paths.
- Live a life of integrity.

D—Directed Prayer

Lord, I want to thank You by living as I should.

September 6

A Little Night Vision

Be sensitive to the Holy Spirit's leadership.
Acts 16:6-10

A—Advice from the Bible

During the night a vision . . .
(Acts 16:9, HCSB)

B—Biblical Example

The Apostle Paul's missionary journeys reveal strategic planning and the Holy Spirit's leadership. Derbe, a province of Galatia, was as far as the missionaries went on the first journey. A decision was made by Paul to continue west to the Roman province of Asia on the second trip. He wanted to go to Bithynia, but the Holy Spirit halted the party. This change in plans had a profound effect on Paul. God turned the group around. Paul and Silas went west to Europe, not east to Asia. (Later Apollos would bring the message of salvation to that city, Acts 18:19—19:41.) The missionary party then came to the port city of Troas. This city was the pivotal port between the continents of Europe and Asia Minor. Paul and his helpers had been busy, but somewhat frustrated. A vision came while Paul was working there. He saw a man from Macedonia begging the missionaries to come and help them. Macedonia was a country just north of Greece. The vision occurred one night and the next day Paul, Silas, and Luke set sail for Philippi.

C—Contemporary Application

William Carey is often called the Father of Modern Protestant Missions. His ministry sparked a new era in missions. His work marked the entry of the English-speaking world into the missionary enterprise. Carey was a social-political radical who opposed slavery and supported the American colonists during the American War of Independence. Captain James Cook's journals inspired Carey to become a missionary. He entered India as an illegal alien. The East India Company would not issue a license to missionaries. Some interesting facts about this early missionary are: he never took a furlough from missionary service during the 41 years he served in India. He helped found the first Christian college in Asia that still exists today. He developed the first Bengali Bible and newspaper. He proposed a world missionary conference. His most influential sermon of all time was "Expect great things! Attempt great things!" The phrases "from God" and "for God" were later added by other preachers. Carey translated the complete Bible into six languages.

What can you expect from a call to ministry?

- God surprises us with opportunities for witness.
- God's plans for us are not always the ones we would have chosen.
- God will be with us in any situation to which He leads us.
- God does not want us to delay when an opportunity for witnessing occurs.

D—Directed Prayer

Father, help me not to waste an opportunity to share the good news.

September 7

The Little Lament of the Bow

Expressing our grief is a normal part of life.
2 Samuel 1:17-27

A—Advice from the Bible

> *. . . ordered that the men of Judah be taught this lament of the bow.*
> (2 Sam. 1:17, NIV)

B—Biblical Example

King Saul died in battle against the Philistines as the spirit of Samuel had predicted (1 Sam. 28:19). He was wounded by archers and rather than be killed by the enemy, he fell on his own sword. David was fighting the Amalekites in Southern Judah. After their king was killed, he stayed in the area. On the third day, one of Saul's men reported to David the loss of the Israelite army and the death of Saul and his sons. The king's crown and bracelet were given to David. At this horrible news, David and his men were grief-stricken. They tore their clothes, wept, and fasted until evening. After Saul's death, David sang to soothe his grief and the people of Judah's grief. Saul was God's anointed and did not deserve to die. In biblical times, funerals involved elaborate mourning. All of Israel assembled to lament for him. The song David wrote invited God's people to become mourners. He encouraged them to express their personal grief. The people were to learn this song in order to remember the importance of Saul's death. In the poem he referred to Jonathan's bow. A beautiful way of expressing grief is to give something in memory of the deceased. David gave a song.

C—Contemporary Application

Personal losses were familiar to Horatio Spafford, an attorney. His fortune was lost in real estate investments and his four-year-old only son died from scarlet fever. In 1873, a family vacation was planned to London. Mr. Spafford admired evangelists D.L. Moody and Ira Sankey and wanted to meet these men. An urgent matter prevented this father from joining Anna, his wife, and their four daughters on their voyage to England. During the early morning hours, their ship collided with an iron sailing vessel. Many people were swept away in the icy waters. When the survivors were rescued, Anna sent a cable to her husband saying, "Saved alone." Mr. Spafford immediately booked passage to join his wife. On a cold December night, the captain said to him, "I believe we are now passing over the place." When this grieving father went to his cabin, he wrote the hymn, IT IS WELL WITH MY SOUL.

Some thoughts about grief:

- Comforting people who grieve is an important part of our Christian service.
- The pain of grief often appears to be overwhelming.
- God's promises enable us to overcome losses.
- Happy memories of loved ones are a good source of comfort.

D—Directed Prayer

Lord, help me sense Your nearness during the loneliness of grief.

September 8

From Great Crowds to a Little Road

How to guide a lost person to understand the Bible.
Acts 8:26-38

A—Advice from the Bible

> *. . . go south to the road . . .*
> (Acts 8:26, HCSB)

B—Biblical Example

This Scripture passage focuses on a man named Philip described as a person with a good reputation and full of the Spirit and of wisdom. Our first introduction to his job description was when he took care of widows, prepared food, and waited on tables in Jerusalem. Next, his preaching resulted in a revival in Samaria. Great crowds were attending when God led him to go to a desert road where he met a eunuch. God wanted him to help one person understand the gospel. The ancient kingdom of Ethiopia occupied the area south of Egypt. Eunuchs were frequently employed there as court officials. This man was the treasurer under Candace, queen of the Ethiopians. He was a God-fearer and had been attracted to Judaism. On his way home, he was reading a small scroll of Isaiah. Philip received specific instructions, conveyed by the Holy Spirit, to join a particular chariot on the road. "Do you understand what you are reading?" Philip asked. The Ethiopian replied that he needed help. This witness from God began to explain the meaning of Isaiah's words. The eunuch became a follower of Christ as the result of the right person spending time on a desert road at the right time.

C—Contemporary Application

The popularity of the novel *Gone with the Wind* was amazing. The book was a favorite table subject whenever people gathered together. One day a young woman was sitting beside her history professor in the school dining area. Trying to make conversation with her teacher, she asked, "Have you read *Gone with the Wind* yet?" He replied that he had not. Then the student said, "You had better hurry, it's been out for six weeks." Then the professor asked, "Have you read Isaiah?" She responded with a no. The teacher then said, "You'd better hurry, it's been out for about 2,740 years!" The Bible is a must read book. Sometimes a person must ask for help in understanding the message. Pastors and teachers are good resources for leading a person to grow in spiritual knowledge. From God's Word, a person learns how to become a more effective witness of the Truth.

How can you become a better witness for Christ?

- By telling what you know about Jesus.
- By telling what Jesus has done for you.
- By telling what Jesus has done for others.
- By telling what God's Word says.

D—Directed Prayer

Lord, I know that many books can *inform*, but only the Bible can *transform*. Thank You.

September 9

Joshua's Little River Stones

The Promised Land was a gift received by obedience and faith.
Joshua 4:4-7

A—Advice from the Bible

"What do these stones mean?"
(Joshua 4:6, NIV)

B—Biblical Example

Joshua is an exciting book about the conquests for the Lord. You recall his "we can-do-it" faith when the spies were sent into the promised land. The "no-we-can't" people ruled on the decision of moving forward into the land God had promised. The result of that decision lasted 40 years. The doubters were now dead and a new generation was ready to claim their victory. The first obstacle that stood in the way of Israel's conquest was the Jordan River, which was at flood stage before them. Following God's instructions, Joshua dared to step out by faith. What followed was truly remarkable! The priests and the people walked across the river on dry land. The occasion was so wonderful that God commanded Joshua to erect a special memorial. Twelve men took stones from the river and carried them to the western shore. There a memorial was built to impress succeeding generations about the power of God. Such times of God's great interventions need to be communicated to each generation.

C—Contemporary Application

Joshua is an example of people of vision who have refused to let the "it-can't-be-done" attitude influence decisions. During the dark hours of World War II, most of the people in Europe had given up hope of stopping German aggression. The nightly bombings and the increased number of dead and wounded brought the country to the edge of despair. However, Winston Churchill believed that Great Britain could resist the enemy and maintain their freedom. His motivational radio talks were broadcast daily. The Prime Minister inspired his people to believe in victory. He is remembered for his two fingers raised in a "V for victory" salute. A memorial to his life and success was erected at Bladon, England near Blenheim Palace. School children take field-trips to this site and are taught the importance of being strong and positive in times of challenges. Experiences of many great people are remembered through similar monuments.

Christian families today need to repeatedly tell their children of God's intervention in past generations. Consider the following memorial ideas:

- Share stories about great-grandparents.
- Interview aging relatives about interesting experiences.
- Visit family cemeteries.
- Consider compiling a family history for future generations.

D—Directed Prayer

Lord, lead me to new challenges that will test and strengthen my faith.

September 10

A Little Surprising Anointment
God doesn't need important people to accomplish His purpose.
2 Kings 9:1-13

A—Advice from the Bible

"I anoint you king over the LORD'S people Israel."
(2 Kings 9:6, NIV)

B—Biblical Example

The Old Testament reveals God at work in history and introduces people who were His human agents for accomplishing His purpose. One of these was Elijah the prophet had passed into heaven. Another was Ahab, the king of Israel who had died from battle wounds. Now a new generation of people seemed to be repeating the same mistakes as the previous generations. A prophet named Elisha was summoned by God to accomplish His purpose of anointing a future king of Israel. This prophet did not go to anoint Jehu, but sent one of his younger helpers. The whole encounter required very little time. The young prophet sought privacy for his interview with the future king, a respected captain in the army of Israel. The helper followed Elisha's instructions, then immediately departed. The soldiers thought the prophet was a madman and Jehu thought his soldiers were playing a trick on him. The truth was finally revealed and the army proclaimed Jehu king. God's purpose for this unlikely person was to bring justice against the royal household that had committed all kinds of evil, including the murder of God's prophets.

C—Contemporary Application

Young Emma would never have heard about or accepted Jesus as her Savior if Sunday school teachers had not cared about her. Since her family worked on Sunday, they did not attend church. She never participated with her parents in prayer or Bible study. To describe Emma as a person whom God would someday use to accomplish His purpose was unthinkable. The teen years were difficult, but again God used someone to minister to her and encourage her Christian growth. A way was provided for her to attend college and there Emma began her walk with God. His plan for her life was to teach others, especially women, how to become all that God had created them to be. Her resume became more impressive each year. International Bible teacher and writer were just a few descriptions used to introduce this unlikely person God was using to accomplish His purpose. Now into her seventh decade of life, Emma continues to be an available servant.

Consider these biblical truths:

- God is at work to accomplish His purposes.
- God sometimes accomplishes His purposes through unlikely people.
- God's judgment may seem severe but is necessary to accomplish His purpose.
- God requires absolute obedience in accomplishing His purpose.

D—Directed Prayer

Thank you, God, for using unlikely people to accomplish Your purposes.

September 11

The Little Followers

Jesus used symbols to help us understand who He is.
John 10:1-18

A—Advice from the Bible

The sheep follow him because they recognize his voice.
(John 10:4, HCSB)

B—Biblical Example

John 10 focuses on the relationship between the Master and His own people by using the image of sheep, sheepfold, and shepherds. This sermon grew out of a confrontation the Lord had with the Jewish leaders. Jesus opened the sermon with a familiar illustration, one that every listener could understand. The story is about protection from thieves who terrorized many shepherds by stealing their animals. At night, the shepherd would guard his flock by lying in the opening of the pen. Several flocks might be housed together, but in the morning, each shepherd would assemble his own flock. The sheep recognized his master's voice. The religious rulers of Israel were only interested in personal provisions and protection. The True Shepherd came to save the sheep, but the false shepherds took advantage of the sheep and sought to exploit them. These terrorists wanted to steal the sheep from the fold, slaughter them, and destroy them.

C—Contemporary Application

The World Trade Center towers came crashing to the ground on September 11, 2001. The deafening roar, the flying debris, and the screams of survivors caused the citizens of New York to experience what many people in other parts of the world had already known—the fear of terrorism. All this unrest in the world might make us think that our future is very bleak, yet one shining hope remains that can brighten our view of the future. Our Good Shepherd lives and wants to protect us from the enemy. After a hijacked plane slammed into the Pentagon, many people inside the building were trapped by a cloud of thick blinding smoke. Police Officer Isaac Hoopi ran into the blackness, searching for survivors, and heard people calling for help. He began shouting, "Head toward my voice!" Six people heard the shouts and Hoopi's voice led them out of the building to safety. The invitation of Jesus is similar when we are in danger or when we have lost our way. He calls his own sheep by name and leads them out. When we need guidance or protection, He calls us to heed His voice and follow Him.

Jesus pointed out in the Scriptures passage, four special ministries of the Good Shepherd.

- He dies for His sheep (love).
- He knows His sheep (care).
- He brings other sheep into the flock (authority).
- He takes up His life again (power).

D—Directed Prayer

Thank You that I don't have to live in fear of terrorists.

September 12

A Little Safeguard

We must do whatever it takes to keep our citizens safe.
Proverbs 29:22-27

A—Advice from the Bible

Whoever trusts in the LORD is kept safe.
(Prov. 29:25, NIV)

B—Biblical Example

The Book of Proverbs is an inspired collection of Hebrew wisdom. In the Psalms, the Hebrew's hymnbook is provided; in the Proverbs, the manual for daily righteousness is available to the people of God. Practical and ethical guidelines for pure and undefiled religion are given. The book is traditionally ascribed to Solomon. Verse 25 assures the reader that true security is the result of trusting God and not humankind. The contrast is between "trusting" the Lord and "fearing man." This kind of fear becomes a snare when it gets to the point of letting others control your life. Their opinions and attitudes put pressure on you and can prevent you from speaking the truth or doing what is right. To be free from the bondage of fear, people must put their faith in the Lord alone. A nation is secure when justice prevails.

C—Contemporary Application

After the United States was attacked by terrorists on September 11, 2001, President Bush called on Congress to create a Department of Homeland Security. The job of this agency is to do everything possible to keep citizens safe. Our individual households also need a plan for "homeland" security if we are to keep others from endangering our families. The world of easy access to harmful outside forces presents problems never before experienced in history. Safeguards must become important issues. Here are some suggestions for maintaining household security:

- Take charge of the media. Do not allow the language and morality of what your family sees and hears contradict biblical guidelines.
- Be selective in choosing friends. The standard of your friends may not match your lifestyle. Make your home a haven for peaceful, loving pleasure.
- Build shields of protection. Teach biblical principles to your family and encourage their faith. Seek ways to protect them from the dangers they face.

Some thoughts about terrorism:

- All the unrest in the world might make us think that our future is very bleak. What can give us hope?
- The Lord provides all the guidance and protection we need.
- We can't pretend that problems don't exist, but a Christian can still rejoice.
- As long as God permits, the prince of this world will be at work.

D—Directed Prayer

O Lord, Your guidance and protection are all the safeguards I need.

September 13

Little Songs from a Prison Cell

People who believe in the Lord Jesus Christ are saved.
Acts 16:25-34

A—Advice from the Bible

Paul and Silas were praying and singing hymns to God.
(Acts 16:25, HCSB)

B—Biblical Example

Paul and his companions had gone to Macedonia in response to a vision. A man from that area had called for them to come help the people. However, a combination of racial prejudice and economic loss was the cause for their prison confinement. The apostle and Silas were beaten, put in jail, and placed in stocks. Discomfort and pain were very real, but these Christians used this opportunity to pray and to praise God. At midnight, they were singing! An audience of other prisoners heard the words. Suddenly, the duet was interrupted by an earthquake so violent that the foundations were shaken, the doors were opened, and all the irons that held the prisoners came loose from the wall. The jailkeeper reacted immediately. Fearing his failure at guarding the prisoners, he considered suicide. Paul responded and delivered a welcome message to him—all the prisoners remained in jail. The jailer asked a question. Paul and Silas answered with the same Christ-centered gospel they had been preaching. The instruction to believe in Christ was accepted.

C—Contemporary Application

The practice of singing in a sad situation is not usually done. However, Paul and Silas used every opportunity to praise God. One interesting fact is that they knew how to praise and proclaim the good news. Daniel Webster Whittle (1840—1901) was a POW during the Civil War. Fortunately, his mother had given him a New Testament as he marched off to war, and he committed his life to Jesus Christ. After the war, Whittle became a successful businessman. In 1873 he began preaching in evangelistic services and led revivals throughout the United States. Thinking back to a question asked during his imprisonment, he realized that many things still existed that he didn't know, but he certainly did know Jesus. He wrote, "I Know Whom I Have Believed" as a testimony of his salvation experience. How much do you know? Read 2 Timothy 1:12 as a praise to God. Sing this favorite hymn.

The example of the Philippian jailer's conversion reveals that Christ also makes a difference in us after we are saved:

- He expressed intense joy.
- He now had a different kind of life.
- He had hope and assurance about the future.
- He was secure in the center of God's grace.

D—Directed Prayer

Lord, help me to show concern for all people who need to be saved.

September 14

Don't Sleep with a Little Cloak

Treat others with kindness and justice.
(Deuteronomy 24:6, 10-15, 17-19)

A—Advice from the Bible

Return his cloak to him by sunset.
(Deut. 24:13)

B—Biblical Example

Deuteronomy 24 presents a variety of laws about human relationships. One reoccurring theme is kind and just treatment of others by not depriving them of what is necessary to sustain life. Therefore, concern for the poor was a major emphasis with God's covenant relationship with Israel. The story develops about a poor borrower who would have very little with which to secure a needed loan. He might not have anything but his cloak to use as a pledge for repayment. At that time a person's outer garment was like a blanket, but used as a piece of clothing. During the day it served as a cloak. At night the garment became a bed covering while sleeping. The lender was not to make the poor man's cloak, taken in pledge, as his own covering for the night. The idea for this regulation sought to protect the borrower from the night chill. The lender would only gain gratitude from the borrower's heart. Some things in life are done simply because they are right. Any act of kindness and consideration is right!

C—Contemporary Application

A musician named Ira Wilson wrote the text for the beautiful hymn, "Make Me a Blessing." The year was 1909 and Mr. Wilson would wait 15 more years before seeing the music for the hymn become a reality. This great testimony in song was introduced in 1924 at a Sunday School Convention in Cleveland, Ohio. A thousand copies were distributed and the rest is history. Now think about the present.

Don had the desire to minister to the homeless in Nashville. He encouraged the church members to participate in a program called, "Room in the Inn." After some preliminary plans were in place, the demonstration of kindness began. Men were brought to the church once a week for eating and sleeping. A Christian program presented the good news of the gospel. Packets of personal gifts were distributed. The fellowship of Bible study classes who provided the meals became a favorite time of the year. God blessed the mission vision of Don by leading homeless, lonely people to accept Christ as their Savior.

Consider the following ways to make your life useful to God:
- Make the sorrowing glad.
- Tell of Christ's power to forgive.
- Give as was given to you.
- Be to the helpless a helper.

D—Directed Prayer

Thank you, Father, for the challenge to make my life useful to You.

September 15

A Little Divine Wisdom

The crucifixion is the supreme demonstration of God's wisdom, love, and grace.
(1 Corinthians 1:18-25)

A—Advice from the Bible

"Hasn't God made the world's wisdom foolish?"
(1 Cor. 1:20)

B—Biblical Example

Some of Paul's first-century hearers thought the gospel was absurd. The troubled *church of God* in Corinth had lost their vision for the Savior. They now had refused to uphold biblical morality and doctrinal purity. They had ceased to focus on Jesus Christ and had strayed out of God's will. The apostle was in Ephesus when he decided to write a letter about spiritual renewal. Paul identified the problem as a clash between divine wisdom and worldly wisdom. Some of the believers were exalting their preachers rather than the Lord. The result of these actions caused groups to form and many believers were drifting back to their former condition of pride. How the apostle must have grieved to hear this sad news from the church he had personally started!

Paul knew how to address these worldly thinkers. He used a technique they understood and wrote from his knowledge of classical teaching. He turned the secular scholars' methods against them and addressed the subject of the wisdom of God and the power of God. He declared that worldly wisdom would prevent people from ever knowing God. The preaching of Christ crucified was the right message for all people.

C—Contemporary Application

Religious images are very popular today. Some owners of these objects seem to place more worldly thinking than godly thinking on their purchases. The story is told of an old Russian woman. She devoutly kissed the nail-scarred feet of a statue of Christ in her church every day. One day she was approached by a Soviet military officer. He addressed her with the common term for grandmother: "Babushka, are you willing to kiss the feet of Stalin?" "Yes," she replied, "if he gets crucified for me."

Worldly wisdom is so evident through the media. People spend hours each day listening to "talking heads" proclaim truths about life that aren't true. The focus of their wisdom is some human who seems to be doing great things or writing great books.

The Holy Spirit wants to use this letter from Paul to challenge believers to:

- Repent from sin.
- Have faith in Christ.
- Live according to His Word.
- Be obedient to the Spirit's leadership.

D—Directed Prayer

Father, lead me away from worldly thinking.

September 16

A Little Valley of Dry Bones

God demonstrates His power to reclaim a seemingly hopeless situation
(Ezekiel 37:1-14)

A—Advice from the Bible

It was full of bones.
(Ezek. 37:1)

B—Biblical Example

Ezekiel was a priest who became a prophet. He was an unusual man who was thoughtful, strong, fearless, and a man of visions. This prophet was carried captive to Babylon in 597 B.C. He began preaching four years later and we have a record of his ministry. Israel had completely collapsed as a nation. The city of Jerusalem had been destroyed. The pathetic, disheartened remnant was in the depth of discouragement, but God prepared a. person to minister to the exiles in Babylonia. A favorite phrase connected to the prophet's visions was, "the hand of the Lord was upon him." This expression was used in the vision of the valley of dry bones. He was transported by the Spirit of the Lord to a valley that was full of bones. The Lord asked Ezekiel if he believed the bones could once again become living persons. He gave a faith response "O Lord, you know." The command was obeyed and he watched as flesh and skin formed on the bones. However, the bodies were lifeless. God gave further instructions and the prophet watched the valley come to life. The message was clear. God was going to put new life in the people of Israel and bring back the nation.

C—Contemporary Application

Settlers in the United States began to emigrate to the West during the late 18th and 19th centuries. Caravans composed of up to 100 Conestoga wagons transported the people overland. Along the trail, a valley identified as Death Valley was an obstacle to movements of the pioneer settlers. Lack of water made Death Valley a desert. The pioneers soon discovered ways to survive this barrier. Today, this site is a National Monument in the Great Basin Desert, California, and is the lowest, hottest, driest portion of the North American continent. The area was declared a national monument in 1933 and was made a national park in 1994. My first visit to this area made me think of Ezekiel. The bones of animals were visible in many places. What God did in the Valley of Dry Bones made me wonder what would happen if that experience were replayed at this location. Do you think a revival would begin immediately?

What can God do for our rebellious and sinful nation?

- God can resurrect our nation from spiritual death.
- God can make our citizens new persons in Jesus Christ.
- God can transform a sinful life through the new birth.
- God has unlimited power.

D—Directed Prayer

Lord, send us prophets who can encourage us and prevent hopelessness.

September 17

A Little Security in God's Eternal Plan

If God be for us, who can be against us?
(Romans 8:28-39)

A—Advice from the Bible

God works for good to those who love Him.
(Rom. 8:28)

B—Biblical Example

Some Bible students call chapter 8 the "Christian's Declaration of Freedom." Paul uses this chapter to describe Christian victory. He gives the details and the application of this information to Christian experience. The essentials are true of all who have come to faith in Christ. Paul begins with "no condemnation" and ends with "no separation." The victory comes by the power of the indwelling Holy Spirit (8:1-11). Security comes from a knowledge of what God is doing in the world and the Bible describes this process as "good." Our ultimate good is defined in terms of God's eternal plan to make us like His Son. God works in our lives according to His purpose. When people see a Christian, they ought to see Jesus Christ. (Read 1 John 2:6 for biblical support.) No one can fully understand God's eternal plan, however, by faith, we know the Father is for us and is working on our behalf in the kingdom business. The one condition to this "good" is that we must love God and are fitting into His plans.

C—Contemporary Application

Not many people have heard about St. John Chrysostom. He was brought up as a Christian by his widowed mother and was intended for the law practice, to which end he studied under a distinguished pagan instructor. But John also studied theology, and before long he gave up his profession to become a reclusive monk. This lifestyle was not for him, either. He became very ill, and returned to Antioch, becoming an ordained deacon and priest. For 12 years (from A.D.386) he established himself as a great preacher and wrote eight books on Paul's letters. For political reason, John was sentenced to the Black Sea and did not survive the exhausting journey. The rest of the story is that this banished priest had Romans 8 read to him every day until his passing. He felt the burden of weakness and the strain of faithfulness, but also realized that the eternal plan of God was in place for his life.

The Christian is completely victorious:

- No denunciation!
- No obligation!
- No frustration!
- No separation!

D—Directed Prayer

Nothing can come between us and our Lord. Thank You.

September 18

The Little Tabernacle Plans

God's people are to worship according to His guidance.
(Exodus 25:1-9)

A—Advice from the Bible

Make this tabernacle exactly like the pattern I will show you.
(Ex. 25:9)

B—Biblical Example

God called Moses to ascend the mountain again (24:12) and for six days the cloud covered Mount Sinai. During that time God revealed to Moses His plans for the tabernacle. He was laying the foundation for Israel's unique worship practices. A large part of the Book of Exodus is given to this construction. The tabernacle became the focus of Israel's national life in the wilderness. The tribes circled around this center piece. The facility was actually a tent with two rooms made of wood overlaid with gold. God promised to dwell there among the Israelites, where they would meet Him in worship. A key factor in building the tabernacle was the gathering the materials necessary for construction. After all, the Israelites were wandering in a wilderness! God's plan included a freewill offering from the people. The building also was called a "sanctuary," meaning a holy place, because God dwelt there and because the tent was dedicated to the worship of God. The Lord continues to live among His people.

C—Contemporary Application

The date of September 18, 1793, is remembered in history books as the day George Washington laid the cornerstone for the capitol building of the United States. This facility is the seat of the US Congress in Washington, D.C. Built on a hill popularly called Capitol Hill; the floor space is equivalent to four acres. On my visit to this area, I was most impressed by the Rotunda located directly under the dome. The media today provides much information about the activities that occur in this area of the building. The original design of the Capitol, by William Thornton, a doctor, was made in 1792, and Congress occupied the original north wing in 1800. Seven years later the main building was completed. During the War of 1812, invading British troops set fire to the structure, gutting the interior, but it was reconstructed after the war. The plans were followed by the builders for a better function of our government today.

Some plans God has for His followers are:

- To grow in prayer.
- To seek direction from His Word.
- To witness to others about the Good News.
- To develop the spiritual gifts for use in His church.

D—Directed Prayer

Lord, thank You for the plans You have made for my life.

September 19

A Little Persuasion

Christians are to be willing and ready to speak up for their faith.
(Acts 26:22-29)

A—Advice from the Bible

"Do you think you can persuade me to be a Christian?"
(Acts 26:28)

B—Biblical Example

King Agrippa II had an interesting encounter with the Apostle Paul. This royal ruler was the son of Herod Agrippa I and was only 17 at the time of his father's death. The people considered him an authority on the Jewish religion, so through a series of referrals, Paul came before him to have his case reviewed. The hearing began with Paul proclaiming that God's power had strengthened him as he witnessed about the gospel of Christ. The apostle excluded no one from his witness. His message emphasized that Jesus died on the cross as atonement for people's sins. He then boldly asked Agrippa whether he believed the prophets. The king did not answer immediately, because if he believed the prophets, the king would have to be persuaded that Jesus was the Christ, God's promised Deliverer. The response is difficult to interpret. Some biblical scholars believe that Agrippa's response was a pointless statement in an attempt to end the interview. Others interpret the meaning that the king almost accepted Paul's invitation to become a Christian. The Bible does not reveal whether Agrippa committed himself to Christ or not. However, Paul spoke persuasively and decisively regarding his faith in Christ.

C—Contemporary Application

Philip Paul Bliss was born in his parent's log house in Pennsylvania. He became a Christian when he was 12 years old and joined a Baptist church. Later, Dwight L. Moody enlisted him to become his evangelistic singer. One Sunday at church, the sermon subject was "Almost Persuaded." The pastor closed his message with these words, "He who is almost persuaded is almost saved, but to be almost saved is to be entirely lost." This thought impressed Mr. Bliss and he immediately composed what proved to be his most popular song, "Almost Persuaded." Through the following years, this song became an effective invitation hymn. Mr. Bliss died in an attempt to save his wife during a tragic train wreck in Ohio.

The message of this Scripture is:

- A witness needs a starting point for sharing his faith.
- A witness always relies on the Holy Spirit's power and work.
- A witness will always include every lost person.
- A witness will use his personal testimony of God's grace and salvation.

D—Directed Prayer

Lord, I want sharing the gospel to become part of my lifestyle.

September 20

A Little Guilty Mind

The danger always exists that we shall forget the primary goals in life.
(Numbers 32:20-27)

A—Advice from the Bible

Your sin will find you out.
(Num. 32:23)

B—Biblical Example

The final six chapters of Numbers (31—36) record an assortment of events related to matters which the Israelites needed to deal with prior to moving into the land of Canaan. The people of Israel defeated the Midianites, people who had influenced them to sin against God. The wilderness journey had ended after 40 years of varied experiences. Now, two tribes approached Moses with a request. They want to settle their families on the east side of the Jordan. The region was rich in pasture land for their cattle. Moses became aggravated, thinking the tribes were trying to avoid responsibility for the coming invasion into Canaan. Promises were made regarding how they would continue to help in the settlement of the Promised Land. Moses was satisfied with the conditions expressed in the intentions of the agreement. He reminded them that the conquest of Canaan was more than the nation's desire; it was God's work. This aging leader declared publicly the details of the agreement so that the two tribes would have no escape from punishment for sin.

C—Contemporary Application

The first time I read about Josephine Scaggs was in a mission study book. I was a young girl at the time and the life of this missionary to Eastern Africa challenged me. A story was related that part of her job was to pay a salary supplement to teachers in the Baptist schools and also help some of the pastors. She had a large, heavy safe in her mission office where she kept this money. One night her office was broken into, and the large safe was missing. The local police searched the area and found the unopened safe at the bottom of a nearby pond. They retrieved the object and took it to the home of a native African chief, who was supposed to help with the village discipline. When the chief saw the police coming, he immediately confessed. A guilty mind and the sight of police led him to believe that his sin had found him out.

How does sin find us out?

- When misunderstanding lead to conflicts.
- When we enjoy only part of what God has planned for us.
- When disagreements prevent dialogue.
- When disobedience brings God's judgment.

D—Directed Prayer

Father, I ask that the next generations do not repeat the mistakes of this generation.

September 21

Little Morning Star

God's Word deserves careful attention.
2 Peter 1:16-21

A—Advice from the Bible

The morning star rises in your hearts.
(2 Peter 1:19)

B—Biblical Example

This letter was written by Simon Peter about three years after his first letter. The date was probably A.D. 67. He had written encouragement to the Christians who were suffering persecution; now he wrote about internal problems in the church. The people needed to have a certainty about the second coming of Christ. False teachers had infiltrated the church, making fun of the idea of Christ's return. Peter focused on the Transfiguration for his example. James, John, and Peter had been eyewitnesses to that event. No doubt existed in his mind that God had spoken and they had heard Him! Even the prophets of the Old Testament had proclaimed this event. He wrote that a believer was to pay close attention to the words "day" and "the morning star." The *morning star* is Christ. (For more insight, read Numbers 24:17 and Revelation 22:16.) As the morning star announces the dawn of day, so Christ announces the eternal state in which no night will occur. In the darkness of the present world, the Scriptures shine forth as a lamp. Someday we shall be changed to be like Him. The anticipation of that time rises in our hearts.

C—Contemporary Application

A few days ago my family and I looked into the evening sky and witnessed a bright object in the sky. At first I thought an airplane was passing overhead with all their lights on. My son then informed me that this brilliant light was Venus, a planet.

He explained that this shining, celestial object was the second planet from the Sun. Except for the Sun and the Moon, Venus is the brightest object in the sky. He explained that the planet is called the morning star when it appears in the east at sunrise, and the evening star when it is in the west at sunset. Venus is never visible more than three hours before sunrise or three hours after sunset. Scientist have mapped some 98 per cent of the planet's surface using the Magellan spacecraft. However, my family was having a wonderful time observing God's handiwork in His creation.

How can we give to God's Word the careful attention it merits?

- We can desire the Bible sincerely.
- We can read the Bible regularly.
- We can meditate on the Bible thoroughly.
- We can memorize the Bible diligently.

D—Directed Prayer

Thank You, that Your Word serves as a lamp for my pilgrimage through the darkness.

September 22

A Little Scapegoat

God has provided the means for His children to be holy.
Leviticus 16:20-34

A—Advice from the Bible

Then the man who releases the goat as a scapegoat . . . .
(Lev. 16:26)

B—Biblical Example

Chapter 16 has been viewed as the most important chapter in the Book of Leviticus. Instructions concerning the Day of Atonement are given. What could make a day of rest, fasting, and sacrifices a highlight of the year? The focus of that ceremony was on making reconciling sacrifices for the sins of the whole nation. Only on that one day of the year could the high priest enter the most holy of holies. After the high priest, Aaron, had sacrificed the goat "for the Lord," he dealt with another one that served as a scapegoat. The placing of his hands on the goat's head, while confessing the people's sins, denoted the symbolic transfer of their sins to the goat. Aaron then sent the goat away into the wilderness beyond the camp to which the animal could not return. A person was appointed to do the job of ridding the camp of the "sins." Each of the two goats, involved in the Day of Atonement, was representative of a lesson about forgiveness. The slaughtered animal reminded the people of the high cost of atonement. The scapegoat was used to remind the people that the complete removal of sin and guilt was possible.

C—Contemporary Application

The joys felt by those devout Jews once a year is the Christian's privilege every day, because Christ bore our sins in His own body on the cross. One of my favorite hymns is "Whiter than Snow." James Nicholson, the composer, was born in Ireland, but immigrated to the United States in the early 1850's. He settled in Philadelphia, where he participated in church and evangelistic work with the Wharton Street Methodist Episcopal Church. A special verse from this song says, "Lord, Jesus, look down from Thy throne in the skies, And help me to make a complete sacrifice; I give up myself and whatever I know; Now wash me, and I shall be whiter than snow." The ceremony of the scapegoat is no longer necessary, nor is waiting a whole year to confess personal sins. Rejoice today in the forgiveness He provided once for all.

The observance of the Day of Atonement reminds us that:
- Sin is serious.
- Jesus' death provides forgiveness for those who repent of their sins.
- When God forgives our sins, He remembers them no more.
- Jesus has carried away our sins by dying on the cross.

D—Directed Prayer

Thank You, Lord, that we can experience Your forgiveness and cleansing.

September 23

A Little *Philia*

We are to love one another as God loves us.
1 John 3:11-18

A—Advice from the Bible

This is how we know what love (philia) is.
(1 John 3:16)

B—Biblical Example

John devoted more space to love than any other topic. One problem for understanding the gospel message lies in differences in meaning of words that occur in translating from Greek to English. For example, the dictionary defines "love" as an expression of deep feeling based on family ties, personal affection, sexually-based attraction, or a strong liking for a thing or an activity. In the New Testament, three meanings are given to the word "love." John's message in this passage is simple and powerful: no Christian is free to be indifferent to the needs of other people. Our duty to others becomes clear in God's action in Christ (v. 11). We know this by what God did to express His love in His Son. Being God's people means that we cannot draw lines nor set limits on what we do for needy people. The person who needs help may not be dying; he or she may need only food, housing, or clothing. If a person has these to give and keeps them, how can he or she claim to be an agent of God's love. Verse 18 brings the message to a logical conclusion. Words can never take the place of action when one needs things for the body or the family. Because God saw humanity's great need, John did not forbid our speaking in times of need. However, acts of self-giving show that we are children of God.

C—Contemporary Application

A deadly hurricane recently struck Louisiana. Small towns were completely leveled. Of the 300 to 350 local residents, several died or were injured. At the time of this tragedy, two churches in the town, one Catholic and the other Seventh Day Adventists, did all they could to provide comfort in the hours following the storm. However, two days later, a group of Baptist workers swarmed into their town and rebuilt 60 houses. The total number of volunteers, who came from several states, was 450. These Christians demonstrated the love for one another that John was encouraging in his book. It is important to tell people that we love them, but talk is only half of love.

Practical ways a Christian can show love to another person:
- Mow the yard for a senior adult or prepare the yard for winter.
- Visit someone who is homebound.
- Take groceries to an unemployed family.
- Provide child-care for a young couple who needs a night out.

D—Directed Prayer

Father, help me to demonstrate Godlike love in a personal relationship.

September 24

Habakkuk's Little Question

Christians do not seek tests of our faith, but hard times test us.
Habakkuk 1:1-11

A—Advice from the Bible

How long, O LORD, must I call for help?
(Hab. 1:1)

B—Biblical Example

Habakkuk is the eighth book of the twelve Minor Prophets. The manuscript was written by the prophet Habakkuk and includes all we personally know of him. Chapter 1 begins with a dialogue between the prophet and God. Habakkuk prayed, God answered; but the answer was as disturbing as the problem. He grieved over injustice among the people of God, but did more than just grieve, he prayed to God. He knew that God cared about everyday life. He expected action because he was praying, not just talking about the situation. Wickedness was threatening the very life of God's people. They lived like everyone else. Since the people of Judah ignored God's justice, they would experience Babylonian justice. Nebuchadnezzar and his troops would conquer every city and fortress by God's hand, though they would give credit to their gods. The hard part to believe was that God would use such a cruel and unrighteous nation as the Babylonians against Judah. Since God's people tolerated violence, the nation would be taken by violence. Judah had ignored God's law and Habakkuk saw the horror of what was coming.

C—Contemporary Application

Douglas dreamed of going to some faraway country ever since he was a teenager. The challenge of working in a remote, third world region caused him to prepare through education. After graduating from a seminary, he sought appointment with an international mission group. Finally after two years, his appointment came and Doug and his family departed for a city in south Asia. The first discovery was the lack of Christians—none were found. Sins of every kind were practiced and evil traditions of the past continued to control these uneducated people. Never before had Doug felt the need to pray and rely on God's guidance. Five years passed and no changes were seen in the lives of the Asians. "Why doesn't God do something?" Doug asked his wife. Justice was eventually achieved. A huge tidal wave swept away the majority of the sinful part of the city.

How does Habakkuk's prayer life differ from yours?

- He _____.
- You _____.
- He _____.
- You _____.

D—Directed Prayer

Lord, help me to understand better the bad circumstances of life.

September 25

A Little Salvation

All people need salvation because they are sinners.
Romans 1:14-20

A—Advice from the Bible

The gospel is the power of God for the salvation of everyone who believes.
(Rom. 1:16)

B—Biblical Example

The Letter to the Romans has been called "the gospel according to Paul." One of the primary reasons for writing to the Christians at Rome was to explain the good news that God had provided a way of salvation for all people. The epistle is not only an explanation, but an invitation to put one's faith in Jesus Christ and experience the freedom and joy of God's forgiveness. Out of Paul's conversion experience also came a deep conviction that the Lord was calling him to preach the gospel to the Gentiles as well as the Jews. God had set him apart as an apostle. Before Paul's conversion, he was driven by a false religious pride. He would never have thought that a person could be right with God in any other way than by accepting Judaism and observing all the commandments and religious traditions. Therefore the difference between Paul's former life and his new life in Christ was that his confidence was now in God's power to save and not in his own. The apostle discovered that even in the Old Testament message, God had called for His people to live by faith in Him. A sinner is brought into right standing with God by believing in Jesus Christ as Savior and God gives salvation to all who believe.

C—Contemporary Application

On September 25, 1493, twelve Spanish missionaries set sail from Spain for the New World. Their mission was to formally introduce Christianity to America. Through the years other groups have sought to make the gospel message understandable for all people. While my husband and I were students at the University of Oklahoma, the Wycliffe Bible Translators would attend a Summer Institute of Linguistics. William Cameron Townsend, a missionary to the Cakchiquel Indians of Guatemala, founded Wycliffe in 1942. He believed that every person should be able to read God's Word in his own language. Over 500 translations have been completed and hundreds more are in process. All people need salvation and this organization is seeking to make that truth possible.

Four conclusions can be expressed from this Scripture passage:

- All sinners are in need of God's salvation.
- Breaking God's law in any way makes a persona a sinner.
- Every person has disobeyed God's law in some way.
- Every person is in need of God's salvation.

D—Directed Prayer

Father, help me locate people who do not know You and share the good news.

September 26

Aaron's Little Funeral

Even God's leaders must abide by the rules for the people.
Numbers 20:22-29

A—Advice from the Bible

And Aaron died on top of the mountain.
(Num. 20:28)

B—Biblical Example

Aaron, the first high priest of God in Israel, made a good team with Moses. He provided his brother with the one skill he lacked—effective public speaking. Aaron was a communicator, but was weak in resisting the people's demands for a golden calf. The Israelites again made preparations to approach the Promised Land from the southern border near Canaan. The complaints of God's people continued. In a moment of frustration, Moses struck a rock and brought water to the camp. God pronounced punishment on Moses and Aaron for their lack of faith. He would not permit them the privilege of leading the Israelites into the land that He had promised to His people. Since the Edomites would not allow the tribes to cross their land for a quicker entrance into Canaan, the wanderers had to make a long, circuitous journey to reach their destination. During the trip around Edom, Aaron died at age 123 near the border of Edom at Mount Hor. After forty years of priesthood, he was replaced by his son Eleazar. Moses transferred the holy garments to the new priest and the people mourned 30 days.

C—Contemporary Application

An American pioneer was born in Leominster, Massachusetts, on September 26, 1774. He is better known as "Johnny Appleseed." When he ventured onto the Pennsylvania frontier, he began planting apple orchards. In the early 1800s, Johnny traveled westward planting apple seeds he had collected from cider presses in Pennsylvania He was able to establish large orchards in the course of his wanderings. He spent his life planting and tending nurseries of apple seedlings over hundreds of square miles in what are now the states of Ohio, Indiana, and Illinois. He also followed the teachings of a Swedish theologian and believed in God in a different way than most of the people of his day. However, he was a true frontiersman enduring the hardships of the new country and living the life of a fruit planting legend.

Aaron's legacy is still remembered among the Hebrew people:

- He was a great leader along with Moses.
- He helped lead the great exodus out of Egypt.
- He was obedient to God most of the time.
- He made a mistake and could not enter the Promised Land.

D—Directed Prayer

Father, may my actions never call attention to me, but only You.

September 27

Lazarus' Little Wake-up Call

Born once, die twice; born twice, die once.
John 11:1-4; 38-44

A—Advice from the Bible

Jesus called in a loud voice.
(John 11:43)

B—Biblical Example

The many signs performed by Jesus provoked the hostility of His enemies to a crisis point and He and His followers crossed Jordan into Perea to escape the crowds. During this time a human tragedy was taking place in Bethany. A special relationship between Jesus and this family existed. He often would retreat to their home for rest. The message of a death in this family took at least a day to reach the Lord. Finally, the two sisters, Martha and Mary, saw Jesus coming down the road and ran out to meet Him. Martha blurted out that had Jesus been present this terrible thing would not have happened to her brother. The next verses takes us up to the dead man's tomb. The sisters were not spared sorrow because they loved Jesus, but they were strengthened in their sorrow and were able to bear it because they loved Him, and He loved them. The next drama-packed moments changed the lives of many who witnessed this awakening. Jesus shouted for Lazarus to come forth. The spectators watched and wondered. Just image, a shrouded figure emerged into the light! Jesus had emptied the tomb. A Puritan writer said that if Jesus had not named Lazarus when He shouted, He would have emptied the whole cemetery!

C—Contemporary Application

The story is told about England's Winchester Cathedral. On June 18, 1815, Napoleon Bonaparte and his French army met the Duke of Wellington at Waterloo. Both armies were well equipped for the next conflict. When the battle was over, great casualties were reported on both armies. News about the battle was sent back to London. When the message finally reached Winchester Cathedral, an anxious citizen read: "Wellington defeated." Bad weather kept the rest of the memo from being received. The people were grieved and could not believe this tragedy. However, when the fog cleared the entire message read: "Wellington defeated the enemy." Death is just one side of the picture.

What lessons can you learn from the principal figures in this Scripture passage?

- Lazarus is an example of a _____.
- Martha is an example of a _____.
- Mary is an example of a _____.
- Jesus is an example of a _____.

D—Directed Prayer

Thank You, Lord, that You are our source of life here and hereafter.

September 28

Elisha's Little Formula

Motive is a thought or feeling that makes a person act.
2 Kings 5:8-19a

A—Advice from the Bible

Go, wash yourself seven times in the Jordan.
(2 Kings 5:10)

B—Biblical Example

The selected Scripture passage for today could be made into a great play. The actors would be Elisha, a prophet in Israel; Naaman, Syrian commander-in-chief, a captive Israelite woman who served as a maid to Naaman's wife, and Jehoram, the Israelite king. Naaman was a high ranking official in the Syrian army. He was wealthy, highly honored and respected, but he was a leper. Now enters the slave girl with some good news. A prophet of God in Israel could heal the leprosy. His name was Elisha. Then politics began between the two warring nations. When a letter arrived commanding Jehoram, Israel's king, to find a cure for a military man, the king became desperate. The prophet heard about the situation and suggested that Naaman come and see him. The formula for the cure displeased this sick soldier. Bathing in the Jordan River seven times made no sense. Finally, a servant encouraged his master to forget about the humiliation and follow Elisha's instructions. Complete healing occurred in Naaman's body. The closing act of the play focuses on the Syrian soldier confessing the goodness of the God of Israel. Elisha's formula worked because he was obedient to his God.

C—Contemporary Application

When the great French chemist, Louis Pasteur, was trying to isolate the microbe of hydrophobia, he did so at the risk of his own life. In the lab it was necessary for him to experiment with rabid animals, for example sucking saliva through glass tubes from the mouths of mad dogs. He did so in spite of a lifelong fear of rabid animals that started when a mad wolf ran through the streets of the town where he lived as a boy. Pasteur's reward came on July 6, 1885, when he inoculated a nine-year-old boy by the name of Joseph Meister, the victim of a rabid dog. Pasteur must have rejoiced to see the boy recover, just as Elisha rejoiced to see Naaman walk out of the Jordan River cleansed of leprosy.

God wants His believers to minister to the needs of others by:

- Looking for opportunities to serve Him
- Being available when God calls.
- Exploring international mission areas.
- Taking risks when people don't understand.

D—Directed Prayer

Father, I want to serve the people You bring to my life.

September 29

A Little Farewell Address

The church is one area of our Christian service.
Acts 20:17-31

A—Advice from the Bible

None of you will ever see me again.
(Acts 20:25)

B—Biblical Example

As Paul journeyed to Jerusalem to conclude his third missionary trip and deliver the offering from the Gentile churches, he wanted to visit some of his church leaders one more time. Miletus was on the coast and Paul did not have time to go to Ephesus, so he sent for the elders of the church at Ephesus to meet him at that coastal city. When they arrived, a sad apostle gave his farewell address to these men. His sermon included exhortation and encouragement, but he also explained his actions and defended his ministry. His personal testimony revealed the kind of life he had led. Opposition had followed him everywhere he went. The situation in Ephesus caused him heartaches and pain. He wept as he recalled those difficult times. Much of Paul's preaching was done openly or in the synagogue. The apostle outlined the conditions of salvation: repentance and faith. Now, he was aware that he was seeing the Ephesian church leaders for the last time. His ministry in the Eastern Mediterranean was finished. The time had come to move on to Jerusalem and then Rome.

C—Contemporary Application

George Washington (1732-1799), was commander in chief of the Continental army during the American War of Independence, and later the first President of the United States. He symbolized qualities of discipline and persistence in adversity that his contemporaries particularly valued as marks of mature political leadership. Washington's place in American history is a fascinating chapter in the intellectual life of the nation. He long served as a symbol of American identity along with the flag, the Constitution, and the Fourth of July. This great leader carefully prepared a farewell address to mark the end of his presidency, urging the citizens to follow the goals set by the nation. After leaving office in 1797, Washington retired to Mount Vernon, where he died on December 14, 1799. He was much like the apostle Paul in doing what he believed was right.

What are some of the goals in a Christian's life?

- Follow the Spirit's leadership.
- Obey God's will.
- Complete the ministry God has given you.
- Appreciate and support the people who lead us.

D—Directed Prayer

Lord, I want to be open to Your leadership in my life.

September 30

Little Mouth—Big Message

Believers are to faithfully pass on what God has revealed.
Deuteronomy 18:14-22

A—Advice from the Bible

I will put my words in his mouth.
(Deut. 18:18)

B—Biblical Example

In seeking spiritual counsel the people of Israel were not to resort to magicians and practices of the occult. An appeal to false prophets was useless, for God would provide His people with a succession of prophets like Moses. Such prophets would function under an obligation of truth, not attributing to God that which did not come from Him, nor speaking in the name of other gods. The task of every true prophet is presented. A person doesn't just decide to speak for God, because He chooses His leaders. God not only reserves to Himself the privilege of calling His servant, but He also assumes responsibility to give them His message. The ideal in spiritual service is a God-called messenger with a God-given message. A consecrated heart and a disciplined mind make for a qualified mouth into which God can best place His words. The prophet's responsibility was to speak what God gave. He was to be the mouth of God for people. Two qualifications are involved in speaking what God commands. First, a true speaker will tell all that God commands. He speaks the whole mind of God. Second, a true prophet will speak to the audience God gives. True teaching carries the stamp of God's character and will be true to His nature in content and application to life.

C—Contemporary Application

Philip P. Bliss was one of the most important names in the development of early gospel music. Before his tragic death at age 38, he wrote many favorite songs still enjoyed by congregations today. "Wonderful Words of Life" was written in 1874 and presents the importance of God's message in our daily lives. Remember these words? "Sing them over again to me—wonderful words of life; let me more of their beauty see—wonderful words of life. Words of life and beauty, teach me faith and duty: Beautiful words, wonderful words of life." Whether spoken or sung, an individual must seek to proclaim what God has revealed to him or her.

Each believer is responsible for:
- Determining the truth of God.
- Depending completely on God's Word.
- Knowing and applying God's Word to every day living.
- Discovering the timeless principles of God's Word.

D—Directed Prayer

Lord, make my mouth a message center for You.

October 1

A New Little Cart
God is Holy!
2 Samuel 6:1-11

A—Advice from the Bible

They set the ark of God on a new cart . . . .
(2 Sam. 6:3, NIV)

B—Biblical Example

The Israelite ark of the covenant had been captured by the Philistines and in their possession for 20 years. David's desire was to establish Jerusalem as the religious center of the nations. The ark was extremely important for this project. This chest was overlaid with gold. On top of the ark were cherubim, facing each other. Their wings touched to form the mercy seat, which was considered the seat for a holy God. The ark was pulled by oxen and had accompanied the people of Israel on their journey to the Promised Land until captured by the Philistines (1 Sam. 4:1-11). However, David forgot the requirements for transportation of the ark. Disaster followed. Now, after three months, this reminder of God's holiness was being transported with much celebration on a new **little** cart to Jerusalem.

C—Contemporary Application

Service for God and worship of God are to be taken seriously. Sometimes Christians forget about the holiness of God and treat Him like a friendly neighbor. How often do you hear God referred to as "The man upstairs?" The places expected to be God-honoring are often neglected. A visit to some local churches will reveal floors needing attention and other major carpentry work a must! The objects of remembrance are sometimes abused in the sense of disrespect. Even in times of celebration, some church members forget to worship. David's desire to do the right thing worked out in a wrong way. He forgot to consult God about his desire to relocate the ark. One mistake led to another. Finally, he discovered God's instructions. A word that seems to go with "holy" is reverence. This attitude of deep respect and love for God is absent from many Christian lives. How are the things of God to be handled? How can a person remember that God is holy? How can the word "respectful" be used to describe a follower of Christ?

Consider the following items or places and think of ways respect or disrespect are evident:
- The Bible
- The Lord's Supper
- The care of church property
- Fellowship meals

D—Directed Prayer

Thank You, Lord, for the reminder of Your holiness in all areas of my life.

October 2

Giving Just a Little

Giving generously requires motivation.
2 Corinthians 9:1-15

A—Advice from the Bible

The person who sows sparingly will also reap sparingly . . . .
(2 Cor. 9:6, HCSB)

B—Biblical Example

Paul was passionately defending his apostolic ministry, when he suddenly stopped to pass the offering plate. The major ministry on Paul's third missionary journey was taking up a special offering for the poor Christians in Judea. Churches in Philippi, Thessalonica, and Berea were participating in giving, but Corinth was not doing their part in helping the poor. Paul attempted to motivate the Corinthian believers to become serious givers in the offering being taken for the Jerusalem fund. He challenged them in a positive, pastoral way to use their surplus for the good of those in want and for the glory of God. He also contrasted the Macedonian's attitude toward giving with the Corinthian's slow response to the needy. Their failure to carry out their good intentions was hindering the work of Christ. The giving model of these northern churches was explained by their commitment to the Lord. They practiced stewardship of money as well as stewardship of life.

C—Contemporary Application

An old miser in the church said, "The preacher says I should give until it hurts, but for me, it hurts just to think about giving." One pastor said, "Gather what you need, share what you can, and don't try to hoard God's blessings." Believers who are faithful givers seem to experience more joy in sharing their possessions.

Jay is a personal friend. His vocation as a builder of buildings and developer of land seems to grow more successful each year. One reason for his success is his love for Christ. Growing in giving seems to parallel his growing in Bible study and prayer. God's Word is clear on the subject of giving and the blessings of giving. Jay has a great burden for world missions and goes and gives to help spread the good news of salvation. He started giving just a little, but not for long!

Consider these truths about giving:

- Christians give generously when they really believe that giving is more blessed than receiving.
- Christians give generously when they follow Jesus' example in service and sacrifice.
- Christians give generously when they give in spite of circumstances.
- Christians give generously when they give by faith.

D—Directed Prayer

Lord, I want to please you by being a generous giver.

October 3

Haman's Little Gripe

God calls people today to stand firm against evil actions.
Esther 3:8-11

A—Advice from the Bible

> *A certain people . . . are different . . . let a decree be issued to destroy them.*
> (Esther 3:9, NIV)

B—Biblical Example

The Book of Esther is set in the Persian Empire and most of the action takes place in the king's palace in Shushan, the Persian capital. The villain involved in this passage is Haman, the Hitler of his day. This man was a descendant of Amalek, Israel's long-time enemy. The heroes are Queen Esther and her uncle Mordecai. Her actions prevented the Jews from genocide. Haman was an ambitious, self-serving man. He was appointed Prime Minister—second in command of the empire. When Mordecai would not bow in reverence to him, the angry prime minister took his gripe to the king and decided to do away with all the Jews. Haman deceived the king and persuaded him to issue an edict condemning the Jews to death. This evil individual's earlier plans to assassinate the king were discovered. His plot to gain power ends the next day when Esther names him as the person set to destroy her and her people. The Jewish Feast of Purim is celebrated to honor this event.

C—Contemporary Application

The world has always had difficult people. Satan enjoys great power and authority in this world. He is aggressive in his attempts to destroy the witness of God's people. Sometimes they are members of our churches. I remember a woman who was so negative that people refused to associate with her. Gripping and complaining were her greatest strengths. Many reputations had been scared by her sharp tongue. As the pastor's wife, I felt the need to influence her in positive ways. That was a big mistake! All attempts at friendship were rejected. Her anger soon focused on my family. Friends warned me that I had become her favorite target with lies and deceit. What could I do now? Maybe she was mentally ill? Maybe she was not a Christian? Friends from her past said that this woman had always been this way. Nothing was physically or mentally wrong with her. I had to endure this enemy until God moved us to a new responsibility.

Ways to cope with difficult people:

- Evaluate the situation. What is wrong with their life?
- Don't just wish the person would change. Wishing won't help.
- Develop a plan of action.
- Pray for the person.

D—Directed Prayer

Lord, help me to cope with seemingly impossible people.

October 4

Little Barns

Life is more than the stuff we store.
Luke 12:13-21

A—Advice from the Bible

"I'll tear down my barns and build bigger ones."
(Luke 12:18, HCSB)

B—Biblical Example

People often tried to get Jesus to settle arguments. The Jewish custom of the day permitted the eldest son to receive two shares of inheritance while the other sons received only one. Jesus was not going to get involved in this family squabble over money. However, Jesus did use this opportunity to teach a great truth about attitude toward possessions. He gave a severe denunciation to the man with great assets. He had built his whole life around his wealth and success. The main oversight in the rich man's pursuit of the good life was that he forgot his relationship with God. The personal pronouns, I and my, occur numerous times, and expose his attitude. He believed he had accumulated sufficient wealth to provide for his future. Verse 21 contains Jesus' conclusion about real wealth. The fool (one who acts without thought and care) is the person who lays up treasure for himself, and is not rich toward God. Basically, the key to life is getting things in the right order of priority. Material possessions must command a lesser role than spiritual possessions.

C—Contemporary Application

The story is told of a third-grader who wrote his class essay on the human body. Here is his assessment. "Your head is first and is kinda round and hard, and your brains are in it and your hair is on it. Your face is in front of your head where you eat and make faces . . . Your stummick is something that if you don't eat often enough it hurts, and spinach don't help none . . . Your arms you got to have to throw a ball with and so you can reach the butter. Your fingers stick out of your hands so you can throw a curve and add up rithmatick. Your legs is what if you don't have two of, you can't run fast. Your feet are what you run on and your toes are what always get stubbed. And that's all there is of you, except what's inside, and I never saw that." The rich fool was unable to see "what was inside." He did not realize that he had everything with Jesus. He was *charmed by the world's delight.*

Some errors in the thinking and planning of the rich man are:
- He did not understand his own mortality.
- He did not use his wealth to help people in need.
- He did not acknowledge God as the source of his wealth.
- He did not get to enjoy his lavish lifestyle.

D—Directed Prayer

Father, make me aware of my priorities that involve material things.

October 5

Little Grudge Bearers

Treat others with the same care and concern that you have for your own well-being.
Leviticus 19:18

A—Advice from the Bible

Do not . . . bear a grudge.
(Lev. 19:18, NIV)

B—Biblical Example

The Book of Leviticus covers about one month of time and the contents serve as a guide for worship and a policy or code of laws. God warned His children to avoid the sins of gossiping, hating, being vengeful, and bearing grudges. The purpose behind these sins is often to make the hostile person feel superior. Biblical examples of malice teach that close relationships are threatened by this sin. For example, remember how Jacob cheated his brother and stole his birthright (Gen. 25:19-34)? Esau harbored a deep resentment for years that robbed him of a warm relationship with his only brother.

Hatred toward other people is often demonstrated by retaliation and resentment. Verse 18 directs us to extend the same loving concern we have for ourselves to others. Jesus summed up all our duties toward other people by referring to this command (Matt. 22:39-40). God's holiness is distinctly prominent in the Old Testament. His desire for His children is to live pure, holy lives. A person bearing a grudge against another individual cannot honor God.

C—Contemporary Application

Lucy and Julia are members of the same church. Each one serves in a place of responsibility on Sunday morning, and yet, these women have not spoken in two years. Lucy began her grudge-bearing when Julia was promoted in their office to a higher position and better salary. She felt overlooked by the management and blamed her friend for creating conditions that made her look inept. This grudge created a cold, icy environment in the church. Many people were "turned off" by their behavior, especially in their Bible class. Obviously, Lucy is to blame for these actions. The question is, "What responsibility does this resentful woman need to take to remedy the situation?" Holiness in relationships means to love others as we love ourselves. James 2:8 reminds us that *If you really carry out the royal law prescribed in Scripture, "You shall love your neighbor as yourself," you are doing well.*

Ways to overcome resentment:

- Confess your negative feelings to God.
- Pray for the person who troubles you.
- Take practical steps to resolve the differences.
- Find ways to show love to others.

D—Directed Prayer

Dear God, lead me to forsake my stubbornness toward other people.

October 6

Little Children

Introducing our children to Jesus is important.
Luke 18:15-17

A—Advice from the Bible

Let the little children come to me.
(Luke 18:16, HCSB)

B—Biblical Example

Jesus exposed the self-righteous Pharisees throughout His public ministry. The pride of these Jewish leaders condemned them. On the other hand, the publican's humble faith saved him. The meaning of these two actions is reflected in the parable of the prodigal son and the elder brother. Some things never change! However, in contrast to the proud Pharisee, the children are brought to Jesus. A common practice of Jewish parents was to bring their children to the rabbi to receive a special blessing. That tradition makes one wonder why the disciples tried to prevent this recognized ritual. One excuse for the men's behavior might be their protection of Jesus. The Lord had been very busy and was perhaps weary and needing rest. An obvious lack of compassion is revealed when the disciples attempted to prevent the little children from receiving a blessing from the true Lord. This biblical account teaches a basic lesson: Jesus wants us to be childlike in our faith, but not childish. Children are symbols of total dependence and insignificance. Jesus demonstrated the fact that the kingdom belongs to individuals who are wholly dependent on Him.

C—Contemporary Application

After all these years, I can still close my eyes and hear our young son singing, "Jesus, wuves me, dis I know, for da Biple tells me so." This simple tune is sung by more children worldwide than any other song. The music was composed by William B. Bradbury, who was born October 6, 1816. This American Baptist composer of sacred music was gifted in writing music that all ages of people could sing. He became a pioneer in children's music for the church and public schools. Anna B. Warner wrote the words to this song in 1860 as a joint effort with her sister Susan. The poem was spoken by one of the characters in her novel, *Say and Seal*. These two gifted people will be remembered for their love of little children. Mr. Bradbury once said, "If there is anything that will endure the eye of God, because it still is pure, it is the spirit of a little child . . ."

Things you can learn from this song:
- I have the assurance from God's Word that Jesus loves me.
- I have the assurance of freedom from sin because of the cross.
- I have the assurance of heaven because my sins have been forgiven.
- I have the assurance of God's presence all of my life.

D—Directed Prayer

Thank You, Lord, that I can be certain that Jesus loves me.

October 7

Job's Little Question

Why should a righteous man like Job suffer?
Job 3:20-26

A—Advice from the Bible

Why is life given to a man . . . ?
(Job 3:23, NIV)

B—Biblical Example

The Book of Job is a story about a real man named Job, who lived in a real country and who suffered a real disaster. The writing reveals God at His best and Satan at his worst. Job had a God, a personal faith, an enemy, and questionable friends. The only thing God withheld from Job was an answer to the question, "Why?" An interesting situation occurred with his wife. She seemed to be bitter and unconcerned for his relationship with God. Weeks of suffering had passed without relief. His unnamed wife could not bear to see her husband experiencing suffering this intense. His physical appearance looked hideous. His condition was so infectious that he was forced to move away from his home. Out of complete frustration, she urged him to curse God and die. Job's response to her anguish was complete trust in God. He pointed out to her that accepting good things from God and not accepting adversity was ridiculous behavior. His life was slowly being stripped away and he was forced to stand alone in the presence of God. One day God answered Job's plea and appeared before him. Something always happens when God reveals Himself to a person. All the arguments ceased. All the complaints were forgotten. Job saw himself as God saw him.

C—Contemporary Application

The Book of Job contains about 16 why questions. Pretend that the following situations are happening to your friends. What comfort would you offer during this time of suffering?
- Paul and Sarah's young son was killed by a drunk driver. They ask you why God would do this to them.
- Anne's breast cancer has returned following remission. She asks you why God doesn't heal her.

Think about this: If there is anything a sufferer needs, it is not an explanation, but a fresh, new look at God. How can a person discover this new look at God?

What can be said in a positive way about Job's three friends?
- They came to visit Job when he was sick.
- They remained silent for a week in the presence of his great suffering.
- They finally talked to his face, not behind his back.
- They displayed courage in their convictions.

D—Directed Prayer

Lord, help me to know how to minister to people in the "valley of the shadow . . . ."

October 8

A Little Contentment

Grow where God has planted you.
1 Timothy 6:1-10

A—Advice from the Bible

But godliness with contentment is a great gain.
(1 Tim. 6:6, HCSB)

B—Biblical Example

The Apostle Paul finished his indictment of the false teachers among the Ephesians. Greed was the cause of their pride and contentiousness. They believed that religion served as a means to make a profit and get rich. He pointed out that godliness does make a person very rich, if accompanied by a contented spirit. The value of physical wealth is limited to a person's earthly existence. "You can't take it with you." Paul's contentment centered in his confidence in the Lord. By linking godliness to contentment, Paul eliminated the self-seeking concern of the heretics who were motivated by financial gain and personal discontent. The apostle provided Timothy with a commentary on contentment, supplying the reasons why a satisfied spirit should accompany godliness. He stated the first reason by means of a proverb: we brought nothing into the world and we can take nothing out. If we have the bare necessities of life, food and clothing, we have all we need. Contentment means having our needs met, not all our wants granted! How easily we yield to the endless appeal of media advertising with a worldly version of the "good life." Let's pursue godliness with contentment. What a worthy priority!

C—Contemporary Application

Our young grandson liked to smell the flowers in beds around the house. One day he pulled up a special, hard-to-grow plant and carefully washed all the soil from the roots. I questioned him about his actions. His explanation was that the flower was too pretty to be planted in "dirty dirt." The plant soon wilted and died causing James to cry. An explanation about my plants followed. I told about how the soil was mixed a special way and the location of the plant was carefully chosen. James seemed to understand. Later that day, I thought about this teachable moment and the meaning of being content to grow where God planted me. God knows everything about me. The dirt might not be as rich as some locations, but He has planted me just where I need to be. Discontentment can uproot a person and stop spiritual growth.

Ways to grow where God has planted you:
- Seek the leadership of God's Spirit.
- Allow God to accomplish whatever He wants for your life.
- Accept whatever situation God brings to you.
- Take responsibility for praying and witnessing for Him.

D—Directed Prayer

Father, help me to never ask for reasons *why* things happen, but to learn to be contented.

October 9

Little Ways

Continue to put first things first.
Haggai 1:1-11

A—Advice from the Bible

"Give careful thought to your ways."
(Haggai 1:5)

B—Biblical Example

A friend just called and asked what I was doing. My reply was, "Getting to know Haggai." She responded, "Haggie, who?" This minor prophet of the Old Testament reveals very little about his personal life. However, he must have been a persuasive leader. In a brief time of about four months he was able to motivate the people of Jerusalem to overcome their weariness and begin rebuilding the Temple. Although very few of the prophets were successful in what they set out to accomplish, Haggai completed his idea and goal of the restoration of the house of the Lord. These returned exiles went on to become involved in building their houses and establishing themselves in Jerusalem. This book contains 38 verses and four prophecies. The neglect of the Lord's house became the subject of the first message. The very materials that should have been used to rebuild the Temple were being used to for personal comfort. The prophet found these actions totally unacceptable. The people thought about what they were doing after hearing Haggai's message and the Temple reconstruction began.

C—Contemporary Application

The downtown church property had been sold to a major hotel chain. The small remaining congregation stood nearby as the demolition team began to level their church building. Some of the members cried; others seemed relieved. What had happened to this once growing, ministering place of worship? The beginning seemed to be lack of money to prepare the leaking roof. Then the water stains didn't seem to matter. The floor began to need repair, but this project was neglected from year-to-year. Nothing happened. New members were a past memory and visitors only came once. The staff was reduced to retirees who didn't require a salary. The neglected church property became an embarrassment to the city. Before long, the members decided to take action, but time had expired. The city was going to condemn the building.

Haggai would have said to these remaining members:

- "You ignored the house of the Lord."
- "You kept everything for yourself and gave nothing to God."
- "You have a way of putting God last in your goals and plans."
- "You need to consider how you will serve God in your future plans."

D—Directed Prayer

Lord, help me to think about the ways I am neglecting Your house and remember to put You first in all things.

October 10

A Little Tent

We can be confident of an eternal home.
2 Corinthians 5:1-15

A—Advice from the Bible

For we know that if our earthly house, a tent . . . .
(2 Cor. 5:1, HCSB)

B—Biblical Example

The Apostle Paul began in chapter 5 to give the Christian a glimpse of the invisible, eternal world. Knowledge of life beyond the grave and the realities of the eternal world comes from revealed truth. The unsaved world exhibits a helplessness and hopelessness when facing death because they have been subject to bondage all their life through fear of death. Paul describes the death of a Christian in terms of taking down a tent. Paul described this tent as "earthly." We know our bodies are made from the earth. Eventually, our earthly tent (bodies) will perish. When death does come, the apostle said we have confident hope that God will replace our old tent with a house made by Him, one that will be eternal. A Christian will be exchanging a weak, temporary tent for a mansion. The new house will be suited to the glorious environment of heaven—powerful and spiritual. Christians can view life and face death with assurance.

C—Contemporary Application

Arthur enjoyed life. He had many hobbies and vocations. I met him several years ago at our church. He worked with the building and grounds crew. Severe headaches began to bother him and they became more frequent through that first month. He finally agreed to see a doctor. Several tests later, the doctor gave the diagnosis. Arthur had a cancerous brain tumor. Medical treatment began. Surgery, chemo, and other painful procedures followed. He began to feel better and was encouraged that the cancer was in remission . . . at least for one year. Then the problems began again, only more intense. Christian friends began to minister to Art and his family. I will never forget a visit to his apartment after all treatment had been stopped. He said, pointing to his body, "This is just a temporary body. It was bound to die and return to the dust. And that is okay with me because I know where I am going and I am excited about heaven. Why would I want to remain here when the best is yet to be?"

How could this man have such a positive attitude in this crisis?

- He trusted in God's Word.
- He believed that God has revealed all we need to know about the future.
- He believed that the Holy Spirit lived within him.
- He trusted in his faith to conquer his fears.

D—Directed Prayer

Thank you, Lord, for the testimony of this man who is dying, yet looking forward to his glorious new life in heaven.

October 11

Poor Little Millionaire

God will not be absent when His people are on trial.
Psalm 109:20-31

A—Advice from the Bible

For I am poor and needy . . . .
(Ps. 109:22, NIV)

B—Biblical Example

King David had a personal fortune worth millions, perhaps billions, of dollars. Much of his money was donated for the construction of a temple for the Lord. This king could certainly not be poverty stricken, yet several times in the psalms he refers to himself as being poor and needy. What caused David to use those terms to describe his life? A poor and needy person is one who cannot get out of the jam he is in; he has no resources to deliver himself, and he depends completely on others for help. Sometimes this kind of person may be financially destitute, but often the trouble is in other areas of life. For example, David was enduring many false accusations about himself. He felt angry at being attacked by evil people who slandered him. However, he began to realize that he was completely dependent upon the Lord. David did not take vengeance into his own hands, but was asking that God fulfill His promised judgment of evil people.

C—Contemporary Application

Sometimes Christians describe themselves as poor and needy. Maybe they lack some particular material possession; or lack financial security. Consider these reminders of how blessed you are:

- If you woke up this morning with more health than illness, you are more blessed than the million who won't survive the week.
- If you attend a church meeting without fear of harassment, arrest, torture, or death, you are more blessed than almost three billion people in the world.
- If you have food in your refrigerator, clothes on your back, a roof over your head, and a place to sleep, you are richer than 75% of this world.
- If your parents are still married and alive, you are very rare, especially in the United States.
- If you can hold someone's hand, hug them, or even touch them on the shoulder, you are blessed because you can offer God's healing touch.

Christians are so blessed in many ways. Consider the following:

- Families.
- Church fellowship
- Bible
- **God the Father, Son, and Holy Spirit.**

D—Directed Prayer

Father, thank You, that I am not poor and needy, but a child of the King.

A Little Exploration

Obeying God is better than disobeying Him.
Numbers 13:1-27

A—Advice from the Bible

Send some men to explore the land . . . .
(Num. 13:2, NIV)

B—Biblical Example

God finished giving Moses the law and He commanded the people of Israel to leave Mount Sinai and resume their journey to Canaan. His instructions were provided to the people through His servant Moses. The leadership role of Moses was reaffirmed. This was the time to move on. God gave instructions concerning sending spies to their promised inheritance while the Israelites were camped in the wilderness of Paran. Sending these 12 men into Canaan implied that God was ready for Israel to enter the land of promise. The spies were to travel through the land of Canaan as scouts. Moses acted under God's leadership and selected Joshua for the scouting expedition. Caleb also obeyed and is remembered for his steadfast loyalty to the Lord. The men searched the land for 40 days and returned to give their report. First, they gave the "good news." Then unbelieving spies presented the "bad news" that discouraged the hearts of the people of Israel. They were convinced there was no hope of defeating the inhabitants. The Israelites rebelled against God because of their fear. Disobedience resulted in spending the remainder of their lives in the wilderness rather than in the Promised Land.

C—Contemporary Application

The Spanish and Italian kings were anxious to find a shorter route to Asia for trade purposes. Many explorers were involved in this early quest. Today we celebrate the most successful of the navigators. His name was Christopher Columbus. He believed that by sailing west across the Atlantic Ocean, a route could be found to Asia. So he presented his idea and received financial support from the Spanish king. His fleet included three ships and 90 sailors. The voyage began. Columbus followed his planned charts, based on the stars, and 5½ weeks later, at dawn on October 12, 1492, land was sighted. The island was in the Bahamas and today is called San Salvador which means Holy Savior. This explorer was not aware that he had discovered America. After his scouts checked out the land, Columbus hurriedly returned to Spain with the good report.

Remember these things:

- Every Christian should consider that being chosen to serve God is an honor.
- God directs believers to prepare responsibly for the work He has planned.
- God rejoices when His children take a faithful stand in the face of opposition.
- Disobeying God brings disastrous consequences.

D—Directed Prayer

Lord, help me to be courageous and responsible for the tasks You have planned for me.

October 13

A Little Deception

A warning against false teachers.
Philippians 3:1-2

A—Advice from the Bible

Watch out for evil workers.
(Phil. 3:2, HCSB)

B—Biblical Example

Philippians 3:1-11 is an autobiographical passage that features personal reflections about Paul's life before and after his conversion. He began his message with a note of joy. The Philippians needed this encouragement. Despite whatever problems and hardships we face, we can rejoice. The chapter then continues with a warning against false teachers who perverted the meaning of salvation and practiced a lifestyle that was deceptive. Who were these false teachers? One view is that they were non-Christian Jews who tried to win Gentile converts to Judaism. Another view is that the false teachers were Judaizers. They insisted on retaining the rites and ceremonies of the law and its traditions. They claimed circumcision was essential for salvation and that faith in Christ was not sufficient. Paul's description of these false teachers was very severe. He called them "dogs," "evil workers," and "mutilators of the flesh." These teachers were guilty of working evil instead of righteousness. Paul's warning about false teachers needs to be appreciated today.

C—Contemporary Application

The New Age Movement continues to sweep our land with a strange mixture of Christian ideas and Eastern mysticism. Distortions in teaching include the views that Jesus was not really God's Son and that salvation comes by altering one's consciousness through specific techniques. The popularity of this movement is actually a return to Gnosticism. The Apostle Paul dealt with this group in his Colossian letter. These false teachers stressed knowledge (philosophy) rather than faith and advocated worship of angels as a principle means of attaining salvation. In the 1970s, a new interest surfaced in reincarnation, extraterrestrial life, and psychic healing. Celebrities became involved in Christian Science and Scientology. Rock groups became interested in mystic Indian religions, thus influencing many young minds. A Christian must be alert to these false teachings and seek to help explain the dangers of turning from Christ.

Warnings for today:

- Avoid any teaching that promotes the worship of angels as a substitute for Christ.
- Believe only in the crucified and risen Christ.
- Continue to obey the teachings of Christ.
- Devote yourself to a practice of love and faithful service to God and humankind.

D—Directed Prayer

Father, lead me to an awareness of the deception of false teachers.

October 14

A Little Cracked Pot

When everyone abandons you, you can count on God.
Jeremiah 19:1-13

A—Advice from the Bible

. . . just as this potter's jar is smashed and cannot be repaired.
(Jer. 19:11)

B—Biblical Example

The people of Judah would not become obedient to God. He had tried many times to keep the people worshipping Him. Instead they continued to honor other gods especially Baal. Sacrifices were even offered to the pagan gods. No evidence indicated that these Hebrews would ever change their ways. Time was up! God's judgment was upon them. The prophet Jeremiah was chosen to warn the people of the coming destruction. A very dramatic way was demonstrated. Jeremiah was to take some of the elders and priests to a local dump. To make a point, God instructed Jeremiah to break a pot. These leaders knew that pottery was an essential item for Hebrew families. Near the rubbish of the city, the prophet broke the pot. Repairing the vessel was impossible. God's spokesman then delivered an alarming message—God was going to break His people and the city of Jerusalem. They could not be reshaped and molded into God's people again. Just as you would expect, Jeremiah faced the consequences for following God's instructions. He suffered the pain of loneliness, mockery, apparent failure, and the feeling that God had tricked him.

C—Contemporary Application

Ceramic classes were being offered in our town. This art form always fascinated me and so I decided to enroll in a short-term session. Working with clay was not as easy as I thought. Sometimes the clay mold would crack; other times the material became too hard for reshaping. Jeremiah's courage in using pottery to prophecy became more real to me.

A neighbor also was enrolled in the class and molded a beautiful nativity set. Envy almost controlled my emotions. Not a piece of her clay was out-of-shape. The finished project resembled fine china. I did not realize that this wonderful Christian woman was making this ceramic item for my Christmas present. She has passed on to be with the Lord, but every Christmas, I proudly display this wonderful gift and remember how that ugly clay was transformed in the hands of the right potter.

How can you keep from becoming a cracked pot?

- Stay teachable in the Master's hand.
- Stay courageous in your witness for God.
- Stay alert to friends who are being taunted by others.
- Stay vigilant to the message of God for your life.

D—Directed Prayer

When my way seems drear, precious Lord, linger near.

October 15

Little Lights in the World

Every committed Christian is already a light in a dark world.
Philippians 2:12-18

A—Advice from the Bible

You shine like lights in the world.
(Phil. 2:15)

B—Biblical Example

Many Bible teachers agree that this message of love for his friends is Paul's gentlest letter. The church at Philippi was faithful to the apostle. The believers were not plagued with problems like the Corinthian church. The focus in verse 14 is on attitude. Like most New Testament congregations, the church was always in danger of becoming fragmented by strife and division. Paul challenged the people to resemble their heavenly Father. Words used to describe this conduct are: "blameless, pure, and without rebuke." These actions meant that the believers were to live above reproach. A positive witness for Christ was needed in the world. Jesus had already emphasized the importance of "light" (Matt. 5:16). Paul's reaction to their obedience would be rejoicing. The missionary's example of service through "light-shining" would be described today as extreme sacrifice. However, all he wanted for these special friends was their faithfulness to follow Christ. This achievement would mean that Paul had not labored in vain.

C—Contemporary Application

Two personal experiences demonstrated the power of light. Our first visit to Carlsbad Caverns National Park in New Mexico was overwhelming. A single-file parade of people entered the lighted "hole." The massive underground chambers formed enormous stalactites, stalagmites, and other cave deposits ranging from the delicate to the bizarre. Shadows from these creations produced an eerie sense of wonder. At a certain point in this experience the guide demonstrated how totally dark the cavern was without light. The blackness was unbelievable. I could not see my hand. Finally, the lights came back on and the visitors gave a sign of relief.

I was raised in southwest Oklahoma, and summer in the cellar was expected. Daddy would go in first and check for snakes then he would light a lantern. The darkness of that hole always scared me until Daddy shined the light.

What is our role as Christians in a dark world?

- To hold forth the Gospel.
- To offer salvation to unbelieving people.
- To be a consistent witness.
- To hold on to the truth, regardless of circumstances.

D—Directed Prayer

"This little light of mine, I'm going to let it shine." Yes, Lord!

October 16

Malachi's Little Question

The Lord instructed what to give, where to give, and why to give.
Malachi 3:6-12

A—Advice from the Bible

"How do we rob You?"
(Mal. 3:8)

B—Biblical Example

The name *Malachi* means "my messenger." He was a prophet used by God to create a dialogue between the Lord and His people. A common practice had occurred with these Israelites. Their perpetual backsliding was nothing new. The specific sin was failure to observe certain covenant responsibilities. When people reject the Lord's direction and go their own way, they eventually experience disillusionment. Malachi was reminding the Hebrews of their guilt in keeping the tithes and offerings they were commanded to pay into the treasury of the temple. This income was for the support of the ministry, the relief of the poor, and every other work of God. No defense against the charge of robbing God is offered by the people, but their guilt was denied. The phrase "you are suffering under a curse" probably referred to the drought, crop failures, and famine. These disasters were God's disciplinary punishment for their sins. Storehouse tithing is an act of obedience to God. The Israelites reacted with a cynical response: "Not us."

C—Contemporary Application

All questions, objections, and disobedience regarding tithes and offerings did not die with Malachi's generation. Church leaders hear all kinds of excuses when a financial campaign is approaching. Stewardship makes some members very uncomfortable. How would you respond to the following statements?

- I don't want to be told how much to give.
- I know God owns everything and I know He said He will provide, but I'm really reluctant to tithe because I need the money.
- I tithe but I probably wouldn't if it weren't expected.
- I give my tithe and more—then I figure out how to live on what is left.

Years ago I read this little poem:

It's not what you would do with a million if riches should be your lot,
But what are you doing today with the dollar and a quarter you've got?

Work for the Lord. The pay isn't much, but the retirement plan is great!

- A peace that passes all understanding.
- A power that enables us to face each new day.
- A purpose which gives a reason for living.
- A provision of a place for us for all eternity.

D—Directed Prayer

God of my possession, I choose to honor You with obedient giving.

October 17

The Little Church at Colosse

Growing Christians inspire others to grow.
Colossians 1:1-12

A—Advice from the Bible

We have heard of your love for all the saints.
(Col. 1:4)

B—Biblical Example

The church at Colosse was treated by the apostles as a Gentile church. The Apostle Paul had never visited this city, but Epaphras visited Paul, who was in a Roman prison at this time. The message of this pastor was that false teachings were gaining a following in and around the city. The captive missionary felt the need to write a letter to the believers who were being deceived by lies. He needed to expose their false teaching. The true message was that they had everything they needed in Christ. However, his approach to this subject was first to complement the church for the love they expressed to all people. He identified the recipients as "saints and faithful brothers." The word *saints* means "holy ones," that is, God's set-apart people, chosen by Him and appointed to His service. *Faithful* suggests the idea of believing and being loyal to Christ. Paul thanked God for the evidence of spiritual growth among the Colossians, and especially for the way they cared for the entire family of believers. These people inspired traveling Christians to grow in Christ by their example of hospitality and the genuineness of their faith.

C—Contemporary Application

One of my favorite devotional books is, <u>My Utmost for His Highest</u>, by Oswald Chambers. This gifted man chose as his life motto, "Excelsior!" Low achievement was never considered in his life. He attended a Bible college in Scotland and began to experience how God answers prayer and discovered that climbing in the Sprit was accomplished by kneeling. He became a popular teacher of the Word. Oswald was passionately devoted to the Lord Jesus Christ and desired for other people to discover the truths of God. A simple headstone in the military cemetery in old Cairo marks his last earthly resting place. Engraved on the stone is the testimony of his life from Luke 11:13, "How much more will your heavenly Father give the Holy Spirit to them that ask him?" We might paraphrase this verse to read, "Keep growing!"

Let's evaluate our spiritual growth based on Paul's teaching:
- Growing believers demonstrate faithfulness to God.
- A growing believer shows love for others.
- A growing believer has a knowledge of God's will.
- A growing believer will be concerned about spiritual growth.

D—Directed Prayer

Lord, help me to establish a plan for my continuing spiritual maturity.

October 18

A Little Spiritual Relapse

Good beginnings are no guarantee of good endings.
2 Chronicles 16:6-13

A—Advice from the Bible

When you relied on the LORD, he delivered you.
(2 Chron. 16:8)

B—Biblical Example

Most of the kings of Israel were for the most part wicked. However, several kings of Judah were men of God who sought to lead the people away from sin and back to God. The spread of sin had already invaded both kingdoms and only a matter of time would pass before a total collapse. King Asa commanded the nation to return to the Lord and God honored his efforts by giving the nation ten years of peace. The king gathered all the people together to reaffirm their covenant with Him. For 41 years, Asa was a strong and humble ruler. He brought prosperity to the kingdom of Judah. However, toward the end of his reign, when the army of the northern kingdom of Israel confronted him, Asa sought help from the king of Syria, instead of from God. Because of his foolishness, his reign weakened and his nation experienced wars. What went wrong? Proud of the past achievements, the king forgot to depend on the Lord and thus God no longer showed Himself to be Sovereign on Asa's behalf.

C—Contemporary Application

An ancient Asian fable tells of a turtle that could fly. He would hold on to a stick with his mouth as it was carried by his geese friends. When the turtle heard the onlookers on the ground saying, "Aren't those geese brilliant!" his pride was so hurt that he shouted, "It was my idea!" Of course he lost his grip, and his pride became his downfall. Many believers, who have served the Lord for years, sometimes forget that their successes are a result of God's help and not their own ingenuity. The danger of taking God for granted in daily living can sometimes lead to mistakes similar to King Asa. Self-help books or lectures by people who have "attained greatness" can cause weakness if a Christian becomes dependent on that person's philosophy. Pride can easily become the enemy of a person who forgets that God honors faithfulness to Him. An old saying states that no one is stronger than the one who depends on God.

How are we to depend on our God?
- With deep humility.
- With the absence of pride.
- With devoted loyalty.
- With faithful love.

D—Directed Prayer

Lord, help me to realize that pride can rob me of Your strength.

October 19

A Little Awareness of God

The reality of God's presence is everywhere.
Psalm 139:7-12

A—Advice from the Bible

If I go up to heaven, you are there.
(Ps. 139:8)

B—Biblical Example

This psalm is a tribute to the greatness of God. A personal meditation is addressed to Him. The writer declared that God knew all about him and cared for him with precious and numberless thoughts. Therefore, when a person, who knows and loves God, ignores the Almighty, they quickly learn that running from Him is tiring. The good news of God's omnipresence is that He remains with His creation forever. Some believers, at some point in time, turn their back on God and the Spirit's leading. But the truth remains that no place exists to escape His presence. The psalmist mentions several ways a person might flee, such as from the Spirit, to heaven, to hell, the uttermost part of the sea, and the realms of darkness. Romans 8:35-39 is a good commentary on this psalm. A question surfaces from this passage, How can the truth of God's presence be a comfort in our trials? I like the idea that with God, I can never be lost in a crowd. His hand will guide me.

C—Contemporary Application

Eight years after Columbus discovered American, an English sea captain showed a map to King Henry VII. The map revealed all the unexplored territories of the new world. Over some of these territories were the words, "Here be dragons," and "Here be demons." What a contrast to a map drawn by King David. Over every unexplored territory of the Promised Land, he would have written, "Here be God." Pioneer missionaries and Arctic explorers also marked on their maps and diaries, "Here be God." Sam and Betsy flew from their home in Indiana to the major airport in Uganda. The plane landed and they departed for their new assignment in the bush country. The absence of any "white" people was a reminder that they were in a minority. Language meant nothing. Feeling isolated from all that was familiar, they sat down, looked at each other, and said, "God is here. He is with us. He will never forsake us."

You can confidently write across the unknowns on your calendar: "Here be God" when:

- Sickness invades your body.
- Relocation is necessary for employment.
- Family relations are stressed because of poor choices.
- Children feel attracted to the world.

D—Directed Prayer

Father, help me to remember that You are every where in my life.

October 20

The Little Temple in Jerusalem

God's sovereignty includes all of history, past, present, and future.
Matthew 24:1-8

A—Advice from the Bible

Jesus left the temple and was walking away.
(Matt. 24:1)

B—Biblical Example

The cleansing of the Temple was perhaps Jesus' supreme claim to messiahship (21:12-13). At the time of this Scripture passage, He once again referred to the temple. The disciples had questions when Jesus predicted its destruction. As the Lord and His followers left the area, they called His attention to the buildings. This structure was actually called Herod's Temple and consisted of the sanctuary and several adjacent courts and colonnades (porches). Hugh stones were used in the construction. King David was the first person desiring to build a temple for the Lord. Because of personal problems, he was not permitted to do more than gather the materials for the site. King Solomon, his son, became the first temple builder. At this New Testament account, Jesus' prediction of the Temple's destruction must have seemed impossible. Shocked by what they had heard, the disciples had more questions they wanted to ask. Jesus led the group across the Kidron Valley to the Mount of Olives to explain about the coming tribulation. The events at this location became known as the Olivet Discourse.

C—Contemporary Application

Our trip to London, England, included a visit to the famous St. Paul's Cathedral. The pictures of this edifice fascinated me. Prior to the tour, I read some interesting brochures about the building. A cathedral has been on this site for nearly 1,400 years. This location in London is one of England's oldest, dating from A.D. 604. Sir Christopher Wren (1632-1723) is best known as the architect of St Paul's Cathedral. Wren was born in East Knoyle, Wiltshire, on October 20, 1632, the son of a clergyman. He died at 90 and was buried in the crypt of St Paul's. His tomb is marked by an inscription that reads: "*Lector, si monumentum requiris, circumspice*" meaning "Reader, if you seek his monument, look around you." This visit reminded me of the temple in Jerusalem and how it, too, had survived through the ages.

Today, Christians are a temple for the Holy Spirit. The Bible reveals that:
- "Your body is the temple of the Holy Spirit."
- "You shall receive power when the Holy Spirit is come upon you."
- "The Holy Spirit helps in our weaknesses."
- "Since we live by the Spirit, let us keep in step with the Spirit."

D—Directed Prayer

Holy Spirit, how honored I am that You live in me as Your temple.

October 21

A Little Forty Year Rest

Trust God to provide deliverance when sin is acknowledged.
Judges 3:5-12

A—Advice from the Bible

So the land had rest for forty years.
(Judg. 3:11)

B—Biblical Example

The Book of Judges is about 12 men and Deborah, who served Israel during difficult times. Five judges ruled during peace time; seven were deliverers from the great oppressions of their enemies. God gave Israel the land of Canaan as an inheritance in the days of Joshua. He led them in conquering their enemies. Then the land was divided among the tribes. Israel's conquest of Canaan was incomplete. Instead of driving out the Canaanites, God's people shared with them and lived among these heathen. Baal worship was introduced to the Hebrews. The sin that followed produced results; Israel began worshiping gods and groves. God was the one who sent judgment upon Israel's sin. The cries of the people were heard by God and He sent Othniel as a first deliverer. He was successful because the Spirit of God came upon him. As long as this judge and his generation lived, rest came to the land. The Israelites saw their sin and felt the anger of the Lord. The Book of Judges shows God's mercy and the results of disobedience.

C—Contemporary Application

Spring had come to Washington, D.C. and the blooming cherry trees lined the streets. A cab driver was taking us to the Arlington National Cemetery. This site serves as the United States federal burial ground in north-eastern Virginia and is administered by the Department of the Army. The 612 acres contain the remains of 250,000 veterans, their dependents, and political leaders. Most of those interred here were members of the US armed forces killed in battle. Wars have always destroyed the peace of nations. Strong leaders are required to find ways to obtain peaceful solutions to these conflicts. Can you recall a time when war was not occurring somewhere in the world? When peace finally returns to the people, their lifestyles change. More success is evident. However, when wars begin, people exhibit fear, lack of security, and doubts about their future. The Book of Judges teaches a believer that sin comes, sin leaves, peace comes, peace leaves.

What can be learned from this scriptural experience?

- We know better than to sin against God.
- We can become entangled in sin.
- We can experience a broken fellowship with God.
- We can learn from Israel's fall into sin.

D—Directed Prayer

Father, thank You, that You do not give up on us.

October 22

A Little Watching

God's sovereignty includes all of history.
Matthew 24:36-44

A—Advice from the Bible

"Therefore keep watch, because you don't know . . . ."
(Matt. 24:42)

B—Biblical Example

Jesus' warning of judgment on the scribes and Pharisees in chapter 23, serves as an introduction to His teaching on last things. He reminded the disciples that only God knows the day and hour of His second coming and when that judgment will occur. Therefore, believers must be prepared. The flood in Noah's day is used as a comparison. Despite Noah's warnings, people went about their normal activities until his family entered the ark. Today, most people will be going through their usual routines with no thought of imminent judgment when He returns. A separation of the saved from the lost will occur at Christ's return. Unlike Noah's day, we are to "watch" in the sense of being prepared and to anticipate joyfully. Because of our ignorance concerning the time of Jesus' return, we should faithfully carry out His will for us. Like a thief in the night, Christ will return unexpectedly. Isn't it interesting that Jesus admitted that in His human state He did not know the time of His return? Only the Father knows the exact hour and day of His second coming.

C—Contemporary Application

Throughout church history various persons have contradicted Jesus by predicting the time of His second coming. In modern times, an American Baptist preacher, William Miller and his followers, known initially as Millerites (now Adventists), preached the imminent return of Christ to the earth. They proclaimed that the second coming would occur on a prophetic date between March 21, 1843 and March 21, 1844. The failure of this prediction was called the First Disappointment. Following this, a second date—October 22, 1844—was set, and many Adventists disposed of their property, quit their jobs, took their children out of school, and waited in anticipation of the event. After this failure, many members left the movement. Jesus concluded His teaching with a warning, "Watch."

Christians must remember that Jesus is coming again and:

- Avoid being overly absorbed in the pursuits of life.
- Find great comfort in the promises of God.
- He has saved us from the wrath to come.
- Faithfully complete His will for us.

D—Directed Prayer

Father, forgive us for becoming distracted from our tasks as Your servants.

October 23

A Little Return Home

God uses other people to bless those he loves.
Ruth 1:6-22

A—Advice from the Bible

Naomi prepared to return home.
(Ruth 1:6)

B—Biblical Example

The Book of Ruth begins with a tragedy. A devastating drought caused a family to leave Bethlehem and sojourn in Moab. The husband, Elimelech, died and his two sons soon passed. The grieving widow, named Naomi, survived the family crisis with two daughters-in-law. When she received word that conditions had changed in her homeland, she decided to return immediately. Several issues had to be resolved concerning taking these two women back to Judah. The move would mean leaving their homeland to go to a different land with a different culture and styles of life. Three widows with no family and no means of support also presented a problem. Perhaps another consideration would be leaving the worship of their god, Chemosh. The possibility of relocation would be a harsh experience for all these women. However, Naomi offered a benediction upon Ruth and Orpah. The departing scene was a sad one. Orpah decided to remain in Moab; Ruth did not want to make this drastic break in relationships. The trip home would be difficult because the effects of the severe famine were still felt in the land. Lack of water, grain for the animals, and basic comforts would make the journey a major hardship. God blessed this little family of two. The barley harvest was beginning and gleaning in the fields would supply their needs.

C—Contemporary Application

The Dust Bowl is a common name applied to a large part of Kansas and Oklahoma, that suffered extensively from wind erosion during the 1930s. In good seasons, the land was covered with grasses that held the fine-grained soil in place in spite of the long recurrent droughts. The homesteaders settled in the region, planting wheat and raising cattle. My grandparents and parents were included in this land possession. Beginning in the early 1930s, severe droughts occurred, and the soil began to blow away. Family farms were ruined. Some migrated westward; my family stayed, survived, and was blessed.

How has God used other people to bless you?

- A godly person provided meals for you during a sickness.
- A college scholarship was available because of a generous family.
- A job was provided by a friend when you finished your education.
- A neighbor comforted you during the passing of a family member.

D—Directed Prayer

Bless the Lord, O my soul, and all that is within me.

October 24

A Little Sanctification

Christians can grow in pleasing God.
1 Thessalonians 4:1-12

A—Advice from the Bible

For God has not called us to impurity, but to sanctification.
(1 Thess. 4:7)

B—Biblical Example

The apostle Paul had spent a total of three weeks with the church in Thessalonica. The beginning of this letter to that group of believers indicates his desire to make a return visit. The Christians needed to begin giving evidence of spiritual growth. The culture of this city was thoroughly pagan. Sexual immorality was common. The believers faced the pressures of their evil city every day. Paul's longing was for them to live in personal holiness. He chose the word sanctification meaning "to set apart, to be different." Instructions on the importance of doing God's will are provided. The Thessalonians needed to change their values, habits, and attitudes in order to be different from other citizens. Help is given for controlling their sexual desires. This lifestyle sharply contrasts with the behavior of the unbelieving Gentiles. A reminder is issued that God not only called them to a holy life, but also gave them His Holy Spirit. Holy living was not something Paul had originated. The good news is that the Holy Spirit is present in every believer's life to produce personal holiness. A life of sanctification is not the product of human efforts. The Holy Spirit is the Sanctifier. Our part is to yield to His control.

C—Contemporary Application

Charles Price Jones was America's first African-American hymnist. After both parents died, Charles wandered around, finally ending up in Arkansas. He also became a follower of Christ. Through a series of events he served as the pastor of a Baptist church in Selma, Alabama. In 1895, he moved to Mississippi and experienced a renewed encounter with the Holy Spirit. The experience was described as, "I fasted and prayed for three days, and then He sanctified me sweetly in His Spirit." The topic of his sermons became "Holiness." Criticism followed his renewal, driving him from his church. During these days of trial, Mr. Jones penned the words to "Deeper, Deeper." The lyrics express a desire to live a holy life for Jesus.

How well do you please God in the following areas?
- Leading a quiet life.
- Yielding control to the Spirit.
- Pleasing God more and more each day.
- Thanking God for personal holiness.

D—Directed Prayer

Father, help me to grow in pleasing You.

October 25

A Little Wall of Fire

Safety is not found in the absence of danger, but in the presence of God.
Zechariah 2:1-5

A—Advice from the Bible

I myself will be a wall of fire around Jerusalem.
(Zech. 2:5)

B—Biblical Example

Information about this minor prophet is very limited. He was a priest and his name appears in a list of Nehemiah's priests. Zechariah was involved in the edict of Cyrus, who gave the Jews the privilege of returning to Jerusalem and of rebuilding their temple (Ezra 1:1-4). Chapter 2 introduces a wall of protection. The prophet had a vision of a man with a measuring line, who was trying to determine the length and width of Jerusalem. His intention was apparently to begin rebuilding the fortified walls surrounding the city. The result of this construction project would bring restoration and prosperity. This man was told that this would not be necessary. God Himself would be the city's defense. One reason for not rebuilding the wall was the number of God's people would be so great that the city walls would not be able to contain them. Besides, they would not need walls, for the Lord promised a wall of fire. His presence made building unnecessary. The prophet gives a picture of God watching; of God acting, and of God blessing in spite of all their failure. The Hebrew people were told that God never lost sight of their condition and knew exactly how the world was treating them.

C—Contemporary Application

Construction began on the Great Wall of China in the third century B.C. around 221 and the project was completed in about 204 B.C. This structure often is called "the eighth wonder of the world." The wall was built to protect the Chinese people against raids by nomadic people and invasions by rival states. The fortification finally reached a length of about 1,500 miles. Our astronauts reportedly discovered that this wall is the only man-made structure visible from space. Despite the size, these physical walls were never a secure defense against the nomadic threats and centuries of fighting. God's children have the best wall of protection anyone can have—God's personal presence. In Him we are safe and sheltered.

Believers need to be sure that their measuring lines are adequate for God's plans by:
- Trusting God to protect His people.
- Including God in all personal plans.
- Understanding the God's presence never leaves His people.
- Believing we are safe and secure in God's arms.

D—Directed Prayer

Lord, help me not to fear the world's alarms, but seek refuge in You.

October 26

A Little Resurrection

Bodily resurrection is a great Christian hope.
1 Corinthians 15:12-22

A—Advice from the Bible

How can some of you say there is no resurrection?
(1 Cor. 15:12)

B—Biblical Example

One of the several questions addressed to the Corinthian church was about the afterlife. Apparently conflicting ideas existed even among believers, probably those with Jewish backgrounds believing one thing, and Gentile Christians another. Paul did not identify those who objected to the resurrection. The preaching of the resurrection of our Lord was a major apostolic emphasis. The Corinthians were not denying Christ's resurrection, but the New Testament doctrine of the bodily resurrection of believers. The apostle confronted his readers with the fact that they could not have things both ways: resurrection for Jesus, but no resurrection for His people. To deny this event nullified the gospel story of the empty tomb. If Christ had not been raised, we still would be guilty, unforgiven sinners. No atonement or reconciliation could occur apart from Christ's resurrection which was as necessary for salvation as His death. His resurrection assures believers of complete triumph over death and of the future that will be free from all the limitations of their earthly bodies.

C—Contemporary Application

Picture a group of people standing at the dock in New York harbor, bidding farewell to a friend who has boarded a cruise ship to Europe. The ship is a picture of strength and beauty as it moves out into the blue water. Eventually, the ship is nothing but a white speck on the horizon and then disappears completely. Her friends say, "There she goes." On the other side of the ocean, a friend of this traveler stands on the dock as her ship arrives. Suddenly, as just a speck on the horizon, the ship appears. Then the image gets larger and larger as the ship approaches the dock. And that friend says, "There she comes." Death is that way for the Christian. As the body, carrying the contents of human life slips away from us, we whisper, "There she goes." But at the very moment when we say, "Here she goes," someone on the other side is saying, "There she comes."

We are pilgrims in this present world:
- Our hope is for a better, future life.
- Every decision should be made in the light of eternity.
- Concerns should not be limited to our present life and surroundings.
- Our labor now is not in vain.

D—Directed Prayer

Jesus, I believe that I will be resurrected from the dead just as You were.

October 27

Joseph's Little Brothers
We should graciously forgive others.
Genesis 50:14-26

A—Advice from the Bible

What if Joseph pays us back for all the wrongs we did to him?
(Gen. 50:15)

B—Biblical Example

The end of an extremely important chapter in the history of God's chosen people came with the death of Jacob. He was God's appointed leader. A new administration was organized with Joseph in charge. This change in leadership brought fears to the ten older brothers. The guilt feelings from selling Joseph into slavery still tormented them. Their brother had said he had forgiven them, but they never fully trusted his words. The cowardly brothers sent a mediator to Joseph. Apparently this was the first time in all these years that the brothers had actually confessed their sin to God's new leader and asked for his pardon. Their younger brother assumed that the matter of his brothers' offense against him had been settled many years before. A plea for mercy was not enough; they also offered to make restitutions. They offered to become his slaves! Joseph was not ignoring their sin and guilt, but as he looked back on his suffering, he knew God had a divine purpose through this event. His family in Canaan might well have perished during the seven-year famine had it not been for his captivity. His brothers did not deserve forgiveness, however, their brother comforted them and spoke kindly toward them.

C—Contemporary Application

My husband and I sat in the congregation of Emmanuel Baptist Church in Oradea, Romania. We were on a teaching/preaching assignment. As I looked around at the great crowd of people, I recalled some of the stories we had heard about the Russian rulers and the terrible treatment of some of these Christians. They had survived savage attacks from the Communist soldiers. They had seen pastors arrested, Christian schools closed, Bibles burned, religious libraries destroyed, and church building turned into Red Army headquarters. Yet, decades later, here they sat, lifting their voices in praise. They had forgiven their enemies and moved on to greater service for the Lord.

Why do some people have difficulty forgiving others?
- Their sins are too bad?
- They have never accepted Christ as their personal Savior?
- They are not good forgivers?
- They don't understand the biblical truths about forgiveness?

D—Directed Prayer

Father, please express Your forgiveness through me.

Paul's Little Liberty in Christ

The Christian's Statue of Liberty is the cross.
Galatians 1:1-10

A—Advice from the Bible

If I were trying to please men, I would not be a servant of Christ
(Gal. 1:10)

B—Biblical Example

Apostleship was the highest office in the church and Paul's apostolic authority was being questioned in the churches of Galatia. After a short greeting, he charged the Galatians with having deserted the gospel that he had taught them by paying heed to people who perverted the message. Paul knew that his gospel was genuine; he had received the truth from Christ himself, not from those who were apostles before him. His heart was overwhelmed by the crisis he faced. He could hardly believe that his converts were about to be turned away from the truth in such a short time by the Judaizers, who were trying to entice Christians back into the Jewish religious system. Verse 10 seems to imply that Paul had been accused of gaining popular favor by making religion too easy. Of course he had emphasized the grace of God. Paul had wonderfully combined the love of Christian freedom with a genuine desire for Christian unity, but he was not trying to please men. His allegiance was only to one Lord.

C—Contemporary Application

The Statue of Liberty was dedicated by President Grover Cleveland on October 28, 1886. When I first saw this colossal figure, I thought about all the immigrants who observed this sight for the first time. What a symbol of freedom that moment must have been! The statue was given by France to the United States to commemorate the centennial of US independence in 1876. American donors financed the pedestal and installation of the monument on Liberty Island in New York harbor. The statue was originally called Liberty Enlightening the World, and was a gesture of international friendship. Today, the "great lady" has become a global symbol of freedom. The statue, the island, and nearby Ellis Island were declared a national monument in 1924. The statue symbolizing liberty is in the form of a woman wearing flowing robes and a spiked crown, who holds a torch aloft in her right hand and carries in her left a book inscribed "July 4, 1776."

Reasons why some people have trouble believing in the gift of liberty in Christ:
- People have a desire to earn their freedom.
- People assume they will be saved if they simply do what they believe is right.
- People look for salvation in religious rituals and rules.
- People are prone to self-sufficiency and pride.

D—Directed Prayer

Thank You, Lord, for giving us liberty in Christ.

October 29

Babylon's Little Fall

God is sovereign over all nations.
Isaiah 14:12-22

A—Advice from the Bible

I will cut off from Babylon her name and survivors.
(Isa. 14:22)

B—Biblical Example

Isaiah, like many other prophets, condemned pagan nations. Many of these nations were near Judah. The prophet warned Judah not to put its trust in Babylon as an ally. The people were already enslaved to this nation. At this time, God already was preparing the Medes to bring His judgment against this group. Cyrus the Great would be the Median leader. That judgment would be so severe that all creation would shake with fear and trembling. Babylon would be so devastated that it never would be inhabited again. No descendant would be left to carry on the family name or sit on the throne. As a result of Babylon's defeat, God's people would be set free. Then they would praise God for the defeat of their enemies and the hope that was brought to them. This destruction would be a joyous occasion for God's people. They would sing a song of triumph over the defeated enemy. Like many ancient Near Eastern rulers, Babylonian kings thought they were godlike beings, if not gods. They were well-known for their arrogance, but Isaiah knew they were frail human beings.

C—Contemporary Application

The Berlin Wall was a fortified structure surrounding West Berlin, maintained by the former German Democratic Republic (GDR; East Germany) from 1961 to 1989. During the night of August 13, 1961 GDR soldiers and members of its militia, the *Kampfgruppen* (combat groups), built temporary fortifications which were rapidly replaced by a concrete wall, around West Berlin, These enemies of freedom wanted to keep the German citizens in. It is estimated that, between 1961 and 1989, at least 70 people were killed trying to cross the boundary. The Germans wanted freedom from the Germans! In 1989 the GDR regime collapsed and the demolition of the Wall, by both official personnel and enthusiastic citizens, began on November 9. The Wall is now commemorated by its few remaining sections.

Truths about God from today's verses:

- He is Sovereign over all nations.
- He judges sin wherever it is found.
- He holds us accountable for our sins.
- He loves us regardless of our sins.

D—Directed Prayer

Father, I pray today for difficult world conditions.

October 30

Little Controversies

When faced with opposition, you should follow Jesus' example.
Mark 2:1-12

A—Advice from the Bible

Why does this fellow talk like this?
(Mk. 2:7)

B—Biblical Example

Why would four friends on a roof-top, a crowded house in Capernaum, and Jesus cause so much controversy? Jesus made Capernaum His headquarters during His Galilean ministry. His fame as a healer attracted a great crowd who packed into a house, leaving no more room. The companions of a paralytic man were demonstrating their faith in the Lord as they took him to the roof that was probably made with tiles, and lowered him into the presence of Jesus. The Lord saw their faith through this loving deed of concern. A bold declaration of faith was spoken by Jesus. The scribes were shocked! Most of them belonged to the religious party known as the Pharisees. They immediately charged Jesus with trying to assume the authority of God. The Mosiac law prescribed death for blaspheming the name of God. The error of these men was not in their doctrine, but in their failure to see divine power in Christ. Jesus perceived the thoughts of the scribes, so He challenged them concerning spiritual and physical healing. The result of what followed electrified the crowd. The crippled man walked away from this experience, healed, and glorifying God, in spite of the controversy.

C—Contemporary Application

Roy is the creator of controversy in his little, country church. He decides which preachers to hire and fire; how to manage the financial giving; and whether to have Wednesday night meals. The sad thing about this disruptive man is that he claims to be a Christian, and yet, so many people have been hurt by his negative challenges. His corporate prayers call on God's greatness and power. He believes in the eternal security of the believers—and yet, Roy would have been a leading member of the scribes or Pharisees. People who generate problems in the church need to be confronted about this sin. Prayer is a major source of power in dealing with Roy. The little church will stay little as long as this man is given the freedom to disrupt the work of the Holy Spirit.

Some of the possible controversies in the church today are:
- Style of worship.
- Doctrinal issues.
- Financial giving.
- Color of the new church carpet.

D—Directed Prayer

Lord, when controversies come to our church, lead us to seek Your guidance.

October 31

The Little Witch of Endor

God is against all occultic practices.
1 Samuel 28:3-20

A—Advice from the Bible

Find me a woman who is a medium
(1 Sam. 28:7)

B—Biblical Example

An impending war between the Philistines and King Saul's forces caused Saul to visit a witch. The king was alarmed when he saw the mighty enemy army camped at Mt. Gilboa. He was desperate to know the outcome of the future battle. When Samuel died, Saul was without a spiritual counsel. He inquired of the Lord what to do, but the Lord did not provide guidance. How ironic that the king, in accordance with God's law, had sought to drive from the land the mediums and spiritists, who claimed to be able to contact the dead and foretell the future! Now, in fear and desperation, Saul disguised himself and went to the village of Endor, about six miles from where the army was camped. The spirit of Samuel appeared to the witch and she delivered his message. The exchange between Saul and the departed spirit of Samuel indicates that this was the work of the Lord, not the medium. She was afraid at what happened. Saul had set himself in opposition to the Lord and he was now confronted with His judgment. The king's days on earth were numbered.

C—Contemporary Application

Tonight, "Trick-or-Treaters" may knock on your door, dressed in costumes and carrying sacks for candy. Where did this tradition begin? Hallowe'en is a name applied to the evening of October 31, preceding All Saints' Day. The observances connected with Hallowe'en are thought to have originated among the ancient Druids, who believed that on that evening, Saman, the lord of the dead, called forth hosts of evil spirits. The Druids lit great fires on Hallowe'en, apparently for the purpose of warding off all these ghosts. The ancient Celts also believed that the spirits of the dead revisited their earthly homes on that evening. The Celtic tradition of lighting fires on Hallowe'en survived until modern times in Scotland and Wales, and the concept of ghosts and witches is still common to all Hallowe'en observances. Of similar origin is the use of hollowed-out pumpkins carved to resemble grotesque faces and lit by candles placed inside.

Let life's obstacles and difficulties push you in God's direction:

- Turning to anyone but God leads to disaster.
- God forbids being involved with the occult.
- God has the answers.
- Look to God for courage.

D—Directed Prayer

Father, awaken our world to the dangers of the spirit world.

November 1

A Little Rain and Snow

God sends forth His Word to bless the earth
Isaiah 55:10-11

A—Advice from the Bible

As the rain and the snow come down from heaven . . .
(Isaiah 55:10, NIV)

B—Biblical Example

Isaiah was a prophet in the eighth century before Christ. Most prophets of God in that day were not popular with the people. The message of coming judgment provoked the Israelites to anger against the prophet. However, Isaiah had a deeper meaning in his message. He was pointing out the hope for restoration of God's people and the marvelous blessings God offered to those who would seek Him. The agriculture illustration introduces the process of precipitation. The people could understand this comparison. Teaching in parables was Jesus' favorite way of helping people understand the spiritual lesson He was proclaiming. The interpretation of this lesson was probably rejected at this time in Israel's life. Most people do not like to hear bad news. Just as God faithfully sends the rain and snow to water the earth, so He sends forth His Word to bless the earth. God was comparing His Word to rain. The mysterious powers of germination in nature parallel the wonderful mystery of God's Word when planted in the hearts of people.

C—Contemporary Application

Camping in a state park in southern Arizona heightens your awareness of land without water. The view around us suggested no rain or snow had fallen for months. The dry air made the heat seem bearable, but the horizon offered no encouragement of rain. Finally after several dry days I said, "Let's go north." Jim's reply was, "Okay, in the morning we will leave." However, sometime during the night, rain began to fall on our travel trailer. By morning, the desert seemed to come alive. The transformation of needed moisture on a dry land seemed to produce vegetation over night. Now I could understand what Isaiah was saying about God sending forth His Word to bless the earth. Some people are living every day without the benefits of God's blessing or hearing the Word of God proclaimed. How thankful I am that "rain came to me" as a ten-year-old girl at First Baptist Church, Hobart, Oklahoma.

Reasons to be thankful:

- God's provisions, whether physical or spiritual, are intended for blessings.
- God's Word, when revealed, produces spiritual fruit.
- God's Word accomplishes His desires for us.
- Gods' Word helps Christians discover the abundant life God has planned for them.

D—Directed Prayer

Begin today thanking God for one or two blessing you have experienced last week.

November 2

Precious Little Memories

Reasons to be thankful for other Christians
Philippians 1:3-11

A—Advice from the Bible

I give thanks to my God for every remembrance of you.
(Phil. 1:3, HCSB)

B—Biblical Example

Paul was a prisoner in Rome for Christ's sake. His trial before Caesar would soon be scheduled. These situations were occurring when this letter was written. Paul wanted his friends to know that the suffering he had endured had opened a door of opportunity for the gospel to be preached. A mutual affection between the Apostle Paul and the church in Philippi existed. His remembrance of friends was not just during this time of imprisonment, but often in his life. The church had blessed Paul during these years. Three special ways the Christians had demonstrated their support for Paul was by their sympathy, prayers, and loving acts of kindness. He joyously prayed for them and longed to be with them at this time of personal crisis. One of his friends, Epaphroditus, delivered a gift to Paul. Another friend, who became a Christian in Philippi, was Lydia. The mutual love for Jesus had drawn them together.

C—Contemporary Application

Aging has many special blessings, especially the realization of how precious memories are. I thank God for people who loved me and led me to Christ. For example:

- A Sunday school teacher who "took" me to Bible study as a nine-year-old girl. My parents did not attend church, but this godly woman made sure that I went.
- Bible-preaching pastors at my home church in Hobart Oklahoma. The Word of God was explained in such a way that I heard and responded to the call of salvation as a 10-year-old child.
- Christian teachers and professors who encouraged me in the Word.
- Jim, my husband of over 50 years, who taught me how to live the Christian life.
- Prayer warriors through the years, who prayed without ceasing for our family.
- Our children, Mark and Martha, who sought to become all God wanted them to be.

How about your memories? In the ministry of the Gospel, name the people or places that come to mind when you give thanks:

- A precious family member
- A faithful pastor or church leader
- A caring church
- A special Christian friend outside the church acquaintances

D—Directed Prayer

Begin today thanking God for Christian friends from your childhood.

November 3

Habakkuk's Little Tablets

God answers with a promise
Habakkuk 2:2-4

A—Advice from the Bible

Write down the revelation and make it plain on tablets.
(Hab. 2:2, NIV)

B—Biblical Example

Habakkuk was a very honest man about his relationship to God. He observed how wicked people within Judah had treated the righteous. He also saw how the people of Israel were suffering at the hands of the Babylonian armies. Babylon was becoming the dominant world power at that time. As a prophet of God, he shared his feelings very sincerely with God. He even questioned God for allowing His people to suffer so much. However, the prophet knew he could count on an answer from God because he sought answers. God's instructions were of such importance that the message had to be shared with everyone. The instructions included making the words on the tablets large enough to communicate with a person running down the road. Verse 4 declared that God's people, who live in faithfulness, would survive. These words became the basis for the doctrine of justification by faith as taught by the Apostle Paul (Rom. 1:17). The purpose of the book was to show that God is still in control of the world despite the apparent triumph of evil.

C—Contemporary Application

Judy stopped my house this morning for a brief visit. Our conversation focused on the bad news in the morning paper. Nine articles on two pages were all about evil people. Our discussion continued about how bad the world situation was today. After she left, I began to think about evil world leaders. Of course, Adolph Hitler headed the list. How did this man gain so much power? He began by promising jobs and a return to national prosperity following the depression. By 1933, he was in power as a dictator. He preached the gospel of hatred for democracy and persecuted the churches. The idea of a master race of people became his obsession. The extermination of the Jews was just the beginning of this dream. Fortunately, God intervened and stopped this mad man. He committed suicide in a Berlin bunker in 1945. His evil power had been destroyed, but other people would soon assume the passion for power and seek to destroy human life—even as you read these words.

How do we confront evil powers in the world today?
- Christ has already defeated the powers of evil.
- Christians must recognize the evil powers.
- Christ has taught us how to pray for these evil powers.
- Christians are equipped with the whole armor of God (Eph. 6).

D—Directed Prayer

Begin today thanking God for answers to His promises.

November 4

Little Lies

Knowledge of Christ can help you resist false teachings.
Colossians 2:7-23

A—Advice from the Bible

Be careful that no one takes you captive through . . . empty deceit.
(Col. 2:8, HCSB)

B—Biblical Example

Paul was in prison when he wrote to the church in Colosse. He had never visited this area of Asia Minor. However, Epaphras, Paul's helper, had led the first evangelistic effort. Some of the false teachings in this region were considered dangerous to the faith of these early Christians. The heresy was a mixture of Jewish, pagan, and Christian ideas. The apostle was emphasizing the fact that Christ was sufficient for the total Christian life. Nothing else was needed! The epistle was an encouragement to the readers to remain true to the faith and grow in their faith. How would these false teachers entrap the Christians? Their plan was to take away the believer's freedom by means of empty illusions. For example, the false teachers demoted Christ to an inferior position by insisting that He was unable to bring men and women into relationship with God. Therefore, the Colosse Christians needed to turn to the ritual of Mosaic law, or to pagan deities. Paul stressed that Christ was sufficient for every need. The indictment against sinners was taken away by His death on the cross.

C—Contemporary Application

Kara did not remember a time when church was not the focus of her family life. Vacation Bible School and summer camps were special times in her life. Singing in the choir and participating in mission projects were fun times with her friends. For that reason, her actions in college are so hard to understand. Kara went to a university in the next state. Her roommate had a tremendous influence on this young freshman student. The second semester indicated that something was wrong in Kara's spiritual life. A campus group seemed to have kidnapped her mind. (Most false teachers seek converts from churches.) Kara was fascinated by the philosophy and empty promises of these deceivers. Later in the semester, horoscopes, charts, Ouija boards, and other spiritual practices were enjoyed by this young woman. She is still a captive of false teachers.

Paul identified in verse 7 four characteristics as ways that Christians should live.

- A Christian is to receive nourishment and support from Christ (*rooted*).
- The Christian life is a continuing process of being built (*built up*).
- A Christian should be in the right relationship to God (*established*).
- The Christian is to abound with thanksgiving toward God (*overflowing*).

D—Directed Prayer

Begin today thanking God for good Bible teachers.

November 5

Three Little Words

True worship involves praise to God.
Psalm 150:1-6

A—Advice from the Bible

Praise the Lord.
(Ps. 150:1, NIV)

B—Biblical Example

The last five psalms from the Book of Psalms are hymns of praise to God. These songs probably were sung to celebrate the completion of the Jerusalem city walls under Nehemiah's rebuilding project (Neh. 6:15-16). The words are all about praise, without a single prayer of petition. King David introduced music into the tabernacle and temple services (1 Chron. 16:4-7). The instrumental music was probably loud and joyous.

Imagine you are in the Temple in Jerusalem and the great choir begins to sing, then the congregation is invited to join in the praise music. The crescendo of praise to God had to cause the worshippers to participate with all their hearts. The people were urged to praise God in His temple on Mount Zion in Jerusalem. Then the psalmist encouraged the worshipers to move out of the temple to recognize God as Creator of all things. The focus then turned to the reason for praise: God's acts, including His works of creation and His gracious care and concern for all that He has created. The appreciation for instrumental music is expressed by requesting various instruments to be struck, plucked, and blown during the worship.

C—Contemporary Application

The psalms were probably the first songs to be sung throughout the ages. English translations were published as early as 1562 and made available to some churches. Music has always played an integral part in the life of believers. In 1612, a Psalter was published by clergyman Henry Ainsworth. This book of music from the psalms was carried by the pilgrims on their journey to the new world. Imagine these frightened passengers confined week after week in their small boats, yet, singing the comforting words from The Ainsworth Psalter. Encouragement was needed by these early adventurers. Seasickness, disease, and weather hazards prevented the people from going on deck. However, the words from God's Book ministered to them in special ways. Perhaps they sang the same songs that King David and the Hebrews had sung.

Four essentials to be included in songs of praise are:
- Remembering what God has done.
- Telling other people about what God has done.
- Showing God's glory to other people.
- Offering gifts of self, time, and resources.

D—Directed Prayer

Begin today thanking God for Christian music.

November 6

Little Divisive Issues

What is right? What is wrong?
Romans 14:1-12

A—Advice from the Bible

For we will all stand before the judgment seat of God.
(Rom. 14:10, HCSB)

B—Biblical Example

The church in Rome received a letter from the Apostle Paul. He wanted to introduce himself to them before his visit on the way to Spain. The church was composed mostly of Jews, but also involved many Gentiles. The Gentiles were recent converts from paganism. Tensions began to exist between these two groups. Some believers took a strong position on what was right and what was wrong. Their rigid attitude caused other believers to say, "You are making a problem out of nothing and we are not going along with your ideas." Two main issues became divisive in the church. First, the food sacrificed to idols could be purchased in the local market. One faction felt that buying and eating this meat offered to idols would compromise their Christian witness. The other believers felt that idols were nothing, so the meat offered to them remained good, wholesome food. The second issue was the mutual criticism between the two groups. An attitude of being better than one another prompted Paul to issue this principle of self-denial: Don't do anything that will cause a fellow Christian to stumble!

C—Contemporary Application

Once upon a time there was a small country church with a faithful congregation. A new, inexperienced pastor was called to lead the church. He did not realize that some members were potential trouble-makers. For example, old Brother John knew from experience how to "control" these people. Before long, divisive issues began to surface. First, one group felt that the leaders were planning too many potluck suppers at the church—once a quarter was enough! The other folks enjoyed the strengthening of relationships involved in these meals. This issue was a constant hindrance to worship. The divisive became divided. One group moved down the road about a mile and named their church New Hope Baptist Church. The other group remained at their site, but called themselves Old New Hope!

Christians may need to waive their own rights in these ways:

- Liberals are not to despise conservatives.
- Conservatives are not to judge liberals.
- No Christian should do anything to retard the spiritual growth of a believer.
- Christian behavior should bring peace to the church.

D—Directed Prayer

Begin today thanking God for Christian self-denial.

November 7

A Little Help for the Hungry

Christians are to care for people in need.
Isaiah 58:1-10

A—Advice from the Bible

. . . then if you spend yourselves in behalf of the hungry . . .
(Isa. 58:10, NIV)

B—Biblical Example

Fasting, abstaining from eating food, was a religious ritual for the Hebrews. In Isaiah's day, this procedure had become meaningless. God's prophet boldly announced the Lord's message of condemnation against people who were going through the forms of faith without real humility before the Lord. An outward appearance of seeking God without any meaningful spiritual desire brought displeasure to the Lord. The fast day was the same as any other day. The people continued disobeying His commands by oppressing the poor. The ritual ended with strife and discord. Isaiah explained that God's concept of faithful, genuine fasting involved removing injustice and oppression, helping the hungry, clothing the poor, and doing what was acceptable in God's sight. True fasting included sharing with individuals who had less. The homeless were objects of God's love and shelter was to be provided by His people. Clothing was to be available to the poor. The hungry person was to be fed. These opportunities for ministry involved the inner person of the giver, not just the possessions they provided.

C—Contemporary Application

William Booth desired to do something for needy people. His plan of action would be the creation of the Salvation Army in 1865. This Englishman began his work with military-type plans. Uniforms, flags, drums, and cornets identify the "army." Through the years their appearance on city streets has been a testimony of their caring spirit. Many members have been arrested for disturbing the peace. However, General Booth and his successors have continued their work. Soup-kitchens and overnight shelters kept many depression-era people alive. This international organization also promotes evangelism. The social services provided are offered without discrimination as to race or creed. General Booth and his daughter, Evangeline, had one purpose in mind and that was to demonstrate a Christian witness by caring people. She later replaced her father as commander and was awarded the US Distinguished Service Medal for her work during World War I.

Isaiah named four blessings for the helper that result from fasting:
- The helper will have insight into understanding God.
- The helper will find healing for the wounds of life.
- The helper will be in right relationship with God and other people.
- The helper will find personal protection from the Lord when evil attacks.

D—Directed Prayer

Begin today thanking God for the opportunities to serve hurting people.

November 8

Five Loaves and Two Little Fish

Become personally involved in people problems
Mark 6:33-44

A—Advice from the Bible

"You give them something to eat."
(Mark 6:37, HCSB)

B—Biblical Example

These verses are commonly referred to as "the feeding of the five thousand." All four gospels record this miracle. Jesus and His disciples needed to get away for relaxation and meditation. The disciples had just returned from a tiring mission trip. Jesus had been very busy teaching and healing. The Lord and His disciples were physically and emotionally exhausted. However, the people saw them set out by boat across the northern end of the Sea of Galilee. By the time the boat came to shore, the crowd was waiting. Jesus was moved with compassion for the people. So He began to teach them. The disciples were aware of the remote location and the need of food for the learners. A suggestion was made to send the people away, but Jesus presented a challenge, "You give them something to eat." He would not allow these men to avoid their duty to minister to people. Having told His disciples to become personally involved in the hunger problem, an inventory of their resources revealed only five loaves and two small fish. Jesus commanded the group to be seated. The miraculous power of Jesus was clearly demonstrated in that moment. All the people ate and were satisfied and the twelve disciples each had a basket of food.

C—Contemporary Application

An increasing number of English children were homeless and without any kind of accommodations. That is until a man named George Mueller of Bristol, England, opened the first great orphanage. The year was 1836 and the years to follow were an inspiration to many Christians. Mueller was born in Prussia and baptized into the Lutheran Church. His early life consisted of many problems and indecisions. A turning point came at a Bible meeting one evening when he chose to "stand on the side of Christ." His unique journey of faith began by depending on God alone for all his needs. The idea of opening an orphanage and depending completely on prayer and faith was begun. God provided every need for the next 40 years of Mueller's life.

What attitudes might we display concerning world hunger?

- Send the hungry people away.
- Let someone else deal with the hunger problem.
- Follow Jesus' example of compassion.
- Give or go to help serve people without enough to eat.

D—Directed Prayer

Begin today thanking God for a full stomach.

November 9

Thanksgiving for Little Blessings

Respond to God's blessings and judgments.
Psalm 67:1-7

A—Advice from the Bible

May God be gracious to us and bless us.
(Psalm 67:1, NIV)

B—Biblical Example

Psalm 67 is basically a harvest hymn that praises God for His blessings. The Jews probably sang this joyous song during their temple worship at the Feast of Pentecost. The words express gratitude for God's presence among His people. The soil from which the harvest came was seen as one demonstration of God's favor. The purpose for asking God's blessing was in order that God would be known and acknowledged by all the people of the earth. The words express a worldwide concern for people. The people also needed God's unveiled presence to illumine their lives. God's character as Judge provides the reason for the universal rejoicing and thanksgiving of all people. He will rule His kingdom with a just and impartial government. The dream of all people confessing God as Lord brought joy to the writer's heart. Just think, one day, people of all nations will be converted and joining in offering praise and thanksgiving to God!

C—Contemporary Application

The young man seemed to be following in his father's footsteps. He loved to stand by his dad in church just to hear the older man's powerful voice. Johnson Oatman, Jr. was born just before the Civil War. As a nineteen-year-old boy, he joined the Methodist Episcopal Church and was ordained into the ministry a year later. However, the family mercantile business was his choice vocation. The money helped pay the bills and gave him opportunities to minister without cost. In 1892 Johnson began writing hymns. No doubt the words of his father's voice still rang in his memory. This successful writer averaged composing 200 hymns and gospel songs each year. One of my favorites is *Count Your Blessings*. This song was originally written for young people and was published in 1897. Johnson reminded his singers to consider specifically how God had blessed them. Some suggested times of blessing are when you are tempted, discouraged, burdened, doubting, lacking money, and others. Johnson Oatman's optimistic faith is contagious when you sing his lyrics.

Practice counting your blessings:

- Think of some reasons you have for responding to God's blessings.
- Think of some reasons your church has for responding to God's blessings.
- Think of some reasons why you don't count your blessings more often.
- Think of some reasons why caring for *all* people should be a Christian priority.

D—Directed Prayer

Begin today thanking God for His blessings and judgments.

November 10

Little Doubts

Jesus helps people overcome their doubts about Him.
Luke 7:18-28

A—Advice from the Bible

"Are You the Coming One, or should we look for someone else?"
(Luke 7:19, HSCB)

B—Biblical Example

John the Baptist was in prison because he had offended Herod Antipas. Since he had no way to personally hear about the ministry of Jesus, John instructed his followers to go ask Jesus a question. He wanted to know if Jesus was really the Messiah. Perhaps John's faith was wavering. Apparently, he felt that Jesus' actions did not match his understanding of the Messiah's role as Judge. The circumstances of immense stress caused him to seek an answer from Jesus. John's disciples were sent and repeated his question. John the Baptist simply wanted some evidence that would relieve his doubts. Doubt and faith can exist side by said. This incident in the life of John the Baptist can encourage us to ask our own questions about Jesus. The important thing to remember is to look to Jesus for the answer. The Lord answered John's question with actions, not words. He gave a clear answer by His actions. He then instructed the disciples to go tell John what they had seen.

C—Contemporary Application

David Livingstone was a Scottish doctor and missionary. He also is recognized as one of the most important explorers of the African continent. His stand against any form of human slavery and slave traders is well-known. His travels led him to regions where no European had ever been. The English and American press found his expeditions exciting to their readers, especially his desire to discover the source of the Nile. In the midst of all this public interest, Livingstone seemed to disappear. His welfare became a matter of international concern. After five years, friends began to doubt that he was alive. Their concerns prompted the New York Herald to send a reporter named Henry Morton Stanley on a rescue party. This American journalist found Dr. Livingstone on November 10, 1871. The world's most adventurous journalist greeted the world's most famous missionary with the words, "Dr. Livingstone, I presume?" The international world no longer doubted the survival of this great explorer. Evidences of his actions were soon published worldwide.

Some important resources in times of doubt are:
- Christian fellowship and worship.
- Witness and support of other believers.
- Hear the Word of God preached.
- Dependence upon the Holy Spirit.

D—Directed Prayer

Begin today thanking God for helping us in times of doubt.

November 11

A Little Heart Pride

God promises deliverance for His people.
Obadiah 1-21

A—Advice from the Bible

The pride of your heart has deceived you.
(Ob. 3, NIV)

B—Biblical Example

Obadiah, whose name means "Worshiper of Jehovah," was one of the prophets to preach following the return of some Jewish people from exile in Babylon. His book is the shortest of the Minor Prophets. He prophesied that God would destroy Edom, a neighbor state to Jerusalem. These people had been cruel to God's people when Babylon conquered Jerusalem. This message of judgment is true for all the nations in the present as well as in the future. God will judge all governments, but He will deliver His people. The book begins with a vision about an announcement by God. He stated that although Edom, a nation of descendants of Esau, took pride in their greatness and invincibility, He would make it small and despised. Edom's main sin was pride, however, they were not beyond God's reach. The Lord described the violence for which Edom was judged. All nations must give account of themselves to God.

C—Contemporary Application

The conflict of World War I began when Kaiser Wilhem of Germany took pride in his armies and the power he felt they had over the other European countries. The war spread as the German army crossed over borders to conquer their neighbors. President Woodrow Wilson attempted to bring negotiations between the different world powers in 1916, but the German leaders resisted the offers of peace. The pride of their hearts led to continued fighting and included the United States. General John J. Pershing commanded the American forces. By 1918 the German forces were being overcome. On November 11, 1918 the armistice was signed in France. The fighting had ceased. Today we celebrate Veteran's Day and seek to honor veterans of all wars. Sometimes artificial flowers called poppies are sold as a reminder of the many lives lost and buried at Flanders Field (where poppies grow) in France.

Consider some answers to the following questions:
- What are some things in our nation that you fear have deceived us into pride and a false security?
- Why do some people rejoice in the misfortunes of others?
- How do you think our nation can avoid God's judgment?
- How can pride, arrogance, and self-sufficiency destroy our nation?

D—Directed Prayer

Begin today thanking God for delivering and preserving His people through years of conflicts.

November 12

Timothy's Little Task

An unashamed worker uses the Bible effectively.
2 Timothy 2:14-26

A—Advice from the Bible

> . . . *a worker who doesn't need to be ashamed, correctly teaching the word of truth.*
> (2 Tim. 2:15, HCSB)

B—Biblical Example

Paul was a Roman prisoner, probably anticipating early execution, when he wrote his second letter to his younger friend. The apostle certainly displayed great confidence in Timothy when he left him to care for the church in Ephesus. This city was celebrated for the temple of Diana, one of the seven wonders of the world. Idol worship created an atmosphere that was in conflict with the gospel. Intense divisions on maters of belief existed in the Ephesian church. Paul described the task he had for this young preacher. Among the concerns was that Timothy focus his mind on the Lord Jesus and on the necessity of faithfulness to Him. He was to exert every effort to rightly handle the Word of God. The Word of God is deserving of the utmost respect and should not be misused or distorted to support personal theories. The faith of some believers might waver, but God's people can place their trust on a foundation laid by God Himself. Paul made his meaning clear. Evil desires must be overcome and worthy traits developed. Apparently, Timothy pursued this task.

C—Contemporary Application

The highlight of our trip to Amsterdam (Netherlands) was a visit to a diamond factory. Men and women were bent over an instrument with powerful lights, looking at a small object through the lens. One of the brochures from this visit told the following story: One day in 1908, the Dutch craftsman Joseph Asscher faced the most demanding task of his life: cutting the 3,106 carat Cullinan diamond, the largest ever discovered. Asscher examined the huge gem meticulously, carefully noting every detail of its crystalline structure. Any error in judgment with his cutting instrument could subtract a fortune from the value of the massive stone. Then he raised his hammer and perfectly cut the stones. The best known is the Great Star of Africa, a British crown jewel. Paul instructed Timothy to handle one of God's crown jewels with all the care of an expert craftsman. Every person needs a copy of the Word of God.

Consider these thoughts about God's Word:
- The Word of God can be abused.
- The Word of God can be distorted.
- The Word of God can be handled casually.
- The Word of God cannot be destroyed.

D—Directed Prayer

Begin today thanking God for His everlasting Word of truth.

November 13

A Little Reminder

Mistreating others brings God's judgment.
Micah 1:1-7

A—Advice from the Bible

. . . because of the sins of the house of Israel.
(Micah 1:5, NIV)

B—Biblical Example

The Old Testament often features specially chosen messengers or prophets to announce God's instructions to His people. Micah served as God's messenger to the nation of Judah from about 742—687 B.C. Spanning the reigns of three of Judah's kings, the prophet stood firm with God during a time of increasing disobedience within the nation. Micah came from a small town and was considered a country prophet. He was sympathetic to the needs of the poor, and critical of those who were rich and powerful. Harsh warnings were issued to the people who willfully disregarded God's teachings. Like an announcer at a sporting event, the messenger called for everyone's attention. What he had to say was urgent. God's power would be felt throughout the earth as He disciplined His people for their sins. Micah assured the people that God would not ignore their practice of idolatry and rebellion. He would execute judgment against them. God's judgment came because of their failure to meet His standards.

C—Contemporary Application

Oklahoma is my home state. Many Indian tribes are located throughout the state. The Kiowa Indians have a reservation near my hometown. Their children did not attend our schools, but were sent to boarding schools away from the reservation. These schools were provided by the government. My ignorance of this group of people was exposed during a class in Oklahoma history. For the first time, I was introduced to the terrible mistreatment of the American Cherokee Indian. This period of history had never personally registered as a time of great sorrow. President Andrew Jackson refused to protect this tribe's request of help, so in 1838 federal soldiers forced the Indians out of the southeastern United States. A march from Georgia to Indian Territory (now Oklahoma) was begun in the midst of a drought and continued into a harsh winter. Four thousand people perished through hunger, disease, and exposure. This mistreatment was later known as the Trail of Tears.

What message would Micah have regarding the following sins of mistreatment today?
- Social injustices.
- The homeless.
- Illiteracy.
- Wealthy drug dealers.

D—Directed Prayer

Begin today thanking God for His warnings about inevitable judgments against sin.

November 14

Hannah's Little Thanksgiving Prayer

The joy of answered prayer leads to thanksgiving...
(1 Samuel 2:1-10)

A—Advice from the Bible

My heart rejoices in the LORD.
(1 Sam. 2:1)

B—Biblical Example

The experience of Hannah in the Bible has always been a personal favorite. This woman demonstrated faithfulness to God by keeping a promise. Her actions are not common among people. Remember the situation? Elkanah, her husband, lived in the hill country of Ephraim, about five miles north of Jerusalem. A major problem existed in this family unit. The husband had two wives. One was able to bear children; the other was barren.

Childlessness was a disaster to a woman in the ancient east. How would the family lineage proceed? Hannah's sorrow was sincere even though her husband loved her very much. A turning point came when she sought the LORD through prayer. The promise to give God her child was unusual. However, she was faithful and dedicated Samuel to service for God. Her deep grief was overcome with praise and thanksgiving. God had completely fulfilled her longings.

C—Contemporary Application

The young married couple was sitting on their honeymoon beach, making plans for their future together. The subject of family was soon discussed. Both individuals shared the same concern for any children who might be born into their new family. Valerie said, "I think we ought to offer our first child to God to be used any where, any way that God so chooses."

James responded, "I agree with you. I want my child to love the Lord and serve Him like we are trying to do."

Several years passed and no child was born into the family. Talk of exploring the invitro process was considered. Adoption also was explored. But in God's time, a beautiful boy was born. The couple kept their promise to God and exposed their son to the Christian way of life. The young man now serves as a missionary to people groups in the Pacific Rim area. Valeria and James consider the years their son was home with them, some of the most precious times of their life, but the day came when God called . . . .

Explore the answers to these questions about faithfulness to commitments.

- Why is being faithful to commitments you have already made so difficult?
- How does giving something special reveal your faithfulness to God?
- Why do people make serious commitments to God in the first place?
- How can my prayer life be more effective?

D—Directed Prayer

Begin today thanking God for opportunities to make commitments that matter.

November 15

A Little Mixed Ancestry

Build relationships with all people.
(John 4:3-9)

A—Advice from the Bible

Now he had to travel through Samaria.
(John 4:4)

B—Biblical Example

Three distinct divisions of land existed in Jesus' day. Galilee was in the north and Judea was in the south. Stuck in the middle was Samaria. The Pharisees had become more intense in their attacks on Jesus, so to avoid controversy, He began to journey toward Galilee. Since the destination was Cana in Galilee, the Lord and His followers took the shortest route through Samaria. Jewish people considered Samaritans a disgusting race who had turned both from the nation and the religion of Israel. Samaritans trace their roots to those Jews not dispersed when the Assyrians conquered Israel in 722-721 B.C. These remaining colonists intermarried and began to practice idolatry. Eventually the worship of the Lord became mixed with all kinds of pagan practices. This group of mixed ancestry was rejected by the Jews. Radical treatment followed such as never going through Samaria, but taking a longer route to Galilee to avoid any contact with these despised people. And yet, Jesus chose to enter this area. His actions demonstrated how rejection of prejudice can open doors for evangelism.

C—Contemporary Application

Events in recent years have focused national attention on the importance of racial harmony. The awareness that racial prejudice prevents the message of Christ from reaching a lost world is a serious matter. A missionary friend of ours was attending a major meeting in India. The purpose of the meeting was to determine ways to share the gospel with all races of people. The conference concluded with the celebration of the Lord's Supper. Our friend expressed the bond of Christian fellowship that was experienced that day. A Swedish minister, a Chinese pastor, a Japanese teacher, a German doctor, a Canadian official, several Americans, and a few Indian believers assembled together in the name of Christ. No cultural or racial barriers divided these believers. These people saw their fellow believers as members of the body of Christ

What can I do about differences that exist between groups of people?

- I can follow Jesus' example and "go through Samaria."
- I can build relationships with people of other races.
- I can invite all groups to come to Jesus and receive salvation.
- I can follow the Lord's plan of evangelism.

D—Directed Prayer

Begin today thanking God for missionaries who will cross borders and barriers.

November 16

A Little Chorus of Thanksgiving

Give thanks to God for the wonderful things He does.
(Psalm 75:1-10)

A—Advice from the Bible

We give thanks because You are near.
(Ps. 75:1)

B—Biblical Example

This Scripture passage is one of three psalms (67; 75;107) that celebrate God's presence and power among His people. The setting seems to be a worship service in the Jerusalem temple. The congregation responds to the retelling of the great things God had done in their midst with a chorus of thanksgiving. God had been so good to them and their worship experience called attention to what He had done. The worshippers were sensitive to the nearness of God. He was present in their lives and for this they were grateful. The psalm continues with a statement of God's right to judge and His fairness in judgment. The accountability of all people would become part of the judgment. A warning was issued to all who liked to brag about what they had done. God only would execute judgment against the wicked. Each individual had gathered for worship and vowed to continue to declare God's works as long as they lived.

C—Contemporary Application

Corporate worship should provoke an awareness of God's nearness. Two instances of this kind of worship have happened in my life. The first was an opening night service at the Glorieta Baptist Conference Center near Santa Fe, New Mexico. The worship center would seat 2,000 people and every seat was taken! These worshippers had come from all areas of the world. When the singing began, a call was issued for volunteers to sing in the choir. A hundred or more musicians went to the platform. None of these groups had sung together before this time. Their "special" for the evening was "How Great Thou Art." The nearness of God was so very real to me. This moment was a personal spiritual highlight. The second experience of the nearness of God was in Oradia, Romania. My husband was preaching in the largest Baptist church in Europe. Everything was in a language that I didn't understand, but God's presence was so real to me. The congregation sang to the glory of God and I worshipped as never before.

Reasons for being thankful for God's nearness:

- Everyone everywhere has reason to praise God.
- God is Judge, and He judges in fairness.
- Believers who have been saved need to tell others.
- God provides for all our needs.

D—Directed Prayer

O Lord my God when I in awesome wonder . . . How great Thou art!

November 17

The Little Return from Babylon

Whatever role you have in church is important to God.
(1 Chronicles 9)

A—Advice from the Bible

The first to live in their towns on their own property were . . . .
(1 Chron. 9:2)

B—Biblical Example

The first book of Chronicles is a record of the history of the Hebrew people from Adam through the reign of David. When the time came for the Jews to return to Judah after the Babylonian exile, they were confronted with several problems, One of these was the correct distribution of the land by families. Another difficulty was the maintenance of religious rituals. One of the primary reasons for the writing of this material seems to have been to show the importance of Judah in God's plan. Chapter 9 tells of the preservation of this genealogical material and of the duties of certain priests and Levites. The people returned by groups of heads of fathers' houses, priests, Levites, gatekeepers, and singers. A brief description of the responsibilities of these groups is listed. Each family unit was finally returning to their past experiences. Some of the young exiles had never been to Judah before. The Chronicler especially addressed these young people in terms of their responsibility to fulfill God's plan for these freed people.

C—Contemporary Application

Our trip to Israel had been pleasant. A visit to the sites from the Bible were very meaningful. Our guide outlined the next day's events and said that we would be visiting the Yad Vashem Memorial to the Holocaust. This World War II reminder was not something I wanted to see. However, our group cooperated and entered this dark, urine-smelling place. Pictures of the extermination camps filled the room. As we walked down the halls, our senses were quickened by the reminder of death. The one thing that saddened me most was the picture of a dark sky in an arched design with tiny lights like stars. Each light represented a Jew who was murdered by Hitler. Go back now to that occasion when the exiled Jews returned to Judah and nothing seemed the same. Responsibilities were given to the returnees, much like the returning Jews who survived the extermination camps. But God had a plan for His people and they got to work.

God continues to have a plan for His people:

- A plan that encourages knowing Him through the study of His Word.
- A plan that encourages the discovery of the Holy Spirit's gifts for the believer.
- A plan that encourages faithful stewardship of money, time, and talents.
- A plan that encourages ministry to needy people.

D—Directed Prayer

Father, help me to understand my responsibilities as a church member.

A Little Harvest Psalm

November 18

God hears more than our words; He listens to our thankful hearts.
(Psalm 65:1-13)

A—Advice from the Bible

We are filled with the good things of Your house.
(Ps. 65:4)

B—Biblical Example

This psalm by David is about the harvest season and glorifies God the Creator. Here we are invited to a thanksgiving service. Praise is the attitude of worship and overflows from a grateful heart. The vows made to God are now fulfilled. These vows come from a thankful heart. Verse 4 is a beautiful picture of a forgiven worshiper who enjoys the benefits of being in God's presence. "Every perfect gift is from above" (Jas. 1:17). The psalmist would agree. God waters the earth. Drought is characteristic of God's judgment while rain signifies God's blessing. Being on the blessing side has great benefits. Verse 10 presents three actions by God that bless the farmers. The land owner plows and plants, but God gives the increase. One truth that is significant to the worshiper is that what God starts, He will finish. The result of all the harvest work is a bountiful crop. God has the power to take the driest of situations and bring forth flourishing life.

C—Contemporary Application

Thanksgiving is a time to remember and recognize. Consider the following questions as you prepare for the traditional Thanksgiving Day.

- Where are you going on Thanksgiving Day?
- What or whom are you taking?
- Who is coming to your house?
- How are you preparing?
- Why are you making all these preparations?
- What was the loneliest or saddest Thanksgiving you ever had?
- What one thing are you most thankful for this year?
- What person in your past do you remember at this time of the year?
- How would you express a prayer to God for His great work in your life?
- Are you happier this year than last year? Explain.

Four actions of God that bring hope to a worshipper:

- God hears our prayers.
- God listens to our hearts.
- God created mountains to display His creative work.
- God made the east and the west; sunrise and sunsets.

D—Directed Prayer

- Lord, thank You that we can see Your goodness through the eyes of a grateful heart.

November 19

Little Firstfruits Baskets

Our offering to God reflects our thanksgiving for His faithfulness.
(Deuteronomy 26:1-11)

A—Advice from the Bible

Take some of the firstfruits the LORD your God is giving you and put them in a basket.
(Deut. 26:2)

B—Biblical Example

Deuteronomy 26 focuses on giving offerings. The chapter features two ceremonies to be held after entering the Promised Land. The first was the presentation of the firstfruits. The second ceremony was the presentation of the third-year tithe (vv. 12-15). God commanded His people to offer to Him what their labor had produced. (Remember that these people were not farmers, but wanderers in the desert.) Now a new era was about to begin. Since the land was God's covenant gift to the people, the return of some of the produce represented an act of thanksgiving to Him. In a special ceremony, the people were to offer a portion of the first harvest of the ground. This particular giving seems to have been a one-time event. The offering was only a sample of the firstfruits. The selections appear to have been a wide sampling of all the variety produced in the land. The basket was to be taken by each worshiper to the sanctuary as the Lord had appointed. The place of worship was to be a dwelling place for God's name. He is always worthy of the first and best we produce.

C—Contemporary Application

About this time each year in our church, individuals, Bible study groups, and families prepare special thanksgiving baskets for people in need. The empty baskets are distributed to the givers and a list of possible supplies is attached. The names of people in need come from school teachers, government agencies, and the police department. Included in the gift, are canned vegetables, fruit, sometimes a turkey, and bread. Our church provides Bibles, leaflets about knowing God, and a brochure from our church. Sometimes a receiver of the basket will get in touch with the giver; other times, we never know what happened in that home. However, the reason for giving is not for rewards, but this action is done in honor of God, who has blessed us so richly. One time a mother and two small children visited us on a Sunday. Her gratitude to us was an emotional moment.

What are some reasons people give to help the needy?
- They are trying to buy blessings from God.
- They give to express gratitude and worship to God.
- They have always given and continue to do so.
- They have a real love for hurting people.

D—Directed Prayer

Father, thank You for all the blessings You have provided for my family.

November 20

A Little Joy and Gratitude

God is the source of all that is positive and meaningful in life.
(Psalm 100:1-5)

A—Advice from the Bible

Shout for joy to the LORD.
(Ps. 100:1)

B—Biblical Example

This Psalm is called "Old Hundredth." A tune was composed in 1560 by British Christians and later became known as the "grand old Puritan anthem." Verse 1 begins with a command to take action. Notice that "please" or "would you" are not used. God's people thought of Him as being worshiped in His own land by His own covenant people, therefore, this psalm might have been written during the exile. The privilege and responsibility for worshiping the Lord was extended to the whole world. A fundamental act of worship is to enter the presence of the One we worship. You recognize a person by looking at his face. Remember when Jesus said, "He who has seen me has seen the Father?" Some believers have become very casual about worship. However, the privilege of entering the presence of God Almighty, who created heaven and earth, should always be appreciated. The spirit of the worshipers was to express gladness and joy. One reason for this attitude is that we are His possessions. God's ownership, protection, and concern are for us.

C—Contemporary Application

When the Mayflower dropped anchor in Provincetown harbor on November 20, 1620, after 65 days at sea, the long journey was over. These simple, ordinary folk had nothing of value and their challenges were just beginning. They had fled from religious oppression. The desire to worship God led this band of 1,600, known as Puritans in England, to face the unknown world in order the serve their God. The Mayflower brought together struggling Protestant Christians from many places and varied backgrounds. One common cord bound them together; they had to be free from religious domination. Their first winter in America was unbearably cold, bitter, and difficult, but their joy and gratitude to God helped them survive. If any of the Puritans wanted to return to England, they never said anything about that choice. God would provide.

Reasons why we should worship God:

- He is the source of all that is positive and meaningful in life.
- His love endures forever.
- He is dependable and reliable.
- He desires our thanksgiving and gratitude.

D—Directed Prayer

Begin today thanking God for His goodness.

November 21

A Little Ordinary Meal

Life-changing experiences still happen with the living Lord.
(Luke 24:28-32)

A—Advice from the Bible

He was at the table with them.
(Lk. 24:30)

B—Biblical Example

Two people were headed for Emmaus when a third Person joined in the walk. Cleopas and his companion had been to Jerusalem and witnessed the crucifixion of Jesus Christ and heard about the resurrection. The main topic of conversation was the events of the past week. As they approached the village, the two travelers did not want the fellowship with the stranger to end. They pointed out that night was approaching and travel would be difficult. Apparently these followers of Christ sensed something unusual about Him and wanted to hear more about what He had to say. Jesus accepted their invitation. He waited patiently for this invitation to be a part of their life. The choice is always up to the person. Notice how Jesus became the host at the meal! Here at this ordinary meal, the Lord Jesus guided events to bring out the truth about Himself. He took the bread as he had been accustomed to doing with His own disciples. He blessed the bread and gave thanks for the meal. Then Jesus served the hosts. At this time, the two men recognized who their guest really was, but He disappeared from them as suddenly as He had appeared. Christ's post-resurrection appearances usually were of short duration. The two then went back to Jerusalem to share the good news that Jesus was alive.

C—Contemporary Application

The Thanksgiving celebration was at our house this particular year. Our mothers had come from Oklahoma and our children from their residences. Time was spent talking about past dinners and letting our aging mothers reminisce about their childhood. The third generation also seemed interested in their heritage. Within the year, both mothers had passed on to be with the Lord, and since Jim and I have no brothers or sisters, we made the plans for their memorials. A sudden realization occurred to us during this time of sorrow. Questions about the past would no longer have answers. Everything we had learned about our heritage was all we were to receive

The living Lord wants every person to:
- Experience a relationship with Him.
- Open their eyes to understand His purpose.
- Tell others about their experience.
- Continue to learn from Him.

D—Directed Prayer

Thank You for the excitement of knowing what You have done and what You will do.

November 22

A Little Begging

Sometimes we need to set our watches to His clock.
(Psalm 141:1-5)

A—Advice from the Bible

O LORD, I call to you; come quickly to me.
(Ps. 141:1)

B—Biblical Example

Perhaps countless thousands of men and women through century after century have recited this psalm at the end of the day, in churches, in monasteries, in institutions, and in private. This evening psalm was written by David when he was in danger of being influenced by wicked people. However, he had the presence of mind and maturity of faith to ask for God's help in resisting temptation. The urgency of this prayer request is emphasized. Incense offered to God and lifted hands in prayer seem to be a pattern from the evening sacrifice in Exodus 29:38-42. David desired to know when to be silent, as well as when to speak. Another request was that fancy food and the social life of the wicked might not tempt him. An interesting observation is that this prayer is a preventive one. Talking with God before temptation occurs is always a smart choice. Now, David would not have to turn to the Lord in repentance as recorded in Psalm 51.

C—Contemporary Application

The first Thanksgiving in 1621 was but a memory to the Pilgrims. They have now been in the New World for two and a half years, and the summer's drought was jeopardizing everything. Without rainfall, no crops could be harvested. They prayed daily that God would send rain. The urgency of their request was much like the psalmist in today's Scripture. They begged God to hurry. Finally, an entire day for prayer and worship was scheduled. When they left their meeting, the weather changed. For the next 14 days, moderate showers fell. The Indians watched and were amazed at how the God of the settlers had answered their prayer. A second Thanksgiving was planned on November 22, 1623. The Indians were again invited to join in the celebration. Sometimes our praying is much like the psalmist. We want God to "hurry up" and when He doesn't, we question His delays. Then, the begging and negotiating with the Lord begins. Remember that God doesn't seem to be in the same rush that we are with His answers.

The psalmist was in "constant prayer." What should our constant prayers be?

- For the spread of the gospel to all people.
- For individuals to go and tell the good news about Jesus.
- For churches to reach out to all of the colors of humanity.
- For personal, spiritual growth.

D—Directed Prayer

Forgive me, Father, when I beg You to answer my requests.

November 23

A Little Expression of Thanks to God

Christians are to take time to thank God personally.
(Lev. 7:28-36)

A—Advice from the Bible

With his own hands he is to bring an offering.
(Lev. 7:30)

B—Biblical Example

The Book of Exodus records the building of the tabernacle and the first seven chapters of Leviticus contain instructions regarding five different, but not unrelated, kinds of sacrifices and offering commanded by God through Moses. The worship experiences were to be offered with the assistance of priests, who served in the tent of meeting. One change is noted in the offering of the priest's share. Each of the children of Israel was to bring their fellowship offering with their own hands. They were to take the time and effort to express thanks to God. This offering was waved before the altar and was called the wave offering. Portions of the meat were to provide food for the priests, who cared for God's house. God gave His people many rituals and instructions to follow. These rituals were meant to teach the people valuable lessons about life.

C—Contemporary Application

Many church members and friends amaze me with the projects they create with their hands. Most of these people attribute their talent to the Lord. "He gave this gift to me," is the response when asked how they build, cook, sew, paint, and garden so beautifully. Allow me to pay tribute to some of these worshippers:

- Elizabeth loves to garden. She provides our church with a beautiful entry way of seasonal plants.
- Don is an electrical engineer. He can put light in all the right places.
- Clayton uses a ham radio to communicate with lonely people and serves as the "sound" man for our church.
- Bess is a fabulous cook and enjoys helping in the church kitchen for meal preparations. Every item she prepares is "magazine cover" quality.
- Claire works in stain glass. She created for the church a beautiful "Holy City" from the Book of Revelation.

Reasons for thanking God personally:

- Prepares us to experience God's presence.
- Reminds us to worship God with reverence and honor.
- Creates a response of joy and genuine humility.
- Leads us to confess sins regularly and receive cleansing from God.

D—Directed Prayer

Thank You, Lord, for providing instructions on how we are to respond to You.

November 24

A Little Thanksgiving to the Lord

The Bible stresses the importance of thanksgiving in the life of every believer.
Psalm 107:1-9

A—Advice from the Bible

Give thanks to the LORD for he is good.
(Ps. 107:1)

B—Biblical Example

This psalm was probably written after the Israelites returned from 70 years of captivity in Babylon. God's people rejoiced in their return to Jerusalem. An important emphasis was placed on thanking god for His act of salvation in delivering Israel from bondage. Perhaps the words were written for use in one of Israel's religious festivals. The worshippers were encouraged to praise God because of His goodness. He is perfectly and completely good. These returnees had special reason to thank God. The Lord chose and cared for Israel throughout history. Verses 4-7 describe the plight of a group of travelers who find themselves lost and wandering in a desert. However, God delivered them when all seemed hopeless. He gave them shelter, food, drink, and most importantly—hope. God did all this in response to Israel's cry for help. The remaining verses are an exhortation to those who had received God's blessings to thank Him. The summary statement of this passage is that God will provide for those who call upon Him.

C—Contemporary Application

How and when did Thanksgiving Day begin? This national holiday in the United States is celebrated on the fourth Thursday in November. A man by the name of William Bradford (1590-1657), is responsible. The first Thanksgiving Day celebration in New England was organized by Bradford in 1621. He had sailed on the Mayflower in 1620 and was one of the Pilgrim leaders and American colonial governor. His concern for freedom of worship in the new world lead him to emphasize a need to give thanks to the God who made all things possible. Our family focuses on thanking God during this special day of remembrance. Events from our past years are recalled. Times of great blessings are revisited. Photographs are available of family members who have passed. Memories are shared of the impact these people made in our lives. The goodness of God needs to be remembered in the busy world of today.

Believers are encouraged to say thank you to God for:
- His guidance.
- His daily care.
- His saving demonstrations of mercy.
- His unceasing, unconditional love.

D—Directed Prayer

Thank You, Father, that we can give thanks every day of the year.

November 25

Isaiah's Little Song of Thanksgiving

Faith in God has always provided joy for the believer.
Isaiah 12:1-6

A—Advice from the Bible

Shout and sing for joy for great is the Holy One among you.
(Isa. 12:6)

B—Biblical Example

Isaiah, the prophet, was excited at the promised restoration of his people. He reacted by singing two songs of thanksgiving. In the first song, he gave thanks for the promise of their salvation (12:1-2). In the second, he admonished those who had been restored to share the joy of their deliverance with the entire world (12:3-6). This joy could not be silenced. After the Exodus, the people of Israel also sang a song of deliverance (Ex. 15:1-18). A new exodus now occurred; a new deliverance was expressed at the hands of God, the Israelite's great deliverer. The words of the song center on the activity of God. He is the one who delivered and promised salvation. Isaiah expressed praise to God for the ultimate victory. The "Holy One of Israel" is one of Isaiah's favorite references to God. Since the divine character of God is described as holy, those who believe on Him are to be holy. The recovery of joy is essential. Right standing with the LORD produces the greatest happiness. He has richly provided salvation and sustenance for us ("wells of salvation"). Our praise should express our delight in Him.

C—Contemporary Application

Carrie dreaded the coming holiday season. Her personal life was in crisis. The once happy homemaker now was bitter and grieving. After years of marriage, her husband informed her that he found someone else that he loved and was moving out of the house and her life. The distraught wife cried for days. Some friends advised her to "get on with her life." Others said how much better off she was with him gone. None of these suggestions helped heal her broken heart. Her days were spent in pajamas and a darkened house. However, God, whom Carrie had ignored for years, still loved her and wanted to restore joy to her life. The healing began on a Sunday morning when she went to worship with some caring friends. The pastor's message ministered to her. She slowly rediscovered her Christian lifestyle and her joy became evident.

God does not leave us to face difficulties alone:
- He faces them with us.
- He provides opportunities for strengthening our faith.
- He sends a message of hope and restoration.
- He honors faithfulness.

D—Directed Prayer

Father, I praise You with thanksgiving for the joy You have provided for me.

November 26

A Little Perfect Tabernacle

Rules and rituals have never cleansed a person's heart.
Hebrews 9:11-14

A—Advice from the Bible

He went through the greater and more perfect Tabernacle.
(Heb. 9:11)

B—Biblical Example

God does not accept an unclean person in His service and perfection was not possible under the Levitical priesthood, so God had to raise up the truly ultimate High Priest from the tribe of Judah. The writer of Hebrews emphasized that Jesus' sacrifice cleanses God's people from their sin so that we might be in a right relationship with Him. The ancient Jewish religion was based on a system of blood sacrifices presented on the altar of God for atonement. Because sin resulted in death, the only way to atone for sin was through the pouring out of blood of a pure, undefiled animal. On the annual Day of Atonement, only the high priest could enter the innermost part of the tabernacle. He offered a bull to atone for his own sins and a goat to atone for the people's sins. These animal sacrifices seem foreign to us, but for the Jewish people such practices were a way of showing devotion to God. When Jesus sacrificed His own blood, however, everything changed! Jesus, the living Lord and permanent priest, proved to be the adequate Savior. He removed all barriers to sinful men and women coming directly into God's presence.

C—Contemporary Application

I placed a call to a local business today and I got lost in an automated telephone answering system. "To receive technical assistance, press 24; to inquire about a new service, press 18; to make a payment, press 4; to schedule an appointment, press 14." I listened carefully and pressed what I hoped were the right digits, only to be answered by another menu of options and numbers. Ultimately, I wanted to shout, "Let me speak to a real person!" In this computerized age, live people are missing. Recorded voices give instructions on how to communicate. However, I can always get through to God. My tabernacle is not restricted to just one high priest per year making atonement for my sins. I gained the right of entry to Him through Jesus Christ my High Priest. He has direct access to the Father and intercedes for me on my behalf.

What is the end result of our being cleansed, not only outwardly but also inwardly?

- We can intercede in prayer for other people.
- We can share the difference Christ has made in our life.
- We can express gratitude for Christ's intercession for us.
- We can believe that Jesus permanently holds His priesthood.

D—Directed Prayer

Lord, thank You for my perfect tabernacle.

November 27

The Little Harlot of Jericho

You can never speak to the wrong person about your church.
Joshua 2:1-24

A—Advice from the Bible

They entered the house of a prostitute named Rahab.
(Jos. 2:1)

B—Biblical Example

The opening chapters of Joshua set the stage for the conquest of Canaan. Though the land had been promised to the fathers of the Hebrews, the possession of the land depended upon their relationship with God and their willingness to take the land under His guidance. Joshua sent two spies to check out the military strength of the citizens. The two spies came in contact with Rahab. She was an ungodly Gentile who worshiped pagan gods and sold her body for money. However, the most important thing about this woman was her faith. Rahab took her life in her hands when she invited the spies into her home and protected them from arrest. She told them that the fear of their God had already spread among all the tribes of Canaan. She also made an agreement with the spies that, in return for saving their lives, they would save her and her family when Israel conquered the city. Had the king discovered her deception, he would have slain her as a traitor. Verse 11 is her confession of faith by a person whose life had been imprisoned in pagan idolatry. She believed in one God.

C—Contemporary Application

Herman came to our church as a new Christian. He was excited about his relationship with God, but distressed that his sister did not know the Lord. One day he asked if I would visit her. Of course, I said, "Yes." When I inquired about her address and phone number, he acted vague, but wrote down the information. After several attempts to reach her, she called and invited me to visit with her at the Long Horn Saloon! Now, what? I thought. So I made an appointment to visit her the next week. Yes, I walked into the dark, smelly saloon and met the woman. She did not expect me to come and especially when she discovered I was the preacher's wife. We developed a friendship over the next six months. One Sunday she came to church with her brother and the man with whom she was living. A few weeks later, she accepted Christ and discovered a new life in Him.

How can you succeed in the challenges that are before you?
- Step out in faith.
- Claim the promises of victory.
- Remember that God will never leave you nor forsake you.
- Accept Christian responsibilites.

D—Directed Prayer

Father, thank You for putting different kinds of people in my life.

November 28

Paul's Little Greeting

A Christian should be known as a person faithful to the Lord.
Ephesians 1:1-14

A—Advice from the Bible

Grace and peace to you from God.
(Eph. 1:2)

B—Biblical Example

When Paul wrote these words, he was in prison in Rome. The Ephesians received his letter with deep joy and listened intently as the words were read to them. The apostle immediately identified himself with Christ. He wrote, he taught, and he lived only by the authority of Jesus Christ. The letter begins with a petition for grace and peace. These two words were the essential gifts that God grants to believers. *Grace* is a Greek word and means the free, undeserved initiative that God made toward us when He offered His Son Jesus Christ for our salvation. The word reminds us that mercy comes to us not by law, but by love. When we accept God's grace, we discover His peace. This word is from the Hebrew language. In God's peace we feel reconciled within ourselves and in harmony with God and in relationships to other people. Wouldn't that bring peace to you? Paul demonstrated how vital Christ is. We live "in Christ" and the blessings of grace and peace come from "the Lord Jesus Christ."

C—Contemporary Application

Frederick Baedeker enjoyed going to prison. In 1877 he traveled to Russia to preach and give out Bibles. While there, he was allowed to visit the prisons, and for eighteen years he was the only person who had the right to visit any prison in Russia. So travel he did, from Poland to the Pacific. The secret police always were watching him, but he continued to be one of the greatest distributors of Scripture of all time. Each prisoner was greeted with the words, "Grace and Peace to you." The prisons of that day were unbearable and many of the inmates were at the point of death. A visit by this preacher and a gift of God's Word provided hope to these hopeless criminals. His message to the prisoners was always the same, "There is a stronger God than we, who is still able to set the prisoners and slaves free." His parting words were always the same, "Grace and peace from our Lord, Jesus Christ."

What does *grace* and *peace* mean to you as a Christian?

- Grace means . . .
- Grace means . . .
- Peace means . . .
- Peace means . . .

D—Directed Prayer

Dear Lord, thank You for Your gift of grace and peace.

November 29

Adam's Little Rib

Marriage is God's idea.
Genesis 2:18-25

A—Advice from the Bible

He took one of the man's ribs.
(Gen. 2:21)

B—Biblical Example

Everything up to this point in creation has been very good and pleasing to God. The first thing He saw that was not good was the man's isolation. The man could not fully develop or function alone. He needed to share himself on a personal level and interact with living persons. The solution to the problem was a companion. This person would be able to meet the man's needs. The Creator brought all the birds and animals to the man to see how he would react to them. Each creature was given a name. Obviously the need for companionship could not be met by these named animals. What God did next is a miracle. He did not want the man to witness His work, so a supernatural sleep fell on him. A special living thing was provided, one of the same nature as himself. A body part was chosen for this miracle. A rib could easily be shared. This new companion was uniquely like him. She was not formed from the ground's elements, like the animals, but of identical biological material. Man was delighted with his new companion. Adam now had someone who could relate to him mentally, physically, socially, and spiritually.

C—Contemporary Application

A young man took his girlfriend out for dinner. They ate a delicious meal, during which the young man continually said to the young lady, "You are my life, my all. Marry me and I will buy you the sun and the moon and the stars." But when the waiter came with the bill, the man said, "Separate checks, please!" The creation story of Adam and Eve defines a relationship between a male and a female. When my husband and I married, we were not told how to respond to God or each other. Most of our early years were spent trying to figure out what married couples did. One of our special habits through the years has been friendship. We really enjoy each other's company in all phases of our life. Just like the marriage vows say, "In sickness and in health; in poverty or wealth," a couple can patiently love each other through the years. God's original plan works!

Ideals for a healthy relationship between a man and a woman are:

- Companionship.
- Acceptance.
- Commitment.
- Love.

D—Directed Prayer

Lord, Your plan for a man and woman causes me to rejoice in Your creation.

November 30

Little Christian Infants

Being controlled by your own decisions will stunt your growth.
1 Corinthians 3:1-11

A—Advice from the Bible

. . . mere infants in Christ.
(1 Cor. 3:1)

B—Biblical Example

Paul begins this chapter pointing out the Corinthian's lack of spiritual maturity. Their lives were dominated by fleshly attitudes and appetites rather than by the Holy Spirit. These people were genuine Christians, but very immature. They were like perpetual bottle babies, who kept grabbing after the world's manner of living. These babes had come out of a very worldly, pagan community that had left the marks of sin upon them. They were new in the faith, and not yet ready to receive the deeper truths. But some people in the church were living outside of God's redemptive grace. The apostle begins to present his case for spiritual growth and compares this action with farming. Because Paul took the gospel to Corinth first, he "planted" the seed; Apollos followed Paul and "watered" the crop. Yet, God alone was responsible for the "growth." Paul and Apollos had a common goal to lead people to a saving knowledge of Christ and to nurture converts toward spiritual maturity. These two men were co-workers and looked to God for the strength to bring the believers from spiritual infancy to spiritual adulthood.

C—Contemporary Application

God will not do the work of spiritual growing for us. Imagine a farmer sitting on his front porch. You ask him what he's doing. He answers, "Farming." You ask him what he's growing. He replies, "Wheat." "But your field looks unplowed and unplanted." "That's right," the old farmer answered, "I'm farming by faith. Believing God for a great harvest." "But shouldn't you be doing something?" you ask. He replies, "I am. I'm praying and believing!" The Corinthian Christians needed to learn that God would not do their work for them. The old farmer in the illustration totally misunderstood how to farm effectively. A believer is responsible for moving from infancy to the adult world. The power of the Holy Spirit enables a person to mature and become a spiritually-minded individual

How does belonging to God and laboring for Him change your life?
- You desire to know Him better.
- You appreciate Bible study.
- You understand the power of intercessory prayer
- You think more about international missions

D—Directed Prayer

Father, lead believers to throw away their spiritual bottles.

December 1

A Little Child

God's Light permeates the darkness.
Isaiah 9:6-7

A—Advice from the Bible

"For to us a child is born . . . "
(Isa. 9:6, NIV)

B—Biblical Example

God's prophets became silent causing the people to seek light from God through illegitimate means (8:19-22). Mediums and wizards were sought for help. This practice only increased the people's darkness and hopelessness. Isaiah, however, in his vision, saw past the gloom and doom. A Messiah would come as a child. The people's oppression would be lifted. A time of eternal peace and joy would occur.

How did Judah get into this godless situation? Assyria was the primary power to devastate the people. King Ahaz's rejection of God's message created the darkness. His refusal of God's Word through Isaiah left Judah groping in total spiritual and political despair. The good news for these people came in the form of a Light. God would intervene and set the people free from the oppressor. The result would be great joy.

C—Contemporary Application

December is an exciting month. Plans are made for parties, programs, and presents. Children become more excited each day as decorations are added to the house and stores.

Sam and Becky do not enjoy this holiday season. This childless couple had struggled in their ten-years of marriage. All known methods for providing a biological child had been exhausted. The absence of nieces or nephews added to their sadness. The dream of having a baby this Christmas looked hopeless. The phone rang on December 1. Becky answer, listened, and then screamed for Sam. Good news had arrived from the overseas orphanage that a little three-month-old baby boy was on the way to the states. This longing couple would have Sammy with them in time for Christmas. All gloom and doom disappeared. A new light of joy shined in their home. This season of remembrance would begin as a time of rejoicing and praising God for answered prayer.

Think about these truths:

- God promised to bring forth a child—and He did!
- God promised to deliver His people from the bondage of sin—and He did!
- God promised to bring the Gentiles into His kingdom—and He did!
- God promised to establish this new kingdom that would endure forever—and He will!

D—Directed Prayer

Begin this holiday season by thanking God for sending a little Child to make a difference in your life.

December 2

A Little Righteous Branch

The coming of Jesus fulfilled the Old Testament promises.
Jeremiah 23:1-6

A—Advice from the Bible

> ... when I will raise up to David a righteous branch ...
> (Jer. 23:5, NIV)

B—Biblical Example

This period of history was so depressing and revealed what happens when God is rejected by His people. Jeremiah's people would soon be scattered in the Exile. However, the prophet recorded words of encouragement. God would gather the people and bring them back to the fold like lost sheep that are found. He discovered that the unrighteous kings had been Judah's problem from the start. Five characteristics of the kings describe how they were to function. First, a king was the anointed one of God, meaning he was set aside uniquely for God's service. Second, the king was limited in power. Third, he was subject to the same moral standards as the people of his realm. Fourth, the king was expected to give political and religious leadership. Fifth, the king was the Lord's representative. No wonder Jeremiah had a problem with these ungodly kings. His good news through prophecy revealed the coming of the Messiah. One day Judah would have a King that the people needed. December reminds us that in a few weeks we will celebrate of the birth of THE King. God always keeps His promises.

C—Contemporary Application

Good King Wenceslaus was not a king, but a Duke of Bohemia. The Christmas carol about this man is a favorite among many nations. The story of his life began in A.D. 903. His father was a Christian; his mother a pagan. For years he struggled between these two beliefs. The influence of his grandmother turned him to Christianity. Wenceslaus Hollar became known for his generous giving, especially to the poor. Churches were built. German missionaries were invited to serve in his country.

Unfortunately, this good man was murdered by his evil brother in A.D. 929. Pagan influences soon were forced on the people. This deceased Christian Duke was soon declared a martyr and saint. Not much was known about him until 1853, when John Mason Neale wrote a carol to teach children about the virtues of generosity.

At this Christmas season, consider what "the righteous branch" means:

- The "righteous branch" means that we can be righteous.
- The "righteous branch" means that we can celebrate the birthday of the King.
- The "righteous branch" means that we can live fruitful lives.
- The "righteous branch" means that we are provided everlasting life.

D—Directed Prayer

Begin this holiday season by thanking God for sending us a true King.

December 3

A Little Family Tree

A person with proper credentials commands our respect and gains our attention.
Matthew 1:1-17

A—Advice from the Bible

The historical record of Jesus Christ . . .
(Matt. 1:1, HCSB)

B—Biblical Example

A person will sometimes make the announcement that they are a king or messiah. This claim causes the thinking public to immediately ask for proof. No credentials; no acceptance. Matthew seemed to anticipate these kinds of questions from the Hebrews, so he begins his gospel with a careful account of the birth of Jesus Christ. He frequently alludes to Old Testament passages to show that Jesus was truly the Messiah. Chapter 1 is like a bridge spanning the Old and New Testaments. The writer announces his purpose by introducing Jesus as Messiah-King. Since royalty depends on heredity, it was important for Jesus to establish His rights to David's throne. Genealogies were very important to the Jews, for without them they could not prove their tribal memberships or their rights to inheritances. If a person came to town claiming to be "the Son of David" they had to be able to prove that claim. Matthew, following the Jewish custom, gave the family tree through Jesus' foster father, Joseph. He wanted to remind his readers of two key Old Testament personalities. Abraham was the father of the Hebrews and David was Israel's most famous king. That claim to fame was impressive.

C—Contemporary Application

Genealogies are very important, even more so with the computer internet accesses to numerous genealogy societies. For a fee, professionals will research your family tree. Some of my friends seem to trace their history back to the ark! My husband's family can be traced back to Germany, Russia, and then the migration to America. These ancestors settled in southwestern Oklahoma on farms. They built churches and founded towns. My family can be traced back to great-great-great grandfather Poore, who rushed to claim land in the then Indian Territory, now Oklahoma. Remember reading about the Sooners? No significant relatives in our family trees are named, but the success of their lives makes us proud to be part of their genealogy. The importance of Jesus' birth provides for us a place in His family. This statement is so true, "The Son of God became the Son of Man that He might change the sons of men into the sons of God."

What specific actions can we begin in preparation for the Christmas season?
- Keep Christ central.
- Celebrate His birth.
- Sing Christmas carols
- Gather the extended family for worship of the King

D—Directed Prayer

Begin this holiday season by thanking God for sending us a true King.

December 4

A **Little** Jewish Virgin
A reminder of God's greatness.
Luke 1:26-38

A—Advice from the Bible

The angel Gabriel was sent by God . . . to a virgin
(Lk. 1:26, HCSB)

B—Biblical Example

Luke is the only writer to provide the details of the angel's mission to Mary. Gabriel's unexpected visit interrupted Mary's quite life. (Nothing about her family background or age are available, however, she probably was still in her teens.) This young Jewish maiden lived in a village in Galilee called Nazareth and had recently become engaged to a carpenter. She, like most young Jewish girls, was anticipating married life. This angel event would change her life forever. Since angels didn't make appointments, Mary was taken by surprise and puzzled about his presence. References to her vital faith and commitment to God are revealed in later verses. The angel addressed her as *the favored one*. These words mean "endowed with grace." God had chosen Mary to be the object of His unmerited favor. She had done nothing to earn the honor; she was simply blessed by God's choice of her and the assurance that God was with her. Mary was the one human who was with Jesus from birth to death.

C—Contemporary Application

The Christmas season provides many surprises, but not quite as surprising as Mary's experience. The wrapped packages under the tree tease us. Our daughter, Martha, just can't stand to be surprised. Christmas becomes a real challenge to her "you have to wait" desires. Shopping for the children was always difficult. Their ability to find hidden gifts was amazing. One Christmas, Martha snooped and found a gift for her. I had gone to town, so she decided to feel the gift or maybe shake the package. A special doll was identified. However, she would have to wait for the pleasures of a future event, namely, Christmas Eve, to open the package. Her name was on the gift and she knew what was inside, but only Christmas Eve would reveal the "real thing." The angel revealed the "real thing" to a little Jewish maiden. What a way to start celebrating!

Consider answers to these questions:
- What does the word "miracle" mean to you?
- How does God communicate with people today?
- How would more facts about Mary help your understanding of this event?
- What do you know today about this angel visit that Mary did not know then?

D—Directed Prayer

Begin this holiday season by thanking God for revealing that "nothing is impossible with God."

December 5

A Little Leap for Joy

Rejoice with people who are blessed by God
Luke 1:36-45

A—Advice from the Bible

The baby leaped inside her.
(Lk. 1:41, HCSB)

B—Biblical Example

The timing of the angel Gabriel's mission to Mary in Nazareth was connected to her cousin Elizabeth's pregnancy. Mary was confused by the recent heavenly encounter. She also was unaware that God had already blessed her relative. Gabriel's announcement did not give minute details, but forced Mary to think about the greatness of God's power. This maiden knew *what* had happened; she didn't know *how* this event had happened. The facts of the message were not disputed. Mary left her village and went to visit the home of Elizabeth and Zechariah, 70 miles to the south. When Mary entered the house, Elizabeth was filled with the Spirit. The baby inside her womb announced the Messiah's presence by leaping. The cousins were instantly bound together by the unique gifts God had given them. Elizabeth knew that Mary's son would be even greater than her own, for her son John the Baptist, would be the one to announce the arrival of Mary's son. This young maiden did not remain a virgin all her life. She later gave birth to sons and daughters (Matt. 12:46; 13:54-56; John 2:12; Acts 1:14).

C—Contemporary Application

The holiday season is a great time to focus on your family. Many reunions will begin in a few weeks. Some relatives will travel long distances just to be with loved ones on Christmas Day. Gifts will begin to appear under the Christmas tree. Cooking and decorating will begin in earnest. Strong families have the ability to express open appreciation and affection as they spend time together. These families know that they are there for each other, no matter what problems may come. Mary must have felt this way about her relative, Elizabeth. Sharing personal testimonies strengthen family unity. Perhaps a reading of the family history and remembering past Christmas seasons would serve as a reminder of God's blessings on your clan. Take the family to a special church service that centers on the Savior.

How can you prepare for your family celebration of Christmas?

- Think of specific ways to show love to one another.
- Encourage others to share events and successes from their life this year.
- Participate in discussions about family memories.
- Make the birth of Jesus the central focus of these days together.

D—Directed Prayer

Begin this holiday season by thanking God for the opportunity to rejoice with your family.

December 6

A Message for Little Nazareth

Great things can happen to little towns.
Luke 1:26-33

A—Advice from the Bible

The angel Gabriel was sent by God to a town in Galilee called Nazareth.
(Lk. 1:26, HCSB)

B—Biblical Example

Nazareth played a significant role in the life of Christ, especially with regard to the events of Jesus' birth. However, the site is not mentioned in the Old Testament and not often in the New Testament. The town is located in northern Israel near present day Haifa. One insight to the town's repetition is a question asked by Nathanael, a friend of Philip, "Can anything good come out of Nazareth?" (John 1:46). To be called a "Nazarene" (Acts 24:5) meant to be looked down on and rejected. An event occurred before Jesus' birth that would forever make Nazareth an important town to Christians. Even though Jesus was born in Bethlehem, He grew up in this place. Luke is the only gospel writer to record the interesting details of an angel's mission to Mary. God the Father was the originator of the plan. Gabriel was sent to a specific town called Nazareth. He was about to accomplish the most wonderful miracle of all time in this little village. I visited the Church of the Annunciation in Nazareth. This magnificent structure is the largest Christian house of worship in the Middle East.

C—Contemporary Application

The small, country town of Hobart, Oklahoma, was the place of my childhood. Many memories are stored in my mind about the people, churches, and schools of that southwestern town. At the holiday season, the main street was decorated with lights and greenery. The county courthouse was built in the middle of town and early in December, Santa would arrive and hand out candy. The same Rotarian "Santa" came every year. Most of my memories involve my home church. The children would present a program about the birth of Jesus. One year I played the part of Mary. After the program, all the children went to the church basement and received a paper sack filled with hard candy and an orange. The excitement could hardly be contained. Music about the birth of Christ was sung all the month of December. Great things can happen in small towns. I became a believer in that miracle Baby because my teachers told me about Him.

What lessons can we learn from this event in Nazareth?

- God can use people from little towns for His work.
- God can do things today to bring His plan to our attention.
- God can expect us to obey His commands.
- God can make the impossible possible.

D—Directed Prayer

Begin this holiday season by thanking God for the Christian influence in towns and cities.

December 7

A Simple Little Question

Asking questions of God to gain understanding is not wrong.
Luke 1:34

A—Advice from the Bible

> *How can this be . . . ?*
> (Luke 1:34, HCSB)

B—Biblical Example

The Old Testament closes with the Persian Empire ruling as the world power. Judea was a Persian province. Not much information is available about the history of the Jews during this time period. After about 200 years, the Greeks became the ruling world power. A series of 14 books were written between the Old and New Testament. These writings are called the Apocrypha and are not considered inspired works from God. Therefore, the Hebrew people had not heard from the Lord in 400 years. No prophets, no miracles, no signs, just silence! A sense of just existing had settled into Jewish behavior. Throughout the Old Testament, examples of God's dealing in different ways with the Hebrew nation are presented. And then, one day, a prophet named John appeared with a message the Hebrews had longed to hear. The Messiah was coming! The silence was broken. The Jews had reason to hope again. The angel, Gabriel, delivered the good news to the waiting people. His appearance to Mary was both exciting and dramatic. No wonder she replied to his announcement with the question, "How can this be?"

C—Contemporary Application

Kathy was hanging out clothes to dry on Sunday morning, December 7, 1941. She looked at the beautiful view of Pearl Harbor from her hillside yard. Suddenly, planes began to appear in a low flying formation. The symbol on the sides of the aircraft caused her to ask, "How can this be?" Kathy and her husband are Japanese friends of ours who live in Hawaii. The location of their house provides a panoramic view of the harbor. This couple are loyal Americans, but Japanese by birth. The devastation that followed in the next hours horrified Kathy and Jim. They watched as much of the US Pacific fleet was destroyed. Eight battleships and 10 other naval vessels were sunk or damaged. The radio reported the causalities the next day as 3,000 men and women. "How can this be?" was a question this couple asked for the next few years. From the lull of peace and safety had now come war and all the consequences of conflict.

What encouragement and inspiration can you receive from Mary's question?

- I believe in a God of the impossible.
- I believe in a God of great power.
- I believe in the deity of Jesus.
- I believe in the incarnation of God.

D—Directed Prayer

Begin this holiday season by thanking God for thought-provoking moments.

December 8

Mary's Little Road Trip

God works through real people.
Luke 1:39-45

A—Advice from the Bible

Mary set out and hurried to a town . . .
(Luke 1:39, HCSB)

B—Biblical Example

All the Scriptures reveal that Mary, the mother of Jesus, was a devout, God-fearing woman. Every reference establishes her as a normal mother with natural concerns for her family. She came from a humble home, although she was a descendant of the royal Davidic line. However, after she had responded in faith and obedience to the angel Gabriel's announcement, she left town. God was about to do something miraculous and Mary needed to share with someone about her experience. She could hardly wait to relate the news to Elizabeth. Perhaps leaving her home at this time helped her process the events of the last few days. After all, she was not yet married to Joseph, and nothing is said about her parents and extended family. Going alone from Nazareth to an unnamed town in Judah, the province immediately around Jerusalem must have been frightening. Mary's visit was not a brief social call. She had a plan in mind. Her visit lasted three months. This touching human drama shows how God's news was received, treasured, and appreciated as a priceless blessing by two women who experienced a miracle.

C—Contemporary Application

Many trips will be made during the holiday seasons. Some families are looking forward to gathering together and catching up on the events of the past months. The children's accomplishments will be discussed, career changes will be announced, and some families will plan a special time to recall God's blessings in recent months. Future family members will attend and future births will be declared. Our family had a custom of baking a cupcake for each person with a candle in each cake. These reminders were placed at each setting on the Christmas dinner table. Sometime during the meal, we would light the candles and sing "Happy Birthday, Jesus." Our children never forgot that experience. Another side of the holiday season is the fact that some families do not enjoy being together. Past experiences or memories can sometimes prevent a person from celebrating the real meaning of Christmas. What a waste of precious time!

Think about these facts about Mary:
- She was a real person with real feelings and emotions.
- She wanted to share her good news with her closest friend.
- She humbly praised God for His goodness.
- She is honored for her special role in God's saving plan.

D—Directed Prayer

Begin this holiday season by telling others the good news about Jesus.

December 9

Mary's Little Song of Praise

Sometimes risks are necessary in following the will of God.
Luke 1:46-55

A—Advice from the Bible

My soul proclaims the greatness of the Lord.
(Luke 1:46, HCSB)

B—Biblical Example

Mary and Elizabeth now had something more in common than just family relationships. Both were expecting miraculously conceived babies. Mary's famous "Magnificat" was her response of praise to God. The words include praise for what He was about to do and for the part she was privileged to play in His plan. Mary's song contains quotations from the Old Testament, especially the Psalms and Hannah's song in 1 Samuel. God's Word had obviously been taught to this young Jewish maiden. A phrase, "He has" is emphasized eight times. Mary was overcome with joy at what God had done for her. Two special appreciations are expressed. First, God had saved her. This statement indicates that Mary was a sinner just like all people. She needed to make a decision about her eternal salvation. Second, she had been chosen to be the mother of the Messiah. Because of her belief in God and her obedience to yield to His will, she was used to bring the Savior into the world.

C—Contemporary Application

On of my favorite songs "His Name is Wonderful" was inspired on Christmas day by a traditional Christmas text. Audrey Mae Mieir was born on May 12, 1916 to wonderful Christian parents. She became a gifted pianist and inspiring worship leader. This song was inspired while working in Bethel Union Church, Duarte, California, where her brother-in-law was the pastor. Christmas fell on Sunday and the church was beautifully decorated with pine boughs, a manger, and fragrant holiday candles. Audrey was overwhelmed with the spirit of Christmas. The pastor began reading from his Bible, "His Name is Wonderful" and she began writing the words to this great song. Before the evening worship, Audrey had completed the song and had enlisted a group of young people to sing the words at the evening service. The congregation did not want to stop singing this joyous reminder of our great Savior.

The biblical study today is about joy. At this season of the year, consider these reasons for Christian joy.

- God has a plan for your life.
- God has provided eternal salvation through His Son.
- God has provided you the privilege of participating in His plans.
- God has done great things for you and will continue to bless you.

D—Directed Prayer

Begin this holiday season by writing a personal praise song to God.

December 10

Joseph's Little Dream

Sometimes God intervenes in a person's life and changes his plans.
Matthew 1:18-25

A—Advice from the Bible

An angel of the Lord suddenly appeared to him in a dream . . . .
(Matt. 1:20, HCSB)

B—Biblical Example

Matthew concluded his genealogy of Jesus and proceeded to give an account of the events of the His birth. He began with Joseph of Nazareth, described as a "just" man. When the news of Mary's pregnancy came, Joseph was confused and deeply grieved. Joseph was reflecting on what he should do about the situation as he retired to sleep. He was legally bound to Mary, but all the plans the couple had made were now questionable. But then an angel appeared to him in a dream and encouraged him not to let fear dictate his actions. He was to proceed with the marriage. The messenger from God assured Joseph that Mary's condition was the work of the Holy Spirit. Notice that Joseph did not question the validity of God's revelation .He was told to take Mary into his home and honor her as his wife. Joseph believed and followed the angel's instructions, even though he did not understand what had happened.

C—Contemporary Application

This story is a favorite about the difficulty some people have in believing in Jesus' incarnation. A family could not share the excitement of Christ's birth. The mother and daughters were devout Christians; the father was indifferent to spiritual truths. An annual community Christmas Eve service climaxed with the midnight ringing of the chimes to signify the birth of Christ. The father was invited to attend. "I just can't believe that God would want to become a man," he said. The family left the father reading the newspaper. Suddenly a storm came with blowing snow. He noticed that birds were dashing against the window, trying to get to the light and warmth. He finally trudged down to the barn, flipped on the lights, opened the doors, and walked back to the house. He waited for the birds to fly into the barn, but they continued to beat against the window. A thought flashed across his mind, "I wish I could be a bird for just a minute and then I would tell those crazy birds to fly into the barn where it is safe." Just then the church chimes rang, celebrating the fact that God became a man so He could communicate His love.

To celebrate the birthday of Jesus we must affirm that:

- God was responsible for Jesus' birth.
- Jesus is fully human and fully divine.
- Jesus' birth was the fulfillment of Old Testament prophecy.
- Jesus provides salvation from sin.

D—Directed Prayer

Lord, help me to display the true "Spirit of Christmas."

December 11

No Little Santa Claus

Jesus is the divine Messiah-King who came to earth as a human being.
Matthew 1:21-25

A—Advice from the Bible

You are to name Him Jesus . . . .
(Matt. 1:21, HCSB)

B—Biblical Example

Matthew began his first chapter by focusing on Jesus' royal heritage and divine nature. Mary's Son was to be more than hers. She bore the divine Son of God. Through medical science parents now can identify the gender of a child before the birth event. For Joseph and Mary this knowledge would not have been something new. The couple knew Mary's child was to be a Son. The name chosen by God was a common Jewish name. Jesus is the Greek form of the Hebrew name Joshua. Both names mean "the Lord saves." The designation of "Savior" reveals the reason for Jesus' birth. His mission was to save His people. Their need for salvation was caused by sin. The saving purpose of Jesus is central to the celebration of Christmas. His coming provided infinitely more than inspiration for Christmas carols and cards. He came to deal with our sins. Matthew also uses another name for Jesus, "Immanuel" which means "God with us." That name told who Jesus the Messiah was. Every person must face the question, "What do you believe about Jesus?"

C—Contemporary Application

The legendary Christmas-gift bringer was first called St. Nicolas, St. Nick, or Father Christmas and was celebrated in Europe. The story introduces St. Nicholas, a 4th century bishop of Asia Minor. He was famous for defending young children and giving generous gifts to the poor. The early tales have him riding through the sky on a horse delivering gifts. The United States was introduced to this figure from Holland as immigrants settled in America. Washington Irving wrote the first details about St. Nicholas. However, in 1823 Clement Clarke Moore wrote the classic poem, "The Night before Christmas." This gift-giver now had a new name, Santa Claus. Clement even named the reindeer and described Santa's appearance.

Remember that the name Santa Claus is no substitute for Jesus.

Instead of asking, "What am I getting for Christmas?", ask what are you going to give, such as:
- Meaningful time with my family.
- Worship opportunities that stay focused on Jesus.
- Gifts for people who are less fortunate.
- Decorations that present the Christian message.

D—Directed Prayer

Immanuel, all I want for Christmas is to know You better.

December 12

A Little Decree

God is able to work His will in and through the process of human history.
Luke 2:1-3

A—Advice from the Bible

In those days a decree went out from Caesar Augustus . . . .
(Luke 2:1, HCSB)

B—Biblical Example

The events of Luke 2:1-3 took place in an extraordinary period of history. Caesar Augustus, grand-nephew and adopted son of Julius Caesar, had been ruling the Mediterranean world as the first emperor of the Roman Empire since 27 BC. Jesus was born during the reign of both Roman (Caesar Augustus) and Syrian (Quirinius) rulers. Under the leadership of Augustus, peace had been restored to the empire. His generals were constantly engaged in the expansion of the empire in what are now Spain, France, Hungary, and much of Eastern Europe. Yet, the greatest event of all took place, not in the center of political and military power but in a corner of a lesser region. A census was ordered by Augustus to determine who to tax and who could serve in the military. The date was probably 6 BC. Luke calls this enrollment a *census.* The usual Roman practice was to have each person enroll in his or her place of residence. However, this time the people were ordered back to their ancestral homes.

C—Contemporary Application

The little decree issued by Caesar Augustus changed the world. Little did he know that such an historical event was taking place in his ruling regions. The world would never be the same again. Suppose you read the following items in your newspaper. How would you explain what happened?
- Children's Home Closed. No Needy Children Available.
- Gang Members Escort a Young Girl to Her Home.
- Murderer Turns in Gun to Police.
- No Police Calls Reported on Domestic Violence.
- Unwanted Babies Placed in Loving Homes.
- Cloning Research on the Decline.
- No Rapes Reported This Month
- Prison Staff Downsized.

What is your attitude when you hear the Christmas story retold each year?
- "Ho-hum. Why don't they come up with something new at Christmas?"
- "If I had lived back then and had seen Jesus, I wouldn't have all these doubts."
- "This is the weirdest story I have ever heard."
- "I wish I could get as excited as the angels and the shepherds did."

D—Directed Prayer

Thank You, Lord, that You are in control of history.

December 13

A Little Baby in a New World

Jesus' birth was a joyous occasion that still calls for continuing celebration.
Luke 2:1-7

A—Advice from the Bible

Then she gave birth to her firstborn Son.
(Luke 2:7, HCSB)

B—Biblical Example

The central theme of the Bible is the coming of Jesus Christ. In the Old Testament, the prophets declared, "He is coming." The first-century Christians declared, "He has come" and they predicted, "He is coming again." The focus is always on Jesus. The pivotal event in the coming of Jesus was His birth. The Bethlehem crowds had no idea that the infant Son of God was asleep in their little town. Mary was just an ordinary person, who lived in Nazareth. The trip to Bethlehem was difficult for this young, expectant woman. The night of His birth must have been frightening. Her firstborn would enter the world without grandma, aunts, or cousins. Mary and Joseph experienced this great moment in history together. Her availability to God provided the unique privilege of being the mother of the Messiah. Her new baby would turn the world upside down. This little Jewish homemaker would be the only human who was with Jesus from His birth until His death.

C—Contemporary Application

I sometimes regret that Christmas carols are sung only one month a year. The music and lyrics create a "Christmas mood" like no other kinds of music. One favorite carol that expresses the Scripture passage for today is "Joy to the World." While walking home from a church service in Southampton, England, 20-year-old Isaac Watts told his father that the music sung in their worship services lacked the dignity and beauty that should characterize the Scripture. His father encouraged him to try to create something better. So in the year 1694, Isaac Watts began writing hymns. While reading Psalm 98, he was inspired to write how this psalm fulfilled the prophecy in the birth of Jesus. He wrote:

Joy to the world! The Lord is come!
Let earth receive her King. Let every heart prepare Him room,
And heaven and nature sing.
Joy to the earth! The Savior reigns!

This hymn reminds us to proclaim that Christ has come because:

- Christ is our Savior.
- Christ is our King.
- Christ rules our hearts with love.
- Christ opens our hearts to grace.

D—Directed Prayer

Father, thank You that I only have to remember Jesus to find the joy for this season.

December 14

A Little Group of Shepherds

We should be anxious to spread His peace and good will to others whenever we can.
Luke 2:8-12

A—Advice from the Bible

And there were shepherds living out in the fields.
(Luke 2:8)

B—Biblical Example

Shepherds are mentioned 200 times in the Bible, but none were as blessed as this group on the hills around Bethlehem. This occupation and lifestyle was generally despised socially, and the men were considered as nobodies! The religious people accepted the sheep for sacrifice, but despised the shepherds. A routine day was concluding when a heavenly angel appeared in their midst. God's choice of these misfits for good news on another uneventful night is amazing. Perhaps of all the people involved in this Bethlehem setting, these sheep-keepers were the most open to receive this new revelation from God. Overwhelmed by God's glory, the shepherds' greatest need was for calmness of heart and mind. However they were griped with fear. This reaction was common of biblical people to an appearance of God or of God's angels to them.

The angel then told the men where to find this special gift from God. What a strange place to look—in the manger of Bethlehem!

C—Contemporary Application

A favorite Christmas carol, using the shepherd's experience, was written by Nahum Tate (1652-1715). He was at one time appointed Poet Laureate of England during the reign of William and Mary. However, this talented man chose a life of degradation and died at age 63. George Frederick Handel composed the melody for "While Shepherds Watched Their Flocks."

The following story expresses the excitement the shepherds might have felt on that wonderful night. A little boy in a school Christmas program had but one sentence to say, "Behold, I bring you good tidings." After the first rehearsal he asked his mother what "tidings" meant and she told him it meant "news." When the program was presented at church, the lad was overcome with stage fright and forgot his line. Finally the idea came back to him and he yelled out, "Hey, have I got good news for you!"

Christians are to be the bearers of the *good news of great joy*. Name some ways this can happen.

- By_____
- By_____
- By_____
- By_____

D—Directed Prayer

Lord, help me to rejoice enthusiastically over the message the shepherd's heard.

December 15

A Little Rush to Bethlehem

The birth of Christ inspires believers to worship God.
Luke 2:16-18

A—Advice from the Bible

And the shepherds found Mary.
(Luke 2:16)

B—Biblical Example

The record of Jesus' birth was coming to a climax. The story is a contrast between the drab stable and the revelation of God's glory. The shepherds must now respond to the angelic message and song. Their decision was to follow the angel's instructions. Bethlehem was their destination. This little town was located about five miles south of Jerusalem. These men hurried to the site and the baby was exactly where the angel had stated. The experience out on the hills was shared with the parents of the Child. These words sounded too good to be true. Could the fact be true, that a child born here, under these circumstances and into a peasant family, was going to be the world's Savior? Their faith was tested as never before. In a sense, the shepherds became the first preachers of the Good News. Their departure from the manger was a time of rejoicing and praising God. The word "Bethlehem" means house of bread. Years later Jesus would identify Himself as "the Bread of life." Micah, a minor prophet, had proclaimed this message, *Bethlehem Ephrathah, you are small among the clans of Judah; One will come from you to be the ruler over Israel for Me* (5:2). Prophecy fulfilled!!!

C—Contemporary Application

The site of the Nativity of Jesus is now under the nave of the Church of the Nativity in the heart of Bethlehem and has been continuously acknowledged by Christians. Phillips Brooks was born in Boston and served in Episcopalian pastorates. He visited the Holy Land on December 24, 1865, and traveled by horseback to Bethlehem. The Church of the Nativity was having a Christmas Eve service. Three years later as he prepared for the Christmas season, he wanted to compose a hymn for children to sing during their annual program. He recalled that magical night in Bethlehem and wrote the hymn we now enjoy singing. "O little town of Bethlehem, How still we see thee lie. Above thy deep and dreamless sleep, The silent stars go by."

The best Christmas is one in which Christ is honored by:
- Worshiping the Messiah.
- Sharing the good news.
- Being obedient to the message.
- Glorifying God with your service.

D—Directed Prayer

Begin today thanking God for life-changing experiences.

December 16

A Little Sign

Continue to rejoice over the message the shepherds heard
Luke 2:9-14

A—Advice from the Bible

> This will be a sign to you.
> (Luke 2:12)

B—Biblical Example

This extraordinary announcement by the angels caused fear among the shepherds. The reaction of being terrified at the appearance of God or of angels was common in the New Testament. The instructions given by the angel revealed who Jesus really was. Although this infant was both Messiah and Lord, He was not to be identified by either earthly or heavenly splendor. Rather, He would be wrapped in the same cloths as any other baby of that day. His only distinguishing characteristic was that he would be lying in the feed trough for cattle rather than a bed. Luke, the writer, was consistently interested in the poor. The working shepherds were just one example. The humble circumstances of Mary's baby in a manger must have seemed familiar to the shepherds. These men were acquainted with poverty and having to substitute things of lesser value. However, the shepherds never dreamed they would be part of this major event in history.

C—Contemporary Application

Some people struggle in vain to find meaning in life in the areas of education, wealth, and entertainment. However, they often look in the wrong places. Harriett longed to be happy. Magazine articles on this subject were purchased and read by this Christian woman. Her prayer requests often included this phrase, "If God would only give me a sign, I could understand . . . ." I believe God gave her many signs, but she wasn't expecting anything from God. The last time I saw her, she was still struggling to find answers about happiness. We met in a shopping mall during Christmas week. Signs were everywhere about what the world had to offer, but she could not receive the gift of God's Son as a special part of the Christmas celebration. On the lapel pin of her jacket, the statement, "Jesus is the reason for the season" was displayed. I have lost touch with Harriett, but I want to believe that she finally recognized the true meaning of this event. Select some words that begin with letters from SIGN that describe this extraordinary announcement by the angels:

- S—
- I—
- G—
- N—

D—Directed Prayer

Signs of the times are everywhere. Lord, open my eyes.

December 17

The Angels Little Song

Praise God for His gift of Jesus.
Luke 2:13-14

A—Advice from the Bible

> *Suddenly there was a multitude of the heavenly hosts . . . praising God.*
> (Luke 2:13)

B—Biblical Example

Immediately after the announcement of the birth of Israel's Messiah, a multitude of angels joined the first angel in saying a hymn of praise to God who had given His Savior and His salvation to humankind. The angelic doxology declared that glory belongs to God in the highest. The word *highest* refers to the dwelling place of God Himself in heaven. What a marvelous experience for the shepherds to witness the angels glorifying God in the highest! Two results were evident from God's gift of a Savior. (1) This gift brings glory to God in heaven. (2) His gift gives peace to persons who are the recipients of God's good pleasure. This hymn means that peace will be the experience of those who have received the favor of God, that is, those who are saved. He gives peace with Himself in the person of Jesus, the Savior. No wonder the angels broke out in rapturous rejoicing; so should we when we receive God's favor in Christ.

C—Contemporary Application

"Gloria in Excelsis" was the first Christmas song used as a morning hymn in the Greek church as early as the second or third century. However, many other songs about the birth experience of Jesus were being written. On Christmas Day, 1816, in a Moravian Church in England, "Angels, from the Realms of Glory" was sung. The 45-year-old composer was named James Montgomery. This man's life-experiences included the loss of his missionary parents, who left him in England and sailed to Barbados, never to return again. James' teen years were spent being apprenticed to different crafts. However, none pleased him except working for a newspaper. Years later he purchased the *Sheffield Iris*. His controversial articles caused him many problems with the authorities in Sheffield, England. He was sent to jail on one occasion, but the people of the town made him into a celebrity for this treatment. One encouraging thing about this man was that he remained devoted to Christ, to the Scriptures, and to foreign missions.

The angel's message reminds us that:

- Jesus came to be the most humble of people.
- Jesus came to bring peace with God to all people.
- God in love gave us Jesus so that we could have eternal life through Him.
- Eternal life is for all who believe in Christ Jesus.

D—Directed Prayer

Thank You, Lord, that I can worship Christ the new-born King.

December 18

The Little Love Gift of Christmas

God offers to us His free gift of love.
John 3:16

A—Advice from the Bible

For God so loved the world that He gave His Son.
(John 3:16)

B—Biblical Example

Jesus and Nicodemus were having a night-time conversation. The Lord was explaining that God's love is not like human love. Human love always has limitations. We love some people and dislike others. However, God's love is without limits. The *world* means people in rebellion against God, but all people are loved by Him. The Son was given to the world and also given to the cross. Jesus is uniquely the Son of God. He is the only, one-of-a-kind Son of God. No other person in the world can wear that title. God's love produces effects in the lives of people only as they place their trust in Christ Jesus. We must personally receive His gift in faith; it is for whoever believes in Him. A sad truth is revealed in this verse. People who reject God's love in Christ will perish. That means to be forever lost from the love of God. The acceptors of the Gift will have a quality of life from Christ. *Eternal life* is more than just endless life; it is a new quality of life.

C—Contemporary Application

During the days of the Civil War, the Union and Confederate armies were engaged in a life and death battle outside Richmond, Virginia. As night approached after the first day of intensive battle, the Union army heard cheers behind the Confederate lines. The commander of the Union forces, General Grant, inquired about the reason for the enemies cheering. The report came back and the General was told that the wife of the Confederate commander, General George Pickett, had given birth to a baby boy. The celebration by the war-weary soldiers led to singing and laughter. When he received the news, General Grant ordered a temporary ceasefire, ordered a bonfire lit, and led his troops in a toast in honor of the opposing general's new son. The birth of this son brought peace—at least for a few hours. The birth of God's Son offers permanent peace—peace with God and peace with one another. This fact alone should provide personal hope in a world that seems to have forgotten what the word "peace" really means.

The message of love from God means that:

- God loves the people He has created.
- God's love extends to all people in the world.
- God's love will be rejected by some people.
- God's Son was born here below that we might be born from above.

D—Directed Prayer

Thank You, God, that You provide salvation from sin.

December 19

A Little Visit from the Magi

Wise men set an example of genuine worship.
Matthew 2:1-12

A—Advice from the Bible

Magi from the east came to Jerusalem.
(Matt. 2:1)

B—Biblical Example

The place of Jesus' birth was a small village about five miles south of Jerusalem. When He was born, some interesting men came to visit Him. These men were scholarly and known as magi. They were experts in the study of stars, such as astronomy and astrology. The Magi had observed in the heavens an unusual star that was interpreted to be a sign that the Jewish Messiah had been born. The knowledge of such a birth either came from Jews who lived in their land, or from the Hebrew Scriptures. God may have given them a special revelation. At any rate, these Gentiles traveled a great distance to find the Messiah and worship Him. Their search brought them to Judea. The assumption that the new "King of the Jews" would have been born in the palace of the capital city, led them to Jerusalem. No one in the city was aware of His birth. Disappointment or distance did not discourage their efforts to find and worship the Messiah. King Herod was troubled at the news of the birth of a new king, so the Wise Men departed for Bethlehem. They located the Messiah in a house with Joseph and Mary. Kingly gifts were presented to the Child, followed by respectful worship. The mission was accomplished and the magi departed.

C—Contemporary Application

Magi were a priestly group in ancient Persia. They are thought to have been followers of Zoroaster, the Persian teacher and prophet. The religion of the magi included astrology, demonology, and magic. (The word *magic* is derived from the word *magi*.) By the first century AD, the magi were identified with wise men and soothsayers. Thus, the biblical magi who came from the East to worship the infant Jesus were regarded as wise men. In our church Christmas program, we sing about the Three Kings of the Orient, who followed a guiding star to Bethlehem to pay homage to the newborn Christ child. They brought with them gold, the gift bestowed on kings, frankincense, used to worship at the altar of God, and myrrh, an embalming agent for the dead.

What should your response be to the birth of the Christ Child?

- I want to____
- I hope to____.
- I plan to____.
- I need to____.

D—Directed Prayer

Lord, provide opportunities for me to share what Christ's birth means.

December 20

Little Town of Bethlehem

Caesar Augustus was ruling, but God was in change.
Luke 2:1-7

A—Advice from the Bible

. . . to Bethlehem the town of David.
(Luke 2:4)

B—Biblical Example

The execution of the imperial decree of Caesar Augustus that all his subjects should enroll for tax purposes, brought Mary and Joseph to the town of Bethlehem. A prophecy was declared ages before that this place would be the site of the Messiah's birth (Micah 5:2) and Mary's child was born as foretold. Bethlehem was called "the town of David" and Joseph "belonged to the house and line of David." Jesse, the father of David lived in Bethlehem (1 Sam. 16:1) and thus Bethlehem became David's town. However the place remained small and was later called a village (John 7:42). The Lord Jesus did not gain any reputation from the place of His birth. The One, who is the Bread of life, was born in an obscure hamlet whose name means" the house of bread." Originally called Aphrath, the town also is referred to as Bethlehem-Judah to distinguish it from another Bethlehem (Joshua 19:15-16) in the territory of the tribe of Zebulun. Bethlehem is first mentioned in the Old Testament as the place where Rachel (wife of the patriarch Jacob) was buried (Genesis 35:19). According to the Book of Ruth, the village later became the home of King David's ancestors and of David himself (1 Samuel 17:12).

C—Contemporary Application

God gave a tiny baby to a world torn by strife, poverty, injustice, and greed—just a common gift, yet what far-reaching benefits! Bethlehem would never be the same quiet little place on a map. Later in the 19th century, a war-weary world was anxiously watching the march of Napoleon. All the while babies were born in the world such as:

- In 1809, Alfred Lord Tennyson was born in Summersby, England.
- Oliver Wendell Holmes was born in Boston.
- Abraham Lincoln was born in Hodgeville, Kentucky.

The people's minds were occupied with great battles, not babies. Yet, 199 years later, no doubts exist about the greater contribution to history—the battles or a Baby!

O Little Town of Bethlehem:

- The hopes and fears of all the years are met in thee tonight.
- For Christ is born of Mary.
- The wondrous Gift is given.
- The great glad tidings tell.

D—Directed Prayer

Father, thank You, for a place called Bethlehem.

December 21

The Search for the Little Child

Jesus came to be the Savior of the world.
Matthew 2:3-8

A—Advice from the Bible

Where is the Christ to be born?
(Matt. 2:4)

B—Biblical Example

When the Magi arrived in Judea, they assumed that the new "king of the Jews" would have been born in the palace of the capital city. These visitors went in search of Him to Jerusalem. Perhaps they marveled that no one in the city was aware of His birth. However, to their credit, they did not allow distance or disappointment to discourage their efforts to find and worship the Messiah. Naturally Herod was troubled at the news of the birth of a new king. The entire city of Jerusalem feared what this Roman appointed king might do. They knew no one was safe from the unpredictable behavior of the tyrant. Herod quickly gathered the religious leaders and demanded an explanation from them. This group was probably the Jewish Sanhedrin, composed of experts in the Old Testament Scriptures. The only reason for the king's interest in the situation was to destroy this potential rival to his throne. He responded to Christ in fear and hostility. An interesting point: the chief priest and scribes did not go to investigate the possibility of this birth. Even the visit of the mysterious Magi from the East provided no motivation to find the truth. The king could find no one to help him locate this Messiah.

C—Contemporary Application

Every year at this time, local churches, large and small, seek to present a Christmas pageant and invite the public to attend. Through a combination of music, drama, Scripture readings, and dance, the members present the story of Christ's birth. The most impressive scene to me is the visit of the wise men. They usually enter from the back of the church dressed in royal robes and march to the flourish of drums and trumpets. The audience is awed by this processional. Then, the Magi go on the stage and one by one remove their crowns and bow before the Christ, the King of kings. This scene leaves me wanting to also bow before the Christ in praise and worship. How wonderful that Herod's evil plan was ignored by his people!

What was going on in Jerusalem at this time?

- The Magi were seeking the King.
- Herod was afraid of the King.
- The Magi wanted to worship the King.
- Herod wanted to destroy the King.

D—Directed Prayer

Father, help me worship the King with appropriate gifts.

December 22

The Little Trip to Egypt

Christians can decide to further God's purpose in the world.
Matthew 2:13-15

A—Advice from the Bible

So Joseph took the child and his mother during the night and left for Egypt.
(Matt. 2:14)

B—Biblical Example

The visitors from the East presented gifts fit for royalty before returning to their homeland. However, their visit started a chain reaction of events. Joseph, Mary, and Jesus escaped the wrath of Herod by fleeing to Egypt. Herod's slaughter of the infant boys of Bethlehem was understood by Matthew as fulfillment of prophecy. By now, Joseph was no stranger to receiving guidance through the Lord's angel. He had established a pattern of listening and obeying. Egypt lay within the Roman Empire, but outside Herod's jurisdiction. The journey covered about 100 miles. Many Jews lived in Egypt at this time. The gifts of the magi may have financed the trip and the sojourn in this distant country. Herod never felt secure in his position as king. He displayed a character that would want to destroy a rival king. Joseph avoided unnecessary risks and departed under cover of darkness. The child Jesus was called out of Egypt when Herod died and Joseph brought his family back into Israel. The prophecy of Hosea was fulfilled (Hosea 11:1).

C—Contemporary Application

Our family decided to spend Christmas in the Sacramento Mountains of New Mexico. A map was used to plan our trip. The car was packed with more than we needed and a cabin was rented near Cloudcroft. The kids found a pine branch that became our tree, and evening walks in the snow were favorite times. One highlight, however, was from God, just for us! The Gemini 7 space program was in effect. These flights were made in 1965-1966. We would stand outside with a transistor radio and listen for news from Houston. All of a sudden we heard the Genesis creation story being read aloud by Lieutenant Colonel Frank Borman. You can imagine our surprise to hear God's Word being read from space. We stopped walking and looked up into the night sky. A tiny light was moving across the heavens and we watched until it disappeared out of sight. Once again, we discovered that God is everywhere we go and we praised Him.

A new, Christian friend asks you if you believe God speaks to us through dreams today?

- You would say—
- You would use examples of—
- You would cite other writers, saying –
- You would seek more biblical affirmation—

D—Directed Prayer

Father, thank You, for accomplishing Your purpose through Jesus, Your Son.

December 23

The Murder of Little Boys

We can further God's purpose by choosing to be obedient to His guidance.
Matthew 2:16-18

A—Advice from the Bible

He gave orders to kill all the boys in Bethlehem.
(Matt. 2:16)

B—Biblical Example

King Herod the Great made a secret request of the magi. He asked them to report to him where they found the newborn King and he anxiously awaited their return. However, God redirected the wise men by warning them not to revisit Herod. They went home by another route. The king became enraged, but nothing compared to his anger directed at Jesus. The slaughter of Bethlehem's male babies is not mentioned by the Jewish historian, Josephus. Perhaps the king's crimes and cruelties were too numerous to include all of them. Once again, God intervened to preserve the life of His Son. Mary, Joseph, and Jesus were long on their journey to Egypt when Herod's men came searching for the baby boys of Bethlehem. Through the centuries, Bible scholars have tried to guess how many babies were murdered. Perhaps 20 were slain based on the population of Bethlehem at that time. Today, Christians place great value on human life and oppose any movement that ignores this truth.

C—Contemporary Application

My favorite vacation site is the Hawaiian Islands. One year, my husband was invited to lead a revival in a local church during the Christmas season. A special event of the week was the retelling of Hawaii's history. Native foods, dances, and costumes were featured. I was introduced to an American Samoan prince. He and his family were living in Oahu while their son attended school. We began visiting and I asked him about his southern Pacific Ocean Island. He explained how child sacrifices were once part of the pagan worship. Today Christians worship the Son of God and honor their children. During the Christmas pageants on the island, reference is made to King Herod and the Samoan king, who called for children to be murdered. At the close of the evening, this family placed a beautiful lei around my neck and we rejoiced in God's sending His Son into all the world. How grateful we were that no one would help King Herod carry out his slaughter.

Ways to participate in God's purpose during the holidays:
- Read aloud the Christmas story from God's Word.
- Sing the great hymns of faith about the birth of Jesus.
- Plan a party for friends who need to know the real reason for the season.
- Pray for areas of the world that still abuse children.

D—Directed Prayer

Father, Your Son is so appreciated and loved.

December 24

A Little Prophecy Fulfilled

God promises victory and hope.
Matthew 2:6; Micah 5:1-6

A—Advice from the Bible

But you, Bethlehem Ephrathah, though you are small . . . out of you will come a ruler.
(Micah 5:2)

B—Biblical Example

The Old Testament prophets often proclaimed doom on Judah and then followed that word with a message of hope. Though verse 1 is a prediction of danger, verses 2-5 are a prophecy of hope. Following his pronouncement that invaders would insult the king of Israel, Micah declared that the Messiah would be born in Bethlehem, a small town in Judah. *Bethlehem* means "house of bread." God often chooses to use little things and make much of them so that He receives the glory. This insignificant location would produce a deliverer who would save His people. The prophet contrasted the failure of the proud kings born in Jerusalem with the triumph of the future Redeemer. He would be a different kind of king and was identified as a member of David's line. This king would be an ideal ruler. The only hope for Judah lay in the coming Messiah. The prophecy ultimately speaks of Jesus, and we are identified as His flock. The Christian's hope is founded upon Jesus Christ. All people must look to Him for peace with God and the peace of God in the world.

C—Contemporary Application

A Christmas card was once published with the title, "If Christ Had Not Come." A pastor falling into a short sleep in his study on Christmas Eve dreamed of a world into which Jesus had never come. No stockings hung on the mantel. No Christmas bells or wreaths of holly, and no Christ to comfort and save us. The pastor walked out into the street, but no church was in view. He came back to his library and every book about the Savior had disappeared. A phone call requested a visit to a poor, dying woman. A Bible was opened to bring words of comfort, but the book ended with Malachi—no Gospel and no promise of hope and salvation. The pastor could only bow his head and weep in bitter despair. Two days later he conducted her funeral service. No message of consolation and no hope of heaven were available. The man woke-up and began praising God for His Gift.

Consider answers to the following questions:

- When did the true meaning of Christmas become real to you?
- What do I have to do to accept God's Gift of Jesus?
- Why did God come to earth as a little Baby instead of a mighty king?
- What family traditions have you developed to focus on the true King?

D—Directed Prayer

Father, Your Gift to us is welcomed.

December 25

The First Little Advent

A danger always exists in keeping Christmas, but losing the Baby.
John 1:1-14

A—Advice from the Bible

The Word became flesh.
(John 1:14)

B—Biblical Example

Merry Christmas, Jesus! The Gospel of John is about Jesus and everywhere in the book, Jesus is magnified. Matthew and Luke had already told the birth events in Jesus early life. The Apostle John chose to go back further in history, back to the "beginning." His record of The Incarnation of Jesus was not like a phantom story or a ghostly spirit. John believed that the Lord came to the earth. The other disciples had personal experiences that convinced them of the reality of the body of Jesus. The writer points out that the Son of God came in the flesh and was subject to the sin problems of humankind. How was the "Word made flesh?" The miracle of the virgin birth was the beginning (Matt. 1:18-25).

C—Contemporary Application

The season of Advent is a time for celebrations that focus on the expectation and birth of Jesus. One year I challenged my Bible study class to write an Advent devotional book. Each willing person recorded their thoughts about "the Word became flesh." Advent begins on the fourth Sunday before Christmas and continues to Christmas Eve. The word, Advent, comes from the Latin "*adventus*", meaning "arrival." Various customs are associated with Advent. One that still survives in parts of Europe, notably in Germany, is the hanging of Advent wreaths. These are rings made up of sprigs of evergreens such as holly and ivy, onto which are fixed four red candles. Each Sunday of Advent one candle is lit so that by Christmas all four candles are burning. Our church uses this time to decorate for the Christmas season. We call the program the "Hanging of the Greens." The worship service begins with nothing to view except the bare walls. Then throughout the program different items are carried in and used to make the worship center a beautiful place. Appropriate hymns and solos are used to enhance the experience. Different families are selected to light the four candles on the communion table wreath and read the appropriate Scripture passage. "The Word . . . " is the central message of the season.

Faith enables us to accept the teachings regarding the incarnation because:

- Jesus was born of a woman without an earthly father.
- Jesus lived among people.
- Jesus was sensitive to all human suffering.
- Jesus is the Son of God, the Son of Mary.

D—Directed Prayer

Thank You, Lord, that You are the one true Word.

December 26

A Little Baby in His Arms

People confronted with Christ are compelled to testify.
Luke 2:25-35

A—Advice from the Bible

Simeon took him in his arms.
(Luke 2:28)

B—Biblical Example

After the birth of Jesus, Mary and Joseph probably remained in Bethlehem for a time. As faithful Jews, they needed to be near the Jerusalem Temple in order to fulfill the requirements of the Mosaic law regarding the birth of their child. Jewish custom indicated that after at least thirty-one days of a first-born boy's life, he would be presented in the Temple as the first-born son, holy to God. Another visit was required to make a sacrifice. The parents completed both of these temple services in one visit. Nazareth was too far away for a return trip. As the traditional offerings were concluded, a godly, devout man named Simeon came to Mary and Joseph and took the Child in his arms. This man was introduced simply as "a man in Jerusalem." Much is revealed about his heart, but very little about his heritage. He began to speak his praise to God, declaring that God's salvation is for all people—Jews and Gentiles. Ultimately, Jesus' Temple dedication was totally fulfilled.

C—Contemporary Application

A four-year-old girl came out of the bathroom with a large bandage on her head. "Did you hurt yourself?" her mother asked. "Yes," answered Jordan. "When I skin my knee, you give me a bandage and that helps. I hit my head on my new swing and it began to hurt this afternoon, so I put a bandage on it." Religious people tend to administer the wrong remedy to our spiritual aches. Because believers act devout does not mean that their heart is just. Right attitude precedes right behavior. In Simeon, we met a man who was "just" in God's sight and "devout" in the eyes of all people. He knew the right cure for spiritual emptiness and he was prepared when God led him to meet Jesus. Many of you received gifts during Christmas that you will cherish the rest of your life. Remember that God gave the greatest gift of all time in His Son, Jesus Christ. Recall the joys of this season during the days ahead.

Simeon spoke his praise to God in a song. What would you include in your song?
- About the Baby Jesus?
- About salvation?
- About God's will?
- About God's blessings?

D—Directed Prayer

Father God, thank You for the people who have yearned and waited to know Jesus.

December 27

A Little Rebuke

Believers need wisdom—the timeless, dependable, true wisdom of God.
Proverbs 17:1-12

A—Advice from the Bible

A rebuke impresses a man of discernment.
(Prov. 17:10)

B—Biblical Example

No book of the Old Testament seems to be quite as difficult to outline as the book of Proverbs. The subject seems to change with every verse. When Solomon became king, he had a vision in which God asked him what his heart desired above everything else. The king asked for wisdom. Because he expressed a need for the treasure of wisdom instead of riches or fame, God gave him all three. Therefore, these verses are the wisdom proverbs of the wisest king Israel ever had. The book approaches life from the position that God has all the answers. He is all-wise and all-knowing. Many book stores are filled with motivational books, tapes, and offer seminars in order to help a person become successful. In reality, the key to success is found right in this book. Verse 10 reminds us that to rebuke a sensitive person affects him more deeply than a hundred blows would affect a fool. The sensitive person takes relationships seriously and tries to maintain them. This action leads to successful living.

C—Contemporary Application

A tale of two transgressors illustrates the truth of today's verse. Charlie and Roger were members of the same church. Both were involved in separate immoral relationships. Charlie's wife confided to the pastor that her husband was having an affair. Their 25-year marriage was in serious trouble. Obviously Charlie needed to be rebuked for his unfaithfulness. The pastor met privately with him and urged him to repent. This plea was accepted. His marriage was saved and he was restored to a leadership role. Roger's immoral lifestyle became apparent when he was fired from his job for being a homosexual. He was confronted by the pastor and resented the rebuke. He maintained his right to live as he pleased. Roger's foolish decision cost him everything except his "lover." No one enjoys reproof, neither the giver nor the receiver. But rebuke is needed and can lead to restoration when wisely received. Roger died of AIDS last year.

Believers must deal with the choices life sets before them in order to find:
- satisfaction
- abundance
- service to God
- daily blessings

D—Directed Prayer

Thank You, God, for friends who take a risk and identify my faults.

December 28

A Little History Lesson

Being God's children involves faith and obedience.
1 Corinthians 10:1-13

A—Advice from the Bible

So, if you think you are standing firm, be careful that you don't fall.
(1 Cor. 10:12)

B—Biblical Example

Paul continues his letter to the weak Corinthian Christians on the subject of eating meat offered to idols. He, then, shows how favored Israel fell because of pride and various sexual sins. The Hebrew forefathers were men of unusual privilege and spiritual opportunity. God had manifested Himself to them in a unique fashion in the guiding pillar of cloud and the deliverance through the Red Sea. The Israelites had been nurtured and cared for in the wilderness. However, they did not respond to God's actions toward them and the whole nation was destroyed in the Sinai wilderness. Paul saw this past destruction as an example or lesson to the Corinthians and to others to guard against the sins which destroyed the people of Israel. The apostle's warning was a reminder that their pride would become their downfall. These church attending people were sure that idolatry would never again touch them. But evidently some of these sins against which Paul warns were already being practiced by professing Christians. Paul ends this subject by assuring them that God is faithful and will not permit anyone to be tested beyond his ability to bear, but will provide a way out.

C—Contemporary Application

Much of life poses moral dangers for believers. We should never assume in any situation that we're incapable of falling. My husband and I enjoy the Pecos Wilderness, near Santa Fe, New Mexico. One summer we were hiking to Hamilton's Mesa. Jim had been there many times, but I had not seen this beautiful place. A narrow trail appeared in front of us after hours of easy climbing. The trial was right on the edge of a major cliff. I became concerned and did not want to go any farther. However, I found the courage and carefully walked this dangerous path. On the return trip, Jim asked me if I was afraid to follow this trail. I responded in the affirmative, and then said, "My fear is what keeps me safe." We must watch, pray, and arm ourselves for every occasion so that we will not fall.

Given the opportunity and circumstances any of us are capable of falling into:

- Sins of unbelief.
- Sins of immoral actions
- Sins of backsliding.
- Sins of unfaithfulness to God.

D—Directed Prayer

Lord, help me to put my total trust in You.

December 29

A Little Whirlwind

We can trust God even when we cannot understand Him.
Job 38:1-7

A—Advice from the Bible

Then the LORD answered Job out of a whirlwind
(Job 38:1)

B—Biblical Example

The major events from the book of Job are: (1) Disaster came to him; (2) Friends shared the experience and their opinion; (3) Job cried out to God in anguish and anger. At this point in time, Job's attitude caused a problem. Now he finally received his opportunity to speak with God. The outcome of the confrontation was not what Job expected. The LORD had to deal with Job's attitude before his life could be changed, so God spoke to Job out of a whirlwind, a startling way to get someone's attention! Job did not get to see God, but he did get his wish of speaking directly with Him. This suffering man did not get an opportunity to argue his case, as he had hoped. God quickly put Job in his place and told him to listen. God knew everything that had happened. He asked Job why he dared to question His fairness and wisdom when he knew nothing of the mysteries of God. The major question God asked was, "Where were you when I created the world?" The purpose of the question was to humble Job. This poor suffering righteous man discovered that life is a gift of mercy from a sovereign God.

C—Contemporary Application

A story is told about President Ulysses S. Grant who served our nation from 1869-1877. One evening he was on his way to a reception in his honor when he was caught in a heavy Washington downpour. The president noticed a stranger also walking and shared his umbrella since the man was headed in the same direction. The stranger, as it turned out, was going to the reception as well. "I have never seen Grant." the stranger remarked. "I'm really going to this reception to satisfy my personal curiosity. Between the two of us, I have always thought that Grant was a very much overrated man." Grant replied, "That is my view also." These words were from a military genius, who was able to lead the Union to victory and became the eighteenth president of the United States. However, Job sometimes did think more highly of himself than he should until God met him.

What do you do when you simply cannot understand what God is doing in a situation?

- Pray.
- Search the Scriptures
- Talk with the pastor or a teacher.
- Share your questions with a friend.

D—Directed Prayer

Father, I am so glad I can trust You even when I don't comprehend the situation.

December 30

God's Little Messenger

Christians must not neglect the true worship of God.
Malachi 1:6-14

A—Advice from the Bible

I am not pleased with you.
(Mal. 1:10)

B—Biblical Example

Malachi is the last prophet of the Old Testament. His Hebrew name means "my messenger." Things were happening in the land of Palestine. The Temple had been rebuilt, but the people were not rejoicing over this completion. They were now taking the sacrifices and worship for granted. Many of them were discouraged. Bored and careless would describe their attitudes. The priests who were supposed to lead the Israelites spiritually had become the worst example of serving God. Worship was nothing but a meaningless ritual required by God. However, Malachi began to criticize the priests. He accused them of failing to give the Lord the honor and respect that is due Him. He said they offered God defiled sacrifices. Sacrifices were supposed to be perfect. God's altar was being treated with contempt. These cynical worshipers were offering crippled and diseased animals on the altar. In a bit of humor the prophet suggested that they give these animals to the governor. The prophet recommended that the Temple doors be shut rather than allowing half-hearted worship. He reminded them that God demanded their best.

C—Contemporary Application

Four people come to my mind as I think about Malachi's message to God's children. First, Jeffery attended our church once in a while. He seemed to enjoy the worship, sang, and gave during the offering. However, during the week, he could not talk without using profanity. Second, Sarah was always offering something to the church. The clothes she brought were worn-out; the food was shelf-dated, and the furniture was beyond repair. Third, Franko owned a very prosperous business and enjoyed coming to worship. However, his offering was pathetic. Greed controlled his giving. Fourth, Meg was a "used-to-be" church member. "I've done that before; let someone else take my place." She was "weary in well doing." Her worship consisted of sitting the back pew, visiting a friend next to her. What would Malachi say to these people?

As the New Year approaches, determine to go:

- Back to God's house
- Back to God's Word
- Back to God's work.
- Back to God's grace.

D—Directed Prayer

Lord, help me not to be a second-rate giver.

December 31

A Little Chorus of Praise

Believers can be confident in the victorious Christ.
Revelation 19:1-8

A—Advice from the Bible

I heard what sounded like a multitude in heaven shouting.
(Rev. 19:1)

B—Biblical Example

The celebration of Babylon's fall continues with a song of thanksgiving that God had triumphed over the great harlot. This enemy of God's people was overthrown and now introduced the beginning of God's triumphant rule. A great host in heaven was singing the "Hallelujah" chorus. This term was a Hebrew word, "Alleluia" is the Greek word, meaning "Praise the Lord." They were not rejoicing primarily over the destruction of Rome; rather, they sang because righteousness and truth had prevailed. The work of Christ had saved them. A great multitude joined the chorus and sang, "Hallelujah! For the Lord our God the Almighty reigns." The singers began to make preparations for a marriage. The wedding nuptials were planned for Christ and His bride, the church. She had remained pure and spotless. Her clothing was made of fine linen. Once again the great choir begins to sing, "Hallelujah!" The time for the wedding of the Lamb had come.

C—Contemporary Application

No one remembers Charles Jenners, but his biblical excerpts inspired George Frideric Handel to compose the *Messiah*. This great musician was older at this time and had not experienced any successful music for several years. He was being criticized by people who said that his inspiration was exhausted. And then a manuscript was delivered to him from Jenners. On August 22, 1741 he shut the door of his home and started composing music from those stimulating words. Twenty-three days later, the world had *Messiah*. When *Messiah* opened in London, King George II, who was present that night, surprised everyone by leaping to his feet during the Hallelujah Chorus. Today is New Year's Eve and many people will celebrate as the world does on this evening. However, for a Christian, godly conduct would be a better witness to people who have never experienced the joy of singing, "Hallelujah." I wish for you the happiest new year of your life. Depend on God for guidance and learn to praise Him every day of the New Year.

A verse from Psalm 106:48 could be our Hallelujah chorus:

- Blessed be the LORD, the God of Israel,
- From everlasting to everlasting!
- Let all the people say, "Amen!"
- Praise the LORD!

D—Directed Prayer

Dear God, What a day that will be! Hallelujah!

Lightning Source UK Ltd.
Milton Keynes UK
07 December 2009

147150UK00001B/1/P